Painting the Town

Scottish Urban History in Art

E. PATRICIA DENNISON, STUART EYDMANN, ANNIE LYELL,
MICHAEL LYNCH and SIMON STRONACH

Happy Birthday Dad!

with love,

Alison and Wayne.

X.

Jacket image: *Leith Races*, 1859, William Thomas Reed, courtesy of Capital Collections

Published in 2013 in Great Britain by the Society of Antiquaries of Scotland

Society of Antiquaries of Scotland
National Museum of Scotland
Chambers Street
Edinburgh EH1 1JF

Tel: 0131 247 4115
Fax: 0131 247 4163
Email: administration@socantscot.org
Website: www.socantscot.org

The Society of Antiquaries of Scotland is a registered Scottish charity no. SC01044.

ISBN 978 1 90833 204 2

British Library Cataloguing-in-Publication Data
A catalogue record for this book is available from the British Library.

The authors and the Society of Antiquaries of Scotland gratefully acknowledge funding towards the publication
of this volume from Historic Scotland.

HISTORIC SCOTLAND

Design and production by Lawrie Law and Alison Rae
Typesetting by Waverley Typesetters, Warham, Norfolk
Manufactured in Slovenia

Contents

List of illustrations and maps

Notes on the authors

E. PATRICIA DENNISON (FSA Scot.) is the Director of the Centre for Scottish Urban History at the University of Edinburgh and Chair of the Historic Burghs Association of Scotland. She has written and edited over thirty published volumes on urban history. These include most of the Scottish Burgh Survey series, *Medieval Dundee: A Town and its People* (1990), the first volume of *Aberdeen before 1800: A New History* (2002) and *Holyrood and Canongate: A Thousand Years of History* (2005).

STUART EYDMANN has worked in urban conservation in the private and public sectors since graduating from the Glasgow School of Art in 1975. He lectures in the Scottish Centre for Conservation Studies at Edinburgh College of Art and is a Post-Doctoral Research Fellow in Celtic and Scottish Studies at the University of Edinburgh. He is a fellow of the Society of Antiquaries of Scotland, a member of the Royal Town Planning Institute and Scottish Convenor of the Institute of Historic Building Conservation.

ANNIE LYELL (FSA Scot.) graduated in Scottish Historical Studies at the University of Edinburgh and won the Fraser Mackintosh Prize for Highland History. She has published two books on Scottish local history and set up a database of images of Scotland's historic burghs using material gathered from galleries, museums and other archives throughout Scotland. She is a fellow of the Society of Antiquaries of Scotland and Secretary of the Historic Burghs Association of Scotland.

MICHAEL LYNCH was Professor of Scottish History at the University of Edinburgh until 2005. He is an Honorary Fellow of the Society of Antiquaries of Scotland. A specialist in urban history, his publications include *Edinburgh and the Reformation* (1981), *The Early Modern Town in Scotland* (1987), *The Scottish Medieval Town* (1988), *Aberdeen before 1800: A New History* (2002). His general publications include *Scotland: A New History* (1991) and the *Oxford Companion to Scottish History* (2001).

SIMON STRONACH graduated with a B.Sc.(Hons) in Archaeology from the University of Glasgow in 1992 before pursuing a career as a professional archaeologist. Over the last twenty years he has worked on a variety of projects in Scotland, England, Ireland and

Germany, particularly enjoying, and specialising in, the excavation of urban sites. Most of these were in the Scottish burghs and included directing the excavations preceding the construction of the Holyrood Parliament building. He has used this experience to good effect by contributing to four volumes of the Burgh Survey series and is also an author of numerous published excavation articles. He is a Member of the Institute for Archaeologists and currently works as a consultant for CgMs in Edinburgh.

Acknowledgements

The authors are grateful to many who have supported and encouraged us. To Simon Gilmour and the Society of Antiquaries of Scotland, to Historic Scotland, particularly Noel Fojut, Mark Watson and Rod McCullagh, we owe sincere thanks. The Historic Burghs Association of Scotland played a crucial role at the outset of this project. Its database, held at the Royal Commission on the Ancient and Historical Monuments of Scotland, and commenced during the chairmanship of John Gerrard, gave us the stimulus to begin this project. Robin Evetts of the Association gave us invaluable and unique support, reading texts and offering advice. We cannot thank him enough. The database, along with the Burgh Survey series commissioned by Historic Scotland and other sources mentioned in the Editorial Note, were invaluable bases for our extensive researches.

We wish to express our great gratitude to the Aberbrothock Skea Trust, the Binks Trust, Brewin Dolphin, the Hugh Fraser Foundation, the Lethendy Charitable Trust, the Misses Barrie Charitable Trust and the Strathmartine Trust for their financial support and Adam and Company for banking services.

Our researches would have been impossible without the generous assistance of many. The National Library of Scotland, in particular the Map Room, Chris Fleet and Jenny Parkerson; Diana Murray and the staff, especially Neil Fraser, of the Royal Commission on the Ancient and Historical Monuments of Scotland; the National Records of Scotland; James Holloway and Valerie Hunter (both now retired), Patricia Allerston, Christopher Baker, Hannah Brocklehurst and the staff of the National Galleries of Scotland; Elspeth King of the Stirling Smith Art Gallery and Museum; George Woods of McLean Museum and Art Gallery, Greenock; Norman Atkinson of Angus Council and Andy Phillipson of Livewireimage all gave support throughout this project.

We would like to express our gratitude to John Pickin (now retired), Anne Ramsbotton and Alan McFarlane of Stranraer Museum, Hugh Cheape of the University of the Highlands and Islands, David Patterson of the Edinburgh City Art Centre, the Royal Collection, Pauline Smeed and Gordon Easingwood of Dunbar and District Historical Society, Craig Statham, Local History Officer of East Lothian Council, David Bertie of Aberdeenshire Council, Claire Pannell and Kate Maynard of East Lothian Museums Service, Marjorie Davies and Ewing Wallace of Dunblane Cathedral Museum, Isabel

MacLachlan of *Museum nan Eilan*, Stornoway, George Dalgleish of National Museums Scotland, Janette Park and David Mackie of Orkney Museum, Honor Clerk of the Public Catalogue Foundation, Ian Tait of Shetland Museum, Fiona Marwick of West Highland Museum, Tom Barclay of South Ayrshire Council, Catharine Niven of Inverness, Maria Devaney of Perth Museum and Art Gallery, Gavin Grant of Fife Council, Richard Cooke of Dalhousie Estates, Anna Robertson and Susan Keracher of the McManus Gallery and Museum, Dundee, Andrew Nicoll formerly of Scottish Catholic Archives, Neil Curtis of the University of Aberdeen, Andrea Kusel of Renfrewshire Council, Susan Mills of Clackmannanshire Council, Denise Brace of City of Edinburgh Art Centre, Elinor Clark of South Ayrshire Council, Museum and Galleries, Griffin Co of Aberdeen Art Gallery and Museums Collections, David Main of Aberdeen City Council, Alison Stoddart of Edinburgh City Council, Joanne Turner of Dumfries Museum, Jason Sutcliffe of the Dick Institute, Kilmarnock, Patricia Grant of the Mitchell Library, Glasgow, Winnie Tyrrell of The Burrell Collection, Graham Nisbet of the Hunterian Museum, Niki Russell of University of Glasgow, Special Collections, Lesley Junor of Highland Council, Rosemary Hannay of Tweedale Museum and Gallery, Ann Gunn of the University of St. Andrews, Nathan Pendlebury of the National Museums, Liverpool, Hannah Kendall of the Ashmolean Museum, Oxford, Christopher Sutherns of the British Museum, Louise Burley of the Tate Gallery, Mark Vivien of the Mary Evans Picture Library, Betty Hunter of the History of Armadale Association, and the Cultural Enterprise Office, Glasgow. The varied list of those who have assisted us is testament to how much we owe others for their very generous support.

We are also indebted to private individuals. To the Earl of Crawford and Balcarres, the Earl and Countess of Dalhousie, Jamie Stormonth Darling, Bert McEwan, Margaret Munro, Donnie Nelson, Jill Turnbull, David Laird, Henrietta Simpson, Ann and James Simpson, George Harrison, Douglas Sinclair and Gordon Ritchie, all of whom gave invaluable assistance, we offer our thanks.

For permission to reproduce illustrations we are indebted to the following (illustrations in the Introduction are referred to as figs; illustrations in the Main Text are referred to as numbers):

Aberdeen Art Gallery and Museums Collections: fig. 19; nos 2, 3
Aberdeen City Council: no. 3a
Aberdeen City Council. Licensor www.scran.ac.uk: no. 58a
Aberdeenshire Museums Service Collections, reproduced by kind permission of
Aberdeenshire Council: nos 9, 58, 88, 88a
University of Aberdeen: nos 96, 96a
Angus Council, Cultural Services: nos 6, 73
Angus Council, Cultural Services (from the collections of Montrose Museum): no. 40

Preface

It is forty years since the report of Grant Simpson and other colleagues for the Society of Antiquaries of Scotland saw the light of day. *Scotland's Medieval Burghs: An Archaeological Heritage in Danger* echoed, for Scotland, much of the concern expressed in Carolyn Heighway's *The Erosion of History* (1972) over the irreplaceable loss of urban history and archaeology. The Scottish report concluded with: 'we have a duty to hand on a heritage to the future. If Scotland's interest in her history is more than superficial, the rescue of our towns should command the support of every thinking Scot.'

It is also forty years since our best buildings were given statutory protection as 'listed buildings' and just a little less since Colin McWilliam, through his *Scottish Townscape* (1975), taught us to read the special architectural and historic character of the built environment and the first conservation areas were designated. Since then, much has changed in how our towns are governed and administered and economic circumstances, modern lifestyles and political policies have had an effect too. There is therefore a greater need than ever for policy formulation and decision making informed by a sound understanding of urban history.

The authors of this volume felt that one area perhaps not adequately tapped in our understanding of the historic town was visual image. Books of town photographs proliferate, but less attention has been given to an earlier medium – art, whether paintings, etchings, engravings or cartographic images of various kinds. This is a book celebrating Scotland's urban heritage. It uses images from archives, museums and art galleries throughout Scotland and beyond. The works reproduced here are not necessarily the 'best' examples of fine art, but are chosen for the intrinsic message of explaining the historic town.

Our searches started with the database produced some ten years ago for the Historic Burghs Association of Scotland, now available at RCAHMS. But we soon found that our net had to be spread more widely. The Scottish Burgh Survey series, commissioned by Historic Scotland, proved invaluable, as may be seen from the endnotes. Of the seventy-five towns and cities which are featured in this book, thirty-nine of them have had a Burgh Survey written about them, nineteen of those published in the fuller second and third series. The authors, coming from varied academic and professional backgrounds, also had vital but differing inputs of their own. Images are a treasure trove of information:

historical, archaeological, ethnographic, architectural, technological, the study of which both adds to and challenges our existing knowledge of many aspects of Scottish history.

The book contains over 200 images drawn from over four centuries and covering towns spread across much of the Scottish mainland as well as the Northern and Western Isles. The end date generally coincides with the popular adoption of photography in the third quarter of the nineteenth century. Taken together, they help remind us that urban development is always the accumulation, in time and space, of innumerable deliberate actions and interventions and that the quality of our places is a result of the quality of these decisions.

Change is the norm, but the essential elements of a place can often endure or be enhanced, particularly when managed to ensure this is the case. Many admirable new buildings have had a relationship with adjacent existing buildings and even with those which have gone before. This shows that urban design and town planning and development are not modern phenomena and that we can learn much from the past. Our current system for the management of change and policies for regeneration are built around the needs and interests of the distinctive architectural merit and heritage of our historic buildings and urban spaces. It is fundamentally important that all involved have access to information and guidance to assist an understanding of how our towns and cities evolved and what makes up their special character.

Of course, there has to be change, but it should be managed and thoughtful, with a deep understanding of an historic town's past and a full recording of that which is to be lost. And for that which is to be conserved, ways must be found in which not merely old buildings can be re-used, but also that lines of properties, streets, back lanes and grain of the townscape are translated, wherever possible, into functioning modern areas that respect modern life and conventions, from cars and pedestrians to cinemas and supermarkets.

As our towns and cities continue to evolve it is hoped that the resources of Scotland's corpus of townscape painting, of which this publication is but a small part, will continue to inspire and guide regeneration and investment. That should, we hope, help to ensure that the places which emerge remain worthy of the special eye and hand of artists still to come.

Edinburgh
November 2013

Editorial note

There are a large number of online resources to facilitate research into Scotland's towns and they have been used extensively in the making of this book. Taken together, they permit far deeper and more comprehensive research into Scotland's urban past, whether buildings, industries, townscapes or images, more readily than ever before.

The agency formerly known as Historic Scotland publishes a searchable database of the *Descriptive List* entries for all Buildings of Special Architectural or Historic Interest which provides full building records, including description, notes and references to approximately 50,000 listed buildings. *Scheduled Monument* records can be accessed by monument name to view legal documents and other information including descriptions and statements of national importance, where available. The executive agency of the Scottish Government also gives access to records of all sites on the *Inventory of Gardens and Designed Landscapes in Scotland* including maps, galleries and site histories.

Canmore is the online window into the database of the body formerly known as the Royal Commission on the Ancient and Historic Monuments of Scotland (RCAHMS). It brings together the results of the survey and collections material in one place and combines location information, site details and images on more than 300,000 archaeological, architectural, maritime and industrial sites throughout the country. The database is continually being supplemented by new research findings and information supplied by the public. Additional, up-to-date information on some buildings is also offered through the site of the *Buildings at Risk Register for Scotland*.

ScotlandsPlaces is a website that allows users to search across different national databases using geographic locations. Users are able to enter a place name or a coordinate to search across these collections or use mapping in the website both to define and refine their search. The results pages provide the data relevant to the search conducted, from each of the project partners including RCAHMS, the National Records of Scotland and the National Library of Scotland (NLS).

A recent and important addition to the online resources provided by Historic Scotland, which partly supersedes other services, is *Pastmap*, which is designed to act as a 'first port of call' and a 'single gateway into every aspect of the historic environment in Scotland, from archaeology and historic buildings, to industrial heritage and designed landscapes'.

The *Dictionary of Scottish Architects* is a database providing biographical information and job lists for all architects known to have worked in Scotland during the period 1840 to 1980, whether as principals, assistants or apprentices. The resource is searchable by name or location of architect, practice, or building, as well as by client. It can be found at www.scottisharchitects.org.uk/.

Some local authorities, such as the City of Edinburgh, have published conservation area character appraisals and similar studies for the historic parts of their urban fabric. These often contain valuable information on how the areas have evolved, including historic maps and photographs. Unfortunately, the volumes in the Burgh Survey series, published reports on the historical development and archaeological implications of development for the most important historic towns, are not yet available online.

The Scottish Church Heritage Research project *Places of Worship in Scotland* offers a searchable database comprising records of all the sites and buildings, rural and urban, used by communities of all faiths and which form part of the collective experience of the people of Scotland.

One of the largest sources of images is the *Scottish Cultural Resources Access Network (SCRAN)*, although care needs to be exercised with the variable quality of the accompanying commentary. The National Library of Scotland is host to a significant number of online maps. For present purposes, the *Towns Plans/Views, 1580–1919* is an invaluable mine of information, though not entirely comprehensive; it is cross-referenced to its online collection of the drawings of Timothy Pont which date to the 1590s and those of John Slezer made in the 1690s. By the 1820s, with the survey of maps drawn by John Wood, almost all of Scotland's towns had been mapped. Some details of towns can also be gleaned from the NLS online collections of county maps, *Counties of Scotland, 1580–1928* and military maps, including the 'Great Map', compiled by Willam Roy 1747–55. Also available on the NLS website are the *Great Reform Act Plans and Reports* of 1832 and *Ordnance Survey* maps and indexes, which date from the 1840s onwards.

The descriptions of local parishes made by ministers of the church in the 1790s and 1830s or 1840s, usually known as the *Old Statistical Account* (OSA) and the *New Statistical Account* (NSA) are freely available online, as is Groome's *Gazetteer*, a comprehensive description of localities first published in six volumes in 1882, but now accompanied with an electronic search facility. Also available to search by date, topic and name is the nineteenth-century British Library Newspapers Database, an online collection of both national and some local newspapers lodged in the British Library.

Pictorial images are increasingly becoming available online via the site www.bbc.co.uk/arts/yourpaintings, although the coverage is as yet far from comprehensive. Much of the holdings of the National Galleries of Scotland is freely available for online search. Less user-friendly in its design for online use but nonetheless useful is *The Government Art Collection*. Local image collections vary in size and detail. One of the most comprehensive and detailed is the Virtual Mitchell; it is accompanied by an older and at times more idiosyncratic resource, TheGlasgowStory. Three of the other most comprehensive sets of local resources are *Capital Collections* (for Edinburgh), *In the Artists' Footsteps* (Dumfries and Galloway), and *Your Paintings* (Paintings at the McLean Museum and Art Gallery in Greenock, Inverclyde). Also useful are the art collections of the Bank of Scotland and the Royal Bank of Scotland, both of which encompass the previous holdings of a large number of local banks, long since defunct.

The contents of the authoritative *Oxford Dictionary of National Biography*, extensively rewritten in recent times, and the *Oxford Art Online*, which includes both *The Benezit Dictionary of Artists* and *Grove Art Online* are both available online, by subscription. The entire contents of the *Proceedings of the Society of Antiquaries of Scotland* (*PSAS*), with a searchable index, are available online.

List of abbreviations

APS	*The Acts of the Parliaments of Scotland*, eds T. Thomson and C. Innes (Edinburgh, 1814–75)
Bann Misc.	*Miscellany of the Bannatyne Club*
BL	British Library, London
BM	British Museum, London
BOEC	*Book of the Old Edinburgh Club*
Canmore	Computer Application for National Monuments Record Enquiries
Cavers, *Slezer*	K. Cavers, *A Vision of Scotland: The Nation Observed by John Slezer, 1671 to 1717* (Edinburgh, 1993)
Cowan and Easson, *Religious Houses*	I. B. Cowan and D. F. Easson (eds), *Medieval Religious Houses: Scotland* (2nd edn, London, 1976)
CDS	*Calendar of Documents Relating to Scotland*, 5 vols, ed. J. Bain *et al.* (Edinburgh, 1881–1986)
DNB	*Oxford Dictionary of National Biography* (online, 2004–)
DOST	*Dictionary of the Older Scottish Tongue, from the Twelfth Century to the End of the Seventeenth Century*, eds W. A. Craigie and A. J. Aitken *et al.* (London, 1937–)
DSCHT	*Dictionary of Scottish Church History and Theology*, ed. N. M de S. Cameron *et al.* (Edinburgh, 1993)
ECA	Edinburgh City Archives
Groome, *Gazetteer*	F. H. Groome, *Ordnance Gazetteer of Scotland: a Survey of Scottish Topography, Statistical, Biographical, and Historical, 6 vols* (Edinburgh, 1882–5)

GUL	Glasgow University Library
McGibbon and Ross	D. MacGibbbon and T. Ross, *The Castellated and Domestic Architecture of Scotland from the Twelfth to the Eighteenth Century*, 5 vols (1887–92)
NGS	National Galleries of Scotland
NLS	National Library of Scotland
NMRS	National Monuments Record of Scotland
NRS	National Records of Scotland (formerly Scottish Record Office and National Archives of Scotland)
NSA	*The New Statistical Account of Scotland, 1834–45* (1845)
OS	Ordnance Survey
OSA	*The [Old] Statistical Account of Scotland*, ed. Sir John Sinclair (1791–9)
PSAS	*Proceedings of the Society of Antiquaries of Scotland*
Pryde, *Burghs*	G. S. Pryde, *The Burghs of Scotland: A Critical List* (Glasgow, 1965)
RCAHMS	Royal Commission on the Ancient and Historical Monuments of Scotland
RCRB	*Records of the Convention of the Royal Burghs of Scotland*, 7 vols, eds J. D. Marwick and T. Hunter (Edinburgh, 1866–1918)
RSCHS	*Records of the Scottish Church History Society*
RMS	*Registrum Magni Sigilii Regum Scotorum*, 11 vols, ed. J. M. Thomson *et al.* (Edinburgh, 1882–)
ROSC	*Review of Scottish Culture*
RPC	*Register of the Privy Council of Scotland*, 38 vols, ed. J. H. Burton *et al.* (Edinburgh, 1877–)
SBRS	Scottish Burgh Records Society
SCRAN	Scottish Cultural Resources Access Network
SHR	*Scottish Historical Review*
SHS	Scottish History Society
SL	Slezer collection of views, NLS
SP	*The Scots Peerage*, ed. Sir J. Balfour Paul, 9 vols (Edinburgh, 1904–14)
SRS	Scottish Record Society
TA	*Accounts of the Lord High Treasurer of Scotland*, 13 vols, eds T. Dickson *et al.* (Edinburgh, 1877–)
Tolbooths and Town-houses	*Tolbooths and Town-houses: Civic Architecture in Scotland to 1833* (RCAHMS, Edinburgh, 1996)

Glossary

Anti-Burgher	Scottish Secession Church which separated from the main body (Burghers) in 1747
aquatint	print made by etching on copper using resin and nitric acid
ashlar	squared and smoothly finished masonry, usually sandstone
backland	area to the rear of the burgage plot behind the dwelling house on the frontage. Originally intended for growing produce and keeping animals; site of wells and midden heaps. Eventually housed working premises of craftsmen and poorer members of burgh society
baxter	baker
bodycolour	watercolour mixed with white pigment to make it opaque
bridewell	gaol or house of correction
burgage plot	toft, or division of land, often of regular size, having been measured out by liners, allocated to a burgess. Once built on, it contained the burgage house on the frontage and a backland. In time, with pressure for space, the plots were often subdivided – repletion. Plots were bounded by ditches, wattle fences or stone walls.
burgess-ship	being in a position to enjoy the privileges and responsibilities of the freedom of the burgh
burgh of barony	a burgh under the jurisdiction of a baron or landowner
callant	lad, servant
camera obscura	an apparatus which projects the image of an object or scene onto a sheet of paper or mirror so that the outlines can be traced
cartouche	a scroll-like ornamental decoration
chorography	topography; a survey and delineation of features over an area of terrain
commone gudis	common good funds, corporate property owned by a burgh
court	courtyard; small, sometimes communal, open space surrounded by buildings in a burgh.
crenellation	a post-medieval architectural motif signifying nobility
diorama	exhibition of pictures seen through an opening with lighting effects
entablature	upper part supported on a classical architectural arrangement of capitals and columns, as in the decorative panel above a house door; collective name for the three horizontal members (architrave, frieze and cornice) above a column

feu	a fixed sum or fee akin to a rent
fermtoun/kirktoun	a rural settlement or village
feuar	the owner of a heritable property
forestair	staircase, usually unenclosed, constructed outside building giving direct access from the street to an upper floor
forestall	to sell goods before taking to the official market
frontage	front part of burgage plot nearest the street, on which dwelling was usually built
fulling	scouring or beating, as a means to clean or finish woollens
gamrel	wooden spar used to separate legs of carcass for butchering
glebe	the land assigned to a parish minister in addition to his stipend
harl	roughcast of lime and aggregate applied to the exterior of a building
harrow	spiked frame or other contrivance for smoothing and pulverising land and covering seeds
heid dyke	the outer wall of a field; main wall at the end of a burgage plot
heritor	landed proprietor in a parish, liable to pay public burdens
hingin lum	primitive chimney head constructed from timber as opposed to one of masonry
'Improvement'	an approving term, used mostly from the eighteenth century onwards, for change which broadened after its initial use for agriculture to a broader social and economic context
lade	mill-stream
landward	the rural part of an urban-based parish
liner	burgh official who fixed and maintained property boundaries
lyme and stane	mortared masonry construction as opposed to dry stone or clay
maltings	industrial building where malt (germinated grain) was made and stored
market repletion	the infilling with buildings of the former market place
pantile	S-shaped clay roof tile originally adopted from the Low Countries
penny geggie	fairground entertainment with paid entry
piended roof	hipped roof, where external angle formed by the sides of a roof when end slopes backwards instead of terminating in a gable
pillory	wooden frame, supported by an upright pillar or post, with holes through which head and hands were placed for punishment

police burgh	a burgh which adopted the powers available under the 1833 Burgh Police Act to provide efficient policing, water supply, sewage, lighting and other services
port	town gate; gateway or entrance to a town; an opening; a gun loop in masonry wall
quoins	dressed stones at the angles of a building; rusticated quoins: where the dressed *quoins* are alternatively long and short
repletion	*see* burgage plot
riding	an annual ceremony inspecting the boundaries of burgh lands
rig	*see* burgage plot
rood	area of land; land held by a town for cultivation and grazing
roup	sale by auction
royal burgh	burgh deriving its charter and privileges directly from the crown
salt pan	large basin, often dug out of rock, within which salt is extracted from sea water by evaporation
shambles	flesh market; slaughter-house
solum	piece of ground belonging to a person; ground on which a building actually stands
staffage	the subordinate figures, animals and objects in a landscape
tack	lease
tacksman	lessee; in the Highlands, one who holds a lease and sublets
teind	tithe
teasing, scibbling and carding	stages in the processing of wool. Teasing is usually done by hand. The wool is pulled apart, separating the fibres and removing debris on a willey. During scribbling the fibres are cleaned and mixed together, before they are passed to a carding machine. Carding opens the fibres, knots and impurities are removed, and then the fibres are combed and blended to produce a loosely twisted 'sliver' that can be spun into yarn.
tenement	building constructed or divided into dwellings for a number of separate households
toft	*see* burgage plot
tolbooth	the most important secular building, meeting place of burgh council; collection post for market tolls; often housed town gaol
triforium	a gallery or arcade over an aisle
tron	public weigh-beam

Venetian window	tripartite window of classical precedent with a wider central opening and two flanking narrower ones, the central portion often arched or surmounted by a pediment
vennel	narrow lane or alley
wappinschaw	literally, a weapon showing; a muster of men under arms
waulk mill	building or small hut where wool was fulled
willey	willowing machine
willowing machine	machine in which a spiked revolving cylinder, usually contained in a spiked box, loosens or cleans cotton and other fibres
worry	to strangle
wynd	narrow lane or street; alley

Introduction: Setting the Urban Scene

The character of medieval and early modern towns in Scotland

Inhabitants of most of Scotland's towns in the period before 1700 would have had little difficulty in finding their way around their own town or indeed any other. Almost all urban settlements were linear in shape, with a herringbone pattern of narrower lanes and closes feeding off the main street, which might widen at one or more points to accommodate a market place. This was in part the product of towns being laid out to a precise plan: Mainard the Fleming planned St Andrews and probably also Berwick-on-Tweed in the twelfth century; both Glasgow and Haddington were laid out in the same century by Ranulf of Haddington. The main variants in lay-out were the result of respecting natural features of the terrain and the need to find dry, stable ground for building on, ready access to drinking water and a reliable local food supply. Viewed in a wider perspective, it was advantageous for a town to be located close to a natural harbour, or a crossing point of natural trading routes or a ford.

The world of the medieval town dweller was a small and familiar one. Maps were not needed since an annual inspection of the marches – marked out by boundary stones – took place, on foot rather than a 'riding'. Few towns had a population of more than a thousand, even in 1500. To many English urban historians, such settlements would not even qualify as a town. In Scotland, however, scattered urban settlements, given a precise set of privileges when elevated to burgh status, acted as the market places for a large hinterland. A burgh almost invariably had only one parish church, a fact which sharply distinguished urban development in Scotland from that in England. But this one church might well serve a vast area to landward, as was the case with Haddington. Hence many burgh churches were larger than might be expected of a modest population within the bounds of the town.

The same town dwellers of the twelfth or thirteenth century would have had little difficulty in recognising the key features of any burgh – its ports, the tolbooth, the weigh-beam or tron, and the market cross, symbol of the burgh's privileges which set it apart from the surrounding countryside – or in finding their way around if they had returned a couple of centuries later. Backlands may have been built on, some gap sites may have been filled in and a market may have moved but the essential lay-out would have remained the same. Only in a few cases would new religious houses have been founded after the thirteenth century, with the friaries of the stricter Observant Franciscan order being the one significant exception: nine new houses of this order were founded, usually at the edge of urban settlement, in the period between 1463 and 1505, including the friary (f.1463 x 66) depicted on John Geddy's map of St Andrews (c. 1580), which in the course of a little more than a century had been embraced within the city's boundaries (92).[1]

By the fifteenth century, the most striking changes might have come within a burgh's own parish church. In larger towns, the church may have been extended or elevated to collegiate status. It became a microcosm of the gradual changes at work within urban society as the economy diversified and trade increased. The parish church was a mirror of a conservative and deeply hierarchical society: the most privileged – those who held the status of being both a burgess and a member of the merchant guild – sat nearest the high altar and, at times, beyond the psychological barrier of the rood screen; members of the craft guilds, given formal incorporation in larger burghs in the late fifteenth or early sixteenth century, sat in a strict hierarchical order near their own altars, dedicated to their own occupational saint; the remnants of burgh society, amounting to the two-thirds of adult males who did not enjoy 'freedom' – or burgess-ship – made do at the west end of the church, farthest away from the high altar. Alternatively, the poor or an under-class of undesirables were often excluded altogether, as was the case in Aberdeen, Dundee and Edinburgh.[2]

The burgh church was a theatre in which 'freedom' and status were displayed ostentatiously. It was also an art gallery in which the privileged members of society collectively – or, at times, individually – displayed their standing. In large burgh churches, such as St Mary's in Dundee or St Giles' in Edinburgh, over forty separate altars, aisles or pillars were decorated with the badges of their founders, in the guise of a saint or a new, fashionable cult, often imported from the continent. For the merchant guild, the touchstone of status was the cult of the Holy Blood, adopted from Scotland's staple port of Bruges; for the wives of the burgh elite, it might be the cult of St Katherine of Siena or another intercessionary saint such as St Anne, mother of Mary and grandmother of Christ; and for members of an incorporated guild it would be the saint typically associated with their craft, such as St Eloi for the hammermen or metalworkers or St Crispin for the skinners.

After the Reformation of 1559–60, most of the art connected with civic ceremony, craft guilds and burgh churches disappeared. Very few traces of this late medieval urban art survive. Two rare exceptions are now museum pieces: one is the so-called 'Fetternear Banner', a banner depicting the cult of the Holy Blood, commissioned for the Edinburgh merchant guild which would have been used in civic processions; the other is an altar piece dedicated to St Bartholomew, patron saint of the glovers, which survived the riot triggered by an inflammatory sermon by John Knox in Perth's burgh church of St John's in 1559

(85). The art galleries of saints and saints' cults in burgh churches disappeared, often under a coating of green paint, as in Aberdeen, Edinburgh and Perth. There may be other, odd survivals of pre-Reformation art, even if much altered. One such is a painting of King William the Lion (1165–1214), which appeared in an inventory of the contents of the Aberdeen Trades Hall made in 1696 (fig. 1). This painting was 'renewed' in 1715 by a local painter by any means 'as cheap as possible'.[3] How much of what remained was faithful to the original, which belonged to the house of the Trinitarian Friars founded in King William's reign, is difficult to say, although it is likely that a cleansing operation had taken place in or before 1715.

Although many of the visual icons of craft, guild and civic identity such as altars and banners disappeared, the sense of privilege and hierarchy persisted and even strengthened. Craft lofts in churches were decorated with the arms of the trade, as were new, elaborate ornamental chairs to lend authority to the office of craft deacon and new seals.[4] Some burgh seals were purged of their saints; some other seals, such as that of the old pilgrimage centre of Dunfermline remodelled in the 1590s, stubbornly held on to an old cult, in this case St Margaret. Market crosses were recast, usually with a symbol of royal authority such as a unicorn (discovered as an icon of monarchy in the fifteenth century) rather than a cross, as at Inveraray (54) and Melrose (72). Within burgh churches, a broad-brush iconoclasm had relented after 1600 to allow some portraits

1. *William the Lion*, n.d.

of wholesome Biblical saints on wall panels in local churches; and four seventeenth-century needlework panels or tapestries, including one depicting *The Finding of Moses*, made for occasional display in St Nicholas Kirk, Aberdeen, also survive.[5] In other cases, the power of a local landowner might suffice to add adornment to funerary monuments; the example of the Skelmorlie Aisle in the parish church of Largs is an extravagant example of such a practice but not a unique one (66).

In the Middle Ages, the character of a city was usually to be found in the vista of its churches – a view confirmed in the last glimpse of medieval Edinburgh, as remembered by one of its earliest Protestants while in exile (28). Increasingly in early-modern Scotland, prestige came to be associated with new municipal buildings, which would be the key elements in the townscape as depicted by later artists and map-makers alike. As a result, fashions in the bird's eye or view map were fast changing: Geddy's map of St Andrews depicted its cathedral, churches, religious houses and the bishop's castle on top of a street plan. Some sixty years later, Wenceslaus Hollar (1607–77) depicted urban civilisation as the accumulation of buildings and institutions which suggested order and civic humanism – Edinburgh's new castellated tolbooth, its schools and its university in addition to its churches and the royal palace in the adjoining burgh of Canongate (30). Prestigious burghs commissioned elaborate monuments as their 'market cross', as at Edinburgh and Aberdeen (1686), festooned with heraldic symbols to underline their status as *royal* burghs (*see* 3). Baronial-style tower houses were built as new tolbooths or elaborate new ports were constructed, with ostentation rather than defence in mind, such as the Edinburgh's main gate at the Netherbow, which sported a statue of a departed king from 1606 onwards – the first public sculpture since effigies of saints had been outlawed at the Reformation (33). Wealthy crafts commissioned new elaborate coats of arms or prestigious chairs for their deacons or built new guild halls, such as that for the tailors in Edinburgh's Cowgate (1621), Stirling's Cowane's Hospital (1649) or Aberdeen's Trades Maiden Hospital, highlighted in William Mosman's landscape of 1756 (2).

The physical damage and loss of life inflicted on various burghs – including Dundee, Dunbar (20), Kirkcaldy (64), Dysart (27) and other Fife burghs as well as Aberdeen and Edinburgh – during the wars of the 1640s and 1650s brought about a prolonged crisis of confidence which, so some towns claimed, lasted for much of the rest of the century.[6] The 1690s brought about an intense combination of extreme weather, harvest failures and famine which postponed economic recovery still further. The age of significant population growth, which had begun sometime after 1500, was over. With the possible exceptions of Edinburgh and Glasgow, both the economy and even the population of most towns probably contracted in this period. The era of recovery and rebuilding did not usually arrive much before the 1720s or 1730s.

Dynamics of the changing townscape as seen in art, maps and town plans
Early burgh development was not recorded contemporaneously, although it becomes clear, as a result of painstaking and piecemeal re-creation of the details of the layout, such as the delineation of burgage plots, that the overall design was conceived as a carefully integrated whole. The well-known view of St Andrews by John Geddy (92) can be used to trace the sequence of development – longer plots came before shorter, which resulted from the intrusion of new streets or market repletion. The Geddy map of *c.* 1580 can be compared with the inset street plan of St Andrews, part of the manuscript county map of Fife compiled by James Gordon of Rothiemay – described as *noviter delineata* – in 1642.[7] Although the main layout remained very similar, development and the infilling of burgage plots is evident at the west end of the burgh, around the site of the former Franciscan friary. Perhaps more

valuable, because of its novelty, is the plan of Cupar, complete with carefully delineated streets and burgage plots and a key listing twenty-one features, including a drawing of the burgh church, in another inset in the same manuscript map of Fife (fig. 2). Despite being a royal burgh dating from at least the fourteenth century, settlement (as depicted here) was still confined to the street frontages without spillage into the backlands, although there had been some building beyond the burgh's east port (marked no. 13 on the map).

The first surviving plan of a planned burgh is comparatively late – that of the new burgh of Edzell, drawn up shortly before its paper creation as a burgh of barony in 1588 (36). In fact, this was a burgh which never happened; its eventual lay-out, in the nineteenth century, bore little relationship to the plans drawn up three centuries earlier. Yet it can be assumed that the design of planned villages in the eighteenth century – almost 150 of them have been traced[8] – followed much the same process of careful outline planning. Ultimately of more significance than isolated planned villages, such as Eaglesham or Newcastleton, was the planning of 'new towns' and their associated suburbs. The distinction between a 'planned village' and a small 'new town' is a fine one and it often turns, as was the case with Keith in Banffshire (*see* 60), on the extent of *subsequent* development. In this case, the neat three-street grid-iron plan devised in 1750 by a land surveyor for the Earl of Findlater spilled outwards in the two decades after 1810 as a result of economic development and a rising population.[9]

Otherwise, the term, for Scotland, needs careful handling for there were no planned new large urban conurbations or one-industry towns such as Manchester, Stoke or St Helens

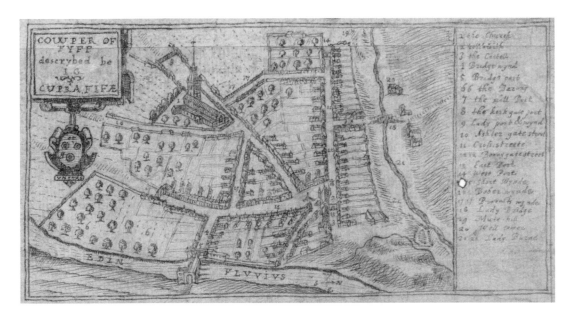

2. James Gordon of Rothiemay, *Cowper*, 1642

5

in England.[10] Nor did most eighteenth-century 'new towns' bear much resemblance to their twentieth century namesakes: they were not new, large greenfield urban settlements, such as Cumbernauld or Glenrothes, with a self-sufficient infrastructure. What usually happened with Scottish 'new towns' were limited extensions of settlement, either for residential use – one of the first was Edinburgh's George Square (1766) and another the westward expansion of Glasgow's grid pattern of streets between 1750 and 1770 – or they were industrial zones, as in Falkirk (38). In the case of Paisley (82, 83), there were both. The initial laying out, in a grid style, of new streets intended for residential development came first, in the 1780s, and was located on both sides of the River Cart. By 1800, the new town residential development on the east bank of the river was largely taken over by different sectors of the fast-growing textile trades, linking what had now become an industrial zone with outlying rural villages. In it, factories jostled for space with low-grade housing for the new, largely immigrant workforce. The new street names, such as Cotton Street and Gauze Street, proclaimed the change. In the process, the ancient abbey complex was virtually swamped. Another variant of the 'new town' was the creation of a new suburb near but not adjoining an existing small settlement, usually dependent on a single nascent industry, such the herring fishery at Pulteneytown (f. 1807), near Wick (99a). This particular new town, one of the most remarkable architectural ventures of the Georgian era, was laid out in two zones, one residential and the other wholly industrial; one was a miniature Bath, characterised by fashionable crescents and squares; the other was severely functional and rectangular.[11] Unlike Paisley, the two zones remained apart.

The linear lay-out of most Scottish burghs, at least prior to the last quarter of the eighteenth century, lent a 'sameness' to panoramic landscapes. Artists frequently countered the perils of template panoramas by framing their townscapes with detail in the foreground, to lend a sense of human activity. Such detail was rarely extensive. In the eighteenth century, Scottish towns had no Hogarth and nothing of the vividness of his *Gin Lane* (1751). In a way, this was surprising. The single most important external influence on Scotland's culture, education and trade until at least 1700 was the Netherlands. By the seventeenth-century Dutch townscape painters, such as Jan van der Heyden of Amsterdam (1637–1712), were accustomed to filling their canvas with a myriad of commonplace detail of life in city streets, markets and ports.[12] Very little of this school of art permeated to Scottish painting before the nineteenth century. One of the earliest examples was *The Panorama of the City of Glasgow* (1817) by John Knox (1778–1845) (48).

In Scotland, that kind of picture of ordinary working life was, for the time being, mostly confined to studies of rural and especially peasant life, such as Alexander Carse's *Oldhamstocks Fair* (1796) (81) or David Wilkie's *Pitlessie Fair* (1804) (89). This was the reflection in art of a revival of the Scots vernacular first espoused in the work of Allan Ramsay (1684–1758), consolidated by Robert Ferguson (1750–74) as in his *Hallow Fair*, and immortalised by Robert Burns (1759–96) in his *Holy Fair*. It involved a celebration of the pastoral and of peasant life and reflected a much older tradition of rustic revelry which went back to popular folk literature in Middle Scots such as the late medieval poem, *Christis Kirk on the Grene*.

Both Ramsay and Ferguson had a sharp eye for the drunkenness, lechery and hypocrisy of the urban scene. Ferguson described with relish the drunken debauchery in which a day at the Leith races usually ended (*see* 68). And Ramsay, in works such as 'Lucky Spence's last advice', the death-bed confession of a brothel madam to her prostitutes, exposed the seamy underworld of Edinburgh society in the 1720s. Yet, despite the many linkages and cross-fertilisation in Edinburgh's cultural scene in this period – involving philosophy, music, decorative art and the fledgling theatre – painting was mostly confined to the seemly and lucrative trades of the portrait and heraldry.[13] The closest to depictions of 'real' urban life, though often with strong elements of caricature, came in some of the work of Paul Sandby (1731–1809), mostly in his Edinburgh scenes, such as *Horse Fair at Bruntsfield Links* (1751) (32), though also in his vivid depiction of a market in an anonymous garrisoned town somewhere in the Highlands (56) and in individual figures captured in his sketch books, such as this 'The Hingie' (fig. 3), an anonymous woman hanging out of her window, and fishermen, probably fishing for salmon, hauling in a net (fig. 4). Other glimpses of Edinburgh life – and often low life – in his sketch books remain unpublished and largely unknown.[14]

Otherwise, human activity in many townscapes was confined to 'staffage'. This might either entail vegetation, in the Dutch landscape style, as in Paul Sandy's view of Leith in 1747 (67) and Robert Paul's (1739–70) view of Paisley (1767), in which the townscape is

3. Paul Sandby, *The Hingie*, c. 1746
Attributed to Paul Sandby, 'Sketchbook of Drawings Made in the Highlands'

4. Paul Sandby, *Local Salmon Fishermen, Inverness, c.* 1746
Attributed to Paul Sandby, 'Sketchbook of Drawings Made in the Highlands'

framed within an idyllic rural setting. Or, it might also use fairly anonymous human figures reposing in a sylvan setting, as in James Paterson's various studies of Arbroath, Brechin, Forfar (40) and Montrose in the 1820s, or (more rarely) working in the fields, as in John Clerk of Eldin's (1728–1812) panoramic view of Dunbar with a horse and ploughman in the foreground (20a), or in the studies of Glasgow from the south (47) by students of the Foulis Academy (1762), and in Sandby's *View of Leith from the East Road* (1751) (67b). One remarkable exception is the anonymous view of the textile mills in Galashiels in 1845, with Sir Walter Scott brought back to life along with his favourite deerhound in the foreground (44). Sometimes, the staffage portrays the artist himself as an integral part of the landscape, as in Paul's Port Glasgow (90), Paterson's Forfar, a view of Kinghorn by James Stewart published in 1840 (63) and in a panoramic view of Stirling of *c.* 1679 which features both artists (94). In the case of a map, a surveyor with his measuring compasses is portrayed in James Gordon of Rothiemay's map of the two Aberdeens of 1661 (1, 2a). It is, however, often difficult to be certain whether such additions lent authenticity to a picture or mere decoration.

Patronage: royal, aristocratic and municipal before 1800

Patronage was vital to the development of the art of the townscape. It was Timothy Pont (*c.* 1565–*c.* 1615) who first captured a landscape of power, with symbols for tower houses, kirktouns, fermtouns and much else. His sponsor or patron is unknown, although the point has attracted much speculation. It is inconceivable, despite Pont's connections to the royal court via his father, the leading figure in the Kirk, Robert Pont (1524–1606), that he could have undertaken such a wide-ranging and costly survey of much of the mainland of Scotland on his stipend as an absentee parish minister.

Burghs were accorded special treatment in Pont's map drafts: they are named in elaborate italic capitals; the key symbols of their status – whether church, tolbooth or burgh walls – are highlighted. Not many towns had a wall surrounding settlement. Pont was careful to indicate burgh walls where they did exist. So Elgin is shown as dominated by both its cathedral and its walls (37). Each of the drafts is a miniature pen portrait: Glasgow with its bridge, the vital link to its vast hinterland, exaggerated; and Forfar's market cross and tolbooth precisely delineated. Some of his portraits raise question marks of history: Tain is conspicuously depicted with a near-circular burgh wall, which archaeology has yet to find, if it ever existed (37a). And, in the case of Nairn, Pont seems to claim that the 'Ruins of the old Cast[le]' were by his time beneath the waves (76a). Each burgh was usually sharply distinguished from its surrounding countryside.

Taken as a whole, what did Pont's depiction of burghs amount to? His period was one in which the mental map of Scotland was fast being remodelled, with a feudal realm refashioning itself as a state. His depiction of large tower houses, with their storeys carefully noted, reflected the rise of landowning classes, both old and *arrivistes*. His burgh vignettes, taken together, suggested a series of concepts: like the nobility, they were and had long been 'chief vassals' of the crown; they were the branch offices of new state formation; and his visual record showed the rise to greater prominence of the third estate of the realm which, despite its small size in terms of population, paid a fifth of all national taxation. In short, Pont's maps were visual exercises in charting power and power-brokers within Scotland's localities using the new discipline of chorography – a word first recorded in English in 1559.[15] Taken together, his maps provided an impression of the standing of each of the three estates of the realm as surely as did the meticulous detail observed in the new ceremony of the 'riding of parliament'. And in the process, Pont's manuscripts, like the 'riding', also mirrored a new sense of national identity.[16]

Royal patronage did not disappear with the removal of the Stewarts to London in 1603. Each of the successive visits to Scotland of Charles I (1625–49) – in 1633, 1639–40 (when his progress northwards with a royal army stopped short at Berwick) and 1641 – provoked landscape portraits, mostly commissioned *after* the visit in an effort to regain the political initiative in calculated displays of the imagery of power. Such were Cornelis van Dalen the Elder's (1602–65) portrait of Edinburgh cowed by the equestrian image of its mighty monarch (1638) (fig. 5); by Alexander Kierincx (1600–52) in his recreated images of two – or perhaps more – of the King's power bases in Scotland, at Seton and Falkland (39) in 1639–40. What is immediately noteworthy is the fact that Charles I,

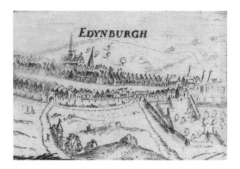

5. Cornelis van Dalen, *The High & Mighty Monarch Charles, c.* 1638

a collector of artists and engravers as well as of works of art, invariably commissioned foreign artists for all these works on Scotland.

The detailed portrait of Edinburgh and Canongate by Wenceslaus Hollar (30), arguably first created in 1641 during the three-month stay of Charles I in Edinburgh late in that year, suggests a less direct pattern of patronage. There is no evidence to suggest that this view of the capital was directly commissioned by the king but Hollar had gradually ingratiated himself into court circles since arriving in England in 1636. He had initially been recruited by the Earl of Arundel, while on an embassy to Cologne, to act as a copyist of works in his art collection. Within months of his arrival, Hollar, styling himself as 'engraver' to Arundel, had produced a panoramic view of Greenwich dedicated to Charles's queen, Henrietta Maria. By 1641 he had joined the household of the young Duke of York (1633–1701), the future James II and VII (1685–88/9), probably as a drawing master.[17]

Surrogate royal patronage also existed, seen at its best in the large portrait of Stirling (94) painted late in the reign of Charles II (1651–85) by two artists – Johannes Vosterman (1643–99) and Jan van Wyck (*c.* 1645–1700). Like Hollar, Vosterman touted for work in and around the court in the late 1670s and early 1680s but had no regular patron. Van Wyck, in contrast, enjoyed the patronage of a number of leading nobles, including the king's favourite, the Duke of Monmouth. Predictably, the painting of Stirling was a representation in the form of a dramatic landscape of one of the key icons of the Stuart monarchy – the historic royal castle and the King's Knot below. Much aristocratic patronage lies hidden within landscape paintings. The period after the departure of the Stewart monarchy for London in 1603 had the effect of fostering a country house culture: new tower houses, built for display rather than defence, had picture galleries displaying the lineage of the family and viewing platforms to survey its lands.[18]

Artists often strove to place noble houses centre stage in their picture. Even though John Slezer (*c.* 1650–1717) had a dedicated section of his *Theatrum Scotiae* (1693) devoted to private aristocratic houses, he also regularly featured them in his views of towns. This was the case with Culross (15) and his *Prospect of the Town of Dunkeld* (1693), with the mansion of the Duke of Atholl literally in the centre of the engraving (26a). James Stobie in his 1783 inset view of the same town followed in Slezer's footsteps (26). Even after 1800 artists could pander to aristocratic tastes and patronage. John Clark (fl. 1824–8), conscious of the promise of his publishers to subject his paintings 'to the inspection of Gentlemen of taste, resident upon the spot',[19] often chose a vista which highlighted a noble mansion; such was his view of Banff (1824), which showed Duff House dominating its foreground. In contrast, the view of Banff by James Wales (1747–95), which was commissioned by its town council in 1775, eschewed Duff House completely, focusing rather on the splendid new bridge which it had paid for (9).

Two of the most striking images to emerge from early modern Scotland were bird's-eye maps – of Edinburgh (1647) and the two burghs of Aberdeen (1661). Both were commissioned by the respective town council and both were the work of James Gordon of Rothiemay (1617–86), son of the map-maker Robert Gordon of Straloch (1580–1661). It might well be thought that these highly detailed maps represented a major landmark in these two burghs' sense of themselves. Why had these town councils commissioned these works? In the case of Aberdeen, the reason is clear as it is given in the Latin 'Description' on the map itself: it was a celebration of survival for 'no citie in Scotland ... did suffer more hurt then Aberdeen did, nor oftener' in the Covenanting wars (1).

The case of Edinburgh, by 1647 debt-ridden and almost bankrupted by ten years of internal strife and war, is a little more difficult to fathom. A decisive clue lies in the map's dedication to the provost, Archibald Todd and four bailies. Todd had been elected to power in October 1647, restoring to power a conservative-minded council anxious to preserve its integrity in the face of the growing storm of radical Covenanting opinion. Less than three months later, the council backed the Engagement, which promised a return to moderate support for Charles I and a restoration of Edinburgh's place as capital of his realm. Little wonder that Rothiemay's elaborate bird's eye view, dedicated to 'the most ancient and noble' burgh of the realm, depicted centre stage the new parliament house, finished at ruinous expense in 1639, alongside St Giles' and the new tolbooth. The key, in Latin as well as the vernacular, confirms that this was an image designed for a readership extending well beyond Scotland's borders.[20]

Sadly for Edinburgh, this glittering image of itself was overtaken by events. Within three years, it was taken and occupied by an English army; its main buildings, including its churches and tolbooth looted, and its council riven by internal dissension.[21] It would not fully recover until the early 1680s, the period when James, Duke of York younger brother of Charles II (1651–85) and heir to the throne – held court in Edinburgh and the capital became a pantheon of the arts and humanities. The impetus was aristocratic in tone and much of it was fuelled by a new breed of patrons – Edinburgh's burgeoning ranks of lawyers. New offices were devised, including those of Geographer-royal and Historiographer-royal; the privy council aided John Adair's (*c*. 1650–1718) project to map Scotland's counties, drawing on the earlier work of Pont and Gordon of Straloch. And the dream of building a new capital on a green-field site away from the congested streets and wynds off the High Street was first mooted. It would take a century, however, to become a physical reality.[22]

It was not until the 1720s that a different kind of organised patronage emerged and for some considerable time it was confined to Edinburgh. In 1729 the Edinburgh School of St Luke, the earliest academy of artists in Scotland, was founded by 'Noblemen, Gentlemen, Patrons, Painters and lovers of painting'. This was an ambitious scheme, inspired by – if not modelled on – the *Accademia di San Luca*, founded in Rome in 1577 as a means to promote the work of artists above that of mere craftsmen. Ironically, if unsurprisingly, two of the founders of the Edinburgh School were craftsmen. They were James Norie (1684–1757), the founder of a family firm of decorators, and Richard Cooper (1701–64), an

6. Roderick Chalmers, *The Edinburgh Trades*, 1720

English engraver who moved to Edinburgh in 1725 after a period in Italy, where he first began an impressive collection of prints and drawings. Others involved in the beginnings of the School were the poet Allan Ramsay, the architect William Adam, and various art dealers and painters. In one sense, the School was a natural development in the long struggle for influence waged by Norie and his colleague Roderick Chalmers (fl. 1709–30) within the Incorporation of St Mary's Chapel, originally a trade guild, to elevate its status (fig. 6): *The Edinburgh Trades* (1720).[23] In another, it reflected the flowering of the arts as a whole in Edinburgh and their cross-fertilisation. Very much a creation of the capital, the School, however, eschewed its birthplace as a subject for its art.

The School was short-lived but the networks which established it remained influential, in the capital at least, for much of the remainder of the century. A series of artists started their careers working for the Norie firm, including Alexander Runciman (1736–85), Jacob More (1740–93) and Alexander Nasmyth (1758–1840). To some extent the same can be said of Richard Cooper. Certainly, much of the story of engraving in eighteenth-century Scotland until the 1760s can be subsumed into his career.[24] He was particularly active in the publication of maps – of Scottish counties, rivers and coastline. On occasion, his maps included a townscape: such was his edition of William Edgar's survey map of Stirlingshire (*c.* 1746), which has a crude picture of Cambuskenneth Abbey and the town of Stirling beyond as an inset, although the perspective is heavily exaggerated (fig. 7).[25] Like Norie, Cooper was not simply an artisan. His interests ranged across the arts, as did his work. Like Norie again, he was a friend and patron of artists and poets: he owned one of Edinburgh's first theatres and employed the French artist, William Delacour (1710–68) – noted for his watercolour landscape of Edinburgh (1756), one of the first full painted townscapes of the city (fig. 8) – as a scene painter. Cooper's son, Richard (1740–1814), was a distinguished artist who studied in Rome and was a friend of both Runciman brothers, Alexander and John (*see* 33), and of Jacob More.[26]

7. William Edgar, *Stirlingshire*, 1745–6

In Glasgow, the Foulis Academy of Fine Arts, founded in 1753, followed a different and more structured course, specifically linked to the city of its birth. Intended as a school of art and design, it was created as a marriage between business and culture; it was financed by some of the city's richest merchants whose wealth was largely based on the tobacco trade

8. William Delacour, *View of Edinburgh*, 1759

but it was also backed by the university, which acted as a home to both the printing press run by the Foulis brothers, Robert (1707–76) and Andrew (1712–75), and the academy. Its pupils were given a wide-ranging, classically based education as well as training in art, architecture, printing and engraving. Although landscape was not at the forefront of the curriculum, nevertheless the work of pupils of the academy produced a body of work which, collectively, amounted to a comprehensive dossier of Glasgow's townscape (47) and that of nearby towns and ports, such as Paisley, Greenock and Port Glasgow (90), in the 1760s and 1770s. One particularly striking image, even if crudely drawn, shows the Bridgegate underwater (fig. 9) – a reminder of the vulnerability of the low-lying part of the city to flooding, seen at its worst in 1795 when the Hutchesontown Bridge was swept away (48). Much of this collection of urban views was done by anonymous pupils but some of the most striking work was that of Robert Paul. By 1800, both the Foulis Press and Academy had gone. Its longer-term impact is debatable. The list of its pupils was long and impressive, though most specialised in areas other than landscape. Two exceptions were David

9. Foulis Academy, *View of the Bridgegate, Glasgow, looking West, c.* 1770

14

Allan (1744–96) and Charles Cordiner (1746–94), one of the few artists to capture scenes in the northern Highlands in this period (17a). Allan's primary interests lay in rural society and culture but he did produce a series of drawings of life in and around Edinburgh.[27] Cordiner's landscapes of Inverness (1780) (fig. 10) and of Duff House with Banff in the background, where he was the local Episcopalian minister, were particularly fine examples of his watercolours.[28] On the other hand, very few of the Academy's pupils pursued careers in the city.[29] Glasgow's loss, to a great extent, became Edinburgh's and London's gain.

Military maps, plans and views, 1650–1800

It is one of the curiosities of Scottish history as it is often written, that, confronted by the dramatic story of Cromwellian invasion, the reimposition of order after the Restoration of 1660, and successive Jacobite plots and risings, a simple fact is often eschewed. Scotland was under military occupation for most of the century and a quarter after 1650. Most maps and views of Scotland in this period were, as a direct result, the work of military engineers. Despite so much of this period being dominated by military strategy, very

10. Charles Cordiner, *Inverness*, 1780

little in comparative terms has survived. The cartoon map of the Battle of Pinkie (1547), later reproduced by Holinshed in 1577, shows very little of Musselburgh other than the strategic bridge over the River Esk. Of more interest to the urban historian, in the far right-hand corner of the map, is the first and only glimpse of Leith before a French citadel was constructed around it in the 1550s (74). Little survives too, somewhat surprisingly, from the period of Cromwellian invasion and occupation. A primitive map of the Battle of Dunbar (1650) survives but tells little about the town itself. A very unusual drawing, made by an ordinary English soldier *c.* 1653, showing the newly built citadel on the promontory of Stornoway's primitive harbour, was discovered in recent times (fig. 11).[30] Otherwise, maps and drawings were confined to depictions of the large citadels – Ayr, Inverness, Leith and Perth which were begun but not always finished in the 1650s (7).

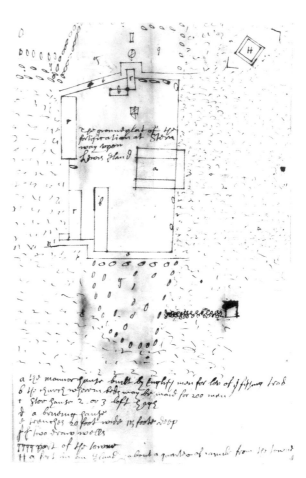

11. *The Groundplan of the Fortification at Stornaway upon Lewis Iland, c.* 1653

One reason for this is that at least parts of the survey work were, in effect, a state secret, such as the mapping work of Paul Sandby for the Board of Ordnance after the last Jacobite rising of 1745–6 and the military survey of 1747–55 conducted by William Roy (1726–90) (*see* 54a). There is very little, however, to compare with the explosion of mapping, military diagrams, and colourful views of battle scenes and sieges of towns which marked the Thirty Years' War (1618–48) in Europe or the wars of Louis XIV (1667–97).[31] In Scotland, by contrast, military mapping carried out by the Hanoverian state largely consisted of the charting of *terra incognita*.

The work of the German-born army officer and military draughtsman, John Slezer, began in Scotland with a survey of the country's defences in the troubled times of the late 1670s, amidst Covenanting resistance and rebellion. It was impecuniousness, driven by persistent arrears in his army pay – under different, successive regimes – which probably prompted Slezer to turn his military surveys into a more general money-making project, which eventually appeared as *Theatrum Scotiae* (1693). As early as 1677, Slezer had received a private commission, from the Duke of Lauderdale, for plans and views of Thirlestane Castle.[32] It also seems likely that he received payments as well as free burgess-ships from Dundee in 1678 (*see* 22), Linlithgow in 1682 (70), and Edinburgh in 1684 for his various views of these burghs. However, the accuracy of many of Slezer's views, especially those of towns, may be called into question; this, it is argued, was the case in one of his three views of Glasgow (46). This applies to the picturesque detail of people, boats and animals – or staffage – which is likely to have been added by his colleague, Jan van Wyck or by apprentices. But it also applies, at times, to perspective, both of townscape and individual buildings. Three examples are clear: one of his two views of Dunfermline sets some of the buildings in the scene in mirror image (SL. 45); his prospect of Perth tries to impose a linear shape parallel to the Tay on a town which, in fact, stretched westward away from the river (*cf.* 86); and his 'Prospect of Stirling from the East' (SL. 6) superimposed on the foreground an exaggerated perspective of Cambuskenneth Abbey in the immediate foreground, which is out of touch with the distant landscape of the town, castle and bridge.

The work of the engineers of the Board of Ordnance, reformed in 1683, produced more than 800 maps and plans of Scotland between 1689 and 1814. Most were concerned with depicting old castles and newly built fortresses and their position in the landscape or with roads and topography seen through strictly military eyes. But a few views of towns – as distinct from strongholds within towns such as Dumbarton, Edinburgh, Inverness and Stirling – resulted. The earliest extant maps of Inverness (7c) and Perth (both 1716) were the result of a surge in activity by the Board's engineers in the immediate aftermath of the Jacobite rising of 1715–16.[33] A series of partial plans of Inverness followed between 1716 and 1732 but the town was not fully mapped again until the survey by John Wood in the 1820s. The next surviving plan of Perth appeared as an incidental detail in James Stobie's county map of Perthshire and Clackmannan of 1783 (86a). Such obvious lacunae in the cartography of Scotland – both rural and urban – would occasion surprise amongst historians of English mapmaking.

The wholesale defeat of the last Jacobite rising of 1745–6 brought a regime which was determined to master the topography and logistics of an alien landscape. Although there had been considerable mapping of key strongholds in Scotland after the failure of the abortive rising of 1715, the period from 1746 onwards saw a systematic campaign of cartography, charting the terrain, roads and strongholds over much of Scotland. Behind this ambitious and ruthless project, no less than a mission to lay the foundation of a British state, lay a determination to conquer a *terra incognita* and to subdue an alien people by 'extirpateing their barbarity with their chief marks of distinction, their language and dress', in the words of Lord Milton (1692–1766), one of the key Scottish 'managers' of the new 'North Britain'. The work of William Roy on the military survey of Scotland between 1747 and 1752 resulted in the 'great map'. For a time, his only assistant was a topographer, Paul Sandby (1731–1809).[34] Together, they produced highly detailed relief maps of mountains and coastline, with the king's roads etched in red, the colour of the uniform of the Hanoverian army.[35] Paul and his brother, Thomas (1723–98), also produced a series of watercolours of the army of occupation based in the Highlands. Their depictions of Fort Augustus (41, 41a) and Fort William (42) are graphic images of a highly organised military force based in a wild and alien landscape.[36]

Yet there were other faces to Paul Sandby, the artist. His obvious fascination with landscape resulted in a series of watercolours, such as Castle Duart, Isle of Mull, and other drawings of military strongholds, including the castles of Bothwell, Dumbarton, Edinburgh (31a) and Stirling.[37] He also portrayed almost a complete range of Scottish society, both Highland and Lowland. His sketch of an anonymous Highland market place, almost certainly either Inverness or Fort William (56), together with a haunting image of Highland prisoners (41a), provide an authentic glimpse of a subdued, alien race. His sketch books, largely unpublished, offer a range of images of life – and often low life – in Edinburgh, and especially in its seamy suburb of the Grassmarket (31).[38] In his portrait of a fair on Bruntsfield Links, just outside Edinburgh, his satirical brush portrays a range of human excess (30). Yet he also recorded with approval peasants hard at work harvesting in the fields in one of his views of Leith (67a). And he knew enough about the politics of post-Jacobite Scotland to portray, with more approval still, the manners of the aristocracy and gentry in the Campbell stronghold of Inveraray (54), in one of the very few glimpses of the town prior to its wholesale make-over by successive dukes of Argyll.

'Improvement': land surveyors, 'new towns' and urban clearance, 1750–1830

The 'rage for Improvement', usually associated with the rationalisation of rural land and the foundation of planned villages, had its urban counterparts, seen in grid-style lay-out plans (in imitation of Edinburgh's New Town but often in advance of its actual long-delayed completion), civic squares, the creation of discrete open spaces or in a celebration of individual buildings, such as Aberdeen Trades Hospital (2), the Mechanics' Institute, Brechin (10), or the new Town Hall in Inverurie (58). This, in a sense, was the rebirth of a much older convention in 'view maps', which in the Middle Ages had portrayed a city as a collage of its key buildings, especially its churches, seen as late as 1550 in Alesius's (1500–65) view of his home town of Edinburgh (28).

'Improvement', however, celebrated a quite different shape of townscape from the historic linear layout of Scottish medieval burghs. In most cases, such 'Improvement' did not amount to a comprehensive plan for the transformation of urban settlement.[39] That tended to come later, as at Kilmarnock, where the old medieval shambles at the core of the burgh was swept away in the two decades after 1804 (62). The main objective was the achievement of elegance, captured both in greater comfort and better standards of accommodation or in new shapes of townscape. Civic squares and new straight-line street vistas, envisaged along neo-classical lines, adorned what were usually exclusively residential areas. These were, in effect, upper- or middle-class estates, set apart from commerce and trade which had traditionally formed the core of urban living. Almost invariably built of stone, and conditioned by space and order, they were far removed from the densely packed, overcrowded living conditions that had characterised medieval and early modern burghs (*see* 45 for an example, depicting Glasgow's Saltmarket).

As such, many so-called 'new towns' were suburbs located in green-field sites outside long-established urban settlements. Such was 'the New Town at the North Ferry' – Broughty Ferry – first laid out on a grid pattern outside the old fishing community in the 1790s, though its real growth did not come until after the arrival of the railway in 1839 (11). They were drawn up by estate surveyors and the main motive with most was clear, although most plans were dressed in the language of 'Improvement' and progress. Detailed plans of plots and projected streets (often with landowners' names) almost invariably extolled the possibilities – and profits – of planned settlement (fig. 12). This was not necessarily a development of the later eighteenth century, although the rise in population and the increasing potential for planting profitable industry in the rural landscape also gave added impetus to such works. The rise of New Lanark was the most striking example of iconic, new-style buildings set in a rural landscape – in this case a highly dramatic landscape – and it was celebrated many times over (78).

A significant variant in planning driven by landowners was urban clearance – the wholesale realignment of a townscape or the abandonment of part of it to accommodate the privacy or ambitions of local aristocracy. Some cases are reasonably well known. One such is Inveraray, where selective demolition of houses too near the Duke's castle began in the 1720s. By the 1740s, when Paul Sandby sketched the centre of the old town (54), the plan had changed towards wholesale clearance and the building of a 'new town' and a new, more splendid castle, discretely set well apart from each other. The project, however, took more than half a century to complete. A particularly blatant case of wholesale clearance was inflicted by the 4th Duke of Gordon on Fochabers, a small burgh of barony founded in 1599, where the population had grown to over 600 by the eighteenth century, as can be seen in William Roy's map of 1747–55. When his fifteenth-century castle was rebuilt in the 1770s, he moved the whole village a mile farther away to the south so as to set his new palace in solitary splendour in 1,300 acres of deer park.[40] Another celebrated example is that of Cullen, a royal burgh which traced its origins to the late twelfth century. Between 1820 and 1822, the whole town, including its market cross, was moved some two miles towards a new settlement at the shore called Fishertown to allow the Earl of Seafield to improve his estate. All that was left in its original position was the burgh church, while Seafield's mansion, Cullen House, was left in splendid isolation.[41]

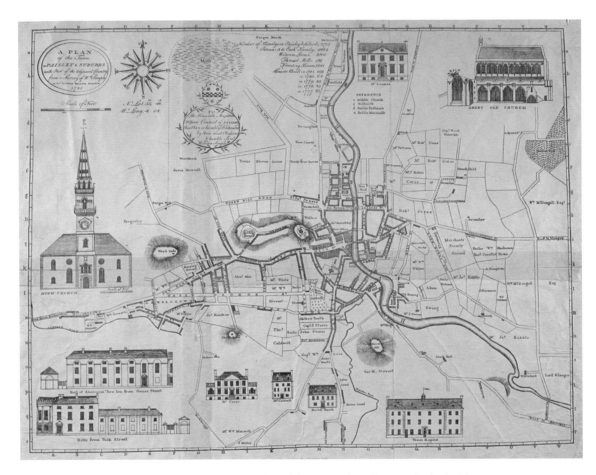

12. William Semple, *A Plan of the Town of Paisley & Suburbs*, 1781

Two less well-known but larger-scale examples of this phenomenon were Dalkeith (16) and Hamilton (53), where wholesale changes were made to the townscape, in both cases under the guise of 'Improvement'. Stornoway also saw successive efforts by the major landowner in Lewis to keep the population of the town at arm's length from his estate (97).

The Duchess of Hamilton in effect cleared much of the 'hie toun' of Hamilton to lend added privacy to her estate. The owners of Dalkeith Palace barred access to the main road to the river crossing which ran through their estate, blocking up nearby houses and windows in the process, and forced a circuitous route around a new estate wall – a road which remains hazardous to this day. In a further case, that of Stornoway, the quest for physical 'apartness' and privacy was carried on for a century or more by successive landowners.[42] As has been seen, an earlier but abortive effort at clearance for much the same reason was made by David Lindsay of Edzell, an ambitious local laird, who commissioned a plan for a 'new citie of Edzel' in 1592 in order to move the nearby settlement of Slateford farther away from his castle (36). In the event, Lindsay's grandiose scheme did not come to fruition.

Maps, view maps and pictorial views in the eighteenth century

Views of towns and town life were not only the work of artists proper. There are a series of inter-connections between artists, engravers and cartographers. William Daniell (1769–1837), John Clark and Paul Sandby, who all feature prominently in this book, were artists who also from time to time acted as engravers. The cartographer James Stobie also doubled as an artist in his county map of Perthshire, which had a series of pictures of country seats as well as views of Dunkeld (26) and Perth (86) to flatter his aristocratic patrons and to enhance the map's sales. As a result, the dividing-lines between landscape or townscape, 'view maps' and cartographic maps proper are often blurred. Gordon of Rothiemay's map of Old and New Aberdeen (1661) also has a townscape in a separate frame (*see* 1, 2a). The map of Scotland (1714) of Herman Moll, a Dutch map-maker working in London, had

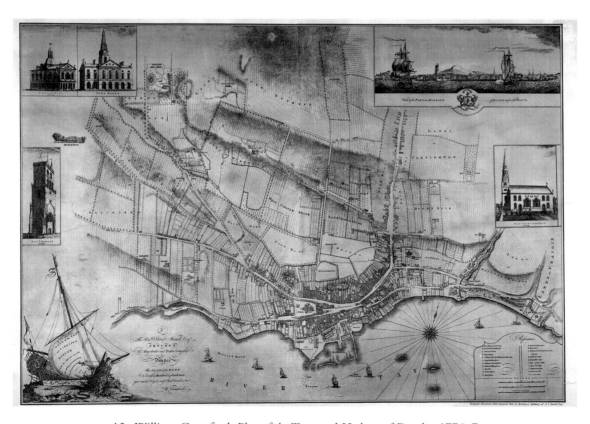

13. William Crawford, *Plan of the Town and Harbour of Dundee*, 1776–7

inset views of seven burghs and four fortresses but most were virtual carbon copies of the views drawn by Slezer twenty years earlier.[43] New townscape views were rare until the third quarter of the century and often were the direct result of new, more sophisticated mapping surveys. Such was William Crawford's *Plan of the Town and Harbour of Dundee* (1776–7), the first modern plan of the town drawn 'from an accurate survey' at a seismic point in its history, signalling a series of improvement schemes involving both new roads and new buildings; it had inset pictures of five of the key buildings in the town, including the newly built Trades Hall as well as a panorama of the burgh from the estuary (fig. 13).[44] William Semple's plan of Paisley (1781) has some of the iconic buildings in the town drawn around the edges of the plan (fig. 12), as does a 1771 map of the county of Berwickshire by Andrew Armstrong (1700–94) with a blow-up of the new town of Greenlaw – an extension to the old burgh of barony – in an inset, showing a sketch of the planned County House, jail and church (fig. 14), as well as existing buildings, which are conventionally mapped.

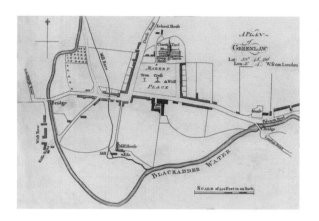

14. Andrew and Mostyn Armstrong,
A Plan of Greenlaw, 1771

By the 1770s, the process of production of new-style, detailed county maps was well advanced in England and Wales, to such an extent that by 1800 only two English counties lacked a modern, large-scale map.[45] Scotland, by contrast, was largely uncharted. As a result, the number of private surveyors was much fewer – the most notable being John Ainslie (1745–1828) and James Stobie (fl. 1775–1804), who had been factor to the Duke of Atholl. Stobie's four-section map of the counties of Perth and Clackmannan (1783) was a veritable art gallery, having no fewer than a dozen landscapes. In the south-east section, four views of country houses were depicted, along with an attractive, if ambiguous view of Perth from the north-west (86) – not a common vantage point for the town. The south-west sheet had five views – three of country seats, a plan of Perth (only the second surviving recognisable street plan of the burgh, the first being part of a military survey of 1716) and a view of Dunkeld from the south (26a), which was distinctively different from that of Slezer in 1693 (26a). Like many other county maps, it was published in both Scotland and London. Stobie used a London-based engraver, Peter Mazell, who was also involved in other pictorial works of Scotland in the same period, such as *Remarkable Ruins and Romantic Prospects of North Britain* (1788–95) by Charles Cordiner, minister of Banff.[46] It seems likely that, in order to maximise profits from the venture, Stobie sold the engravings of views separately as well as *in situ* on the county map.

Maps by Captain Andrew Armstrong and his son, Mostyn (fl. 1769–91), of half a dozen Scottish counties followed. His map of Ayrshire (1775), in six sections, has a prominently placed selling point – a cartouche view of the Ayrshire countryside and an anonymous castle, picturesque and evocative rather than accurate or readily identifiable. Virtually the whole of the sixth section is devoted to a very detailed map of Ayr, within an elaborate quasi-classical decorated border. In it, the New Town, to the north of the river, is given equal prominence with the historic burgh, with projected streets and plots laid out, as well as a proposed dry dock which would never materialise (fig. 15).

More elaborate still was Armstrong's map of the three Lothians (1773), in six sheets. The south-east sheet was almost entirely taken up with a fairly conventional (copied) map of Edinburgh, with streets both actual and projected, also referenced in an accompanying list. More than half of the south-western sheet depicted a grandiose

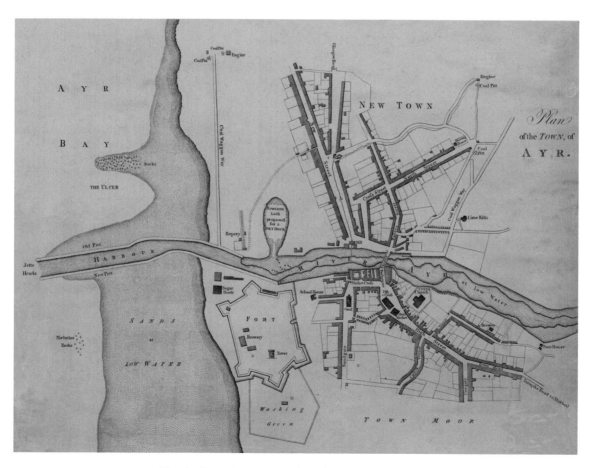

15. Andrew Armstrong, *Plan of the Town of Ayr*, 1775

23

cartouche and panoramic illustration, even more obviously an imaginative composite of nowhere land, of burgh walls, ruined tower, river and a lone herdsman (fig. 16). These elaborate and ambitious examples of a county map by a private surveyor managed to include within them three fashions: conventional mapping, now often based on more technical and accurate trigonometrical surveying, new town plans, and imaginative views of buildings and their setting in the landscape.[47] In it, the map and the artistic viewpoint became essential partners. It is inherently unlikely that the view of Dunkeld on Stobie's map (26) or other views in his virtual art gallery maps were the original work of the map-maker, although he does ascribe all but two of the views to himself, marking them 'Stobie delint'. Just as map-maker surveyors needed specialists to add the 'staffage' of human figures and animals to their view maps, so conventional map-makers needed artists to add inset landscape decorations to their county maps.

The artistic view, of course, had one enormous advantage. New-style mapping, involving complex technical surveying, drafting, engraving and publishing, was prohibitively expensive.[48] A number of schemes for county maps foundered for lack of finance and

16. Andrew and Mostyn Armstrong, *Map of the Three Lothians*, 1773

some, in order to save costs, were based on estate surveys. Stobie's county map was partly based on the work he had done for the Duke of Atholl in creating new, detailed maps of his extensive estates in Perthshire.[49] One effect of the cost imperative was that maps were copied and recopied, in atlases, hand guides and elsewhere, at times despite being out-of-date or overtaken by other developments.

17. Charles Ross, *A Plan of Glasgow*, 1773

A different tactic was to increase sales by adding 'human interest' elements in maps. Although Ainslie's early work was more sober than that of some of his rivals, he, too, was increasingly prey to the allegory, elaborate cartouche, visual symbolism and the spectre of 'bare ruined choirs', as in the north-west section of his six-sheet map of Fife and Kinross (1775) and his north-east section of the four-sheet map of the Stewartry of Kirkcudbright (1797), showing the ruined castle of Kirkcudbright. In his highly detailed map of Scotland (1783), he became even more extravagant. On the eastern sheets of his nine-section map, he depicts a herdsman of Highland cattle and three fishermen, hauling in a half-net; bizarrely, two of the figures wear a tam o' shanter. 'Scotland the brand' was already in draft form well before the age of Sir Walter Scott. Ainslie's map of Kirkcudbright referred to him as a land surveyor but did not claim to be based on an actual survey. His target market was clear: he addressed it to the 'Nobility and Gentry of the Stewartry'. By contrast, the *Map of the Shire of Lanark* (1773) by Charles Ross of Greenlaw (1722–1806), a land surveyor whose work was characterised by a meticulous attention to detail, did do so.[50] In the south-west section, he included a detailed and relatively little-known street plan of Glasgow, which pre-dates Robert Collier's 1776 map, often taken as the first usefully detailed survey of streets and development. It is a useful confirmation of detail as to the westward development of Glasgow in the early 1770s but interestingly, it also, as did Collier, marked out land east of Bridgegate as 'laid out for building' (*cf.* 47) (fig. 17). Although Ross's map also contained an imaginative scene of river, local architecture and typical workers' tools, this can help gain a series of contemporary impressions which, taken together, add up to a portrait of the county's economy, which was close to life as well as allegory (fig. 18).

Panoramic compositions of townscapes, in contrast, were much cheaper than modern-style mapping and they would become cheaper still with the increasing use of steel plate engraving from the 1820s onwards. Even so, landscape painters, too, often found it necessary to seek commissions or subscribers. A good example is to be found in the work of James Paterson, a Montrose drawing master, who composed views of a number of towns in Angus in the early 1820s, including Arbroath, Brechin, Forfar (40) and Montrose (73). His portfolio also included views of country seats, such as Rossie Castle and Langley House, recently built on the profits from the West Indies sugar trade. Yet private commissions were not confined to the wealthy. Paterson offered to add private houses to future editions of his landscapes.[51] Another tactic was a lottery. As well as having it engraved for sale, Robert Seaton, another local drawing master, raffled his original painting of the Castlegate, Aberdeen (1806), a familiar scene enlivened by colourful local personalities, including his patron, a local Episcopalian minister, and the local hangman, for five shillings a ticket (fig. 19).[52]

The cult of the 'landscape portrait' was part of a wider exploration of local and cultural identity, sometimes termed as the search for the 'Scottish historical landscape'.[53] In towns, it was natural that the quest should focus on important buildings and styles of

18. Charles Ross, *A Map of the Shire of Lanark*, 1773

buildings, particularly because most burgh churches were pre-Reformation structures. Alternatively, a cult, partly fostered by artists' experiences of Roman or Greek antiquity on the Grand Tour in the later eighteenth century, focused on Scotland's own architectural ruins, the result of decades of Protestant iconoclasm or neglect after the Reformation of 1560. One such example was Charles Cordiner's depiction of the ruins of Dornoch Cathedral (17a).

In ideal circumstances, maps and artistic views complemented and confirmed each other: one such example was the view of the west end of Paisley Abbey, blocked by the building used by a rival congregation (as clearly shown on John Wood's map of 1828) but suddenly revealed when the building was demolished (83a). It was, however, unusual for art and cartography to work in such harmony. In the case of Glasgow, it was art which predominated at first, in the work of Slezer in the 1690s and various exponents of the Foulis Academy in the 1760s and 1770s. It was not until the later 1770s that the first detailed maps of the city were published, beginning with Robert Collier's plan of 1776 and John McArthur's more extensive map of 1778.

Landscape and townscape painting, 1750–1830

One of the more curious effects of the work of Paul Sandy, an agent of the British state which was wholly hostile to Highland society and culture, was to begin the forging of an interest in the *terra incognita* of the Scottish wilderness. Ironically, the man sometimes described as the father of the topographical tradition in English landscape owed much of his early reputation to his landscape watercolours of Scotland, and especially those of the Highlands. As early as 1764, Thomas Gainsborough described him as 'the only Man of Genius … with respect to real Views from Nature in this Country'.[54]

19. Robert Seaton, *View of Castle Street on Market Day*, 1806

Although the famous tour of the Hebrides made by Dr Johnson in the company of James Boswell in 1773 still had a distinct air of eccentricity about it as a venture, by the end of the century Scotland was firmly established as a tourist destination. An extensive travel literature grew up, complete with maps and illustrated views of mountains, lochs, and wild landscape. One early example, which combined scenic depictions with a commentary was *Scotia Depicta or, the Antiquities, Castles, Public Buildings, Noblemen and Gentlemen's Seats, Cities, Towns, and Picturesque Scenery of Scotland* (1804), in which the artist was John Claude Nattes (1765–1822) (77). Another, much more comprehensive work was the eight-volume *Voyage around Great Britain* (1814–25) made by William Daniell, based on six separate expeditions between 1813 and 1823 (*see* 20, 43a). With the arrival of a comprehensive railway network in the late 1840s and 1850s, a second tranche of tourist literature, cheaper and less discriminating, flooded bookstalls geared to the interests of the railway passenger: one example was a series called *MacDonald's Tourists' Guides*. Its view of Dunfermline was conflated rather than strictly accurate (25).

It should be borne in mind that it was not always the case that a view might promote more interest in prospective visitors rather than a map. The *View of Inveraray from the Sea* (*c.* 1801) by Alexander Nasmyth showed a dramatic landscape in which the new planned town, the castle and its grounds (depicted centre stage), and the mountains and loch interacted in perfect harmony.[55] But was it enough in itself to attract visitors? A map of Argyllshire of the same year by George Langlands (fl.1771–1810), a land surveyor who had worked on Argyll's estates, was more didactic. It had two insets: one was of the Castle; the other was a plan of the town, complete with explicit advice: 'a few directions to travellers who may come to see the place' (fig. 20). In effect, it was an early example of a route map for tourists. The coincidence in date of an artistic landscape by the painter who had himself laid out the grounds of the castle and a map by another of Argyll's employees suggests that here, taken together, was one of Scotland's earliest travel brochures.[56]

One of the earliest Scottish exponents of this new vogue for wild scenery was Jacob More, who, like Alexander Runciman, had trained in the tradition of decorative painting first begun by James Norie the elder (1684–1757) in Edinburgh in the 1720s. The firm was continued by Norie's son, Robert Norie (*c.* 1711–66), and Runciman. The route from domestic decoration to art took half a century. The Norie family firm initially specialised in decorative painting, often of an admixture of classical scenes and Scottish landscape for internal plaster work and panelling in country houses, mostly around Edinburgh. After the legalising of the theatre in Scotland which paved the way for the opening of the Edinburgh Theatre Royal in 1767, the firm began to specialise in stage sets. In the course of two generations, landscape scenes moved from internal walls to full-scale studies on canvas. Scene painting produced a number of talented artists, including Delacour and David Roberts, whose striking watercolour of the Canongate owed much to a theatrical view of townscape (13).

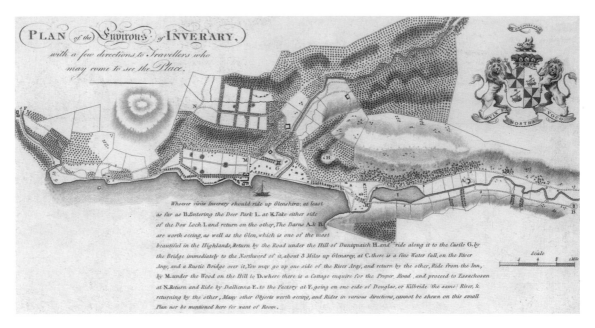

20. George Langlands, *Plan of the Environs of Inveraray*, 1801

The arrival on the scene of theatrical scene painters, together with a new vogue for landscape painted on the interior walls of houses, indirectly led to another innovation. This was the panorama. The device of a 360 degree painting, viewed from a platform within a rotunda, was invented in 1787 by Robert Barker (1739–1806), an Irish-born artist living in Edinburgh. His first exhibition was a *View of Edinburgh*, a circular prospect of the city from the top of Calton Hill, but subsequent displays of British victories in the Napoleonic wars at the panorama on Edinburgh's Mound took advantage of the jingoism of the moment. The next development was the moving panorama: an early version of it was the work of another artist from Edinburgh, Peter Marshall (1762–1826), whose first panorama, of the banks of the Clyde, appeared in Edinburgh in 1809. The popularity of panorama spread quickly. By the 1820s Glasgow had more than one panorama theatre: in 1825 an exhibition of the Battle of Waterloo played at an unnamed rotunda (fig. 21).[57] Another panorama theatre in Glasgow's Buchanan Street boasted of 16,000 square feet (1,486 sq. m.) of canvas in a performance during the Glasgow fair week depicting the Battle of Bannockburn with 'figures as large as life', complete with a military band (fig. 22).[58] In a real sense, such performances, which claimed to give a 'complete sense of reality', anticipated the silent cinema and accompanying music score by almost a century. Most of the enormous pieces of work involved in making a panorama have not survived. One case in point was the panorama of Glasgow devised by John Knox (*cf.* 48). One of the largest to survive, but in the form of an extended fold-out book of aquatint illustrations extending to 60 feet (18 metres) in length, is the *Panorama of the Thames from London to Richmond*, published by Samuel Leigh in 1829.[59] There was considerable controversy as to whether the panorama and its off-shoots constituted art, though most artists recognised its educational value and its theatrical potential.

Another pupil of the Norie family firm, albeit briefly, was Alexander Nasmyth, whose subsequent career and interests followed a different path. His apprenticeship under Allan Ramsay (1713–84), son of the poet of the same name and principal painter to George III, led him into portrait painting on his return to Edinburgh in 1778. Although his dramatic picture of Edinburgh Castle and the Nor' Loch was painted as early as 1780 (32a), much of his landscape work belonged to the period from the 1790s onwards. By the 1820s, Nasmyth had become the first professional – and financially successful – exponent of the Scottish townscape, which demanded an attention to details of architecture, daily life and contemporary fashions. The combination of a dynamic of detail to capture the essence of the townscape is seen to best effect in his large-scale studies of *Edinburgh from Princes Street with the Royal Institution Building under Construction* (1825) (34) and *Edinburgh with the*

21. Exhibition of the Battle of Waterloo,
Buchanan St, Glasgow, 1825

22. Handbill for Rotunda,
Buchanan Street, Glasgow, 1820s

High Street and Lawnmarket (1824). Despite a continuing and highly profitable interest in both the painting and cultivation of country house landscapes, such as those at Dalmeny and Dunglass, Nasmyth was the first to capture the essence of the large city in Scotland. His was a fortunate combination of circumstances: he became the artist and consultant to Edinburgh's New Town project; he was closely involved with the planning of its second new town, around Calton Hill; his work on Glasgow 'excited universal admiration';[60] and the visit of George IV to his Scottish capital in 1820 raised demand for more of his studies of Edinburgh scenes.

Changing urban life in the nineteenth century

The 1830s and 1840s were the two decades which saw the greatest and most seismic changes in the patterns of urban life in Scotland. After 1830, the ambitious work of planning and constructing 'new towns' – usually new suburbs of long-established settlements – on novel and classically inspired criteria of culture, refinement, space and order came to be challenged. The novel forces of change were the demands of industry, commerce and population growth. In the new economy towns began to need mills, factories and engineering works. And they needed more and more cheap housing to accommodate the throngs of migrants and immigrants who worked in the new economy. Industry and working-class housing, as a result, sprang up cheek by jowl with each other. Art captured very little of this. There were some exceptions; one was a nineteenth-century view of Dunfermline from the south which showed the historic abbey framed within two of the town's mill chimneys (25);[61] others were in the work of James Paterson on towns in Angus, such as his view of Arbroath (1825), which shows three of the chimneys of the town's many handloom weaving factories but discreetly hides the rest of them – unlike the graphic picture of reality in a railway advertisement, which showed its forest of factory chimneys (6).[62]

The second novel force to challenge the new towns was the railways.[63] Roads and bridges in the period of new-style planning, much celebrated by artists, had been seen as heralding a new age of space and order. The new bridges at Banff (1779) and Perth (1783), both designed by John Smeaton (1724–92), were celebrated shortly after their opening in art (9, 86). The second bridge at Ayr, built in 1788, featured in numerous views drawn or painted over the following century (8). The new street lay-outs in Aberdeen and Kilmarnock replacing the medieval shambles were the focus of portraits of each town (3a, 62). Railways were very different: they were not planned as part of organic growth. They typically drove wedges through towns, with a brutal disregard for existing patterns of settlement. The town of Coupar Angus was literally cut in two by the advent of the railway (14). The two rival lines into the centre of Glasgow drove everything from their path, including some of the new grid-style plans of the previous three-quarters of a century which had done so much to create the 'merchant city'. The Greenock and Ayr line brutally crossed King Street, Tradeston, in the Gorbals (fig. 23). Their associated demands, for sidings, goods yards and engineering sheds, used up urban space profligately, as David Octavius Hill's portrait of the St Rollox depot for the Glasgow and Garnkirk railway demonstrated (fig. 24 and 50).[64] The new economy – of mass industry, railways and new slums – would be the key setting for the new medium of photography.

Another dynamic steadily gathered pace in the last quarter of the eighteenth century and the first half of the nineteenth. It was the emergence, first in the shape of dissenting congregations, such as the Burghers and Anti-Burghers or Seceders, of new churches. At times, these early congregations were small enough only to need meeting houses rather than new, purpose-built buildings. By the first decades of the nineteenth century, the rise in population, mostly fuelled by mass migration to the new industries, resulted in the spread of a rash of new church buildings. This happened in small one-industry towns, such as Lerwick (69a), as well as in fast-growing 'new towns' such as Paisley (82). The surge in new churches was compounded after the granting of Catholic Emancipation in 1798, which resulted in a confident building programme, especially in the old Northern District, with churches in the heartland of surviving Catholicism, as at Braemar (1839), Dufftown (1825) and Keith (1831) (60), and even at the new one-industry town of Pulteneytown (1836), across the river from Wick, to cater for the seasonal migration in the

23. *View of the Greenock and Ayr Railway crossing King Street, Gorbals, Glasgow,* 1837

summer months from the Highlands and Western Isles for the herring fishery (99). At much the same time, the various growing splits within reformed Protestantism which marked the 1820s and 1830s culminated in the Disruption of 1843 and the construction of hundreds of new buildings to house the large-scale defection from the established church to the Free Church of Scotland. Although images of them abound, in art and architectural plans as well as in photography, some largely unknown in archives, little work has been done to chart the spread, ambitions and characteristics of these new church buildings which, in the case of larger towns, could be very sizeable indeed.

Just as new features began to disfigure or adorn the townscape of the 1830s and 1840s – in a rash of factory chimneys and a proliferation of church spires, often enhanced by the architectural fashion of the Gothic revival – a realisation began to emerge that the patterns of urban life were changing irredeemably. The original, single parish burgh had all but disappeared by the third quarter of the eighteenth century. New kinds of towns, often clustered around a single industry or a grouping of sub-industries such as textiles, were emerging fast. In the larger long-established towns, the coherence of the community

24. David Octavius Hill, *View of St Rollox Railway Depot*, 1831

of the burgh – and with it the credibility of both the status of burgess-ship and guild membership and the authority of burgh councils – had already come under strain in the later eighteenth century. By the 1820s and early 1830s, the self-electing oligarchies which ran burghs had resulted in various combinations of corruption, insolvency and ridicule. The artistic equivalent of John Galt's novel *The Provost* (1822), which wryly laid bare the machinations of Provost Pawkie and his cronies, was the cast of the bloated Dundonian establishment portrayed by a young local portrait artist in 'The Executive' (1821) (24), or the even cruder caricature of a resident ass en route to claim its hereditary burgess ticket in the Canongate (1833) (12).

The combination of the Burgh Reform Acts of 1833 and the Burgh Police Act of the same year provided some of the answers of how to cope with the new kind of urban society which industrialisation and growing population had begun to produce. The electorate in the burghs was sharply expanded and new powers were introduced to regulate town life, both in terms of behaviour and the provision of lighting, water, cleansing and drainage. This was reform of a sort. The direct beneficiaries of this legislation were £10 property holders but they amounted to less than one in forty of the adult male population. Images of town life, as reflected in art, made much of the new urbanity. The new fashions were closely reflected in street scenes; this was a world of 'long coats, gartered long trousers and top hats', depicted in profusion in Joseph William Allen's portrayal of Aberdeen's Castlegate in 1839 (3a), and in views of Inverurie (58) and Wigtown (100a) in the 1850s.[65] It was an urban world in which street lights now featured with regularity, as in this view of Dundee's Greenmarket (fig. 25), although in reality municipal lighting and paving often extended only to the streets where the new minority electorate lived. The second *Statistical Account*, usually written by local ministers of the established church in the decade after 1834, was full of praise for the new order, proud of the new bridewells and gaols, as were map-makers and artists who featured them regularly, as in Alexander Nasmyth's panorama of Edinburgh from Calton Hill (1825), which featured the Bridewell centre stage, as did T. H. Shepherd's *Modern Athens* (1837). The badge of the new order, in defiance of the enormous proliferation

25. *Old Custom House, Greenmarket, Dundee*, 1840s

26. *Teetotal Tower, Renfrew Road, Paisley, c. 1840*

of grog shops, especially in the industrial suburbs of new towns, which was one of the most regular complaints within ministers' accounts of their parishes, was teetotalism and self-help. The response amongst the middle classes and the skilled working classes was widespread and, at times, bizarre, such as the 'Teetotal Tower' in Paisley in 1840 (fig. 26).

The continuing and widening gulf between the two strains of urban society – the one, either assuredly middle-class or aspirational, in pursuit of thrift and sobriety, the other poorer than before, unskilled, under-educated and ill-regarded – is reflected in some portrayals of street scenes, such as the market in front of Dundee's Custom House (probably in the 1840s), or in Allen's almost obscene caricature of female market vendors in Aberdeen's Castlegate (3a). The second of these worlds – at times resembling an underworld – was the subject of a series of pamphlets in both Edinburgh and Glasgow in the 1840s and 1850s, such as George Bell's *Days and Nights in the Wynds of Edinburgh* (1849) and the anonymous investigation

27. William Gibb, *Fish Street, Dundee, c. 1830s*

Fish Street Looking East

28. Walter Geikie, *Libberton Wynd from the Cowgate*, 1830

of Glasgow's slums, *Midnight Scenes and Social Photographs* by 'Shadow' (1858). For the most part, artists faithfully recorded the slums – such as Dundee's Butcher Row and Fish Street (fig. 27) or Glasgow's Saltmarket (45a) – but they eschewed the slum dwellers or sanitised them. That task was mostly left to photographers who recorded this underworld of closes and overcrowded tenements but also the underclass living and dying there. Here, it is telling to compare Walter Geikie's (1795–1837) sanitised view of life in Libberton's Wynd (1830), just off Edinburgh's Lawnmarket, shortly before it was demolished (fig. 28) with the haunting human portrait conveyed in Thomas Annan's photograph of Close no. 46 in Glasgow's Saltmarket. Annan's image is indeed of children of the dead end.

Part II: Depicting the Town: Art and Artifice

Influences at work in Scottish landscape art

The number of glimpses of Scottish towns in either map or view form before 1650 is very limited. The influences which produced or conditioned them may be classified under three headings: some were the direct result of military surveying, especially during Scotland's wars with England; others were drawn with publication in a prestigious foreign atlas in mind; and a third category were the result of royal patronage. Henry VIII's (1509–47) obsession with maps and military strategy was reflected in the 'rough wooing' of Scotland in the 1540s. The so-called 'spy map' of Edinburgh and Canongate, showing an English army assaulting the royal palace of Holyroodhouse in 1544, gives only an outline impression of both burghs. The author's real concerns, each shown as a miniature, are the palace and castle and the great gate at the Netherbow (fig. 29), which withstood a frontal English assault. The Battle of Pinkie (1547), near Musselburgh, and its aftermath produced the first fleeting images of Leith,

29. Netherbow Port, 1544

seen in contemporary 'story' drawings and reproduced as a kind of running cartoon by Holinshed thirty years later (74). These views of Leith contrast sharply with the English coloured map of the town of 1559, now complete with a *trace italienne* citadel built by the French in the 1550s.[66] And a further English military action, this time to help the king's party besieging Edinburgh Castle in 1573, produced the first reasonably accurate view map of the capital, drawn by a military engineer (29).

Another early but very different view of Edinburgh, instructed by the memory of a Protestant refugee who had fled his native town some twenty years before, was printed in the German edition of Munster's *Cosmographia* (Basel, 1550) (28). One of the most prestigious atlases of the sixteenth century was the six-volume collection of Georg Braun and Frans Hogenberg, *Civitatis Orbis Terrarum* (1572–1618). The Edinburgh image within it of *c.* 1582 was impressionistic rather than detailed or accurate but it tried to show, in its portrayal of the burgh's castle, its main east gate and its churches – unfortunately two rather than three – the attributes of a 'metropolis'. Even so, the omissions (such as the palace), its exaggerated streets and its errors (two east gates rather than one) render it little more than a cameo. It is possible that the much more accurate view map of St Andrews, of much the same date, drawn in this case by a native hand, may have been intended for the same atlas (92).

Common to most of these images is the convention of the 'bird's eye view' – half map and half aerial survey – which was much the fashion in continental town atlases until well into the seventeenth century. As that century progressed, the vogue turned increasingly towards the scale map. In it, individual buildings or features are highlighted, often in great detail, but the overall perspective is variable. Such were the view maps of Edinburgh (1647) and the two burghs of Aberdeen (1661) drawn by James Gordon of Rothiemay, who depicts himself with a surveyor's compasses in an inset and also provides a scale of 'walking passes' [sic] (1). By the 1640s, Gordon was a highly experienced map-maker and it is likely that his Edinburgh masterpiece, although commissioned by the town council for political purposes, was intended for the *Atlas novus* (1654) of Blaeu, published in Amsterdam.

The most satisfying early views of Scottish towns were almost invariably the work of foreign artists, such as Kierincx and Hollar, if in their very different ways. Native painters, once deprived of ecclesiastical work after the Reformation, for the most part confined themselves to portraits, heraldic painting and internal decoration of country houses. It was Charles I especially who promoted the political landscape, though in the case of Scotland, as individual or one-off commissions, as was the case (as has been seen) with the two Dutch artists, Cornelis van Dalen and Alexander Keirincx (38).

Johannes Vosterman and his collaborator, Jan van Wyck (94), who also later worked for John Slezer, were only two of a larger group of foreign artists who visited or worked in Scotland during the reign of Charles II, particularly stimulated by the setting up of a virtual royal court at Holyrood during the period of residence of the Duke of York, between 1679 and 1682. The period of 'York in Edinburgh', when the palace of Holyroodhouse was extensively refurbished, brought more foreign artists to the capital, including Jacob de Witt (1640–97), who painted the sequence of portraits of kings for the Long Gallery at Holyrood.[67] This period, however, was also the virtual swansong of royal or aristocratic patronage. In the next century, a much more disparate picture of patronage and clientage would emerge.

It was no accident that most of these artists, save Hollar and Slezer, were Dutch. It is hardly surprising that the Netherlands was one of the main influences on Scottish culture in the seventeenth century; Scotland's students filled its universities and its merchants plied much of their trade there or in the Baltic. Dutch art did exercise a profound effect on the Scottish scene but in an unexpected way. It was the Netherlands tradition of landscape painting which was more influential than its emerging reputation for the art of the townscape. The reason for this is not hard to seek. After gaining independence from Spain in 1609, the urban culture of the Netherlands – a nation of expanding cities and burgeoning trade – underpinned a vision of prosperity, space and order. Townscape artists celebrated the aesthetics of urban living.[68] Compare the fortunes of Scotland's towns in the same period – one of the worst centuries in its history. Towns were besieged and sacked and civilians slaughtered by both foreign and domestic armies; in 1644–5 they experienced a severe outbreak of plague which, in some places, probably claimed one in five town dwellers; a number of towns were brutalised by the Cromwellian regime in the 1650s, with large numbers of graves dug up to make way for the building of large-scale citadels (7); and burghs were subjected to military occupation and free quarter both before and after 1660. The end of the century brought little respite: a combination of severe weather – the last blast of the Little Ice Age – bad harvests and falling trade brought about population stagnation and infertility, which in many places lasted until the 1720s or beyond.

It was little wonder, in such circumstances, that many artists took refuge in the conventions of Dutch *landscape* painting. Towns were framed against a rural or sylvan background. Peace and order were found, not in the internal space and architecture of towns, but by setting the townscape in a wider, pastoral environment. Most views of towns were painted from a distance, using the silhouette of the townscape, which was typically linear, interspersed with spires or towers denoting its key buildings. The art of John Clerk of Eldin was typical of this genre: he specialised in depicting historic buildings in the landscape or towns put within an agricultural setting. Such was his picture of Dunbar (20a). The genre, in Clerk's work and elsewhere, combined the topographical, the picturesque and the antiquarian.

The Grand Tour, invariably culminating in Italy, had a profound effect on both aristocratic would-be patrons and budding artists alike, particularly in the decades after the last Jacobite rising. It brought Scottish artists into contact with their English counterparts and stimulated a variety of influences, both personal and genre. The Tour tended to push artists' subject matter towards the classical and neo-classical or a merging of antiquity with the pastoral. The ruined castle in the landscape, often reminiscent of classical ruins, whether Greek or Roman, was one of its hallmarks. It had little or no impact on the town set within the landscape. One of the few major artists to experience Italy but take a distinctively different path was Alexander Nasmyth. After his return from a second visit to Rome in 1784, he tried to achieve a balance in his work, describing himself as both a portrait and a landscape painter, though increasingly the one featured in the other. By the 1820s, in his mature work, the figures in his townscape scenes were an integral part of a panoramic scene of detail, order and balance. His late works on Edinburgh and Leith are the closest that Scottish art reached out to the urban panoramas of Canaletto. It was little wonder that he was hailed in his lifetime as 'the founder of landscape painting' in Scotland.[69] His counterpart in Glasgow, John Knox, came closest to him in style, if not in contemporary reputation. His *Panorama of the City of Glasgow* (1817) (48) and *The Trongate* (1826), melded topography, architecture and social observation in an effective balance not achieved for Glasgow's townscape before him.

The advent of better stagecoach services, often celebrated in art (*see* 62, 75, 100a), and the invention of the steamboat helped generate an increased demand for views of the Scottish landscape, but the vogue was for wild scenery, whether nearby (seen in Knox's

30. John Fleming, *Greenock from the East*, 1829

paintings of *Landscape with Tourists at Loch Katrine* and *The Clyde from Dalnottar Hill*) or in the Highlands. Better transport links, new bridges and the advent of travel guides and other tourist literature brought increasing numbers of visitors. J. M. W. Turner (1775–1851) came to Scotland no less than six times, first in 1801, in search of the 'sublime' landscape. Save for his well-known studies of Edinburgh, including *Edinburgh from Calton Hill* (1804), based on a sketch made during his first visit, and a series of evocative studies of Linlithgow Palace (71), little of his work touched on Lowland Scotland, although his *View of the Tweed with Melrose and the Eildon Hills* gives a distant view of the town. It was part of the speculative venture arranged by Walter Scott to help promote his *Provincial Antiquities and Picturesque Scenery of Scotland*, which did not enjoy the success either hoped for. Another early visitor to embark on an extensive tour of Scotland was John Claude Nattes, whose watercolours, based on forty-eight 'accurate drawings on the spot', were published in *Scotia Depicta*. Nattes' work covered much of the Scottish mainland, extending from Inverness, Banff and Aberdeen to North Berwick and New Galloway (77), although townscapes generally seemed less important to him than evocative sites such as Elgin Cathedral, aristocratic residences or the homes and estates of his hosts.[70]

Despite the enormous changes taking place in most Scottish towns in the 1820s and 1830s, the townscape remained a minority interest and few artists were willing to portray it 'as it was', complete with factory chimneys, shipping and commercial development. One exception was John Clark, who will be discussed shortly. His view of Dumbarton accurately portrays the cones of three glassworks as dominating the town (18). And his painting of Paisley from Saucel Hill (1825) accurately depicts the old town framed by its two churches and the new industrial suburbs staked out by factory chimneys (82). Another exception was the Greenock artist, John Fleming (1794–1845). His *View of Greenock from the East* (1829) (fig. 30), which, despite its pastoral foreground and its background of the Clyde and hills beyond, is dominated by factory chimneys, mills and docks. Nonetheless, it proved popular enough to be reproduced in various forms and sizes ranging from the near-miniature to full landscape size. The suspicion remains, however, that his living depended more on portraiture and his numerous small-scale views of Highland scenes, published as cheap engravings.[71]

It is a story which could be reproduced for most Scottish artists of the period, with the exception of David Octavius Hill (1802–70), who, before his career in photography, published more engravings of landscapes, townscapes and much else than any other living artist.[72] Three of his works are represented here. Hill had a highly developed sense of commercialism. His portraits of the opening of the Glasgow and Garnkirk railway (1831) posed a contrast between an old Scotland, of plaid and tam o' shanter bonnets, and a new, thrusting mechanical age (50). This had much to do with the commission by the railway company. The culmination of his career as an artist was his series of sixty views brought together in *The Land of Burns* (1846), in which he used a very different 'auld sang'.

31. David Octavius Hill, *Ayr Market* Cross, 1846

This was a highly ambitious publication. It took full advantage of the new technology of steel plate engraving, which sharply lowered the costs of publication by allowing thousands of copies of illustrations to be made rather than the mere hundreds which copper plate engraving permitted. The effect was to reach a new readership but, at least in Hill's work, it also lent a certain 'sameness' to civic art. *The Land of Burns* portrayed a series of similar scenes in various south-west burghs – Ayr, Dumfries, Irvine, Kilmarnock – but it reduced burghs to a collection of stock figures, market crosses, burgh ports, coach arrivals and the like.[73] Hill's approach was imaginative rather than accurate, satirical, allegorical or evocative rather than a mirror image of strictly contemporary urban life. In some of his pictures, such as *Ayr, Market Cross* (1846), this is obvious: the dress is in the fashion of Burns's time yet street lighting is shown; the topographical details are compacted or confused – the Wallace Tower, in 'Mill Lane', is bracketed with the market cross which, in reality, was a few streets distant (fig. 31).[74] Here, the purpose – to depict the town in which Tam o' Shanter spent his night drinking before his fateful ride home – overrides almost all else. In other examples, such as Kilmarnock, the satire is subtler and the balance between past and present as depicted is more ambiguous (62). It is, however, in pictures which are largely devoid of human activity, such as his view of Dumfries, that the viewer must temper any temptation to think of the scene as accurate rather than essentially representational; the street where Burns lived and the church behind which he was buried are the real focal points of the picture (19). Hill was literally inspired by his agenda in the *Land of Burns*. But by the time 'painting the town' reached a wider market, it had – with the exception of only a few artists such as Sam Bough (1822–78) (*see* 27a) – largely begun to run out of ideas and inspiration.

Commissioned works and urban portraiture

Commissions took various forms: some of the better known were made by a burgh council to promote its own town, as in the case of Aberdeen in 1661 and 1756 (1, 2) and Stirling in 1706 (95). In other cases, artists were commissioned to provide illustrations to boost sales of printed books. As has been noted, Sir Walter Scott, an assiduous promoter of his own works, employed no less a figure than Turner to produce illustrations for a travel book he had compiled. David Octavius Hill copiously drew a series of views of towns in Burns country to promote a volume which sought to exploit the Burns fever which gripped much of Scotland from 1830 onwards (19, 62). The prospect of certain buildings portrayed as the centrepiece of an urban panorama can strongly suggest a commission was involved, as in the set-piece portrait of Greenock's new Customs House by Robert Salmon (1775–1845) two years after it was built in 1818 (51a), and in the architectural picture of Aberdeen's new bank buildings, completed in extravagant neo-classical Grecian style in 1840–42, with what was in effect a group portrait of the town council and the Aberdeen establishment prominently featured (3a).

Commissioned works – whether of maps (such as Gordon of Rothiemay's maps of Edinburgh in 1647 and of Aberdeen in 1661) or of townscapes – are like commissioned portraits: they are not necessarily accurate likenesses. One of the earliest examples of a work which was commissioned or, at least, inspired by an artist wishing to ingratiate himself with a town council was the view of Stirling Bridge (1703–7) by John Berrihill of Alloa (95), who had recently been lured to the burgh by the award of a free burgess-ship. His picture extols the natural features and resources of a town and stresses the linkages between townscape and rural landscape, which would often be portrayed in later works by other artists through human figures working in the fields, ploughing, and harvesting. In a sense, such works belonged to the subject which (as with family portraits) reserved the right to demand augmentation or embellishment of aspects of the painting. One example of this was the implausible addition of larger-than-life human figures, animals and ships in Mosman's 1756 view of Aberdeen (2). Rather more harmless was the habit of adding staffage of people or animals or boats, sometimes later. At times, such embellishments were the work of a different jobbing artist such as Jan van Wyck, who provided 'extras' for both Slezer (46) and Vosterman, as in the panorama of Stirling (94). In other cases, such as Mosman's view of Aberdeen (1756), the additions are easier to detect since they are cruder, often out of perspective and probably made later, by another hand.

Staffage is a major obstacle in reaching authentic views of ordinary life in many view maps. The human detail in Paul Sandby's work, such as his beshawled women and servant maids in Edinburgh's Grassmarket and his drunken bystanders on Bruntsfield Links (32), or Gordon of Rothiemay's vivid image of a legless man and a small child in a primitive pram in his inset view of Aberdeen's inhabitants in 1661 (*see* 1a) reek of authenticity in a way that staffage figures in many of Slezer's engravings of the 1690s do not. On occasion, paintings portray named or recognisable individuals, such as the caricatured worthies in the Dundee Executive of the 1820s (24) or the oil painting of Montrose's High Street by Alexander Milne in 1826 which even provides a key to the people depicted (73). In other works of Sandby, however, such as *View of Leith from the East Road* (1751), the figures hard at work in the fields on bringing in the harvest are symbols rather than individuals (67). They represent those Scots who had heeded the advice that the surest way to cure the barbarity associated with the way of life of Highlanders was to civilise them through 'improvement' and the introduction of 'Agriculture, Fisherys and Manufactures and thereby by degrees extirpateing their barbarity … and their idleness'.[75]

Commissioned works – on townscapes as in portraiture – can be 'vanity portraits'. There is one major body of work which is largely exempt from that criticism. It lies in the commission made by the London publishing firm of Smith and Elder to produce a series of townscapes called *Views in Scotland* (1824–5). The commission was given to John Clark. The series was heavily publicised at the time, in both Scottish and London newspapers such as the *Aberdeen Journal,* the *Caledonian Examiner* and *The Examiner*, which announced at regular intervals the publication of individual pairs of pictures. A fuller list was provided in another publication of Smith and Elder, which came out in 1827.[76] It detailed seventy-two towns, thirty-five of which, so it claimed, had already been published, as indicated by an asterisk.

*ABERDEEN	*DINGWALL	FORRES	KELSO	*PERTH
ALLOA	DORNOCH	FORTROSE and	KILMARNOCK	*PETERHEAD
ANNAN	*DUMBARTON	FORT GEORGE	KINCARDINE	PORT PATRICK
ARBROATH	DUMBLANE	FRASERBURGH	KINROSS	*PORT GLASGOW
*AYR	*DUMFRIES	*GLASGOW	KIRKCALDY	and NEWARK
*BANFF	DUNBAR	*GREENOCK	*KIRKCUDBRIGHT	*RENFREW
BERWICK	*DUNDEE	*GRETNA GREEN	*LANARK	*ROTHESAY
BRECHIN	DUNFERMLINE	HADDINGTON	LEITH	SELKIRK
CAMPBELLTON	*DUNKELD	*HAMILTON	*LINLITHGOW	*ST ANDREWS
CARLISLE	*EDINBURGH	HUNTLEY	*MONTROSE	*STIRLING
CLACKMANNAN	three Views	*INVERARY	*MELROSE	STRANRAER
*CROMARTY	*ELGIN	*INVERNESS	NAIRN	TAIN
CULLEN	*FALKIRK	IRVINE	NEWTON-STEWART	WEMYSS
*CUPAR, IN FIFE	FOCHABERS	*JEDBURGH	*PAISLEY	WHITEHORN
DALKEITH	*FORFAR	KEITH	*PEEBLES	WIGTON

Although all but one of the towns on the list was on the mainland – the exception being Rothesay – his travels took him from Cromarty to Kirkcudbright and Gretna Green in the course of a tour of Scotland he made in the summer of 1824.[77] Five of his works are discussed here – Dumbarton (18), Falkirk (38), Paisley (82), Peterhead (88) and Wigtown (100) – although a view of Alloa, (4) too, has been claimed to be by him, probably erroneously.[78]

It is difficult to determine the ultimate fate of the series with any precision. It seems likely that, even working at breakneck pace, Clark could not have travelled to more than seventy far-flung places or have produced over seventy works – all 'sketched and painted on the spot' – in the course of a single summer. The last of the thirty-five, according to a newspaper advertisement – Banff with a view of Duff House – appeared in February 1826.[79] Clearly, he continued with his task and produced more than thirty-five pictures: the painting of Wigtown appeared in 1827 and a view of Tain was published as late as 1828. What is not clear is whether he produced the later works from pre-existing draft sketches. On the other hand, the same book advertised a new series of views by Clark of towns in England and Wales, including two which had already been completed – Bath and Chepstow. The price was to be greater – 12s as opposed to the 10s 6d for each in the Scottish series – and potential customers were invited to nominate candidates for inclusion. And in these later productions – Bath, Chepstow and Tain – Clark had the help of an expert engraver, Robert Havell senior (1769–1832).

There the story peters out. It seems that neither series was completed. The Scottish paintings, it was originally intended, should each measure a uniform 22ins × 15ins (558 × 381mm), be done in aquatint engraving, and were produced two at a time in a variety of frames and finishes. Two of these, advertised in June 1824, were Dingwall and Stirling.[80] A subsequent advertisement, however, claimed that their size had increased to 33 inches by 15 (838 × 381mm), presumably because of the difficulty of capturing all of the linear layout of many Scottish towns. The English series, however, was to revert to the original size, as did the last of the original thirty-five of Scottish towns – Banff.[81] Smith and Elder's advertising, however, also referred to a complete set to be accompanied by a 'Historical and Descriptive Account of the whole series, and of Scotland generally' on completion of the project. That work remains elusive.

This was a highly ambitious venture, a 'great national undertaking' as the advertising claimed, even though fewer than half of the original wish-list appeared and were not of a uniform size. It attracted the patronage of George IV, still clad at least in his head in the tartan of his visit to Scotland two years earlier. The interest of Smith and Elder is readily understandable. George Smith (1789–1846) was a native of Banff and Alexander Elder (1790–1876) came from Elgin. Despite the risk taken, for Clark was paid £1,000 for his work, the Scottish series must have been relatively successful for the firm to announce a further series to cover the towns of England and Wales.

If it is regrettable that not enough is known of the Smith and Elder series of Scottish views, it is doubly unfortunate that so little is known with any degree of certainty about the artist who compiled the most complete dossier of Scottish townscapes at a critical point in their development. In the extensive advertising which accompanied the series, he was described as an 'eminent artist', 'Mr John Clark of London'. The quality and relative accuracy of the series, each 'drawn on the spot', finished in the relatively new technique of aquatint and subject to 'the inspection of Gentlemen of taste, resident upon the spot', are undoubted. In his view of Peterhead, for example, each of the town's prominent buildings are picked out meticulously. His 'true to life' style did vary at times. In the case of Dumbarton, his view portrays with forensic precision the cones of three glassworks dominating the town. Taken from that vantage point, of the north-west looking across the River Leven, perhaps Clark had little choice. His painting of Paisley from Saucel Hill (1825) was more sympathetic, accurately depicting the old town framed by its two churches and the new industrial suburbs staked out by factory chimneys. His portrayal of Falkirk is more artful still: he shows it as a market town in an idyllic rural setting. The heat, dust and dirt caused by the massive Carron Ironworks are only puffs of smoke in the far distance.

There is a problem in discovering more about the most prolific painter of the Scottish townscape. Clearly, Clark was a highly skilled engraver as well as an artist. Justly, he was described in the firm's advertising literature as 'an artist of acknowledged talent … whose superior taste and skill in topographical delineation, are already well known, and have been justly appreciated in his Views in the Netherlands and other places'. This extra clue has proved to be little use in identifying Clark. It has been claimed by some − often modern dealers anxious to authenticate the artist and thus raise the price of their stock − that the artist is John Heaviside Clark (c. 1771–1863).[82] He had done a variety of work, mostly as a jobbing engraver and book illustrator, but had made his name as a painter with graphic depictions of the scene of the aftermath of the Battle of Waterloo (1815) − hence his nickname 'Waterloo Clark'. After 1815 he had specialised in seascapes and other maritime scenes. He had acted as the engraver but not the artist for at least two panoramas, of the Rivers Main and Rhine (1830) but they were not published until after 1824, so the clue as to previous work on the Netherlands is not relevant. Heaviside had been born in Dundee but had moved to England while still a child. He lived in London from 1802–32, occasionally exhibiting at the Royal Academy, before retiring to Edinburgh where he lived to the age of ninety-two. Neither his obituary notice in *The Scotsman*,[83] which was replicated in a number of other newspapers, nor any of the half a dozen books which he wrote on the art of painting, including *A series of practical instructions in landscape painting in water colours* (London, 1827) made any mention of the painting of townscapes. The main publisher for whom he worked was Samuel Leigh, until his death in 1830, not Smith & Elder. Leigh was the publisher of a massive *Panorama of the Thames from London to Richmond* (1829).[84] The artist involved was John Clark. Again, however, the same question persists: *which* John Clark? The case that Heaviside was the John Clark of *Views in Scotland* remains not proven. That artist remains something of an enigma.

Dating and the circumstances of composition

The date ascribed to a painting is not necessarily to be taken as confirmation that the image is an accurate impression of that date. This is also true of maps, such as Gordon of Rothiemay's view of Edinburgh in 1647, which depicts a church never built but was in the planning – the church of the north-east quarter, to the immediate west of the Lawnmarket. With Hollar's near-contemporary, highly detailed view of Edinburgh, the problem of dating is acute, not least because at least three, very different versions of it survive. If initially drawn on the spot, a deduction is possible, based on both content and opportunity, which would radically revise the date of its composition to 1641 rather than the date of 1649, which has sometimes been claimed, or 1670, when one of the three versions was produced. Alternatively, like many jobbing artists and map-makers, it is possible that Hollar never visited his subject. If so, his *information* must pre-date 1648 (30).

In paintings, both dating and relying on the details in a painting accurately to reflect the date of its composition are exercises fraught with complications. The view of Alloa, which has tentatively been ascribed to John Clark, is a case in point (4). An art historian might well cast doubt on this attribution by saying that Clark almost invariably placed human figures in his foreground views of towns, not animals, as here. But the ascription falls when a building in the picture is dated to 1839; Clark's series of town views was completed by 1828. The same building could grow and shrink in different artistic compositions. Compare the two very different versions of the spires in the distant Glasgow townscape of the early 1760s (47). Robert Paul's *View of Paisley from the East* (1767) shows a small town framed in a rural idyll although it had, in reality, already begun to expand into an industrial centre with five times the population it had when captured by Slezer in 1693 (82a). In it, the artist gives an exaggerated perspective of both the ruined abbey and the newly built steeple of the new parish church of Paisley Cross. Paul used the same device in depicting some of the churches in his *View of Glasgow from the south-west*, which hugely magnified the twin towers of the far-away cathedral. By comparison, as has been seen, maps, which necessarily claimed to be up to date (even if they were not), regularly tried to capture new developments and new, iconic buildings. This was the case with Crawford's plan of Dundee (1776–7) (fig. 13, above). The same rationale often also applied to panoramic views by artists, and particularly to John Clark, as in his views of Paisley and Wigtown.

On other occasions, perhaps with a painting designed as prestigious or for presentation, a feature may be depicted although it had, in reality, long since disappeared. Such was the Cromwellian citadel in Ayr, displayed in a picture which can be precisely dated to 1720, *Prospect of Ayr from the East*. It was an almost exact copy of an earlier view of 1693 (7). Yet by 1720, the citadel had long since disappeared as a coherent entity. Another example of artistic sleight of hand is Hugh Irvine of Drum's view of the Castlegate, Aberdeen (3). Although completed in 1803, it depicted an iconic old building which had been demolished some ten years earlier.

Accuracy and artistic licence

The use, from the time of Slezer onwards, of the camera obscura gave a certain added accuracy to the portrayal of townscapes but it could also damage perspective or unduly highlight certain buildings. Others artists could manage an equally faithful rendition of a scene without resort to the camera obscura, such as Alexander Kierincx in his portrayal in 1639 of the palace and burgh of Falkland (39) – a view which competes for accuracy with Slezer's view (1693), compiled half a century later, almost certainly with the benefit of the camera obscura. Such accuracy in a painter's work gives some confidence that other works of much the same date, such as Kierincx's view of Seton Palace (1639), may also be as accurate.

At a lower level, accuracy is not always to be expected in the spheres of human activity. In Slezer's work, as has been seen, the same figures or artefacts (such as boats, carts and carriages) crop up in different scenes. Grazing animals or dozing rustics often 'decorate' the foreground of a townscape. Figures – sometimes figures added later – could be used to 'gentrify' a scene, as in the new suburbs of Paisley, full of licensed premises, drunkenness and crime (*see* 83); or to suggest caricature, as in Sandby's *View of Bruntsfield Links* (30); or to add a sense of nostalgia, as in Irvine's view of Aberdeen's Castlegate in 1803 (3). In other cases, an imagined landscape, as on the painted ceiling of the Skelmorlie Aisle (1636–8), brought together scenes which were geographically remote from each other (66).

Regularly, in drawing academies, pupils would be set the task of copying an earlier work. This applied as much to landscapes and townscapes as to mainstream art. One exercise set by teachers in the Foulis Academy in Glasgow was to copy works of Slezer, such as his view of the city from the south-east (1693) (47). The copy faithfully recorded the staffage – of human figures and boats – which had been added after the original drawing had been made.[85] The effect of reproductions, either as an exercise for pupils or as engravings intended for a wider public, was to give added but unintended authenticity to detail, some of which almost certainly never existed in reality.

Artists often approached both townscape and views of urban life as a creative process rather than a reproductive one. Minor adjustments to the landscape were a regular feature of paintings. Dundee Law was moved eastwards to bring it into view behind the town's new iconic townhouse (23); in the portrait of Brechin's Mechanics Institute, the building was framed by distant, whimsical church spires (10). Nasmyth famously realigned Calton Hill in his 1825 view from Princes Street to add greater symmetry to his townscape (34); the size or height of parish churches in particular and of other key local buildings were often exaggerated, as in the view of Stonehaven's Fetteresso Church (96), or in Hill's portrayal of the observatory near Dumfries (19). Whole townscapes might be compacted or rearranged, as in both Slezer's and Stobie's views of Perth (86). As a result, historians need to approach artistic portrayals of urban landscapes with caution and even suspicion. Like many written or printed documents, paintings can be ambiguous or obscure but they can also lie. To put the point more kindly, the art form very often comes with attitude. Yet, by accurate or contrived means, artists – very often locals imbued with a deep sense of civic pride – often helped to create a town's favourite sense of itself. Such were Aberdeen's Castlegate (3); Ayr's 'twa brigs' (8); Dundee from its estuary (23); Dumfries (19) and Inverness (57), each framed by the river running through the town; and Perth from the heights of Barnhill (87). In the cases of Aberdeen and Perth, the view was replicated on the banknotes of local banks (fig. 32).

32. Banknote of Central Bank of Scotland, *c.* 1834

Paintings could hail the future, especially in the burgeoning sense from the 1820s onwards, of a new sense of civic order. Here, the emphasis was usually on new buildings, often in neo-classical style, and wide streets, sometimes exaggerated as in a view of Wigtown in the 1850s (100a). Nasmyth's masterpiece, *Edinburgh from Princes Street with the Royal Institution under Construction* (1825) hailed the building of a temple of the arts against a

33. T. S. Peace, *Broad Street, Kirkwall*, 1866

backdrop of the utopian city – a new, urban version of the Scottish historical landscape (34).[86] But the same period also witnessed the historicity which underpinned the Gothic revival. The antiquarian architecture of many new urban churches – whether established or Free Church – seemed to reflect a claim that *they* represented the authentic tradition of Scottish Protestantism.

The second and third quarters of the eighteenth century had seen the attempts by poets and artists alike to cling to a tradition of rural life which was fast disappearing. In almost every decade from the 1770s onwards, both antiquarians and painters tried to recapture a civic past, in process of decay or outright loss. Nasmyth's panoramic vision of the future, showing an affluent *bourgeoise* and a contented labour force in harmony, was a world away from the human chaos fondly depicted in James Howe's *Horse Fair in the Grassmarket* (35), although this was the same city in the same period. In reality, Edinburgh's middle classes in the 1820s, as elsewhere, were simmering with a variety of resentments and grievances, as reflected in the series of scathing cartoons penned by Thomas Sinclair (*c.* 1805–81) in and before 1830 (12). In Aberdeen, the same conflict between hailing the future and lamenting the loss of the past can be grasped in contrasting pictures of the Castlegate in 1839 and 1803: humankind is the focus of the earlier work; in the later painting, human figures are only extras in a neo-classical stage set (3a). It is a contrast which could be replicated many times over in town after town as depicted in these years.

Art versus photography after 1840

Art can and has offered unique glimpses of both urban life and buildings which are otherwise lost. They may be particularly helpful in recapturing a sense of life in historic burghs which already by 1820 or thereabouts were without a built heritage, such as Kinghorn (63) or, indeed, Perth (86). A recently discovered view map of Dunfermline, dated to 1766, offers a rare view of the royal palace and the frater hall of the abbey (25a). Tolbooths were frequently replaced in the course of the late eighteenth and nineteenth centuries. In some cases, as that in Annan, painted some years after its demolition (5), or in Inverurie, marking a civic welcome sometime in the 1850s (58a), they exist only in a single artistic image. In other cases, an effort was made to record a building prior to its demolition; such was the case with a rare glimpse of Kirkwall's old tolbooth in an architect's drawing of 1866 (fig. 33).[87] Similarly, photography did not immediately displace art as the preferred means of recording or celebrating urban life. Photography, at least initially, tended to specialise in certain areas of interest: old buildings, including slums, new buildings, and single and group portraits – especially in the workplace. It did not – and could not – match the energy and dynamic which had regularly come to be associated with paintings or drawings of street scenes. The work of David Octavius Hill before and after the discovery of photography in 1839 is instructive: his early painting of the *Twa Brigs of Ayr* is full of life – a stagecoach, the toll, a peep show, a paviour and his tools – all framed by the familiar landscape of the

34. David Octavius Hill, *Twa Brigs of* Ayr, 1846

new and old bridges across the river and the distinctive tolbooth steeple. The picture, in essence, captures in miniature the whole economy and livelihoods of the town (fig. 34).[88] It demonstrates an essential element in Hills' artistic work, which was described in an article in the *Art Journal* of 1869: that piece argued that he was not to be classed as one of the 'school of naturalists' who 'represent nature as they see her'; instead, he was to be thought of as one of the 'poetists, treating his subjects in a manner that gives additional charms to whatever they may in themselves possess'.[89]

It was a town's people, in other words, which gave it life. This was largely the insight of Scottish artists in the nineteenth century but not before – an insight which had already been applied to scenes of rural life by artists such as David Allan, Alexander Carse and David Wilkie in the late eighteenth century, seen in depictions of the fairs at Oldhamstocks (81) and Pitlessie (89). And it was the business of art to record ways of life and the instruments of work and leisure which defined those ways of life. The bustle and frenetic activity of the Glasgow Fair was captured in a satirical picture of 1825 (50). The drunken debauchery which had notoriously come to be associated with the Leith horse

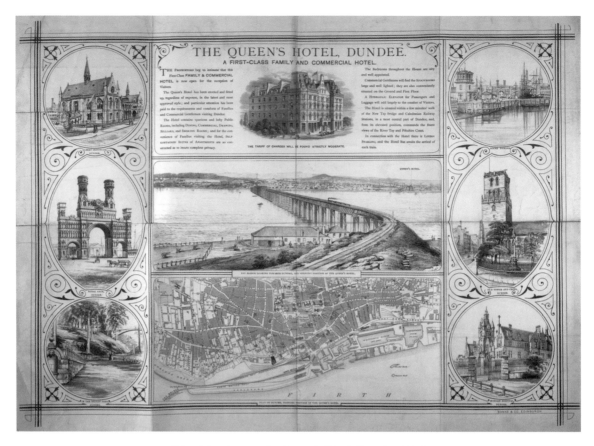

35. *Advertisement for Queen's Hotel, Dundee, 1878*

races was captured in a portrait of its last hurrah in 1859 (68). The same medium was used to depict the North Lindsay Street Fair in Dundee, complete with a cameo of the poet, William McGonagall, reciting his lines while harangued by local urchins, as late as *c.* 1876.[90] Or, a series of prints of drawings of key buildings, with the estuary and railway bridge as the centrepiece, was used to attract visitors to the newly opened Queen's Hotel in Dundee in 1878 (fig. 35).[91]

Paintings used street scenes, often arranged around the burgh tolbooth, to convey subconscious messages of space and order, such as pictures of Falkirk in 1820 or Irvine in 1840.[92] Art continued, well into the nineteenth century, to emphasise the intimacy of the interaction between town and countryside, as in a picture of 1843 of Coupar Angus (14). Art and photography typically brought into play different notions of spatial awareness. Typically, as for example in the work of an Edinburgh artist, William Gibb, depicting Dundee in the 1830s, art conceived of the town as defined by its peoples or by its buildings rather than by its streets (fig. 27). In depicting grid-style new towns, which were often the triumph of the drawing-board over natural topography, as with the rebuilding of Dumfries in the 1830s,[93] artists strove to celebrate an alternative harmony – a new-found classical balance of refinement and gentility. Alternatively, images could be used to convey the history of a town – as in this scene depicting Aberdeen's turbulent past, including its burning by the forces of the Marquis of Montrose in 1644 (fig. 36).[94] In this case, the commission was paid

for by an insurance company, the Aberdeen Assurance Company, founded in 1801: the none too subtle advertising message on its letterhead was that neither the burgh's patron saint nor the local fire tender could provide the peace of mind that insurance could achieve.

In the 1860s, Charles Lawson, a Dundee-based artist and printer, was commissioned by a wealthy local hotelier and antiquarian, Alexander Crawford Lamb (1843–97), to capture a townscape on the brink of disappearing. Lawson produced over 600 sketches of buildings, closes and interiors immediately prior to

36. *Advertisement for Aberdeen Assurance Co., 1801*

the City Improvement Act of 1871.[95] Some of the results, including earlier sketches made by William Gibb in the 1830s, were published in a large volume edited by Lamb, *Dundee: its Quaint and Historic Buildings* (Dundee, 1895) (fig. 37). It was the last significant collection of the artistic impressions of a major Scottish townscape before photography largely displaced topographical painting and drawing, though that continued to feature in depictions of individual buildings where interpretation and nuance were as important as accuracy. The Dundee venture, the initiative of a wealthy local eccentric, is to be compared with a project which was more typical of its time: the commission awarded in 1868 to Thomas Annan (1828–87) by the Glasgow Improvement Trust to document through photography the city's slums before demolition.[96] In the 1850s and 1860s, photography became as much an agent of social change as the other dynamics urging civic improvement.

Parallel to these attempts to capture visions of the last traces of city slums, much of which dated to the seventeenth century or even earlier, were the imaginative recreations of earlier days, seen in pastiche in the 'Old Edinburgh' section of the 1886 Edinburgh Exhibition,[97] or in the calculated rebuilding in historicist mode of parts of the Old Town. James Howe's chaotic depiction of the Grassmarket in *c.* 1830 acts a cue here (*see* 35). Civic improvement, in nearby George IV Bridge and Victoria Street, triggered by the Edinburgh Improvements Act of 1827, for the meantime passed by the

37. Charles S. Lawson, *Butcher Row and Nethergate, Dundee, c.* 1870

Grassmarket, which still languished in poverty and disrepair. Within a few years, however, the Grassmarket also underwent a make-over. One of the first of the new buildings, calculatedly designated by the Act of 1827 as being in 'the old Flemish style', was the new corn market, built in 1849 on the south side of the street. In the process, the slums of the Old Town were refashioned anew – as an historic 'Old Town'.[98] This was a reaction against the severe, neo-classical lines of the New Town. In this confusing turn of fashion, new became old and old became new. Former artists of urban Scotland might have enjoyed the conundrum.

M.L.

Endnotes

1 Cowan and Easson (eds), *Medieval Religious Houses*, 130–3.

2 E. P. Dennison, D. Ditchburn and M. Lynch (eds), *Aberdeen before 1800: A New History* (East Linton, 2002), 296, 298, 462, n 51; E. P. Dennison, 'Power to the people? The myth of the medieval burgh community', in S. Foster *et al.*, *Scottish Power Centres from the Early Middle Ages to the Twentieth Century* (Glasgow, 1998), 116.

3 E. Bain, *Merchant and Craft Guilds: A History of the Aberdeen Incorporated Trades* (Aberdeen, 1887), 182–3.

4 For examples and illustrations of post-Reformation craft deacons' chairs, *see* Bain, *Merchant and Craft Guilds*, 173–81; *ibid.*, for examples of new craft emblems, all of which date to the 1680s or 1690s: pp. 194 (hammermen), 212 (bakers), 236 (wrights and coopers), 253 (tailors), 265 (cordiners), 292 (weavers) and 305 (fleshers).

5 G. Hay, 'Scottish post-Reformation church furniture', *PSAS*, 88 (1953–5), 47–56; *see* www.kirk-of-st-nicholas.org.uk/.

6 'Register containing the state and condition of every burgh within the kingdom of Scotland in the year 1692', *SBRS Miscellany* (1881), pp. xxv–lxii, 51–157.

7 *See* NLS website, County Maps, Fife. The street plan of St Andrews did not feature in the published version of the map in Blaeu's *Atlas Novus* (1654).

8 T. C. Smout, *A History of the Scottish People* (London, 1969), 296.

9 R. J. Naismith, *The Story of Scotland's Towns* (Edinburgh, 1989), 92–4.

10 P. Clark (ed.), *The Cambridge Urban History of Britain: Volume II, 1540–1840* (Cambridge, 2000), 733–5, 807–15.

11 D. Maudlin, 'Robert Mylne, Thomas Telford and the architecture of improvement: the planned villages of the British Fisheries Society, 1786–1817', *Urban History*, 34, no. 3 (2007), 453–80.

12 C. Brown, *Dutch Townscape Painting* (National Gallery Themes and Painters in the National Gallery, no. 10, n.d.), 16–17.

13 Ramsay's own son, Allan Ramsay of Kinkell (1713–84), amassed a fortune through a list of sitters, first in Edinburgh and latterly in London, which became steadily ever more prestigious.

14 NGS has two of Sandby's unpublished sketch books.

15 The word 'chorography' was first recorded in England in 1559: *OED*: 'The art or practice of describing, or delineating on a map or chart, particular regions or districts.'

16 I. C. Cunningham (ed.), *The Nation Survey'd: Timothy Pont's Maps of Scotland* (Edinburgh, 2001), 27, 30, 33–4, 127–32, 140–4.

17 *DNB*, Wenceslaus Hollar.

18 C. McKean, *The Scottish Chateau; the Country House of Renaissance Scotland* (Stroud, 2001), *passim*.

19 The promise by Clark's publishers, Smith and Elder, was printed as part of an advertisement for the series at the back of a book, first published by the firm in 1824: *A practical view of the present state of slavery in the West Indies* by Alexander Barclay of Jamaica.

20 L. A. M. Stewart, *Urban Politics and the British Civil Wars: Edinburgh, 1617–53* (Leiden, 2006), 278–9. The Rothiemay map of Edinburgh (1647) was intended for inclusion in Blaeu's *Atlas Novus* (1654) but, in the event, did not appear in it.

21 Stewart, *Edinburgh*, 288–95.

22 H. Ouston, 'York in Edinburgh: James VII and the patronage of learning in Scotland', in J. Dwyer *et al.* (eds), *New Perspectives in the Politics and Culture of Early Modern Scotland* (Edinburgh, 1982), 133–7; M. Lynch, *Scotland: A New History* (London, 1991), 262, 298, 353.

23 D. Macmillan, *Scottish Art, 1460–1990* (Edinburgh, 1990), 84–6.

24 http://sites.google.com/site/richardcooperengraver/.

25 SCRAN, William Edgar, Map of Stirlingshire (1745).

26 *DNB*, Richard Cooper the elder; Macmillan, *Scottish Art*, 92–3, 118.

27 *Ibid.*, 126–32, plate 66.

28 The two landscapes of Cordiner were published in his *Antiquities and Scenery of the North of Scotland in a Series of Letters to Thomas Pennant* (London, 1780).

29 G. Fairfull-Smith, *The Foulis Press and the Foulis Academy: Glasgow's Eighteenth-Century School of Art and Design* (Glasgow, 2001), 7–13, 65–75; *cf.* Macmillan, *Scottish Art*, 225–6.

30 E. P. Dennison and R. Coleman, *Historic Stornoway: The Archaeological Implications of Development* (Scottish Burgh Survey, 1997), pp. 25–7, fig. 9.

31 *See* K. Bussman and H. Schilling, 1648: *War and Peace in Europe* (Münster and Osnabrück, 1998), 85–185; J. Childs, *Warfare in the Seventeenth Century* (London, 2001), *passim*.

32 Cavers, *Slezer*, 3.

33 C. Fleet, M. Wilkes and C. W. J. Withers, *Scotland: Mapping the Nation* (Edinburgh, 2011), 77–8.

34 *DNB*, William Roy.

35 L. Colley, 'Paul Sandby. Picturing Britain', *The Guardian*, 7 November 2009.

36 J. Bonehill and S. Daniels, *Paul Sandby: Picturing Britain* (London, 2009), 79.

37 *Ibid.*, 76, 92–4.

38 *Ibid.*, 122, 124–7.

39 Naismith, *Story of Scottish Towns*, 101–3.

40 R. Gibson, *The Scottish Countryside: Its Changing Face, 1700–2000* (Edinburgh, 2007), 105–8, prints the large-scale contemporary plan drawn up by the duke's factor which shows the individual dwellings in the 'old town' of Fochabers and the site of the 'new town'.

41 I. H. Adams, *The Making of Urban Scotland* (London, 1978), 68.

42 Dennison and Coleman, *Historic Stornoway*, 33.

43 *See* Fleet *et al.*, *Mapping the Nation*, 6–7.

44 For Crawford's 1776 map, *see* www.dundeecity.gov.uk/maps/dundee.htm. The 1793 map did not have insets of the buildings or the panorama. *See* also C. McKean and P. Whatley, *Lost Dundee: Dundee's Lost Architectural Heritage* (Edinburgh, 2008), 18–19, 53–4.

45 C. Delano-Smith and R. J. P. Kain, *English Maps: A History* (Toronto, 1999), 88–91, 97.

46 Peter Mazell may have been born in Dublin of Huguenot extraction. *See* W. G. Strickland, *Dictionary of Irish Artists*, 2 vols (Dublin and London, 1913), ii, 104–5.

47 Delano-Smith and Kain, *English Maps*, 89, 91.

48 *Ibid.*, 101–3.

49 Fleet *et al.*, *Mapping the Nation*, 133.

50 *Ibid.*, 138.

51 SCRAN, *see* James Paterson.

52 Aberdeen City Libraries, B25_04.

53 A. Mackechnie, 'Scottish historical landscapes', *Studies in the History of Garden and Designed Landscape*, 22 (2002), 214–39.

54 Letter from Thomas Gainsborough to Lord Hardwicke, in L. Herrmann, *Paul and Thomas Sandby* (London, 1986), 23–5.

55 The 1801 view of Inveraray by Alexander Nasmyth is reproduced in Macmillan, *Scottish Art*, 140.

56 NLS website, Counties of Scotland, Argyllshire (1801).

57 Cartoon of Buchanan Street rotunda, *Glasgow Looking Glass* (25 June 1825), GUL Special Collections, Bh14-x.8

58 Poster for Glasgow panorama, Battle of Bannockburn, GUL Special Collections, Eph. E/650.

59 *See* www.leighpanorama.com.

60 J. Ballantine, *The Life of David Roberts* (Edinburgh, 1866), 13–14.

61 E. P. Dennison and S. Stronach, *Historic Dunfermline: Archaeology and Development* (Scottish Burgh Survey, Dunfermline, 2007), cover. Another rare exception was William Bell Scott's, *Iron and Coal* (1861): *see* Macmillan, *Scottish Art*, 207–8.

62 *See* SCRAN, 'Town of Arbroath' (1825); *cf.* SCRAN, 'Arbroath in 1838', which shows almost twenty factory chimneys.

63 Naismith, *Story of Scotland's Towns*, 122.

64 This was one of a series of illustrations in a commissioned work by David Octavius Hill, *Views of the Opening of the Glasgow and Garnkirk Railway* (Edinburgh, 1832).

65 J. F. McCaffrey, *Scotland in the Nineteenth Century* (Basingstoke, 1998), 17, 24, 26–9, 36.

66 M. H. Merriman, *The Rough Wooings: Mary, Queen of Scots, 1542–1551* (East Linton, 2000), 336.

67 Macmillan, *Scottish Art*, 78–81.

68 Brown, *Dutch Townscape*, 31–6.

69 Macmillan, *Scottish Art*, 140; Sir David Wilkie to Mrs Barbara Nasmyth, 18 April 1840, cited in S. Smiles (ed.), *James Nasmyth, Engineer: An Autobiography* (London, 1883), 232; *DNB*, James Nasmyth.

70 *DNB*, John Claude Nattes. A catalogue of over a hundred drawings by Nattes is in NLS, MSS, 5203-6.

71 *See* www.inverclyde.gov.uk/community-life-and-leisure/mclean-museum-and-art-gallery/museum-collections/fine-art/scottish-painting-john-fleming/?galleryindex=5.

72 *DNB*, David Octavius Hill.

73 *The Land of Burns: A Series of Landscapes and Portraits, Illustrative of the Life and Writings of the Scottish Poet* (Blackie & Son, Glasgow, 1846).

74 The street lay-out and the position of the market cross and Wallace Tower can be established by the maps of Andrew Armstrong (1775) and John Wood (1822): NLS website, Counties, Ayrshire (1775) and Town Plans/Views, Ayr.

75 P. Langford, *A Polite and Commercial People: England, 1727–1783* (Oxford, 1989), 216–17; Bonehill and Daniels, *Paul Sandby*, 14.

76 The list of Clark's Scottish completed works is reproduced from an unpaginated advertisement at the end of the second edition of Alexander Barclay, *A practical view of the present state of slavery in the West Indies* (London, 1827); *see* n. 17, above. Oddly, no mention of Clark's work is made in Macmillan, *Scottish Art*.

77 The evidence of the date of Clark's tour of Scotland and the fee paid is relatively late and may not be fully accurate: Leonard Huxley, *The House of Smith Elder* (London, 1925), 10. His view of Inverness was published in 1823.

78 Alloa was on the original long list but was not confirmed as published. This view of Alloa is in the care of Clackmannanshire Council Museum and Heritage Service, which dates the picture as *c.* 1840 and attributes it either to the Greenock-based painter John B. Fleming (1794–1845) or John Heaviside Clark. The attribution to Fleming, whose work was largely confined to views of the Clyde and west coast, seems unlikely; that to Clark even more so.

79 *The Aberdeen Journal*, Wednesday, 8 February 1826.

80 *The Examiner* (London), Sunday, 6 June 1824.

81 The advertisement, in the first edition of Barclay's book, published in 1826, described a smaller size of 22×15 inches and indicated only thirteen views had already been published. The later notice of 1827 listed thirty-five as completed.

82 The BM identifies Heaviside as the artist of five prints of Scottish towns (1824) in its care. The website for the Government Art Collection similarly ascribes Heaviside as the artist of seven views of Scottish towns; *see* www.gac.culture.gov.uk/.

83 *The Scotsman*, 15 October 1863.

84 *See* www.Leighpanorama.com.

85 *See* S. Mullen, *It Wisnae Us: The Truth about Glasgow and Slavery* (Edinburgh, 2009), 9.

86 Macmillan, *Scottish Art*, 141–2.

87 The view of Kirkwall's tolbooth, which was demolished to make way for a new townhouse, forms part of the scene drawn by a local architect, T. S. Peace, *Broad Street, Kirkwall* (1866).

88 Naismith, *Story of Scotland's Towns*, 16.

89 *Art Journal* (1869), cited in *DNB*, David Octavius Hill.

90 McKean and Whatley, *Lost Dundee*, 139–40.

91 The 'Silence of the Lamb', ephemera: Dundee Central Library, Local Studies Collection.

92 *Tolbooths and Town-houses*, p. xii, 2.

93 *See* Naismith, *Story of Scotland's Towns*, 91, for Castle Street, Dumfries.

94 *Tolbooths and Town-houses*, 2.

95 McKean and Whatley, *Lost Dundee*, pp. xiv–xvi.

96 Thomas Annan's images were published in three editions as *Old Closes and Streets of Glasgow* (Glasgow, 1871, albumen prints; 1877, carbon prints; and a posthumous photogravure edition in 1900).

97 *See* M. Glendinning *et al.*, *A History of Scottish Architecture from the Renaissance to the Present Day* (Edinburgh, 1997), 352–3.

98 J. Gifford *et al.*, *The Buildings of Scotland: Edinburgh* (Harmondsworth, 1984), 21, 84, 226–8, 235–7.

Painting the Town

1   Aberdeen, 1661

This view of Old Aberdeen was completed by James Gordon of Rothiemay (1617–86) in 1661. Gordon was a graduate of Aberdeen, the minister of the parish of Rothiemay in Banffshire, and the son of an earlier map-maker, Sir Robert Gordon of Straloch (1580–1661). Both father and son worked as compilers of maps and both featured in the *Theatrum orbis terrarum* (1654) of the Amsterdam printer, Joan Blaeu (*c.* 1599–1673). Gordon was a historian as well as a cartographer, and his map, presented to the town council of (New) Aberdeen in 1661, was accompanied by a Latin *Description* of both burghs of Aberdeen, which suggests wider antiquarian interests beyond mere cartography.

The part of his map which deals with Old Aberdeen shows a small settlement laid out in the traditional manner of Scottish burghs – burgage plots or tofts running in a herringbone pattern back from a single, main arterial thoroughfare. There is no evidence of infilling or repletion of the tofts, which would suggest that there was little pressure for space. Indeed, a census of inhabitants taken in 1636 suggests a population of only 832 men, women and children.[1] There were probably a further fifty to one hundred personnel at King's College, shown clearly on the east side of High Street, which would make a total population of only about 900.[2] Behind the houses on the street frontages the long tofts ran to the 'back dykes', beyond which lay the town's common fields, which were probably accessed by small gates set into the back dykes.

Standing prominently at the head of the secular town was the market cross. It was here that the weekly Monday market was held, and wooden booths probably lined the frontages along much of the High Street.[3] The most outstanding focal point of the burgh, however, was the cathedral and chanonry. The church building dominated the townscape in the later Middle Ages, although the ecclesiastical complex held itself apart from the small burgh by 'high strong walls and dikes (for defence in troublesome times)'.[4] Before the Reformation, within these walls were the manses and gardens of the canons. Their property was of a considerably higher standard than those of the townspeople, whose homes were largely of wood, with thatched roofs. The manses, by contrast, had slate roofs and were fine buildings of stone and lime, with well-dressed sandstone being brought from distant quarries.[5] A water supply was provided by a 'water draught' (no. 8 on Rothiemay's key).

1. James Gordon of Rothiemay, Detail of *A Description of New and of Old Aberdeens* (1661)

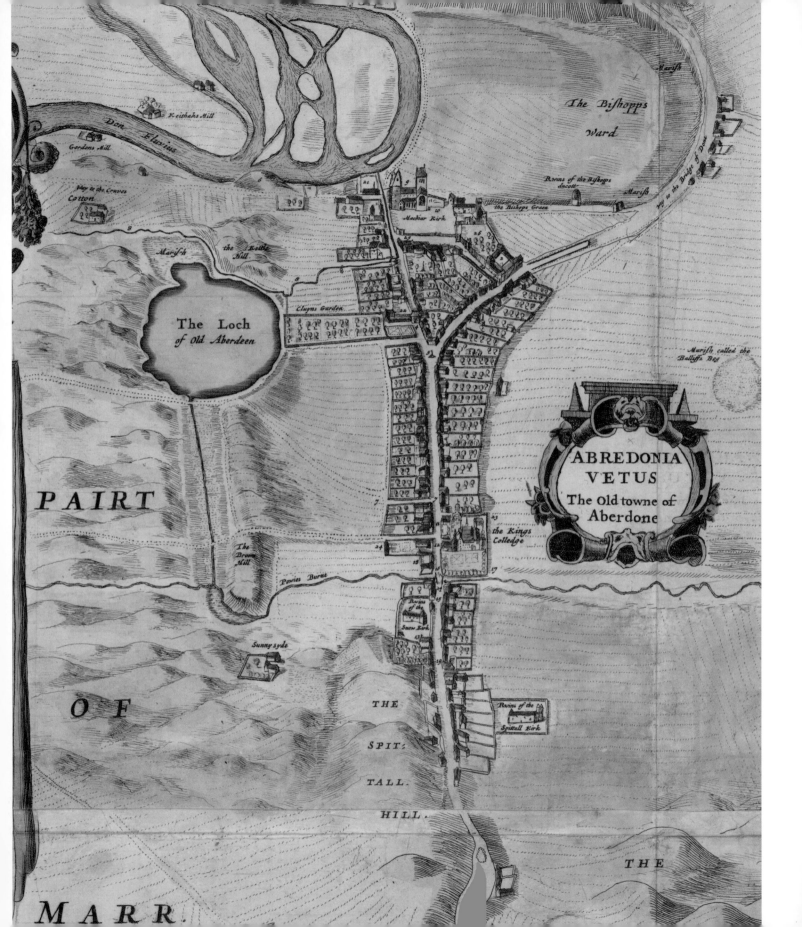

The Bishopps Ward

The Bishopps Ward

Ruins of the Bishops Pallace

the Bishops Green

Marish

Way to the Bridge of Don

Don Flavius

Keithoks Mill

Gordons Mill

Way to the Crawes

Cotton

Marish

the Kettle hill

Machar Kirk

Marish called the Baillffs Bog

The Loch of Old Aberdeen

Cluyns Garden

ABREDONIA VETUS
The Old towne of Aberdone

PAIRT

The Broom hill

Powies Burne

the Kings Colledge

Sunny syde

OF

Ruines of the Snow Kirk

THE

SPIT:

TALL.

Ruins of the Spittall Kirk

HILL.

MARR.

THE

The town had suffered greatly during the Reformation, being a burgh of barony dependent on a bishop. The interior of the cathedral had been looted and its roof stripped of its lead, leaving it in a semi-derelict state. The town itself felt impoverished financially and culturally. The plan refers to 'ruins' – of both the Spittal Kirk and the 'Snow Kirk' (*St Maria ad Nives*, which briefly became the parish church of the burgh in the half century before the Reformation),[6] and the bishop's dovecot. Political events of the seventeenth century also took their toll. By the turn of the century the great tower of the cathedral had fallen into ruin, to join those of the bishop's palace. But stone was a reusable commodity: the decaying manses were either converted for lay use or their sites utilised, for example as a Trades Hospital. A new tolbooth and school were built early in the century and remedial work was done on the manse and the cathedral, which had been re-adopted as the parish church soon after 1560.[7] In 1725 stones from the Dunbar Aisle in the cathedral were used to 'help build anew the south side of the college' along with other repairs. Gordon himself left an account of a renewed bout of iconoclasm inflicted on the fabric of the cathedral by Covenanting forces in 1640. The damage, however, was mostly reversed by extensive repairs carried out, despite the 'trublous times' of the 1640s.

Equally dominant on the townscape was King's College, founded by papal bull in 1495, although for its first ten years teaching was conducted in the manses of the chanonry, until sufficient funds to guarantee stipend, bursaries and completion of Bishop

1a. Detail of panorama in *A Description of New and of Old Aberdeens*, 1661

Elphinstone's building of the university. Rothiemay draws it in fine definition. These two complexes – that of the cathedral and of the college – must have dominated medieval life in the town.

Gordon's elaborate map of the two Aberdeens and its carefully drawn picture of dishevelled refugees – depicting a legless man, but also with women and children more prominent than men – in the foreground of an inset panorama, was a history lesson: it was at one and the same time a lament and a celebration of the two burghs' survival of the Covenanting period. During that time, as his *Description* put it, 'the civill warrs did overrun all' and, perhaps more controversially, claimed that, 'no citie in Scotland . . . did suffer more hurt then Aberdeen did, nor oftener'.[8] The burgh recovered, if slowly. But for Thomas Pennant, a visitor travelling in the region in 1769, Old Aberdeen remained 'a poor toon'.[9]

Endnotes

1 MS, Old Aberdeen Town Council Minutes, ii, 3–11.

2 G. G. Simpson, *Old Aberdeen in the Early Seventeenth Century: A Community Study* (Aberdeen, reprinted 1980), 5.

3 The market day was changed to a Thursday, but since the burgesses of the considerably wealthier New Aberdeen complained that a market on this day in Old Aberdeen forestalled their market, it was altered to a Tuesday (J. Milne, *Aberdeen: Topographical, Antiquarian and Historical Papers on the City of Aberdeen* (Aberdeen, 1911), 18.)

4 W. Orem, *A Description of Old Aberdeen, the Chanonry, Cathedral and King's College of Old Aberdeen in the Years 1724–25* (Aberdeen, 1832), 79.

5 Milne, *Aberdeen*, 16.

6 E. P. Dennison and J. Stones, *Historic Aberdeen: The Archaeological Implications of Development* (Scottish Burgh Survey, 1997), 101–2.

7 A. Short, *Old Aberdeen in the Eighteenth Century* (Aberdeen, 1985), 5–7; D. Stevenson, *St Machar's Cathedral and the Reformation, 1560–1690* (Aberdeen, 1981), 4.

8 G. Desbrisay, '"The civil warrs did overrun all": Aberdeen, 1630–1690', in E. P. Dennison, D. Ditchburn and M. Lynch (eds), *Aberdeen before 1800: A New History* (East Linton, 2002), 238–66.

9 T. Pennant, *A Tour of Scotland, 1769* (London, 1771), 116.

2   Aberdeen, 1756 and 1661

Thⁱs panoramic painting, *View of Aberdeen*, 1756, was commissioned by the town council. It was intended to be placed over a fireplace in the townhouse. The artist was a native of Aberdeen, William Mosman (*c.* 1700–1771), who is better known for his portraits of landowners and aristocracy. He was briefly a pupil of the Scottish portrait painter based in London, William Aikman (1682–1731), who specialised in commissions for portraits of the aristocracy. By 1732 Mosman was in Rome, where he studied for six years. His exact whereabouts after he returned to Scotland in 1738 are not known, although he increasingly specialised in portraits of clients from the north-east. These included *William Duff, 1st Earl of Fife* (1741) and the full-length portrait of *Sir Thomas Kennedy of Culzean, 9th Earl of Cassillis* (1746).[1] By the early 1750s Mosman had settled in Aberdeen. By the 1760s he had established a drawing school in the town.

The picture depicts the royal burgh of New Aberdeen from the hillside of the small fishing settlement of Torry, to the south of the River Dee. It gives a view of the harbour and estuary before the river was diverted in the 1770s and 1780s to afford a deeper draught for shipping. As a result, the size of some of the ships in the picture is implausible. Before then, larger ships had to navigate the small islands at the mouth of the estuary and then, because there might be less than two feet of water at the Bar, hug the Torry shore where the water was deeper; cargoes were then offloaded and conveyed across the estuary in small boats to the quayside.[2] Mosman's shipping is largely window-dressing.

There are clear similarities between Mosman's view of 1756 and the landscape view which was reproduced at the foot of James Gordon of Rothiemay's *View of Aberdeen and Old Aberdeen* (1661)[3] (*see* fig. 1). As in the 1661 view, some of the figures in the foreground of Mosman's painting – a mixture of elegant ladies, salmon fishermen with long nets and cattle – seem out of proportion, both in relation to other figures and to the cluster of dwellings on the south bank of the river. So obvious are these oddities – and the sharp contrast between giants and pygmies – that it is possible that the larger figures were added later, by a different artist. A work of 'official' art, especially one that was commissioned, often became a work in progress.

Again, as in Rothiemay's work, key buildings are highlighted by Mosman and at times are distorted. Yet, when more closely examined, Rothiemay's earlier view can be shown to be more accurate than that of Mosman, with one important exception. Rothiemay

2. William Mosman, *View of Aberdeen*, 1756

provided a key with twenty-two place names and he depicted the burgh's churches in their proper sequence from west to east, along with topographical landmarks such as St Katherine's Hill and the Spital, the road to Old Aberdeen. The main concession to artistic

2a. James Gordon of Rothiemay, Inset in *A Description of New and of Old Aberdeens*, 1661

licence was his depiction of St Machar's Cathedral and King's College – 'the oldtown colledge' – as being visible to the west of the Spital Hill rather than hidden behind it, but their inclusion is almost as an aside, as if in a separate frame, depicted where they

2b. Trades Hospital with sparkling waters in front

are at the left edge of the picture. Rothiemay's brief was to portray both burghs of Aberdeen. Mosman, commissioned by New Aberdeen, had, in contrast, no interest in including the rival college in Old Aberdeen, which was at the time in acrimonious competition with the royal burgh's own Marischal College.[4]

In *View from Aberdeen*, the distortions and inaccuracies extended to buildings, as well as the staffage in the foreground. The parish church of St Nicholas, although one of the largest burgh churches in Scotland, is depicted as larger than life, with an exaggerated spire. The Townhouse, which had its spire added in *c.* 1726, occupies centre stage, again magnified. And the Trades or Trinity Hospital, located at the quay side in front of St Nicholas rather than farther east, is highlighted and made an improbable size. There is no hint, in the sparkling waters which reflect the outline of the Trades Hospital, of the sandbank called the Trinity Inch, which was the main barrier to ships docking at

2c. The 'giants' of Torry

the quayside.[5] Mosman's intention was clear – to paint a picture of Aberdeen as a centre of education, trade, manufacturing and prosperity. If he used a camera obscura to capture this view, as has sometimes been surmised, he also relied on his imagination to finesse upon its findings. Although *View of Aberdeen*, unlike Rothiemay's panorama, was a unique work, intended for the private pleasure of the burgh's political elite rather than reproduction, the view of the estuary from Torry would become one of the most iconic images of Aberdeen, copied by successive generations of artists and photographers.

Endnotes

1 D. Macmillan, *Scottish Art, 1460–1990* (Edinburgh, 1990), 99.

2 G. Jackson, 'The Economy: Aberdeen and the Sea', in E. P. Dennison, D. Ditchburn and M. Lynch (eds), *Aberdeen before 1800: A New History* (East Linton, 2002), 163–5. The perils of Aberdeen's shallow estuary are clearly depicted in John Slezer, *View of New Aberdeen from Torry* (1693).

3 The Mosman view of 1756 was reproduced as the cover of *Aberdeen before 1800: A New History*. The Rothiemay view of 1661 is reproduced in *ibid.*, colour plate 38, between pages 228 and 229. A digitised version is available on the NLS website, Towns Plans/Views, 1580–1919, Aberdeen (1661).

4 D. Ditchburn, 'Educating the Elite: Aberdeen and its Universities', in Dennison *et al.*, *Aberdeen before 1800*, 332–3.

5 *See* George Taylor's map of Aberdeen (1773), reproduced in *Aberdeen before 1800*, 105, for a graphic depiction of the silting of the Dee estuary.

3 Aberdeen, Castlegate, 1803 and 1839

Art can deceive as well as inform. One of these two paintings portrays a building which no longer existed. The other has centre stage a building which had yet to be built. The earlier painting of the historic centrepiece of New Aberdeen by Hugh Irvine of Drum (1783–1829) dates to 1803. It was composed at a turning-point in the burgh's architectural and social history. The Union Bridge (1801–5), the central pin in a new, mile-long thoroughfare from west to east linking the town to its natural routeways to south and north, was in the process of being built. The burgh's historic market centre, in Castle Street or Castlegate was planned to form the axis linking Union Street and King Street, the gateway to the River Don and the north. However, the great scheme stalled when the city was bankrupted by its own ambition. Up until then, the burgh had lacked an entrance; now it had an entrance but no new town. The plans to lay out an iconic new street on either side of the bridge, which spanned the Denburn, were put on hold. The street was partly laid out, from 1801 onwards, building sites were cleared, and the core of the medieval burgh, the Shiprow and St Catherine's Hill, was clinically dissected, but very few new buildings were begun, still less completed. The new town was something of a ghost town.[1]

The Castlegate is readily recognisable in Irvine's painting. The tower of the seventeenth-century townhouse, with its later spire and clock (1726), was one of the burgh's familiar landmarks. Prominent are the Castlegate Well (1706), a rectangular water fountain, and the Mercat Cross (1686), a highly elaborate ceremonial symbol, depicting the line of Stewart monarchs from James I to James VII.[2] Yet it is one of the curiosities of this painting that, although dated 1803, it chooses to ignore the most striking of the new buildings which *had* been built: the Aberdeen Banking Company's (f. 1767) four-storey essay in extravagant architecture by James Burns (1801), built of white granite with dramatic Tuscan pillars and a heavily decorated balustrade, which dominated the street's south-west corner and featured proudly on its banknotes. Instead, Irvine chooses to portray an older four-storey, crow-stepped building occupying the strategic position on the west side of the Castlegate. In Rothiemay's map of 1661, it was marked as being the Music School. But it seems to have been demolished before 1789, when Alexander Milne's map of Aberdeen depicted a gap site.[3]

The painting is not a picture of the Castlegate at its self-proclaimed date of composition, 1803. Work on the banking company's building had been in train since 1794, when Irvine was only eleven.[4] Is it rather an exercise in historicity, coated with nostalgia? Or, is it an essay

3. Hugh Irvine of Drum, *Castle Gate, Aberdeen*, 1803

in what Aberdeen had been, before the intrusion of its planned new town? The scene is framed by the Castlegate Well on the right of the picture and the Mercat Cross at its centre, and the picture isframed by human activity: from the blind beggar and milk sellers on the right to the fisherwoman, bowed by her creel, and the blue-clad town officers in centre stage.

The same view of the Castlegate was painted by Joseph William Allen (1803–52) and engraved by a local printer, John Hay, in 1839. By this time, most of the vision for the new Aberdeen, first mooted in the 1790s, had been completed. Here, there can be no doubt where the artist's real interest lies. The picture is dominated by the Aberdeen Banking Company building on its left and Archibald Simpson's two exercises in granite-built, neo-classical Greek revival: the Athenaeum-Union Building, which helped redefine the placing and importance of the Mercat Cross, and the pillars fronting the North of Scotland Bank at the corner with King Street, on the right. The latter building must have been created from projected architectural drawings since its foundation stone was laid only in 1840. Another clue as to the provenance of Allen's painting is the figure atop the Bank, complete with crown, orb and sceptre; it is probably the recently crowned Queen Victoria (1837–1901). The eventual terracotta-coloured statue, designed by the local artist James Giles (1801–70), would be that of Ceres, Goddess of Plenty.

3a. Joseph William Allen, *Castle Street*, 1839

72

The key figures in the painting are the rather awkwardly drawn men in top hats. In a copy of the print held in the city's archives, nineteen of these figures are identified:[5] they include the founder of the bank, Alexander Anderson, and its manager, Henry Paterson; the local MP, Sir Alexander Bannerman; the provost, James Milne, who had been a director of the bank from its foundation in 1836, as well as at least five other members of the council including the town clerk.[6] By contrast, the primitive faces of the women selling their wares in the market place are crude caricatures. Allen had been criticised by some of his fellow-artists for work which suggested haste in composition and lacked a finishing touch.[7]

The two paintings were separated by less than four decades. But otherwise they were much farther apart. This was not surprising: the two artists could scarcely have come from more different backgrounds. Irvine was the son of the 14th laird of Drum, a family which had owned lands near Banchory since 1324. A friend of Byron, he had travelled widely and had an established presence in Rome, as a collector and exporter of art. Allen, by contrast, was a jobbing artist who died destitute. This English landscape painter, born in Lambeth as the son of a schoolmaster, worked from 1834 onwards as a drawing master in the City of London School. The circumstances of Irvine's work are readily understood. What drew Allen to Aberdeen, where he painted two nondescript watercolour landscapes of the harbour and the estuary of the River Dee (both 1838) is less obvious: most of his landscape work was confined to north Wales, Cheshire and Yorkshire. The painting of the Castlegate, however, has more than a hint of the bespoke commission about it. For Allen, the Castlegate was essentially a two-dimensional architectural drawing, complemented by the presence of the city's establishment. For Irvine of Drum, it was a human stage.

Endnotes

1 R. MacInnes, 'Union Street and the "great street" in Scottish town planning', in T. Brotherstone and D. J. Withrington (eds), *The City and its Worlds: Aspects of Aberdeen's History since 1794* (Glasgow, 1996), 25–39; J. Macaulay, 'The growth of a new town', in E. P. Dennison, D. Ditchburn and M. Lynch (eds), *Aberdeen before 1800: A New History* (East Linton, 2002), 408–21.

2 W. A. Brogden, *Aberdeen: An Illustrated Architectural Guide* (Edinburgh, 1986), 7–10.

3 NLS website, Town Plans/Views, 1580–1919, Aberdeen (1661) and (1789).

4 www.aberdeencity.gov.uk/web/files/LocalHistory/granitecity_trail_leaflet.pdf - 2011-10-22 -.

5 We are grateful to Judith Cripps, former City Archivist, and Stella Fraser, Aberdeen City and Aberdeenshire Archives, for this information.

6 The directors and chief staff of the bank are identified in A. Keith, *The North of Scotland Bank Limited, 1836–1936* (Aberdeen, 1936), 22–4, 45. For Alexander Anderson, *see ibid.*, 13–15, *passim*. Henry Paterson, the manager of the bank, had been recruited from the National Provincial Bank of England. The MP was Sir Alexander Bannerman (1788–1864), who had been elected to parliament in 1832 and had also been appointed Dean of Marischal College in 1837. The town clerk was John Angus, an advocate. Also portrayed were Thomas Blaikie, a baillie, and three other members of the council of 1838–9, Alexander Fraser, James Hadden and William Philip (*Aberdeen Journal*, 17 October 1838). Blaikie succeeded Milne both as provost and chairman of the bank on his death in 1841. Also prominently placed near the centre of the painting, alongside its sitting MP, was a fellow radical, Sir Michael Bruce of Stenhouse and Scotstown, a local landowner who had unsuccessfully stood for parliament in 1831. *See* www.historyofparliamentonline.org/volume/1820-1832/constituencies/aberdeenshire.

7 *DNB*, J. W. Allen.

4   Alloa, *c.* 1840

This painting shows Alloa around 1840 viewed from the north-west, with the River Forth in the background. The town is given a productive agricultural setting with men hard at work with horse-drawn ploughs, well-fed cattle and bountiful enclosed fields. The road from Stirling runs down into the town on the right; it is wide but rutted, with a flanking walking area.

The burgh developed close by Alloa House or Tower, the ancestral home of the Earls of Mar, on good ground close to the Forth. As recorded in the prospect by Slezer in the 1690s,[1] 'the town formerly almost surrounded the tower, as in the rude ages they afforded mutual benefits to each other'.[2] It then consisted of a few narrow streets and a market place in a seemingly irregular arrangement of townhouses and agricultural buildings at a crossing of the Brothie Burn, which provided the power and water for the town's first industries.[3]

The Mar family extended the castle into a stately home of considerable scale and architectural interest. John Erskine, the 6th earl (1675–1732), a committed improver and prolific architect and garden designer, on paper at least, was instrumental in developing the harbour and coal mining at Sauchie and exploiting water resources to support industrial development. Attention was also paid to improving the town, and a formal Lime Tree Walk was created to link it with the harbour and to help set out a planned new town. This was just part of a much larger project envisaged by the 6th earl that comprised 'a unique creation: a Scottish historical landscape garden with an industrial base'.[4] The town would have developed more rapidly and differently had the Erskine estates not been forfeited after John's role in the 1715 Jacobite rebellion and his exile in France. However, during the eighteenth century the family continued their interest by purchasing many old houses by the tower and combining and widening streets as well as laying out new ones.

The Craig Ward or King's Ferry was a safe river-crossing point and there was a substantial stone quay with good anchorage. Harbour activity expanded with the introduction in 1710 of a Customs House, which was responsible for all upper Forth ports.[5] Although the harbour suffered continually from silting by mud, it was subject to improvements over time. An animal-drawn railway wagon road was introduced in 1768 to carry coal from Sauchie to the harbour and was still in place at the time of Wood's plan of 1825.[6] Shipbuilding was carried on from 1790 and there was a dry dock. The earliest brewery dated to 1774 and there were whisky distilleries with associated cooperages.

4. Anon., *A Prospect of Alloa, Clackmannanshire, from the North looking towards the Forth, c.* 1840

A glassworks was founded *c.* 1750 by Lady Frances Erskine, daughter of the 6th earl. It was leased in September 1767 to the Alloa Glasshouse Company and there has been glassmaking there ever since, making it the oldest glassworks in Europe still operating on its original site. The glassworks had access to a pier and took coal directly from the wagon road. There were also brick and tile and tan works, sawmills and timber yards, rope works and sail-making. From 1813 there was spinning and manufacture of wool, using mainly home-grown materials, in a number of factories producing knitting, hosiery and tweed yarns. This period also saw the introduction of steamboat communication with Leith and Stirling.

The buildings depicted and the dress of the figures allows the painting to be dated at around 1840. At this time the town's population was around 5,400 and it was entering a new period of prosperity.[7] Previously a 'creek' of Bo'ness and then of Grangemouth, Alloa was made a sub-port in 1838, and an independent port in 1840, its district extending along both sides of the Forth from the new bridge of Stirling to Kincardine, and there were even proposals in 1843 to bridge the Forth there.[8] Around this time it was noted that 'the plan of the town is irregular; but in the principal streets most of the old houses have been replaced by handsome buildings, and many of the shops are of peculiar elegance … The streets are well paved and regularly cleaned, with the exception of the old town, part of which is in a ruinous state. The town is expanding rapidly towards the west, where several elegant villas have been erected.'[9] By the 1880s it was said that 'Alloa yearly assumes a more and more prosperous aspect, its filthy "Old Town" now being almost a thing of the past, its "New Town", founded in 1785, having of late years been greatly extended by the erection of blocks of dwelling-houses and numerous tasteful villas.'[10] Parts of the old town were to be redeveloped for industry on a large scale including the Kilncraigs Mills of Patons & Baldwins.

In the painting we can identify a number of buildings. From left to right, there is Alloa Academy (1824), the Infant School (1839), the Meadow Brewery (*c.* 1764), Tobias Bauchop's 1680 tower of the old parish kirk of St Mungo's with its graveyard, and the Grange Distillery (1795). The central focus of the composition is the fresh sandstone of James Gillespie Graham's picturesque perpendicular Georgian Gothic St Mungo's Parish Church (1816–19) with its tall, slender spire, a precursor of his design for the parish church at Montrose. Beyond the distillery are the brick cone furnaces of Alloa glassworks. One of the traditional brick-built glass cones of around 1825 still exists and is the only surviving structure of this type in Scotland, although they were prominent features of many nineteenth-century towns, including Dumbarton (18), Leith (67, 68) and Portobello (91). The harbour became less viable with the introduction of the railways and improved roads although glassware, distilling and brewing remained important industries.

The painting has been attributed to either John Fleming (1794–1845), who lived and worked as a portrait and landscape painter in Greenock for most of his life, or to John Heaviside Clark (*c.* 1771–1863). Born in Edinburgh, Clark worked in London from 1802 as a landscape painter and book illustrator, and died in Edinburgh. Although both men produced paintings of a number of towns for later reproduction as prints, there are difficulties with both attributions. Much of Fleming's work was confined to the west of Scotland and there is no record of any work involving Alloa. Although Clark's publisher did list Alloa as one of the towns he painted, much of that work was done between 1824 and 1828, too early for at least one of the buildings depicted.[11] The work may be by another, as yet unknown, artist.

Endnotes

1 Cavers, *Slezer*, 26.

2 *OSA*, viii, 594.

3 A. Swan, *Clackmannan and the Ochils. An Illustrated Architectural Guide* (Edinburgh, 1987), 22.

4 Margaret C. H. Stewart 'Lord Mar's Garden at Alloa 1700–1732', in J. Frew and D. Jones (eds), *Aspects of Scottish Classicism. The House and its Formal Setting 1690–1750* (St Andrews, 1988), 33–140, at 33.

5 Swan, *Clackmannan and the Ochils*, 20.

6 J. Wood, *Plan of the Town of Alloa from Actual Survey* (Edinburgh, 1825).

7 *NSA*, viii, 44.

8 Swan, *Clackmannan and the Ochils*, 20.

9 *NSA*, viii, 52–3.

10 Groome, *Gazetteer*, i, 42.

11 *See* Introduction.

5   Annan, 1878

This painting was made in 1878 as a record of the old townhouse, which had been demolished in 1870 before a new town hall in Scottish baronial style was constructed to designs by architect Peter Smith of Glasgow. It is one of two almost identical pictures[1] in existence and, as inscribed on its frame, it was presented to John Nicholson, Esq., Provost of Annan, 'by a few friends in appreciation of his aid in opening the new town hall on 22nd January 1878'. The painting also carries the name of M. R. Kilpatrick of Carlisle, who may have been the framer as there is no artist of that name recorded. It is known, however, that the companion image was by local artist George Wright (1851–1916), who was born in the town and attended school there before being apprenticed to a local painter, decorator and signwriter. He showed an early talent for landscape painting and undertook visits to Europe, but his best work is of Scotland's hills and rivers. Following a serious injury to his arm he became art master at Annan Academy.

Annan, a modestly scaled town close to the mouth of the River Annan, was founded in the late twelfth century. The superiority of the burgh lay with the Bruces, Lords of Annandale. By the 1530s, when the town became a royal burgh, it consisted of a single street running eastwards from a ford on the river. Threat of attack inhibited economic growth and the demolition of the castle in the seventeenth century led to a general decline and, despite the construction of a bridge around 1700, Daniel Defoe could say little more than that it was a place 'in a state of irrecoverable decay'.[2] The poet Thomas Gray (1716–71) visited in 1760 and noted that it consisted of 'huts of mud with no chimneys', perhaps referring to the rural vernacular rather than the town's buildings as, in the same year, Bishop Richard Pococke noted the presence of plenty soft red freestone that 'they used for door frames and window frames for their thatched cabins'.[3] However, in the 1790s it was noted that 'houses are in general decent and well built'[4] and Dorothy Wordsworth contrasted two kinds of houses in 1803:

> Those houses by the roadside which are built of stone are comfortless and dirty; but we peeped into a clay 'biggin' that was very 'canny', and I daresay will be as warm as a swallow's nest in winter. The town of Annan made me think of France and Germany; many of the houses large and gloomy, the size of them out-running the comforts.

5. George Wright, *Old Town Hall of Annan, taken down 1876*

One thing which was like Germany pleased me: the shopkeepers express their calling by some device or painting; bread-bakers have biscuits, loaves, cakes, painted on their window-shutters; blacksmiths horses' shoes, iron tools, etc. etc., and so on through all trades.[5]

Cotton spinning was established in 1785. A formal harbour was created in 1812. A new three-arch bridge was erected in 1824, and there was trade with Liverpool and Whitehaven, London and Newcastle markets in grain, wool, bacon and livestock. Sandstone was exported and local industries included manure manufacture, tanning, distilling, bacon curing and sawmilling. By 1832 it could be reported that 'Annan is a clean, neat and very thriving town'[6] and shortly afterwards it was noted that 'the town itself is well built, and the streets are capacious and generally well paved. The church and town-house are each well adorned with a handsome spire.'[7] The population doubled between 1800 and 1850, and the introduction of the railway to Dumfries and Gretna improved prospects. By 1880 the town was thriving with many improvements, new hotels, commercial premises and public buildings. However, the cotton industry never recovered following a fire in 1878, after which the town became overshadowed by Dumfries and Carlisle.

The old building had been erected in 1740 and gained its steeple, in characteristic local red sandstone, in 1795 although this had been removed in the 1850s for safety reasons. The painting is therefore self-consciously nostalgic; the appearance of the 'characters' and their associated activities, such as the sheep being driven over the bridge into the town to the left of the main building, are clearly from previous times.

Annan had a tolbooth from early in the seventeenth century and a charter of 1612 confirmed its right to have a council house with a prison.[8] There is a record of the building being thatched in 1722 and slated around 1790. A steeple with a clock and bell 'for the advantage and adornment of the burgh' was added in 1740, as were a clock and bellhouse in 1785, but those were removed in 1841.[9] The building had five rooms, one of which was used as a meal house. By the 1850s a library had been established in the ground-floor right-hand room.[10] The street and market cross are not made up and there is a single street light on a bracket affixed to the gable of the townhouse. The building was modest in scale yet robustly handsome with its projecting quoins, window and door masonry, the whole building lime-washed in the local tradition of light painted walls with contrasting colour on the surrounds. One building on the left has a gable front and forestair that suggests antiquity, while the others are everyday late-Georgian buildings of modest pretensions. John Wood's plan suggests that the building beyond the block was the Blue Bell Inn, which faced towards the bridge.[11] This example of a Victorian local artist capturing his town in transition has a companion in the paintings of Broughty Ferry (11), Inverkeithing (55) and Wigtown (100a).

Endnotes

1 Both paintings are in the collection of Dumfries and Galloway Council at Annan Museum.

2 Quoted in J. Gifford, *Dumfries and Galloway* (London, 1996), 94.

3 A. Turner Simpson and S. Stevenson, *Historic Annan: The Archaeological Implications of Development* (Scottish Burgh Survey, 1981), 10.

4 *OSA*, xix, 448.

5 W. Knight (ed.), *Journals of Dorothy Wordsworth* (New York, 1904), i, 166.

6 *Great Reform Act Report, Report on the Burgh of Annan* (London, 1832), 137.

7 *NSA*, iv, 526.

8 *Tolbooths and Town-houses*, 202; Simpson and Stevenson, *Historic Annan*, 10.

9 A. Steel, *Records of Annan, 1673–1833* (Annan, 1933), 82.

10 *OS* Sheet LXII.8.17 Annan (1859).

11 J. Wood, *Plan of Annan from Actual Survey* (Edinburgh, 1826).

6   Arbroath, 1838

The town of Arbroath, originally known as Aberbrothock because of its location on the Brothock Burn, developed as an ecclesiastical centre focused on the Abbey. As an abbot's burgh, it had by 1182 the rights to hold a weekly market, dispense basic justice and to create a harbour. The importance of the town suffered with the partial destruction of the Abbey at the Reformation but small-scale industry, fishing, hand-loom weaving and shipping continued as the mainstays of the local economy and Arbroath was re-established as a royal burgh in 1599.[1] A new harbour was constructed in 1725 and resulted in increased maritime traffic, both native and international, including trade with the Baltic ports. In the early nineteenth century fishermen from the neighbouring village of Auchmithie and from other Scottish ports were encouraged to settle in the town, land for building homes being offered at the foot of the town near the harbour.

However, during the last decades of the late eighteenth century the town saw considerable new industrial growth through the introduction of powered flax weaving, including the establishment of extensive new textile and engineering works. Production of sailcloth supported a greatly expanded population with workers migrating from the surrounding countryside. In addition, there were new bleach fields, rope works, tanneries, calendaring works, asphalt and tar manufactories, chemical works and shipbuilding yards.

By the turn of the nineteenth century the road from Dundee to Arbroath was one of the busiest turnpikes in the country for, in addition to the local traffic between the two ports, the route also carried the important coaches between Edinburgh and Aberdeen, which were noted for their high standards and punctuality.[2] The introduction of a steam rail link was therefore recognised as highly desirable if the town was to maintain its good communication links and compete economically.

Under Lord Panmure (William Ramsay Maule, 1771–1852) a committee was formed to promote a bill for the new railway, which was supported by trustees of Dundee Harbour and the Dundee and Arbroath Councils. Construction of the line was supported by both local industrialists and landowners, with Panmure proving especially helpful by releasing feued land to the project for a nominal fee. Panmure had a vested interest as two-thirds of the railway passed through his own land. The Dundee textile operators, many of whom had operations in Arbroath, were also keen to endorse the initiative and

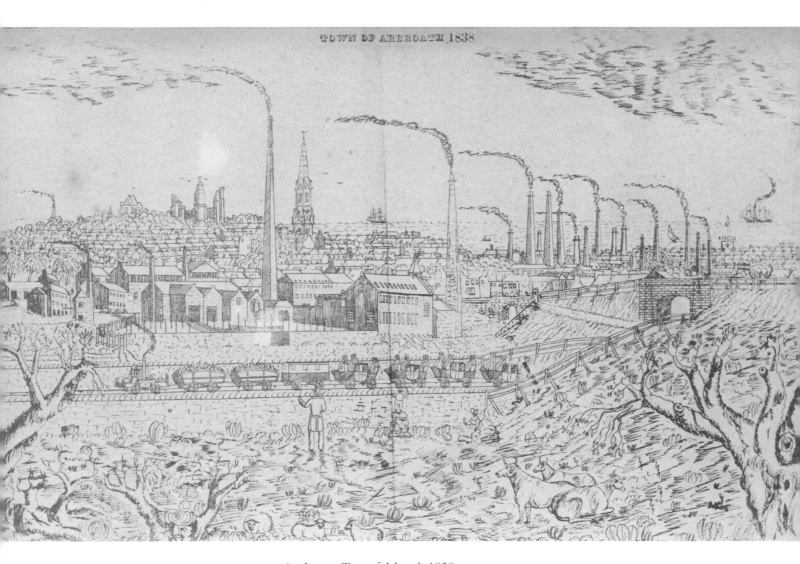

TOWN OF ARBROATH 1838

6. Anon., *Town of Arbroath*, 1838

became investors as the railway offered the prospect of the transportation to Arbroath of raw jute landed in Dundee. This may account for the large number and prominence of the factory chimneys in the image.

The Bill became an Act on 19 May 1836, the same day as that for the separate Arbroath and Forfar Railway. There were also many local investors and it was significant that a town of this modest scale could provide support for two railways at the same time.[3] There was rivalry between the two railway developments but, on their completion, animosity was eased by the provision of a horse-drawn carriage through Arbroath. This anonymous illustration shows the town of Arbroath viewed from the west of the Dundee–Arbroath line and was drawn to commemorate its opening on 6 October 1838.[4] Its terminus was at Ladyloan, and that of the Arbroath–Forfar line, opened in January 1839, was at Catherine Street. The two railways were built with different gauges but a standard was agreed in 1846 when they were combined, with a cutting being formed to join them.

The engineer of the Dundee–Arbroath line was John Miller (1805–1883) of Miller and Grainger, who was also associated with the Glasgow and Garnkirk Railway (49) and the first locomotives were made at the Wallace Foundry in Dundee.[5] It is recorded that the first train comprised five first-class and five second-class carriages carrying 500 people.

6a. George M. MacGillivray, *The Opening of the Dundee and Arbroath Railway*, 1838

A brass band was located in the leading coach and the seventeen-mile trip from Dundee to Arbroath took forty-five minutes, with a 'stop en route to oil the axles'. Hundreds of people lined the way to cheer the spectacular cavalcade. The drawing is therefore not an accurate depiction of the event but rather a symbolic impression of the day, perhaps intended for mass distribution.

According to a report on the opening in the *Dundee Courier* three days later, the first-class carriages were 'fitted up in a most comfortable and elegant style, with plate glass windows and sides, and cannot be surpassed by any description of carriage. The second-class carriages are also exceedingly comfortable, and are supplied with hair cushions, and in every respect as easy as the first class, only they are open at the sides.'[6] There were no third-class carriages at first but these were added later as demand increased.

The new line attracted day-trippers and holidaymakers and supported the development of Arbroath, Broughty Ferry, Monifeith, Carnoustie and East Haven as visitor destinations. As an advertisement for Arbroath the town's other principal attributes – the Abbey, a fine parish church, the Bell Rock Light signal tower and sea travel by both sail and steam – all feature. The artistic quality of the image contrasts greatly with those produced to mark the opening of the Glasgow and Garnkirk Railway but nevertheless has great charm and stresses the importance of such developments to the local communities which they benefited. The opening was also the subject of an oil painting by the Dundee artist, George M. MacGillivray, which shows the actual first train en route but closer to Dundee.[7] While this naive image is less accomplished as a work of art it is no less informative.

Endnotes

1 Pryde, *Burghs*, nos 91, 159.

2 P. Marshall, *The Railways of Dundee* (Headington, 1996), 25.

3 *Ibid.*, 26.

4 Angus Archives, GB 618 PA 1981 525LF.

5 Marshall, *Railways of Dundee*, 29.

6 *Ibid.*, 29.

7 *The Opening of the Dundee and Arbroath Railway, 1838* (Dundee Art Galleries and Museums).

7   Ayr, Inverness, Leith and Perth: Cromwellian citadels, 1650s

This is a coloured, later copy by an unknown artist of the engraving of Ayr which John Slezer made in 1693 for his *Theatrum Scotiae*. It was made as a presentation copy to Alexander Lord Polwarth on his appointment as envoy extraordinary to Denmark in 1716.[1] As in the original, the copy shows Ayr from the north-west rather than the east as stated in the title. Both versions are striking illustrations of the physical impact on Scotland's towns resulting from Cromwell's invasion and the country's forced incorporation into a Commonwealth with England, declared in the centre of Edinburgh in 1652.[2] An extensive programme of construction with the aim of pacifying the country included four citadels, at Ayr, Inverness, Leith and Perth – key nodes in a matrix of many smaller forts.[3] These tightened the martial grip of Cromwell's right-hand man, General Monck, and were a more lasting declaration of the new order.

The effects of the citadels' creation were immediate and dramatic. At Perth, substantial parts of the town were demolished to provide stone, including a schoolhouse, hospital and 140 houses.[4] Hundreds of tombstones were also incorporated. In Leith too, religious sensitivities were ignored, and the citadel was erected over the site of St Nicholas' chapel and burial ground,[5] as well as by demolishing tenements, houses, shops and a barn.[6] In Ayr, the citadel subsumed the parish church of St John's, and its tower stands on the right side of the Slezer view. A minister of Kirkhill in Inverness declared the citadel there a 'sacrilegous structure', built from stones robbed from Kinloss Abbey, Beauly Priory and St Mary's Church.[7] More surprisingly, he also lauded the benefits that the citadel brought: its construction provided employment, and the resulting facilities and increased trade meant that 'they not only civilised but enriched the place'.[8] A military plan of Inverness made around 1716 (*see* fig. 7c) shows a star-shaped fort on the banks of the Ness to the left of, and dwarfing, the burgh.[9] It is clear that the citadels were considerable additions to the towns they subjugated. Ayr, Inverness and Leith all contained a core of well-built stone buildings, several storeys high and set in ordered rows around a parade ground. Comprising barracks, hospitals, stores and the like, these buildings can be seen to the right of St John's Tower, defended by a great moat and sloping stone ramparts with angled bastions at the corners. In July 1657 490 men plus officers were stationed at Ayr.[10] To put this in context, in 1745 it was estimated that the population of the whole town numbered only 2,000.[11]

Within the image:
Prospectus Civitatis AERÆ ab Orientale. The Prospect of the Town of AIR from the East.
This Plate is Most Humbly Inscribed To the Rt Honble Alexander Lord Polwarth Envoy Extraordinary & Plenepotentiary from ye King of Great Britain To ye King of Denmark & ye King of Prussia

London. Printed for Rob. Wilkinson, 58 Cornhill - and - Bowles & Carver, 69 St Pauls Church. Yard.

7. John Slezer (adapted), *Prospect of the Town of Air from the East*, 1716

The occupation's impact was not restricted to large towns for smaller forts were built in every corner of Scotland.[12] Although they were not as imposing as the citadels, they remained impressive, as can be appreciated from an informal and revealing sketch entitled 'groundplan of the fortification at Stornoway upon Lewis Iland' and dated 1653 (*see* Introduction, fig. 11).[13] This was presumably created by a soldier or officer stationed in the fort and, though lacking artistic flair, it clearly shows a building that could be used as a dormitory for 200 men, a brewery, 'manor house' and store rooms. These smaller forts were not trifling structures.

The regime's network of control was of a scale and ambition that must have astonished the Scots, but it was also short-lived. As testified by letters from Monck, a critical weakness of Cromwell's Scottish government was the vast expense it took to maintain.[14] This led to swingeing taxes and widespread poverty. All the citadels were abandoned after the Restoration of Charles II in 1660 and it is instructive how quickly and thoroughly they were demolished. Ayr is the only one that survived to any extent, with much of the coastal defences left intact, perhaps because they continued to serve as protection from the sea. Even so, Slezer's image also tells of the citadel's dismantling, with the landward defences largely removed.

7a. James Skene of Rubislaw, *Gate of the Old Citadel of Leith*, 1818

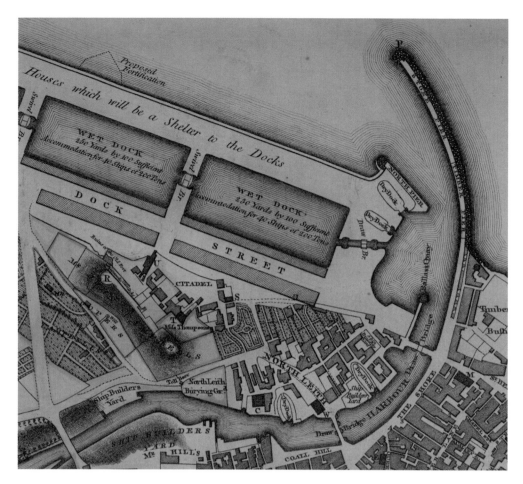

7b. John Ainslie, *Old and New Town of Edinburgh and Leith with the proposed docks*, 1804

No internal buildings now survive above ground. Therefore any depictions of them are of particular value and one appears to have survived largely unrecognised. A watercolour, titled *Gate of the old citadel of Leith* by James Skene in 1818, shows what he noted (in the bottom right corner) to be the 'last remnant', with a group of buildings beyond. If Skene's painting is compared with a plan made by John Ainslie in 1804 it can be concluded that it shows the western gate and the interior of the citadel, with the docks of Leith marked by a forest of masts on the left. Ainslie's plan notes that the large building marked 'U' is the 'Old Barracks for Cromwell's soldiers'. The citadel buildings were converted into dwellings following the Restoration and Skene has painted smoke emanating from many domestic chimneys.[15]

As well as being apparently ignorant of the survival of the barracks, it is intriguing that Skene has also chosen to ignore the eastern gate, marked 'S' on Ainslie's plan, which still stands today, and we can wonder if he was exaggerating for dramatic effect. Skene was a close friend of Sir Walter Scott and played an active role in the Society of Antiquaries.[16] We can assume he was sympathetic to the preservation of historic buildings at a time of rapid development. This development is symbolised in his painting by the stonemasons labouring in the foreground, presumably reworking stone from the citadel's defences to develop Leith's new docks. Perhaps we should regard this image and its misleading description as antiquarian propaganda.

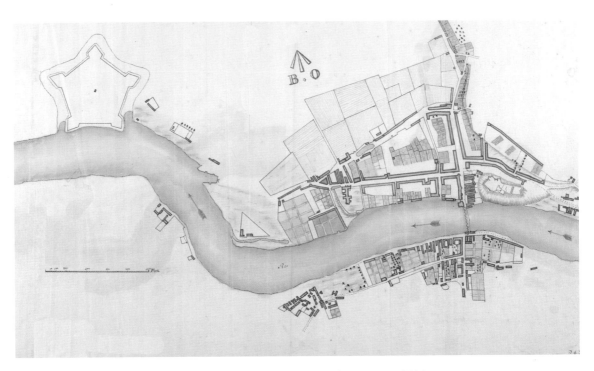

7c. Lewis Petit, *Inverness in North Brittain, c. 1716*

The transformation of the citadels, from state-of-the-art military bases to vulnerable antiquities, took only 150 years. With the notable exception of Ayr, their erasure from the Scottish towns they dominated has been almost complete. Archaeological excavations in Perth and Leith have temporarily exposed the monumentality of these structures to modern eyes,[17] but otherwise we must rely on the work of artists such as Slezer, Skene and an anonymous soldier to remind us of their formidable former presence.

Endnotes

1 *DNB*, Alexander Lord Polwarth.

2 A. A. Tait, 'The Protectorate citadels of Scotland', *Architectural History*, 8 (1965), 9–24.

3 *Ibid.*, 12.

4 M. Roy, 'The excavation of the south-western bastion of Cromwell's citadel on the South Inch, Perth', *Tayside and Fife Archaeological Journal*, 8 (2002), 145–68.

5 S. Mowat, *The Port of Leith: Its History and its People* (Edinburgh, 2003), 190.

6 J. Turnbull, *The Scottish Glass Industry 1610–1750. 'To serve the whole nation with glass'* (Edinburgh, 2001), 117.

7 S. Cruden, *The Scottish Castle* (2nd edn, London, 1963), 234.

8 C. H. Firth, *Scotland and the Protectorate: Letters and Papers Relating to the Military Government of Scotland from January 1654 to June 1659* (SHS, 1899), p. xlvi.

9 NLS, Military Maps of Scotland website, MS 1647, Z.02/78b.

10 *Ibid.*, p. xlviii.

11 *OSA*, i, 92.

12 Tait, 'Protectorate citadels', 10.

13 E. P. Dennison and R. Coleman, *Historic Stornoway: The Archaeological Implications of Development* (Scottish Burgh Survey, 1997), 25–6.

14 Firth, *Scotland and the Protectorate*, p. lv.

15 J. Gifford, C. McWilliam and D. Walker, *The Buildings of Scotland: Edinburgh* (London, 1984), 449.

16 W. D. H. Sellar, 'William Forbes Skene (1809-92): historian of Celtic Scotland', *PSAS*, 131 (2001), 3-21.

17 *See* Roy, 'South Inch, Perth' (2002); G. Brown, *Results of an Archaeological Investigation at Dock Street, Leith: Phase 2* (unpublished report, 2002).

8   Ayr, 1820s and *c.* 1845

Ayr was erected a royal burgh between 1203 and 1206, making it one of the oldest in the west of Scotland.[1] This lively watercolour of the town was painted by Henry Gibson Duguid (1805–1860), an artist who specialised in topographical views, mostly of Edinburgh where he taught drawing and music.[2] The scene shows the northern approach to the town by the new bridge over the River Ayr.[3] Opened to traffic in 1788, it replaced the medieval bridge beside it, known as the auld brig. These river crossings dictated the layout of the town. The early township grew along the Sandgate, seen on the far side of the new bridge, because there was a convenient ford at this point.[4] When the old medieval bridge was built, it fed into the High Street which became the new focal point. The Sandgate suffered serious problems with blown sand, solved only in 1725 when the sandhills were levelled.[5] When the auld brig was condemned and the new bridge opened, the Sandgate again became the main route into town. Thus Ayr is one of the few towns in Scotland to have had two tolbooths and two crosses on two different thoroughfares.[6]

Duguid's picture gives the impression that the viewer is actually entering the town, the woman and girl carrying scythes and the couple leaning against the parapet appearing only mildly interested in the new arrival. Those on the bridge are too busy chatting to notice or, like the man herding cows, too involved with the job in hand.

On the far side of the bridge is the High Tolbooth, nicknamed the 'Dungeon Clock'. It stood in the centre of the Sandgate rather than the High Street, as its predecessor had. Built in the early seventeenth century and largely reconstructed in the eighteenth century, this tolbooth was 131 feet high. It is possible to see the outside staircase leading up to the court-house within. There were two secure cells below, 'the woman's house' and 'the thief's hoal', and a common jail in a building to the rear.[7] As this tolbooth was demolished in 1825, it is reasonable to assume that Duguid painted this picture in the early 1820s.

The pointed steeple to the left of the tolbooth was the 'auld toure'. A 'rude massive square building', this two-storey bell tower and house of correction for local beggars stood on the High Street.[8] The auld toure, also known as the Wallace Tower, was another building soon to be demolished. The auld brig had escaped demolition because of a new site was ultimately chosen for its replacement. It continued to serve as a footbridge thereafter.

8. Henry Gibson Duguid, *The New and Old Bridges at Ayr*, 1820s

The companion piece, from a similar vantage point, was drawn by an unknown artist about 1845. It shows the magnificent spire of the new town buildings that replaced the old tolbooth. Of all the classical town spires erected in Scotland in the late eighteenth and early nineteenth centuries, Ayr's was the tallest at a lofty 210 feet.[9] Although close to the old tolbooth, this building no longer blocked this busy thoroughfare but stood on a corner site between the High Street and the north end of the Sandgate, renamed New Bridge Street. This gave the new town buildings not one but two impressive frontages.

The same picture shows the new Wallace Tower built in 1833 and the elegant new building at number 2 New Bridge Street, on the right of the road just across the bridge. Also clear from this picture is the wide sweep of the main road into town compared with the narrow vennel between the auld brig and the High Street. The new bridge was widened in 1840. Duguid's version shows it in its original narrow form.

8a.   Anon., *Ayr from the North*, 1845

It is interesting to speculate why Duguid chose this subject so far from Edinburgh at this early stage in his career. One possible influence was that of the poet Robert Burns (1759–1796), whose work included a humorous but moving piece called 'The Brigs of Ayr'. Popular during his lifetime and feted on his various sojourns in Edinburgh, Burns's fame intensified after his death. The first of a worldwide network of Burns Clubs was started in Greenock in 1801, and by 1815 a Burns Mausoleum had replaced the plain slab in the Dumfries churchyard where the poet was buried. Places associated with the poet soon became sites of pilgrimage.[10]

Burns inscribed 'The Brigs of Ayr' to John Ballantine, a leading provost of the town who was instrumental in the building of the new bridge. While in London securing the necessary act of parliament for its construction, Ballantine hired the services of the famous Enlightenment architect, Robert Adam (1728–1792).[11] Adam enjoyed a high reputation for his designs but not his ability to cost them.[12] This may explain why Adam's original plan had been modified by the time work began on the new bridge in 1786.

In his poem, Burns imagines an exchange between the two bridges at the dead of night after the Dungeon-Clock and the Wallace Tower had struck two. The auld brig, its 'vera wrinkles Gothic in his face', foretells the doom of the new with the dire warning: 'I'll be a Brig when you're a shapeless cairn!' So it proved to be. In 1877 the new bridge was badly damaged by a great flood; the auld brig survived. Burns may have had second sight, as he claims in his poem, or he may have been voicing concerns raised about the cost-cutting exercise undertaken when the new bridge was built. It was replaced in 1878. At the beginning of the twentieth century, the decayed state of the auld brig again brought with it the threat of demolition. Its costly rescue owed much to the generosity of Scottish and St Andrews Societies all over the world which responded to the name of Robert Burns.[13]

Endnotes

1 Pryde, *Burghs*, no. 31.

2 We are grateful to Helen Smailes, Senior Curator of British Art, National Galleries of Scotland, for her advice.

3 We are indebted to Tom Barclay, Reference and Local History Librarian (South Ayrshire), for his advice.

4 R. Gourlay and A. Turner, *Historic Ayr: The Archaeological Implications of Development* (Scottish Burgh Survey, 1977), 4.

5 J. H. Pagan, *Annals of Ayr in the Olden Time, 1560–1692* (Ayr, 1897), 50.

6 *See* NLS website, Counties of Scotland, 1580–1828, for A. Armstrong, *A New Map of Ayrshire, 1775;* and *ibid.*, Town Plans/Views, for J. Wood, *Plan of the Town and Parishes of* Ayr, 1818.

7 Pagan, *Annals of Ayr*, 53.

8 *Ibid.*, 55.

9 *Tolbooths and Town-houses*, 11.

10 *DNB*, Robert Burns.

11 J Strawhorn, *The History of Ayr, Royal Burgh and County Town* (Edinburgh, 1989), 113.

12 *DNB*, Robert Adam.

13 J. A. Morris, *The Brig of Ayr and Something of its Story* (Ayr, 1910), 59.

9   Banff, 1775 and 1838

This charming view of Banff was painted by James Wales (1747–1795). Born in Peterhead, Wales was educated at Marischal College, Aberdeen. He appears to have been largely self-taught as an artist.[1] He began his career as a portrait painter, producing small portraits for a guinea or less.[2] A commission from Banff's town council for a 'landskip' of the town was more lucrative. Wales was paid four guineas for this picture in March 1775.[3] As the trees are in full leaf and this was said to be 'a painting of the town in 1774',[4] we may assume that Wales began work that summer.

On the right of the picture is part of Banff's elegant, seven-arched stone bridge over the River Deveron. Work on this bridge began in 1772 but was not completed until 1779. Strangely, there are no signs of construction work, despite summer being the building season. This suggests that Wales was working from plans rather than the bridge as it was. Understandably, the town council wanted to celebrate the building of this vital bridge. Not only had they achieved government funding, the second such grant in seven years, but also they had secured the services of John Smeaton (1724–1792), Britain's foremost engineer, who had already constructed major bridges at Coldstream and Perth (86).

For centuries the eastern approach to Banff involved fording the Deveron or crossing it by ferry. This was not only inconvenient but could be dangerous. The river was tidal a mile upstream and flooding was a regular occurrence. Until the first bridge was built in 1765, hardly a year passed without some fatal accident at the river crossing.[5] One such, in 1739, resulted in Alexander Steinson, tacksman of the ferry, being imprisoned for negligence because the boy he left in charge was not up to the job and eight people drowned.[6]

The first bridge cost nearly £6,000. Three years later, it was washed away much to the annoyance of James Duff (1729–1809), 2nd Earl of Fife, whose parkland forms the riverbank. As principal proprietor of the Deveron, a prolific salmon river, Duff earned 'a very handsome revenue' from net fishing; here being carried out by the three fishermen in the foreground.[7] Having already secured one government grant, his lordship was clearly irritated at having to repeat the exercise. However, he informed the magistrates of Banff that he intended 'to help forward another' because he thought 'the life and comfort of every individual of the place in some degree connected with a Bridge upon that river'.[8]

9. James Wales, *View of Banff in 1775*

In 1772 Duff, who was Member of Parliament for Banffshire, received assurances from the Duke of Argyll and Colonel Skene, Commander of his Majesty's Forces in North Britain, that a new bridge would be built.[9] The decision to build it farther upriver than its predecessor was based on a design and costs provided by Smeaton. His estimate of £4,500 was small for the size of the contract, but he was confident that the close proximity of a local quarry would enable him to keep costs down.[10] Despite Colonel Skene being granted free access to the town's quarries, the final figure was almost double the original estimate. The bridge seen here remains little changed to this day.

The role played by Colonel Skene and the readiness of the government twice to fund this project is a reminder that the last Jacobite rebellion had been put down less than thirty years before and the army still played an important part in Highland affairs. The large ships sailing on the Moray Firth beyond are probably intended to draw attention to Banff's strategic importance as a port and the construction of a new harbour completed about this time.

Lord Fife's position in the town is implied by the elegant people strolling in his park and the carriage making its way to Duff House, his principal family seat, which is out of

9a. William Henry Bartlett, *Banff*, in William Beattie, *Scotland Illustrated*, 1838

sight on the left. This is a highly unusual omission. Successive Scottish landscape artists such as John Clerk of Eldin (1728–1812), Charles Cordiner (1746–1794), Hugh William Williams (1773–1829) and John Clerk (fl. 1824–8) all include Fife's majestic mansion in their views of Banff. It sems likely that the town council stipulated that Duff House should not be included when they commissioned this fine view of their town. Duff House features prominently in the centre of the attached vignette by William Henry Bartlett (1809–1854) which appeared in *Scotland Illustrated*, published in 1838.

The 1st earl had begun construction of Duff House some forty years earlier to a design by William Adam, but the two fell out so badly that the house was left unfinished and unloved till the 2nd earl inherited in 1763. Banff's appearance as a walled town is misleading. What we are most likely seeing are the 'dykes' that enclosed Lord Fife's parkland.[11] The carriage shows the route taken by the driveway to Duff House. While it carried straight on from the end of the bridge, the public road to town had to turn sharp right towards the coast.

The impressive mansion house on the skyline is Banff Castle, a contemporary house though its forerunner was medieval, first documented in the thirteenth century.[12] It was built by James Ogilvy (1714–1770), 6th Earl of Findlater and 3rd Earl of Seafield. Horace Walpole described the young Ogilvy as 'formidable',[13] and his career would seem to bear this out. A passionate improver, Ogilvy used much of his own wealth to promote local trade, fisheries, manufacturing and agriculture.[14] His widow was still living at Banff Castle when this picture was painted.

The artist, James Wales, left Scotland to pursue his career in London, but fierce competition forced him to travel to India where he finally found success. He died in Bombay and was buried in the cathedral where a tablet was erected to his memory.

Endnotes

1 *DNB*, James Wales.

2 *Transactions of the Banffshire Field Club* (1817–1926), 22.

3 *Ibid.*, 24.

4 *Ibid.*, 22.

5 W. Cramond, *The Annals of Banff*, 2 vols (Aberdeen, 1841), i, 289.

6 *Ibid.*, i, 212.

7 *OSA*, xx, 354.

8 Cramond, *Annals of Banff*, i, 321.

9 *Ibid.*, i, 321.

10 *Transactions of the Banffshire Field Club*, 26.

11 *Annals of Banff*, i, 322.

12 R. Gourlay and A. Turner Simpson, *Historic Banff: the Archaeological Implications of Development* (Scottish Burgh Survey, 1977), 2.

13 *DNB*, James Ogilvy, 6th Earl of Findlater and 3rd Earl of Seafield

14 *OSA*, xx, 375.

10   Brechin, *c.* 1838

In the early 1830s, Brechin had a population of some 5,000 people. The most remarkable feature of the parish, according to a local minister, however, was the 'striking changes' that had taken place since the turn of the century, particularly an increasing desire for knowledge and a general love of reading.[1] This building, with its elaborate, castellated Tudor façade, built in 1838–9 in the heart of the town, symbolised this new spirit of progress and self-advancement.

Many of the changes taking place in Brechin resulted in amenities that are now taken for granted. A board of health was set up to improve hygiene, gas lighting was installed in streets, shops, public and private buildings, and a system of piped water was laid from the town wells to homes and businesses. In 1836 the street on the right of this picture, then called Nether West Wynd but soon to be renamed Church Street, was levelled and macadamised, part of a programme of road improvement and a refashioning of Brechin as a model county town.[2]

Educational provision was also improved with the remodelling of the public schools – grammar, parochial and burgh. This was the subject of heated debate before agreement was reached and three teachers were employed: a rector to teach languages and higher education and two schoolmasters, one to run the parochial school and another to teach reading, writing and arithmetic in the burgh school.[3] All three schools were housed in one building.

In contrast, the decision taken in 1835 to set up a Scientific and Library Institute in Brechin was passed unanimously. Mechanics' Institutes, already widespread, were an answer to new demands for skilled labour by employers and a desire for self-improvement among the skilled working classes. They offered a basic knowledge of the scientific principles behind modern machinery and new methods of manufacture. They also tackled adult literacy, an increasingly important and desirable skill with the advent of cheaper newspapers.[4] Mechanics' Institutes first appeared in Scotland in the early 1820s, some of the earliest starting in towns such as Aberdeen, Dundee, Greenock and Kilmarnock. Not everyone, however, approved of educating the masses. In Greenock, the minister praised the concept but worried that 'infidels and anarchists' would use it for their own ends.[5] Funding was often a problem, with many of these Institutes relying on financial support from the

10. Anon., *The Mechanics Institute, Brechin, c.* 1838

middle and upper classes. Economic depressions, like that of the early 1840s, could spell the end of these Institutes.[6]

Two common problems in setting up Mechanics' Institutes were the provision and maintenance of suitable premises and funding. The Brechin Institute was more fortunate than most. It attracted a patron in the form of William Maule (1771–1852), Baron Panmure, a local landowner, who not only gave the Institute its hall outright but also endowed it with a cheque for £1,000.[7] In 1838, to meet the demands of rising pupil numbers, he offered to rebuild the public schools at his own expense. He also proposed the addition of a second storey to accommodate a large lecture hall and library for the Mechanics' Institute. The result was this magnificent piece of civic architecture, 118 feet (36 metres) in height, captured by an unknown artist shortly after its completion in 1839. A controversial figure, dissolute and self-indulgent, Maule was also known for acts of extreme generosity and benevolence.[8] According to David Black, town clerk of Brechin for thirty-six years, the town had no greater friend.[9]

The architect was John Henderson (1804–1862), the son of one of Maule's gardeners at Brechin Castle. It was thanks to Maule's patronage that Henderson rose from being a carpenter's apprentice to become one of Scotland's leading architects, noted for the many churches he designed and built all over the country.[10]

10a. J. M. Corner, *Church Street, having Mechanics' Hall in the Distance*, 1838

On 28 June 1838 a gala day was celebrated in Brechin. Not only was it Queen Victoria's coronation day but also the day when the foundation stone of the building in this picture was laid. It began with a grand procession marching to the music of a local band. The route took them down new streets like Southesk Street and Panmure Street, each decorated with arches of flowers to mark this public opening. Celebrations included a puppet theatre for the children, the first such 'Fantoccini Theatre' ever seen in Brechin, and culminated in a grand firework display that evening. Many of these entertainments were paid for by Maule.[11]

When the building was formally opened as a Literary and Scientific Institute in February 1842, the first lecture delivered was aptly titled 'On the diffusion of knowledge, and the means by which it may be promoted'. From the outset, every effort was made to ensure that as many people as possible were able to benefit from the education opportunities offered by both the schools and the Institute. All fees were kept to a minimum and the well-stocked library in the Mechanics stayed open until nine at night since many workers, such as those in the spinning and bleaching industries, worked a twelve-hour day. On 8 June 1846 a museum was also opened in the Mechanics' Institute.

David Black, Brechin's long-serving town clerk, wrote a detailed history of the town first published in 1864. Included is the attached wood-cut, by J. M. Corner. It shows the Town Hall on the High Street with a view up Church Street towards the Mechanics' Institute, above which a flag is flying. According to Black, the old Brechin tolbooth was thought to have stood on the same site as this town hall. Built in 1789 the town hall held a court-room on the ground floor with a town hall above. The building on the right is the Brechin Baking Company.[12]

In his history, Black mourned the passing of the stagecoach in this picture. Two coaches a day passed through Brechin, which lay on the main road between Edinburgh and Aberdeen. The arrival of the railway, however, made the service redundant. The *Defiance*, a 'sprightly dashing conveyance', made its final journey through the town in 1848.[13]

Endnotes

1 *NSA*, v, 134.
2 D. D. Black, *The History of Brechin to 1864* (Edinburgh, 1867), 199–218.
3 *Ibid.*, 201.
4 H. Holmes (ed.), *Scottish Life and Society, Institutions of Scotland, Education* (East Linton, 2000), 355.
5 *NSA*, vii, 471.
6 Holmes (ed.), *Scottish Life and Society*, 177.
7 Minutes of the Brechin Mechanics Literary and Scientific Institute, 10 February 1842.
8 *DNB*, William Ramsay Maule, 1st Baron Panmure.
9 Black, *History of Brechin*, 223.
10 *DNB*, John Henderson.
11 Black, *History of Brechin*, 209–10.
12 *Ibid.*, 281–2.
13 *Ibid.*, 221.

11   Broughty Ferry, 1835

Broughty Ferry developed in the vicinity of Broughty Castle as a small fishing port on the north bank of the Firth of Tay, where a ferry operated to Port-on-Craig in Fife. The castle, on a rocky promontory flanked by beaches, was built *c.* 1496 but fell into decay after 1603 and survived as a romantic ruin and in the ballad tradition:

> It fell upon Christmas day,
> Burd Helen was alone.
> To keep her father's towers,
> They stand two miles from town.
>
> Glenhazlen's on to Broughty Wa's,
> Was thinking to win in,
> But the wind it blew and the rain dang on,
> And wat him tae the sken.[1]

There had been tanneries, fulling mills, linseed-oil making, bleach-fields and thread mills but these had all closed by the start of the eighteenth century. There was once a 'very fine salmon fishery here, below at the castle walls'[2] and by 1790 there were around a dozen fishermen's huts. In 1840, just after the time of the painting, there were thirteen boats and fifty families dependent on white fish and herring.[3] This was to increase to a peak later in the century, although the local fishing industry was unable to compete with the emerging steam-driven vessels and it declined drastically. Other industries included rope making, a foundry, brewery and bakehouse. Coal was landed from English ports.

By the late eighteenth century the potential of the place as a fashionable resort was already recognised when it was noted that 'the village of the Ferry ... is uncommonly dry and wholesome and, perhaps, better fitted for sea-bathing than any other place on the east-coast of Scotland'.[4] From the 1790s land was feued for development, and plans were drawn up for a 'New Town at the North Ferry'[5] on a grid lay-out north and east of the fisher community, located above the pebble beach to the west of the castle. Housing of all types followed, including many fine villas erected by Dundee's 'merchant-princes of that jute metropolis'[6] and purpose-built holiday accommodation.

11. Alexander Smith, *Beach Crescent and Broughty Castle*, 1835

There were coaches to and from Dundee, and also a regular steamboat service from the city, with special trips for bathers and day-trippers. This caused some concern as the boats 'during the summer months, bring down an inundation of the worst population of Dundee on the Sabbath day. Hence drunkenness and riot, in spite of all moral exertions to put a stop to the evil.'[7]

The painting is by Alexander Smith, a local house painter and amateur artist. It captures a part of the town just before the railway but one already developing into a fashionable resort. We see the first of the elegant houses on what became known as Beach Crescent, many with gaily painted façades and bay windows and dormers to take advantage of the fine views as were also found at Portobello, outside Edinburgh (91). There are enclosed front gardens and a general 'clean and neat'[8] character although the street is not yet surfaced. The castle forms an attractive ruin at the end of the picturesque terrace, fishers' cottages are conveniently left out of view to the left and there is little indication of the acres of suburban development behind.

Fisher folk sit within a timber shelter, a woman preparing bait, while gentlemen in top hats chat informally with a sailor. The motif of the fisher woman features in a number of other paintings and prints of Broughty Ferry[9] and she appears in the local song tradition too:

> It was in the month of August one morning by the sea,
> When violets and cowslips they so delighted me,
> I met a pretty damsel, for an empress she might pass,
> And my heart was captivated by that bonnie Broughty Ferry fisher lass.
>
> For her petticoats she wore so short, fell straight below her knee,
> Her handsome leg and ankle they quite delighted me;
> Her rosy cheeks and yellow hair, none with her could surpass,
> With her creel she trudges daily, does my bonnie Broughty Ferry fisher lass.
>
> 'Good morning to you, fair maid,' I unto her did say;
> 'Why are you up so early, and where go you this way?'
> She said, 'I am going to look for bait, so allow me for to pass,
> For my lines I must get ready,' said the bonnie Broughty Ferry fisher lass.[10]

The fishing people and traditions of Broughty Ferry were thus viewed by the people of Dundee in the same quasi-romantic manner as the residents of Edinburgh regarded those of the community of Newhaven in the nineteenth century.[11] A man in a coble gathers nets close to the shore, and other boats are beached, no pier or jetty being shown. Elegant ladies and gentleman promenade, and a housemaid with a basket heads to buy fish. The town bellman makes a public announcement, although he appears to be ignored by his audience. Industry is not far away, as witnessed by the chimney in the background.

With the arrival of the Dundee and Arbroath Railway in 1838, the town became even more desirable as both a residential suburb and a holiday resort, and it expanded considerably. By 1840 the population was 2,200 residents but this increased greatly during the summer months. Tension developed between the people of Dundee and the well-off commuters who lived in Broughty Ferry and paid no rates to the city which provided their wealth, employment and social facilities:

When the city merchants, cool an' cute,
Have fortunes made frae jam or jute
They flee tae 'scape the smeel an' soot
Away tae Broughty Ferry.

Tae 'scape the smeel an' but the tax
(oor laws are shuir a trifle lax)
They tak' the honey, lave the wax
These Nabobs o' the Ferry

An' thus we see braw villas stand
Wi' whigmaleeries on ilk hand
As raised by some enchanter's wand
Round bonny Broughty Ferry.[12]

The loophole disappeared in 1913, following the promotion of a private Bill in parliament, which incorporated the town into Dundee.

Endnotes

1   *Broughty Wa's* in F. J. Child, *The English and Scottish Popular Ballads* (Boston, 1886), iv, 425.

2   'Nova Fifae Descriptio. Angvsia, Angvs', *Blaeu Atlas of Scotland* (1654), 83.

3   *NSA*, xi, 552.

4   *OSA*, viii, 200.

5   F. Mudie, D. M. Walker and I. MacIvor, *Broughty Castle and Defence of the Tay* (Dundee, 2010).

6   Groome, *Gazetteer*, i, 191.

7   *NSA*, xi, 553.

8   *NSA*, xi, 552.

9   For example, *Old Jetty, Broughty Ferry (Baiting the Line)* by George M. MacGillivray (Dundee Art Galleries and Museums).

10 N. Gatherer, *Songs and Ballads of Dundee* (Edinburgh, 1985), 124, 132.

11 S. Stevenson, *Hill and Adamson's The Fishermen and Women of the Firth of Forth* (Edinburgh, 1991).

12 *City Echo* (1907), quoted in *Broughty Ferry Complete Guide,* accessed at www.cometobroughty.co.uk/htm/town-history.htm.

12   Canongate Cartoons, 1830

This lithograph was produced by Thomas Sinclair (*c.* 1805–1881). Born in Orkney, he studied lithography in Edinburgh, where he had established his own firm, based in West Register Street, by 1825. Lithography was a relatively new technique and Sinclair's work was of high quality. Although a few maps can be traced to him,[1] his main work seems to have been in satirical prints, typically drawn with expansive speech bubbles identifying the protagonists, about the various controversies – *recherché* as well as populist – which rippled through Edinburgh society in the late 1820s and early 1830s. This print, entitled *A Residenter in an Ancient Burgh on his Way to procure a Burgess Ticket*, was one of a set of three targeting the various issues linked to burgh and parliamentary reform and the thorny issue of pew rents. The vignette showing *Mechanics of an Ancient Burgh going to Church to claim the Superiority of their Seats* poked fun at the fact that the new Canongate parish church could not accommodate all of its congregation. By 1692 only those with communion tickets and persons of 'known quality' were permitted entrance. The price of each – one shilling – suggests that his target audience was much the same as that of *The Scotsman*, selling at 10 pence per issue (including 4 pence of stamp duty): the new, disenfranchised professional and middle classes.

Sinclair had published a set of twelve prints in 1828 making fun of the controversy about which books of the Apocrypha were authentic. One, *The Procession of the Annuity Money Receivers to Bank Street*, depicting ministers in their Geneva gowns queuing outside the Bank of Scotland to be paid, tapped into the long-running grievance of Edinburgh inhabitants taxed to support the Established Church whether they belonged to it or not.[2]

The three reform prints of 1830 were his last known publications in Scotland. By 1833 he was in Philadelphia and by 1838 he had set up his own lithographic business. Thomas Sinclair & Son, as it later came to be called, became a firm renowned for quality lithographic work in colour in a variety of subjects, including landscapes, portraits and animals and birds.[3]

By 1830–2, in Scotland as in England, the agitation for political reform had reached fever pitch. The burgh reform movement had first emerged in Scotland in the 1770s, but the unholy, usually unspoken alliance between the corrupt oligarchies which controlled burgh politics and the Ministry which ruled Scotland from London effectively kept the campaign for reform of burgh government away from the Westminster parliament. The

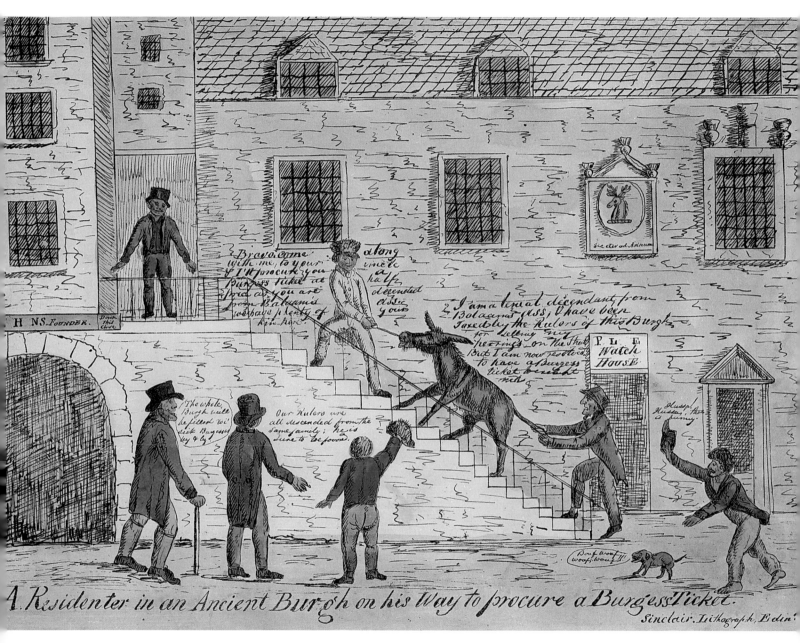

12. Thomas Sinclair, *A Residenter in an Ancient Burgh on his Way to procure a Burgess Ticket*, 1830

issues involved in burgh reform were complex and increasingly intertwined with the failure to secure progress on any one issue. One was related to the franchise, where the level of abuse varied; in Edinburgh, the election of the MP was limited to twenty-five voters. The other was concerned with the corruption and financial scandals stemming from the nepotism of the self-serving cliques which controlled the urban economy as well as government.[4]

This cartoon poked fun at the Canongate trade incorporations and their privileges. It suggested that entry to burgess-ship – the right to freedom of the burgh, a coveted privilege from medieval times – was so discredited that those who held power were 'asses'. Only burgesses had the right to attend head courts, held three times a year, where burgh business was decided upon, or in many cases merely homologated, or become a member of the burgh council. Only burgesses could be a member of the gild merchant, which controlled trade and the market. Trade incorporations were the formal alliance of members of a specific craft. Mostly established before 1600, they had entrenched their old privileges and power in what was by the 1820s a very different, new economy.

12a. Thomas Sinclair, *Mechanics of an Ancient Burgh going to Church to claim the Superiority of their Seats*, 1830

Here, in this cartoon, the ass being cajoled up the stairs to enter Canongate tolbooth on the first floor is proclaiming his right to be accorded the freedom of the burgh. Citing the Old Testament's *Book of Numbers*, he claims that

> I am a lineal descendant from Balamis ass. I have been taxed by the rulers of this burgh for selling my herrings on the street.[5] But I am now resolved to have a burgess ticket.

Clearly, the ass has fallen foul of the authorities by 'forestalling' the official market and selling his wares illicitly. From medieval times forestalling was one of the most heinous infractions of market rulings. Even so, the ass intends to enter the higher echelons of burgh society. The man pulling the rope is encouraging the ass:

> Bravo, come along with me to your uncle and I'll procure you a burgess ticket at half price as you are descended from Balamis ass. We have plenty of yours like him.

Misuse of power often stemmed from nepotism. As one onlooker says, 'Our rulers are all descended from the same family. He is sure to be favoured.' The clear implication is that the uncle is in the tolbooth and in a position of authority, perhaps as a bailie or provost. But even he is an ass. The man on the left responds: 'The whole burgh will be filled with sich [such] burgesses by and by.' The trade incorporations, it is suggested, were bolstering their own anachronistic position, filling the burgh with people of little worth – asses. The Burgh Reform Act of 1833 extended the franchise for both parliament and burgh councils to £10 property owners and forced councils to publish their accounts. This was reform of a sort: it helped reduce the level of corruption and abuse of power but only one in thirty-eight adult males were given the vote.[6] As for the ass's misdemeanour, the Act, unlike its counterpart in England, did not solve its problem: the centuries-old ban preventing the unfree from trading escaped abolition.[7] The ass still needed his burgess ticket.

Endnotes

1 *See* two maps of the River Findhorn (1823, 1826), connected with a legal dispute (NLS, Signet.s.56; NLS, EMS.s.814).

2 BM, Satirical prints, nos 15574–85, 15887–91 (1828). The annuity tax procession is BM, 15592. Another print, *The Meeting* (1828), showed a dispute between academics throwing books at each other (BM, 1991, 0615.73).

3 G. C. Groce and D. H. Wallace, *The New-York Historical Society's Dictionary of Artists in America 1564–1860* (1969). *See* www.library.upenn.edu/collections/rbm/keffer/sinclair.html, 0615.73).

4 W. Ferguson, *Scotland: 1689 to the Present* (Edinburgh, 1968), 243–5; J. Innes and N. Rogers, 'Politics and government, 1700–1840', in P. Clark (ed.), *The Cambridge Urban History of Britain: vol. ii, 1540–1840* (Cambridge, 2000), 554, 570.

5 The prophet Balaam, according to the *Book of Numbers*, rode on an ass and was accused of mistreating the animal.

6 J. F. McCaffrey, *Scotland in the Nineteenth Century* (London, 1998), 26–7.

7 Innes and Rogers, 'Politics and government', 547.

13   Canongate, *c.* 1828–38

This somewhat melodramatic and, in places, fanciful view of the Canongate was painted by David Roberts (1796–1864). Showing artistic talent from an early age, Roberts was apprenticed at ten and a half to the Edinburgh house-painter Gavin Buego. Having finished his seven-year apprenticeship and a short spell decorating Scone Palace, he became a scene-painter to James Bannister's touring 'company of pantomimists'. Returning in 1817 to house painting in Perth and Edinburgh, he worked as a journeyman painter on Dunbar House and Craigcrook Castle. In 1818 Roberts was engaged as scene-painter by Montagu Corri for the Pantheon, a circus and theatre in Edinburgh. His scenery so impressed that he transferred in 1819 to the Theatre Royal, Glasgow. There he met Alexander Nasmyth (1758–1840) whose work, he later claimed, formed the basis of his style.

Returning to Edinburgh, to the Theatre Royal, Roberts met and worked with the English marine painter, Clarkson Stanfield (1793–1867), who encouraged both his scene-painting, for which his reputation was steadily growing, and his general work. In 1822 Roberts submitted three paintings to the Fine Arts Institution, Edinburgh; all were accepted and two depicting Edinburgh scenes were sold. He continued his collaboration with Stanfield on dioramas and panoramas in London. He returned to Edinburgh during holidays to paint scenery. Roberts travelled extensively in Europe in the later 1820s and 1830s but maintained his love of Edinburgh, campaigning for preservation of important buildings, such as the John Knox House and Rosslyn Chapel. In 1834 he was invited to submit a design for a monument to Sir Walter Scott and in 1856 he produced designs for a new National Gallery.

Becoming noted as an important architectural artist, he was elected a full member of the Royal Academy in 1841. Roberts was supported by many patrons and collectors, including Queen Victoria and Prince Albert. This came at a time when Roberts fulfilled one of his ambitions – to travel to the Near and Middle East. Leaving Britain in 1838 for the first time on these travels,[1] the influence of these visits is reflected in much of his work, although not this painting, which has, rather, an Italianate influence, and so possibly dates the work to pre-1838.

This view, looking westwards up Canongate High Street towards Edinburgh, displays many of the attributes acquired during his eclectic life. His role as a scene-painter is

13. David Roberts, *The Toll House Edinburgh*, c. 1828–38

reinforced in this dramatic image, with its interest in light and impression rather than in detail, with the modification of buildings away from reality towards an almost 'fairy-tale' style. He contentedly moves or alters buildings to suit his desired composition, much as Nasmyth did with his Edinburgh views and Turner also to some extent with Linlithgow (*see* 34, 71). Parts of this image may be viewed as a fantasy, given that this was painted in the nineteenth century, at a time of increasing overcrowding and industrialisation, with inevitable concomitant lack of sanitation – cholera hit in 1832, and influenza and typhoid five years later. Epidemics of typhus, relapsing fever and typhoid fever made several visits in the 1840s, along with scurvy, with cholera reappearing in 1848–9. Whooping cough, smallpox, scarlet fever and tuberculosis were an almost inevitable part of life. Something very threatening and frightening was happening in Canongate in the 1830s and 1840s.[2] None of this is portrayed in this magnificent study of architecture.

Roberts portrays accurately a narrow street hemmed in on both sides by tall buildings. Canongate and Edinburgh, because of their topography, had, when pressure for space arose, no option but to expand upwards rather than outwards.[3] These tenement blocks housed varying stratified ranks of society, with the poorer living on the least desirable floors – the attics and the cellars. The street is thronging with people; crowd scenes were among Roberts' favourites, the 'extras' on the set. Congestion on the High Street was inevitable, particularly as coach travel became the vogue for the wealthier members of society. It is little wonder that the market cross, which had for centuries stood in the middle of the thoroughfare, was moved to the side, close to the churchyard wall in 1737 'for the convenience of passage in the street'.[4]

At the head of the street, highlighted in pale colour, overshadowing the darkened buildings nearer the forefront, is Edinburgh's Tron Church. In 1824 the steeple of the church was burned and subsequently demolished. In 1828 it was rebuilt to a new and considerably taller design.[5] His use of light and darkness to add atmosphere makes it somewhat difficult to see detailing of the church. What is discernible would suggest that Roberts was depicting exactly neither the original nor the new tower.

Prominent in the centre of this image is Canongate tolbooth, with its distinctive clock overhanging the High Street, its exterior staircase leading to the first floor and its roofing of wooden shingles.[6] Roberts recreates the main block of the tolbooth accurately, defining the importance of this building to town life and stressing its importance with a white render visual effect. But the lower, more easterly section of the structure is foreshortened. He shows fewer windows than existed and an abruptly truncated eastern gable. Why was this? It appears that it is to make way for the Italianate structure at the right-hand side of the image.

If this is illustrating Canongate Parish Church, it bears very little relationship to reality. But possibly the most striking piece of fantasy is the siting of the church. In reality, the parish church is set back from the roadway, with elegant railings round it. Roberts' church is hard up to the pavement, where the populace might walk right past the entrance. The townscape effect of a gable-fronted church built directly onto the road was something Roberts would have been quite familiar with from his time working in Rome and he has no difficulty importing it into the Scottish setting. It is possibly to add more visual impact to this expression of unreality, this stage set, that the tolbooth has been foreshortened. Roberts has drawn a city of imagination at some indeterminate time in the historical past, which is the visual equivalent of a story by Sir Walter Scott or a Victorian historical stage drama.

Endnotes

1 *DNB*, David Roberts.

2 E. P. Dennison, *Holyrood and Canongate: A Thousand Years of History* (Edinburgh, 2005), 147–8.

3 Edinburgh's topography goes a long way to explaining this. Flatting was not adopted, however, in heavily populated English cities, and flatted accommodation appears in Scottish towns where lack of space was not an issue. One explanation is the legal system: the boundaries of burgage plots were strictly monitored in Scottish burghs, and Scots law was relaxed about multiple ownership over a single solum.

4 W. Maitland, *The History of Edinburgh from its Foundation to the Present Time* (Edinburgh, 1753), 156.

5 J. Gifford, C. McWilliam and D. Walker, *The Buildings of Scotland: Edinburgh* (Edinburgh, 1984), 174.

6 Dennison, *Holyrood and Canongate*, 38.

14   Coupar Angus, 1843

Published in 1843 by an unknown artist, this view of Coupar Angus from the south shows many of the most significant features of the town. The parish church had been partially rebuilt in the 1780s, partly using stones from the ruins of the old Cistercian abbey: 'an arch, of beautiful architecture, situate near the centre of the … churchyard, was demolished for the purpose of furnishing stones for the … church'.[1] This siting of a kirk within the precinct of the erstwhile monastery was a direct result of an agreement between King James VI (1567–1625) and Lord Coupar, the burgh superior, in 1618. Initially part of the parish of Bendochy, parishioners in Coupar Angus had to cross the Water of Isla to attend church. At times of flood this could prove dangerous; to this day in the dry season the causey stones of the ford are still visible. Henceforth the kirk of Coupar Angus, when eventually built, was to serve as the parish church for the town and the parish of Bendochy, south of the Isla.[2]

Ruins of the abbey, often referred to as the gatehouse, partially shrouded by trees, may be seen in the centre of the view. Buildings to the west show vividly how the lands of the abbey complex became colonised. This area, known as 'the Precinct', so recalling its previous function, was soon cannibalised by the locals, if the seventeenth-century register of baptisms may attest to occupation.[3] To this day, many domestic dwellings reveal the use of abbey complex stones in their structure. The tall building with a spire was the tolbooth, permission for its erection being given in 1607 on achieving the status of a burgh of barony.[4] It was here that dues, or tolls, to use the market were collected. It underwent a major transformation when the steeple or tolbooth tower was erected by public subscription held in 1762 and was completed seven years later. It was to serve as a gaol on the ground floor and as a meeting-house for local courts on the upper floors, regality courts and bailie courts until then being held in the open air at nearby Beech Hill.[5]

The foreground scenery stresses the rural character of Scottish towns well into the nineteenth century. The man to the left is sowing seed by hand, the seed being stored in a sheet or cloth wrapped round his body. The horses draw an appliance to harrow the land and so cover the scattered seed. A stagecoach is seen travelling into town, approaching the foot of the High Street, on the road that led to Dundee. This would not have been the traditional pre-Reformation alignment of the Dundee road, as this one portrayed lay on

14. Anon., *View of Coupar Angus from the South*, 1843

erstwhile abbey lands. Was this originally an approach to the abbey's south gate? To cater for travellers, hostelries were set up. The Royal Hotel, once called the Defiance Inn, took its name from the stagecoach that stopped there daily on the Edinburgh–Perth–Aberdeen run. Across the road the White House or White Horse Inn, now the Strathmore Hotel, was also a hostelry for travellers. Until very recently some of the stabling and tethering rings for visitors' horses were visible to the rear of the hotel. A scheme to assist communications and benefit the growing local manufactories was projected in the 1760s. George Young, a linen manufacturer in the town, had a survey prepared, with the intention of linking Forfar and Perth by canal, but nothing came of this innovatory idea.[6]

The second image is a sketch made earlier, in 1820, part of a series of studies of the ruins of the Abbey and of other ecclesiastical sites throughout Scotland made by George Henry Hutton (d. 1827), formerly a professional soldier and an amateur antiquary. A handwritten note at the foot of the drawing indicates that this is a view 'looking north, Augt 29, 1820'. It also jots the word 'tolbooth'' underneath the tower of the town house. It is, in fact, the same view as the main image, although the perspective of the one-storeyed houses at the edge of the town is different. Otherwise, it is clear that little changed between 1820 and 1843, although much would do so shortly afterwards.

The town's contacts with the rest of Scotland were strengthened with the opening of the railway in 1837. The Newtyle and Coupar Angus Railway Company had been

14b. George Henry Hutton, *Ruins of the Abbey, looking North*, 1820

incorporated in 1835, employing the services of the local surveyor William Blackadder. Although its seal depicts a locomotive with symbols of speed and time, and bears the motto 'Time is Precious', the service was horse-drawn for much of the time until it was incorporated in 1847 into the Dundee, Perth and Aberdeen Railway Junction Company. The arrival of the railway had a great impact on the lives of the townspeople. A new hotel was built beside the railway station for the accommodation of travellers. Once called the Railway Hotel, it is now the Red House Hotel. But of possibly more profound significance for the townspeople, who now numbered about 2,600, was the siting of the railway line. Coupar Angus had always been 'divided' by natural features, the Coupar Burn running across the line of the High Street putting the northerly section in Perthshire and the southerly in Angus. The railway, however, ran right through the town, dividing it in half at the top of the High Street. Henceforth, until the closures of lines by Dr Beeching in the 1960s, access to the two halves of the town was by level crossing.

Endnotes

1 *NSA*, x, 1144; E. P. Dennison and R. Coleman, *Historic Coupar Angus* (Scottish Burgh Survey, 1997), 30.
2 For the long delays in building the parish church, *see ibid.*, 26.
3 NRS, CH2/395/1, for example, 12 April 1688.
4 Pryde, *Burghs*, no. 281.
5 *Tolbooths and Town-houses*, 56.
6 *OSA*, xi, 91.

15   Culross, 1693

Captain John Slezer (*c.* 1650–1717), a German-speaking military engineer, probably from the Rhineland, came to Scotland in 1669. To augment his income he set in preparation two books, one to illustrate Scottish towns, palaces and abbeys, which he hoped might be subsidised by parliament, the other to depict important country seats, which would be funded by private subscription. Parliament agreed to the first proposal but, in the event, never paid him. The resultant work – the *Theatrum Scotiae* – was published in 1693, consisting of aspects of both proposed volumes. The insights he gave into Scottish life, particularly into towns in the late seventeenth century, are invaluable, but he died in debt in 1717, in spite of having been appointed Captain of Scotland's Artillery Train and without being fully reimbursed for this project.

This prospect of Culross was made from a group of rocks in the Forth, which are easily accessible at low tide to this day. The figures fowling in this plate, however, give a distorted view of the rocks, which are, in reality, much smaller. Prominent on the skyline are the ruins of the abbey of Culross and the extant church. To the east, Culross House, with its extensive gardens, almost overshadows the little town.

Culross Abbey had been founded in 1215 x 1217 by Malcolm, thane of Fife, for the monks of Kinloss, Moray. Attached to the Cistercian monastery was a church dedicated to the Virgin Mary and St Serf. By the late fifteenth century the lay brothers had left, the abbey then being occupied only by choir monks. An element of decline set in, with the western half of the abbey being abandoned and the nave demolished around 1500 and the present tower added. At the time of its closure there were nine Cistercian monks practising in the monastery.[1] By 1633 the church became the parish church for public worship. The original parish church stood about a quarter of a mile to the west, outwith the monastery precincts, and continued in use after the Reformation as a burial ground.

Culross House was built in 1608 for Edward Bruce, Lord Kinloss, on elevated ground with excellent views over the Forth valley and extensive, beautifully laid-out gardens. Sir George Bruce (*c.* 1550–1625), brother of Lord Kinloss, a mining industrialist and landowner, was the youngest of the three sons of Sir Edward Bruce (1505–1565) of Blairhall, near Culross, then in Perthshire, and Alison Reid of Aitkenhead, a sister of the bishop of Orkney. Sometimes described in documents as a 'merchant' or 'burgess of

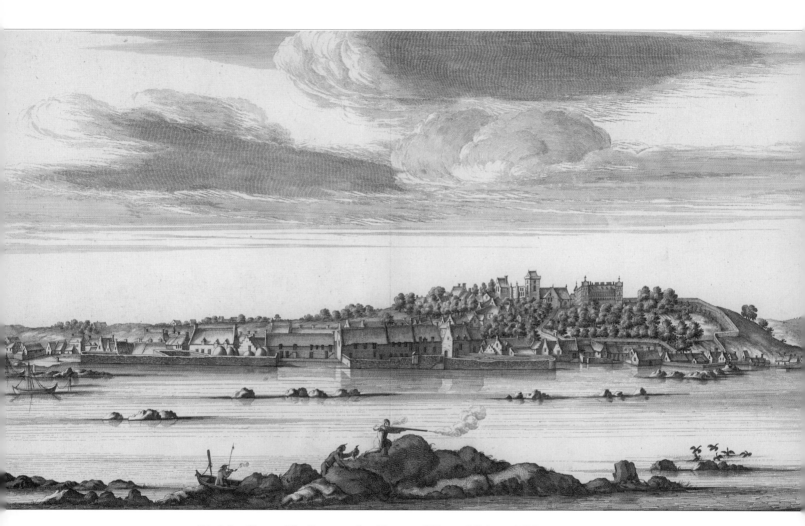

15. John Slezer, *The Prospect of ye House and Town of Colross*, 1693

Culross', Bruce came from an established and well-connected landed family. Both George Bruce and his brother Edward were privy councillors. George himself filled a number of important offices, including member of the Scottish parliament for Culross after it was elevated to the status of a royal burgh in 1592.[2]

George Bruce's business dealings were clearly profitable, to judge from his attractive mansion, often mistakenly now referred to as 'the Palace' (built in stages between 1597 and 1611), at the foot of the steep hill leading to the abbey, and from the impressive tomb in Culross Abbey church. He was a ship owner and merchant, as well as a substantial landowner. His principal lands, purchased in 1602, were at nearby Carnock. James VI (1567–1625) knighted him, probably in 1610, and visited his house and industrial businesses in 1617.

In 1575 Bruce was granted the lease of the former monastic coalworks at Culross, 'for his great knowledge and skill in machinery such like as no other man has in these days; and for his being the likeliest person to re-establish again the Colliery of Culross'.[3] Bruce used innovative mechanical drainage, ventilation and haulage techniques – notably an 'Egyptian wheel' – to exploit these deep under-sea coalmines. Indeed, so important were the Culross coal workings that in 1663 the Culross chalder became the standard measure

15a. View of the salt pans

in Scotland.[4] Some of the extracted coal was used to supply the heat for the evaporation of seawater at Bruce's saltworks. By 1625 he had as many as forty-four salt pans in and around Culross.[5] Salt was a vital commodity, being used extensively as a preservative for meat after the autumn slaughter. It has been estimated that to produce three tons of salt, ninety-seven tons of seawater were needed to evaporate. This would require about forty-eight tons of coal.[6] This explains the plethora of saltpans on the Forth coast – the closeness of fuel and seawater.

Slezer's view shows clearly the salt pans in the foreground. Since approximately 97 per cent of the water would be lost to evaporation, pans were placed as near as possible to the sea and saltwater supply and often, as shown in this view, projected out into the sea.[7] Once evaporated by heating, the salt was kept safely in storehouses called girnels. So precious was salt as a commodity that, until the repeal of salt duties in 1825, girnels were locked by customs and excise officials.

In their day, Bruce's mines and saltworks were a tourist attraction, being probably the largest and the most technically advanced in Scotland. Shortly before his death in 1625 Bruce's showpiece enterprise was largely destroyed by a great storm, but Culross enjoyed commercial and industrial significance, particularly for its saltworks, until the end of the century.

Endnotes

1 *OSA*, x, 147.

2 Pryde, *Burghs*, no. 65.

3 A. S. Cunningham, *Culross: Past and Present* (Edinburgh, 1910), 53.

4 *OSA*, x, 144.

5 C. A. Whatley, *The Salt Industry and its Trade in Fife and Tayside, c. 1570–1850* (Abertay Historical Society, Dundee, 1984), 26.

6 I. H. Adams, 'The salt industry of the Forth Basin', *Scottish Geographical Magazine*, 81, part 3 (1965), 155.

7 *Ibid.*, 153.

16   Dalkeith, 1822, 1770 and *c.* 1776

Pictorial views of Dalkeith before photography are scarce. This preliminary etching by the amateur antiquarian, John Clerk of Eldin (1728–1812), is a rare exception. Clerk drew a large number of etchings, mostly of historic buildings set within a landscape, and often of the area around Edinburgh. It was only to be expected that, with his estate of Eldin at nearby Lasswade, Clerk would turn his attention to the historic burgh of Dalkeith. The three figures in the foreground are approaching the Luton Bridge across the North Esk from the north. With the exception of two houses portrayed at Bridgend on the town side of the bridge, little detail is discernible of the linear settlement of the burgh, save for the distinctive steeple of the parish church of St Nicholas, which had been dismantled in 1752 and re-erected in 1762, shortly before this sketch was made.[1] Otherwise, Clerk's rare glimpse of Dalkeith tells little. For that, one has to turn to another visual resource – maps of the town.

This plan of Dalkeith was drawn in 1822 by John Wood (*c.* 1780–1847) who made a series of townscape maps between 1819 and 1846. A variety of other sources suggest that they are all highly accurate. What is intriguing about this plan is that Wood delineates a major High Street, lined with a church (the collegiate church of St Nicholas) and markets, and the burgage plots of the inhabitants, also showing clearly a big, open market place. What is somewhat bizarre is that the High Street leads to nowhere. This is very unusual. Many Scottish towns had, in effect, truncated High Streets, often ending in a port, or town gate, but the roadways continued as more minor routes further into the hinterland. Dalkeith's is blocked. Clearly visible, is the blockage – the Duke's Gates to Dalkeith Parks surrounding Dalkeith House (also variously named Castle or Palace), favoured often by the monarchy.[2] What has caused this enigma?

One clue may come from a 1556 charter detailing the resignation of a tenement on the south side of the High Street. The resignation was effected at the green of Dalkeith which was 'near the castle'.[3] But early maps show no possibility of space for a town green in Dalkeith, although they were commonplace in many other Scottish towns – unless it was within the Duke's Gates! It may be of significance that when the lordship, barony and regality of Dalkeith was transferred to Francis, Earl of Buccleuch, in 1642, it was described as 'extensive lands, lordship, regality, town and burgh of barony and regality of

16. John Wood, *Plan of Dalkeith*, 1822

124

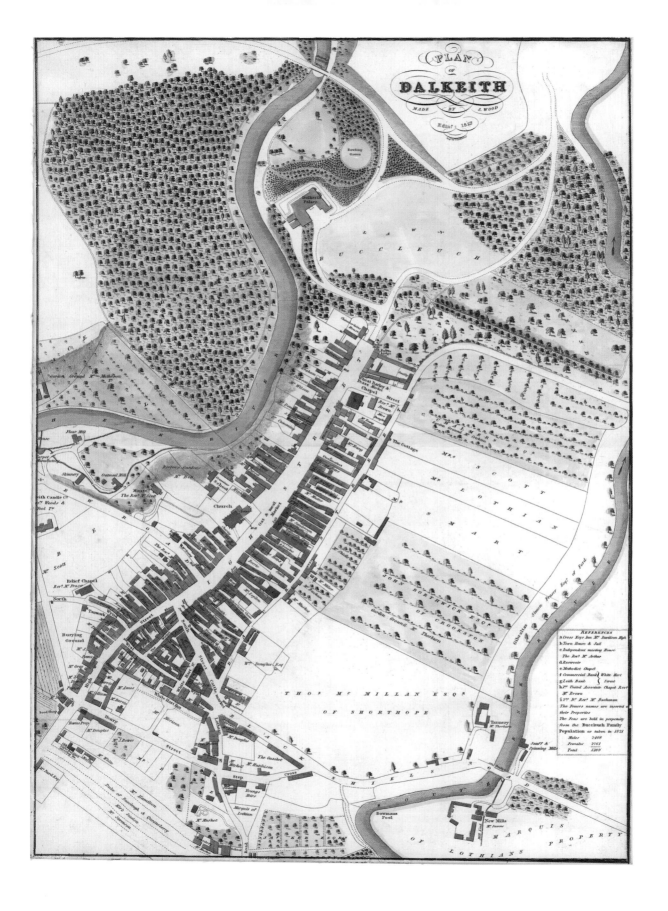

PLAN
OF
DALKEITH
MADE BY J. WOOD
Edin.¹ 1822

Bowling Green

Dalkeith Palace

L A W N

B U C C L E U C H

Wheat Barley & Pease
Chapel
Street

The Cottage

S C O T T

L O T H I A N

S M A R T

JOHN BOTHWICK ESQ.
OF CROOKSTON

Garden Ground Mr. Thorburn

THO.ˢ MC MILLAN ESQ.ˢ
OF SHORTHOPE

Tannery
Mr. Thorburn

Snuff & Spinning Mills

Bowmans
Pool

New Mills
Mr. Snow

MARQUIS PROPERTY

OF LOTHIANS

REFERENCES
a. Cross Keys Inn Mr. Davidson High
b. Town House & Jail
c. Independent meeting House
   The Rev.ᵈ Mr. Arthur
d. Reservoir
e. Methodist Chapel
f. Commercial Bank
g. Leith Bank
h. U.ᵗᵈ Associate Chapel Rev.ᵈ
   Mr. Brown
i. Dr. Rev.ᵈ Mr. Buchanan
The Feuers names are inserted
their Properties
The Feus are held in perpetuity
from the Buccleuch Family
Population as taken in 1821
   Males   2408
   Females   2761
   Total   5169

Dalkeith with its liberties, with the castle, gardens, orchards, forests and parks, grain and cloth mills, fisheries, rabbit warrens, tenants, coal mines, prebendary and patronage of the collegiate church'.[4] Twenty-two years later, when the same was granted to James, Duke of Monmouth and Buccleuch, the lordship was similarly described, but the policies around the castle were described as 'all the lands included within the stone dyke of the ... park'.[5] So clearly by this date, 1664, or possibly earlier, the castle was surrounded by a stone wall with gates, which abruptly ended the High Street.

What is also unclear is the route to the Cow Bridge, which was the crossing over the South Esk River, just as the traversing of the North Esk was over the Lugton Bridge, on the road alignment still existing today. With the Dalkeith Parks enclosed with a stone wall, the road south from the end of the High Street was forced to take a circuitous route around the wall and from there move eastwards towards Musselburgh, across the South Esk. Remains of demolished housing – blocked doorways and windows in the stone wall just to the south of the Duke's Gates – attest, as in Hamilton (*see* 53), to clearance of parts of the town too close to the aristocratic residence.

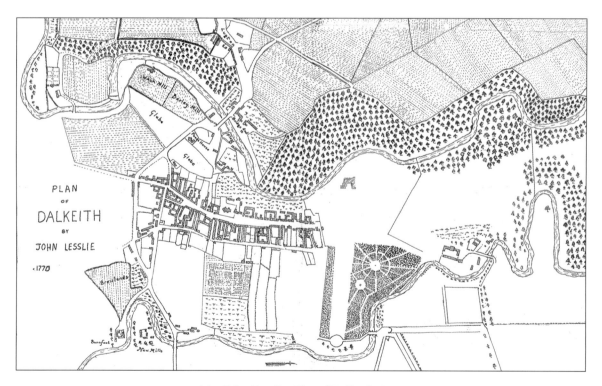

16a. John Lesslie, *Plan of Dalkeith*, 1770

16b. John Clerk of Eldin, *Dalkeith from the North West, c. 1776*

A copy of a map drawn by John Lesslie in 1770 (the whereabouts of the original is unknown) may hold some clues. As in the Wood map, the High Street is shown to come to an abrupt end. The castle/palace is clearly shown, although un-named, in splendid isolation. The route to the west of the town, crossing the South Esk, roughly on the current alignment, is depicted. So also is a crossing to Cow Bridge in the centre, as well as the circuitous route crossing the South Esk to Musselburgh. Interestingly, a pathway leading to a bridge over the South Esk is portrayed to the right. (The nearby buildings depicted are associated with the palace – kennels, laundry and the like.) If a hypothetical line was drawn from the end of the High Street to this pathway, the route is virtually on the same alignment. Is there here evidence of a once extended High Street that was assimilated into the Dalkeith policies, along with the town green – another example of urban clearance? Perhaps only archaeological investigation can answer this.

Endnotes

1 E. P. Dennison and R. Coleman, *Historic Dalkeith: The Archaeological Implications of Development* (Scottish Burgh Survey, 1998), 36–7, 49–52.

2 *Ibid.*, 21, 22–3. 28, 34.

3 D. Laing (ed.), *The Bannatyne Miscellany*, ii (Bannatyne Club, 1836), 170, no. 653.

4 *RMS*, ix, 445, no. 1191; *see also* NRS, GD 150/644, Morton Papers.

5 *RMS*, xi, 339, no. 673.

17   Dornoch, 1839 and *c.* 1776

The town of Dornoch grew round the cathedral that dominates this watercolour by James Giles (1801–1870). Born in Aberdeenshire, Giles painted extensively in the eastern Highlands where his patrons included Queen Victoria and the Earl of Aberdeen. Giles painted this scene in 1839, shortly after a major reconstruction of the cathedral had been completed. The tranquillity of this scene would suggest that the eventful history of town and cathedral was a thing of the past but another chapter was about to begin.

Dornoch is unlikely to have been a greenfield site when Gilbert of Moray, newly elected bishop of Caithness (1222–45), chose to build his cathedral there in 1223.[1] Based on some ambiguous documents, historians have suggested that there was an earlier religious community at Dornoch, possibly as far back as the ancient Celtic Church of the culdees. Recent archaeological excavation close to the cathedral has uncovered part of an early medieval settlement, with evidence for metal working, which would seem to support this theory.[2]

Traditionally, the part-Norse, part-Gaelic diocese of Caithness, including the county of Sutherland, had been based at Halkirk, near Thurso. Gilbert's decision to relocate to Dornoch may have been influenced by the violence meted out to two of his predecessors. Certainly, the move distanced him from the powerful Viking Earls of Orkney and brought him closer to the rule of David I, King of Scots (1124–53), and the protection of a kinsman, the thane of Sutherland.

Giles's painting demonstrates how Dornoch developed round Gilbert's cathedral. The tall building on the left is all that remained of the imposing sixteenth-century Bishop's Palace, reputed to have had three such towers.[3] It is often referred to as 'Dornoch Castle' and it is not difficult to see why. The picture also shows the striking contrast between the lofty cathedral and palace and the much smaller, more basic buildings that surround them. These would originally have housed the chapter house, guest house and living quarters of the numerous clergy attached to the cathedral.

It is interesting to note the different roofing materials used. Some buildings are thatched and some slated, while others use large stone slabs. Slate could be sourced locally as there was 'a quarrie of sleat hard by the toun of Dornoch' according to Sir Robert

17. James Giles, *View of Dornoch from the East*, 1839

Gordoun's 1630 history.[4] Other quarries at Dornoch provided the sandstone that was used to build the piers of the cathedral.[5]

On the left of the picture it is just possible to make out an old bridge. This crossed the Dornoch Burn to the pasture-land where a mare is suckling her foal. The woman standing in the burn may be washing her clothes in a mill race, if a reconstruction of the town which appears in Bentinck's 1926 history is correct, and the ruined building behind is that of the Bishop's mill and kiln.[6]

Much of the town and Gilbert's cathedral were destroyed by fire in 1570 when John Sinclair, master of Caithness, attacked Dornoch, the only town in Sutherland, as part of a long running battle between the ruling houses of Caithness and Sutherland. It was about this time that Robert Stewart, the last bishop of Caithness, retired to St Andrews. Stewart had been appointed bishop of Caithness at the age of nineteen. Lacking any form of religious qualification, he relied on his powerful royal kinsmen and a sister who was married to the Earl of Sutherland. Stewart embraced the Protestant faith with ease

17a. Charles Cordiner, *The Nave of Dornoch Cathedral, c.* 1776

following the Reformation of 1560.[7] In Dornoch, as with so many Highland communities, the new faith was slow to establish itself.

A terrible storm hit Dornoch in November 1605 inflicting severe damage on a cathedral already in need of repair. That it rose again as we see it here, was due to Elizabeth (1765–1839), duchess and countess of Sutherland. The scale of the restoration was formidable and can perhaps best be judged by a sketch of the roofless nave made by Charles Cordiner in *c.* 1776.[8] The ambitious scheme, carried out entirely at her expense, was completed in 1837. By that time, using the fabulous wealth generated by her husband's English estates, the family had bought over the bulk of the county of Sutherland. Like the many other improvements they undertook, however, the 'drastic refashioning' of the ancient cathedral into the building in this picture, appears to have been carried out without sufficient consultation and to have caused much ill feeling.[9]

As patrons, the Duke and Duchess of Sutherland had presented the minister and his assistant to this cathedral. Four years after Giles's picture was finished, the Church of Scotland finally split over the right of lay patrons to nominate parish ministers. One third of its ministers left to found the Free Church of Scotland, including Angus Kennedy, minister of Dornoch Cathedral, and George Kennedy, his assistant and son. Perhaps it is as well that the duke, who died in 1833, and the duchess, who died six months before Giles painted this picture, were unaware of this new chapter in the long history of the cathedral town of Dornoch.

Endnotes

1 R. Fawcett, *Scottish Cathedrals* (London, 1997), 32–3, 122.

2 R. Coleman and E. Photos-Jones, *Early Medieval Settlement and Ironworking in Dornoch, Sutherland: Excavations at The Meadows Business Park* (Scottish Archaeological Internet Report 28, 2008).

3 A.T. Simpson and S. Stevenson, *Historic Dornoch: The Archaeological Implications of Development* (Scottish Burgh Survey, 1982), 19.

4 Sir Robert Gordon, *Genealogical History of the Earldom of Sutherland* (Inverness, 1630; reprinted 1813), 6.

5 W. D. Simpson, Appendix, in C. D. Bentinck, *Dornoch Cathedral and Parish* (Inverness, 1926), 383.

6 Bentinck, *Dornoch Cathedral*, 142.

7 J. Dowden, *The Bishops of Scotland* (Glasgow, 1912), 249; G. Donaldson, *Reformed by Bishops: Galloway, Orkney and Caithness* (Edinburgh, 1987), 53–67.

8 C. Cordiner, *Remarkable Ruins and Romantic Prospects of North Britain* (1795). The sketch is reproduced in Fawcett, *Scottish Cathedrals*, 33.

9 Simpson, Appendix, 377.

18   Dumbarton, 1824

This scene, which artfully combines the industrial and the bucolic, was painted by John Clark, watercolourist and aquatint engraver, who sometimes signed, as here, as I. Clark. It portrays people and animals at leisure above the waters of the River Leven but it also reveals much more about the town of Dumbarton and its geographical location. Immediately arresting are the twin peaks of the volcanic basalt Dumbarton Rock. This was the chosen spot of the Britons of Strathclyde for their principal stronghold and political centre. Known to them as *Alcluith* (Clyde Rock) and to the Irish annalists as *Dun Breatann* (Fort of the Britons), it was probably occupied from the fifth century AD onwards and frequently survived attack and siege.

Virtually surrounded by the waters of the Clyde, the Rock had an important role to play in guarding the approaches by river to inland Scotland and the upper reaches of the Clyde, with its emerging towns such as Renfrew (founded 1124 x 47), Rutherglen (1124 x 53) and Glasgow (1175 x 78). The view shows the Clyde to be a busy water-route for both sailing barks and the newly invented steam ships. But it was not until the eighteenth century, when an artificial channel was cut through a rock barrier at Dumbuck, a little more than a mile upstream of Dumbarton Rock, that any seagoing vessel could reach the heart of Glasgow, although at high tide smaller boats with a shallow draught might be successful.

The medieval town was contained within a sweeping S-bend in the Leven, a fast-flowing, meandering river prone to flooding. The River Leven is tidal to approximately two miles above the town. A high spring tide, allied to spate conditions from melting snow from Highland hills, invariably meant floods. This would have profound implications for the township, at times almost giving the impression that the town was an island within the river. The north end of the town, in particular, was vulnerable. Around 1580 the river burst its banks, flooding this area. Known as the Broad Meadow, this land was to lie under water, known as the 'Drowned Lands', unreclaimed until the nineteenth century. Townend, at the north of the town, became separated from the rest of Dumbarton.[1] The novelist, Tobias Smollett, a pupil at Dumbarton Grammar School in the 1730s, recalled feeling cobbles or paving stones under the water as he paddled the old pathway from the collegiate church and school to Townend.[2]

18. John Clark, *The Town of Dumbarton*, 1824

Also prominent in the picture is the bridge crossing the River Leven from Cardross to the town itself. Widened and repaired on a number of occasions since then, it retains its basic five-arch design with rounded cutwaters and full-height buttresses. For centuries a ferry was the manner of crossing, arriving at Dumbarton at the Boat Vennel, later called Brewery Lane, or at very low tide a nearby fording place might be used.[3] In 1765 John Brown of Dumbarton was commissioned to build a bridge near to the old fording point. This had an impact on the townscape: a new thoroughfare was built in the town to give access to the bridge, also giving rise to the development of a new suburb – West Bridgend – shown here. Although, as may be seen in this view, there were croftlands to the west of the bridge, for example Arthur's Croft, sometimes called Bridgeland,[4] much of the new property that was developed here in the nineteenth century was substantial housing, such as Springbank, Rosebank, Bellfield and Levengrove. It brought advantage also to Archibald, 3rd Duke of Argyll, one-time provost of Dumbarton, and his successors, as no longer did they have to float their coaches on a raft over the Leven to their castle at Rosneath.[5] The cattle market also benefited; cattle no longer crossed by ferry or were forced to swim or travel by raft, risking drowning in times of storm or high tide.[6]

The most significant sight on the townscape is the triple cones of the glassworks. This new industry arrived in Dumbarton in 1777 and quickly expanded. The Dumbarton Glassworks Company was set up by James Dunlop as a speculative venture, and in 1793 it purchased Glasgow Glassworks Company and later in the decade added Greenock Glassworks Company, making this a formidable industrial concern, with warehouses as far afield as Liverpool, Hull and London. Later falling into decline, they were demolished in 1850. The publishers of the series of townscapes drawn by Clark emphasised that each was subject to the 'inspection of Gentlemen of taste, resident upon the spot'.[7] So it is likely that the figures portrayed in the foreground are the Dixons, the town's major glassmaker and one of the wealthiest families in Scotland.

Other features of the town may be noted. In the middle distance the spire of the Riverside parish church, built in 1811, may be seen. Its interior closely mirrored social status in the town. On the south side was the pulpit, with opposite, in prime position, the gallery for the town magistrates and council; at the east end were the galleries of the guild brethren and the 'castle loft' for the soldiers and officers of the Dumbarton Rock garrison.[8] Above the guild's loft and the soldier's loft a small gallery almost reached the roof. This provided the seating for the single women of the town and became know as the 'Hens' Bauk'.[9] At the west end were the lofts of the trades and beneath were seats for the grammar school children.[10]

The townscape suggests well-built housing, mostly of stone, with no evidence of thatched roofing – a sign of increasing prosperity as Dumbarton entered its nineteenth-century industrial era. Clustered around the glassworks was the 'Artizan' settlement which housed the workforce, a harbinger of similar developments which would transform the town. New industries were to develop, in particular whisky distilling and shipbuilding with the arrival of William Denny & Brothers as its nucleus. All would jostle for space in the transformed town.

Endnotes

1 F. Roberts and I. M. M. MacPhail (eds), *Dumbarton Common Good Accounts, 1614–1660* (Dumbarton, 1972), p. iii.

2 E. P. Dennison and R. Coleman, *Historic Dumbarton: The Archaeological Implications of Development* (Scottish Burgh Survey, 1999), 23.

3 *Ibid.*, 55.

4 NRS, B16/2/5; MS Dumbarton Burgh Register of Sasines, 1753–64, 3.

5 *Ibid.*, 33.

6 *RPC*, third series, vi, 498.

7 *See* Introduction.

8 Dennison and Coleman, *Historic Dumbarton*, 35.

9 E. McGhie, *Dumbarton Parish Church in History* (Dumbarton, 1995), 28.

10 Dennison and Coleman, *Historic Dumbarton*, 36.

19   Dumfries, 1846 and 1878

These two images of Dumfries and the River Nith reveal much about the history of the town in the nineteenth century. The picture of 1846 by David Octavius Hill (1802–1870) was one of more than sixty illustrations he provided for the collaborative work, *The Land of Burns* (1846). This was a highly ambitious publishing venture: the de luxe edition, in two volumes, was the most lavishly illustrated and expensive publication produced in Scotland to that date, despite the use of steel-plate engraving to lower costs. This edition was aimed at a middle-class readership, in the Scottish diaspora as much as within Scotland itself. It was also published in twenty illustrated parts, each costing two shillings; this was obviously designed to take advantage of the widespread popular appeal which Burns's works had generated, especially after 1830, in a world of Burns festivals and annual processions.[1] The 1844 Festival, marking the eighty-fifth anniversary of the poet's birth, had seen a procession of 50,000 people from Ayr to Alloway.[2]

Hill's portrayal of a near-idyllic, modest-sized town in the evening, with sheep grazing on the Whitesands, its inhabitants fishing, punting and boating, and neat, well-ordered streets and housing may have sought to evoke an impression of Dumfries in the time that Robert Burns (1759–1796) lived there rather than of the town in 1846. Between 1791 and 1793 Burns, who had taken up a post as an exciseman, lived in Bank Street, which adjoined the Whitesands, between the Old Bridge and the church of St Michael's, which is the steeple prominently depicted in the picture.[3] Another reason for highlighting St Michael's was that the poet was buried in the Greek-style temple of the Burns Mausoleum, built in its grounds in 1815. Other touches typical of Hill's work include portraying the scene with the sun setting over the river – in this case in the south-east! – and the foreshortening of the distance from the bridge to the church steeple to make a symbolic point.

This image of Dumfries, however, was not far removed from the portrayal of it in the *New Statistical Account*, written in 1833. It described a town dominated by agriculture and small-scale handicrafts, especially of hats and stockings. It did not suffer, the minister concluded with satisfaction, from the working-class 'discontent and insubordination in all manufacturing towns' which characterised the reform movement in the 1830s. One such town which experienced considerable unrest was undoubtedly the Canongate (*see* 12). The appearance of Dumfries had improved since the time of the original *Statistical Account*

19. David Octavius Hill, *Dumfries*, 1846

in the 1790s and it had undergone a 'general enlargement', from a population of 5,600 in 1791 to 11,600 in 1831, although it remained without large-scale industries.[4]

The second image of Dumfries is taken from another celebratory work, the Revd George Gilfillan's *The National Burns* (Glasgow, 1878). The theme was much the same as Hill's of thirty years before but the target audience was more modest; it was produced in fifteen parts, each costing two shillings.[5] The artist, James Ramage (*c.* 1825–1887), like Hill, was also a photographer, who had been exhibiting for the previous twenty years.[6] Although he depicted almost the identical scene, Ramage's art produced a picture which had more accurate perspective and was much less impressionistic than Hill's.

It shows that considerable change had taken place in the interim years. The Old Bridge, however, remains, as it does to this day. Although local tradition can insist on thinking of it as a survival from medieval times, a new stone bridge had been built in the seventeenth century. Originally of nine arches, three had been demolished on the Dumfries side in 1794.[7] Although both pictures show the remaining six arches, only Ramage's view makes clear that the bridge was only for foot traffic, with a flight of steps

19a. James Ramage, *Dumfries*, 1878

on the Dumfries side. A new metal suspension bridge, built in 1875 for pedestrian traffic, is shown farther downriver. The fact that the Whitesands had long housed a timber market is made more obvious in Ramage's view. There is also in his scene a hint, in the contrast between the tidal water on the near side of the Old Bridge where fishing is still being done and the still water beyond, of the caul or primitive weir built to channel water to the Maxwelltown mills.[8] The eighteenth-century town windmill, which had been converted to an observatory in 1836 (and is now part of Dumfries Museum) high on a hill on the Maxwelltown (Kirkcudbright) side of the river, is more accurately drawn to scale than the imposing, iconic edifice in Hill's view.

The main factual difference between the two views are the factory chimneys depicted in 1878. On the Dumfries bank, close to St Michael's, is the large-scale Nithsdale woollen factory – described as 'almost palatial' in Groome's *Gazetteer* – and its enormous chimney stack, 174 feet (53 metres) high, built in 1859. Here, it pours smoke into the air. Almost directly opposite it, on the Maxwelltown bank, the picture shows smoke also rising from one of the two Troqueer woollen factories, built in 1867 and 1870.[9] Adjacent to these factories was a line of mills along Mill Road in Maxwelltown: they included a large granary and kiln on the hill facing the river and the town's corn mill on the waterside near the suspension bridge. Both can be seen in the picture.[10]

As with all artists' views, a scene is only a moment captured in time. The final intriguing point to consider when viewing these two very different townscapes is that both artists were also photographers. Hill, in both his arts, was a 'poetist' (*see* Introduction). Ramage was not, in either of his.

Endnotes

1 J. Wilson, R. Chambers and D. O. Hill, *The Land of Burns: A Series of Landscapes and Portraits, Illustrative of the Life and Writings of the Scottish Poet* (Blackie & Son, Glasgow, 1846). *See DNB*, David Octavius Hill.

2 J. Burnett, *Riot, Revelry and Rout: Sport in Lowland Scotland before 1860* (East Linton, 2000), 196.

3 For the true position of Bank Street, *see* the John Wood map of Dumfries (1819): NLS website, Town Plans/Views.

4 *NSA*, iv, 15–16, 18, 23.

5 G. Gilfillan (ed.), *The National Burns including the Airs of all the Songs and an Original Life of Burns* (Glasgow, 1878).

6 For James Ramage, *see* Photographic Exhibitions in Britain, 1839–1865: http://peib.dmu.ac.uk/detailphotographer.php?photogNo=834&inum=6&listLength=7&orderBy=coverage

7 Canmore, *Dumfries, Old Bridge*.

8 Canmore, *Dumfries, Whitesands Caul*.

9 Groome, *Gazetteer*, ii, 390–7.

10 The town mills on the Maxwelltown bank are detailed in the OS map of 1850. The later factories are detailed in the large-scale OS map of 1893.

20   Dunbar, 1822 and *c.* 1780

This peaceful view of the entrance to the Old Harbour of Dunbar belies the hustle and activity that this haven sometimes experienced. Drawn in 1822 by William Daniell (1769–1837), it was promoted twenty years later, in 1842, when Dunbar's Victoria Harbour, or New Harbour, was opened. The view probably formed part of the hand-coloured aquatints for Richard Ayton's *A Picturesque Voyage round Great Britain* (1814–25). Dunbar had not had an ideal harbour before the seventeenth century and used a safer anchorage at Belhaven. At this point, a harbour of sorts was built at Dunbar itself, probably between a causeway between Lamer Island and the shore, providing protection from northerly winds, and the curved east pier of the later harbour, which offered a level of security from easterly winds. The inadequacy of the harbour facilities was summed up by William Brereton, who visited the town in 1635. The town, he said

> is so environed with shelfs [*sic*], bars and sands, as there is no manner of haven, though the main sea beat upon the town, which indeed is not seated upon a river, which might furnish it with an haven or a navigable channel; only here is an haven made of great stones piled up, whereinto at a spring tide a ship of one hundred ton may enter, but not without much hazard.[1]

The Old Harbour became known as Cromwell Harbour. Oliver Cromwell had occupied the town, at one point staying close to the harbour, during his campaigns in Scotland and the humiliating defeat of Alexander Leslie's army on 3 September 1650, when 4,000 Scots were killed and over 10,000 captured.[2] The town itself had suffered from the occupation. Most of the shipping had been commandeered; and the costs of garrisoning the troops and the provision of supplies by the townspeople had taken its toll.[3] A storm damaged the harbour so severely in December 1655 that the following year the town had been forced to petition parliament for assistance towards repairs. They had claimed that there was great damage to the whole country from Berwick to Leith. This had left no safe shelter for herring fishing which was the only livelihood of many. To assist with the rebuilding, Cromwell's government granted £300.[4]

This resulted in the construction of Broad Haven and the Old Harbour, largely as we see them today. Several types of masonry are evident in the walls relating to the two

20. William Daniell, *Dunbar, Haddingtonshire*, 1822

phases of construction. But since that time, numerous repairs have been conducted, usually following storms.[5] A lower wharf was built in 1761 inside the curved pier for unloading coal.[6] The Old Harbour became host to whaling vessels in the eighteenth century. By the time of Daniell's visit in 1822, over 200 boats congregated at Dunbar during the herring season, a number that doubled by the middle of the nineteenth century, partly as a result of the opening of Victoria Harbour. The view shows the masts of both fishing boats and traders in the protection of the harbour. Small fishing boats are setting out to gather their catch. Hugging close to the pier may be seen warehouses and maltings, the essential back-ups to a successful harbour. And in the distance, standing in splendid isolation in Daniell's view, is the parish church and a watch-house, built in 1822 to ward off grave-robbers, sometimes called Resurrectioners, in their search for newly dead bodies for medical research.

20a. John Clerk of Eldin, *View of Dunbar, c.* 1780

Situated on a small knoll, the church was a prominent feature on the landscape. It has been claimed that the medieval parish church was on the site of an earlier church or chapel. It is not surprising that the parish church is set apart from the town, for parishes were often founded before burghs and were designed to serve the landward country folk as well as nearby towns. Dunbar was not created a burgh until 1370.[7] The church was the first in Scotland to receive collegiate status. The foundation was instituted by Patrick, Earl of Dunbar and March, at whose instigation William, bishop of St Andrews, granted a charter of erection in 1342.[8] The canonries of Dunbar were appropriated to the Chapel Royal at Stirling in 1501, when that church was itself given collegiate status. Bellenden's translation of Boece's description of the collegiate church relates that 'Nocht far fra it [Dunbar Castle] is ane toune under the same name with ane magnificent and riche college of Channons foundit and honoribily dotat [endowed] be the Erlis [of March]'.[9] The church ceased to be collegiate at the Reformation in 1560.

By the end of the eighteenth century the fabric of the church was deemed 'very old' and the interior was the 'worst and most inconvenient perhaps in Scotland'.[10] The view depicted by John Clerk of Eldin (1728–1812) about 1780 gives a fine aspect of Dunbar from the west, showing clearly this old parish church and its prominent bell tower, set apart from the town. After much heart-searching, a decision was taken to demolish the church and rebuild. The most suitable site was that which the old church occupied, but there were concerns that a new-build might affect the vaults and burial aisles already in existence. Finally, agreement was reached. Sir George Warrender conceded that the new church might be built over the family vault, as long as the heritors arched over the burial ground at their own expense and at such a height to allow access from outside. The Duke of Roxburghe desired the same, asking that the monument in the Duke's Aisle should be preserved and also the entrance to the family vault from outside the church. This monument commemorates George Home, Earl of Dunbar (d. 1611).[11] Mr Hay of Belton, who had also put forward some objections, was persuaded to collaborate.[12] James Gillespie Graham of Edinburgh was chosen as the architect. His design omitted the conical bell tower above the square steeple, which is the main difference between Eldin's and Daniell's views of the church.[13]

Endnotes

1 P. Hume Brown (ed.), *Early Travellers in Scotland* (Edinburgh, 1891), 135.

2 E. P. Dennison, S. Stronach and R. Coleman, *Historic Dunbar: Archaeology and Development* (Scottish Burgh Survey, 2006), 38; M. Lynch, *Scotland. A New History* (London, 1992), 279.

3 I. and K. Whyte, *Discovering East Lothian* (Edinburgh, 1988), 162; Dennison, Stronach and Coleman, *Historic Dunbar*, 38.

4 *APS*, v, ii, 763a–b; S. Bunyan, *A Walk Around Historic Dunbar* (Haddington, 1991), n. p.

5 A. Graham, 'The old harbours of Dunbar', *PSAS*, 99 (1966–7), 173–90.

6 J. R. Hume, *The Industrial Archaeology of Scotland: Lowlands and Borders* (London, 1976), 117.

7 Pryde, *Burghs*, no. 95. Pryde also discusses the possibility of a burgh having been founded in the thirteenth century.

8 Cowan and Easson, *Medieval Religious Houses*, 219.

9 T. W. Fish, 'Dunbar of old', *Transactions of the East Lothian Antiquarian and Field Naturalists' Society*, ii (1929–30), 29; S. A. Bunyan, 'Dunbar parish church', in *Dunbar Parish Church, 1342–1987* (East Lothian Antiquarian and Field Naturalists' Society, 1987), 27–8; J. Miller, *The History of Dunbar from the Earliest Records to the Present Time* (Dunbar, 1859), 96.

10 *OSA*, ii, 473; J. McNie, *Dunbar Parish Church: Place and People* (Dunbar, 2002) gives details of this church and that which replaced it.

11 George Home was knighted in 1590, acquired the lands of Spott in 1792, and was appointed Lord High Treasurer of Scotland in 1601 and Chancellor of the Exchequer in England. He was made Earl of Dunbar in 1605 and one of the commissioners on the Borders in 1606.

12 NRS, HR69/1 Heritors' Minutes, 3 September and 22 October 1818.

13 We would like to thank Pauline Smeed and Gordon Easingwood of Dunbar and District History Society for their advice on Dunbar.

21   Dunblane, 1853 and 1880s

These two views encapsulate much of the town of Dunblane. The first, a coloured lithograph by the celebrated artist David Roberts (1796–1864), showing the stone bridge over the Allan Water, dates to 1853.[1] The second, by W. E. Lockhart (1846–1900), is a watercolour depicting *Dunblane on a Rainy Day* in the 1880s. Lockhart produced over 400 paintings, twenty-nine of which were exhibited at the Royal Academy. This aspect of the town was a favourite subject among artists, one of the most memorable being Francis Grose's (1731–1791) *Entrance into Dunblane, Scotland*, a pen and watercolour from *c*. 1788–90, to be repeated in the 1830s by J. M. W. Turner (1775–1851), who made a series of sketches of this view.

The building of the first bridge over the Allan Water by Bishop Finlay Dermoch around 1409 was significant for the township. Built of stone, it was said to have been 12 feet wide and 42 feet long (3.6 × 13 metres).[2] The original yellow dressed stone may still be seen from the north side. This would without doubt have given stimulus to settlement on the west bank of the river, which by 1443 was sufficiently substantial to be given a separate name from that of Dunblane – Bridgend – when it was confirmed as one of the Dunblane see's possessions to Bishop Michael de Ochiltree (1429–47) by James II (1437–60).[3]

This first view gives a fine portrayal of the cathedral, showing it in a certain state of disrepair. Other than the destruction of the trappings of Roman Catholicism, there appears to have been relatively little malicious damage to the cathedral fabric at the Reformation of 1559–60.[4] The cathedral certainly deteriorated during the sixteenth century, but mainly through neglect. By 1586 it was reported that the kirkyard dykes were broken and the nave was no longer watertight. A measure of the affection of the townspeople for their church was their offer to repair the roof at their own expense, as long as the bishop maintained it thereafter, as had been the custom. In the event, this offer was not taken up, and sometime around the turn of the century the roof of the nave collapsed. It remained in this state until the late nineteenth century, as may be seen in this view. Until then the choir rather than the nave functioned as the parish church, still fortunately enjoying the beautiful stalls added during the episcopacy of James Chisholm (1487–1545).[5]

The south port, or gate, to the town probably stood at the east end of the bridge, possibly actually on it, giving access to Millrow and High Street.[6] Ports functioned

21. David Roberts, *Bridge over the Allan Water*, 1853

not only as collection points for tolls to use the burgh market, but also as control points in times of danger, such as plague, and at night when the gates were closed at curfew.

The foreground is a somewhat romanticised view of a rural idyll with a thatched building, wheelbarrow and cartwheel. The wearing of kilts and a bonnet to suggest the connection with the Highlands may be a sentimental whim, although certainly Dunblane was considered a suitable place for a school to teach Highland children in 1716, but the presbytery ultimately opted to site it at Callendar.[7] The cattle crossing the bridge are also recollections of the past. Dunblane had been renowned for its cattle markets and fairs, but by the May fair of 1837, only seventeen cattle were put forward for sale and these, it was claimed, were of inferior quality.[8]

It was in all probability soon after the building of the bridge that the High Street was opened, seen in the Lockhart painting to the right. Millrow to the left, and closer to the river, was probably an earlier thoroughfare, providing access to the ford, upstream from the bridge, and the mill, which is known to have stood nearby probably since the fourteenth

21a. W. E. Lockhart, *Dunblane on a Rainy Day*, 1880s

century.[9] At its northerly end Millrow entered The Cross, or Cathedral Square, where the Dunblane market was held.

Possibly confirming that the High Street was a secondary routeway to Millrow is the fact that on its eastern side the burgage plots stretched back from the frontage for a distance. Most were probably terraced to adapt to the topography of the land. But with such large plots, these would be desirable places to live in close proximity to the market. The plots to the west, however, may be seen to be cramped into minimal space between the Millrow houses and the High Street, affording very little breathing space. Millrow itself is seen as a narrow street. It would eventually be widened, so offering better access. It is interesting to note that one house, on the near right, is still thatched, whereas the majority are slated. It is perhaps not surprising that the dwelling pinched between High Street and Millrow in the foreground is a ruin. A further building to disappear is that facing up Millrow – Allanbank House. It, along with others in the street, did not seem to be appreciated by certain sections of the local authorities; they were deliberately allowed to deteriorate, to be subsequently demolished in the 1960s.[10]

In the distance the cathedral is seen, still in the 1880s with the old nave in a state of disrepair but, as major restoration work on the cathedral in the 1870s transformed it back to much of its past structural beauty, there may be a query over the dating of this picture. Not seen in this view are the manses of the cathedral canons, many of which have been likewise restored. Albeit a rainy day, this is a charming scene, showing street life in the late nineteenth century.

Endnotes

1 J. Ballantine, *The Life of David Roberts, RA* (Edinburgh, 1866), 176, 251; he sold the original painting in 1853 for £50.

2 A. Barty, *The History of Dunblane* (Stirling, 1944), 39.

3 *RMS*, ii, no. 270; D. E. R. Watt and A. L. Murray (eds), *Fasti Ecclesiae Scoticanae Medii Aevi Ad Annum 1638* (SRS, 2003), 102.

4 D. McRoberts, 'Material destruction caused by the Scottish Reformation', in *idem* (ed.), *Essays on the Scottish Reformation, 1513–1625* (Glasgow, 1962), 435–6.

5 E. P. Dennison and R. Coleman, *Historic Dunblane: The Archaeological Implications of Development* (Scottish Burgh Survey, 1997), 24, 21.

6 *Ibid.*, 8, 20.

7 Stirling Council Archives Service, MS CH2/123/7, Presbytery Records, 1716–22, fos 15, 20.

8 Barty, *History*, 223.

9 A. McKerrachar, *The Street and Place Names of Dunblane and District* (Stirling, 1992), 18.

10 Dunblane Cathedral Museum, Box 3, 3/3/vi/i, Notes on Allanbank and other properties in Millrow, by courtesy of Gas Board.

22   Dundee, 1693

Captain John Slezer (*c*. 1650–1717) was an army officer and topographer, probably originally from the Rhineland. He first came to Scotland in 1669. In 1671 he was appointed as chief engineer in Scotland, on an annual salary of £10. He was ultimately to be appointed Captain of Scotland's Artillery Train. In an attempt to augment his income, he began in 1678 a project to draw 'all the King's Castles, Pallaces, towns, and other notable places in the kingdom belonging to private subjects'. He hoped that one book, illustrating towns, palaces and abbeys, should be subsidised by parliament and the other, depicting significant country seats, would be supported by private subscription. Parliament agreed to the first proposal but, in the event, never paid him, although *Theatrum Scotiae* was published in 1693 by royal authority. The insights his work gave into Scottish life, particularly into towns and townscapes, are invaluable, but he died in debt in 1717, never fully recompensed.

Slezer visited Dundee in 1678, when he was granted the freedom of the burgh – a considerable honour, bestowed only on the most respected. Two views of the town were produced as a result, one of which is depicted here. This, taken from the east, tells much about the town. In the foreground, probably added later as an artistic extra as often happened with Slezer's views, are washer-women, treading and threshing their loads in traditional fashion, probably with water from the nearby Dens Burn.

Slezer's view shows an active harbour, wharves and bulwarks with storage buildings and associated offices, as would be expected of an important trading town. But the reality for Dundee by the end of the seventeenth century was contraction of trade with France, collapse of Dutch trade, the growth of transatlantic interest and the rise of west-coast ports, and the silting of the burgh's own harbour. The town's plight is highlighted by the fact that in 1556 and 1563 Dundee paid 12.7 per cent of the taxation levied on royal burghs, standing second only to Edinburgh. By 1697 and 1705 its proportion had fallen to 4 per cent.[1] For some, Dundee at this time was a 'place suffering from prolonged depression, lacking resiliency and recuperative powers'.[2]

Standing proudly overlooking the town is the tall steeple of St Mary's Church, at 160 feet (49 metres) high the tallest surviving medieval tower in Scotland. Founded supposedly in the late twelfth century by David, Earl of Huntingdon, in thanksgiving

22. John Slezer, *The Prospect of ye Town of Dundee from ye Eas*, 1693

for a safe return from crusade, it served as the parish church for much of the Middle Ages, but after the Reformation it was subdivided into four and then five distinct congregations.

Of great interest is the depiction of the town wall encircling Dundee. In the late sixteenth century the building of a town wall around the central core of the medieval burgh stressed the continuing need for defence of the town after the Reformation crisis and the earlier English invasions of the late 1540s. Charters of the later sixteenth century refer to tenements as 'wastit and brunt by oure auld innemyies of England'.[3] In 1548 the English themselves had proposed measures to fortify Dundee (although in practice little more than the placement of some form of fort on the rock to the north of Marketgait and some ditching may have been achieved).[4] It has also been argued that the French auxiliaries of Mary of Guise erected a substantial wall, but there appears to be little

22a. *Close-up view of St Mary's Church, houses and defensive walling*

documentary evidence to support this. But certainly by the end of the century the burgh itself, with licence from the crown, had invested heavily in labour and funds to surround the town on the landward side with a stone wall. What we see depicted here are improvements to these defences and reinforcing ditching, effected in the 1640s, the most important being a system of double walling with a ditch between certain sections and a realignment of the defences east of the Murraygait Port, which lies to the right of the picture.

As a result, as may be just detected in this view, tenements were destroyed; it was felt that 'the toune can not be put in ane reasonabil securitie unles that the haill houses in the Walgait, Cowgait and without the Seagait port be presently spectit and demolishit'.[5] So effective and innovatory were these defences thought to be, that Dundee became the repository of other towns' muniments and treasured possessions during the troubled 1640s and 1650s, since it was a 'toun of defence, fortifeit both be sea and land'.[6] In the event, the burgh was unable to protect itself from the onslaughts of the Marquis of Montrose in 1645 and General Monck in 1651.

There was much discussion in the nineteenth century as to whether the Seagait Port, sometimes called East Port, was destroyed, or possibly blocked up, at the time that the reinforcement defences of the 1640s were being erected. Slezer's view holds the answer. Tucked in behind the later defensive wall, the old port still stands proudly, but now useless as a route to the burgh lands to the east.

Endnotes

1 M. Lynch, 'Continuity and change in urban society,' 1500–1700, in R. A. Houston and I. D. Whyte (eds), *Scottish Society, 1500–1800* (Cambridge, 1989), 115.

2 S. G. E. Lythe, 'The origin and development of Dundee: a study in historical geography', *Scottish Geographical Magazine*, 54 (1938), 353.

3 A. C. Lamb, *Dundee: Its Quaint and Historic Buildings* (Dundee, 1895), 19; M. H. Merriman, *The Rough Wooings: Mary, Queen of Scots, 1542–1551* (East Linton, 2000), 361; *RPC*, first series, iii, 520–1, details a petition by Dundee to the crown to be exempt from taxation for five years, to offset the great damage done to the town by the English attacks.

4 Merriman, *Rough Wooings*, 312–13.

5 W. Hay, *Charters, Writs and Public Documents of the Royal Burgh of Dundee, 1292–1880* (SBRS, 1880), 174.

6 J. Nicoll, *A Diary of Transactions and Other Occurrences, January 1660–June 1667* (Bannatyne Club, 1836), 58. In 1914 Linlithgow returned to Dundee four Dundee charters. These had been inadvertently sent to Linlithgow after the Civil War with a bundle of papers sent by Linlithgow to Dundee for safekeeping.

23   Dundee from the Harbour, 1780s

This view of Dundee from its harbour by an anonymous artist is the first known oil painting of the town. Although undated, it can be ascribed with some certainty to the period between the first full-scale map of Dundee by William Crawford in 1777 and a subsequent map drawn by his son, also called William, in 1793.[1]

Beyond the harbour mouth, substantially reconstructed in 1770, and the various small craft moored can be seen the open space of Shore Walk, where the fish market and Merchant's Exchange were located. To the left are municipally owned pack houses or warehouses, built in 1756. In the middle distance, dominating the harbour as well as the High Street and its market place, can be seen the distinctive, elegant spire of the Townhouse, designed by William Adam (1684–1748) and built between 1732 and 1734. To the right of the picture are prestigious houses along the rising line of Seagate; most were positioned on long rigs which stretched down as far as the harbour wall, as can clearly be seen in Slezer's view of 1693 (22). Beyond them, to the east and also on Seagate, towering above other buildings near it, as shown on Crawford's map of 1793, was the seven-storey Sugar House, built by a consortium of local merchants in 1766.[2]

Certain views of various Scottish towns would become iconic, such as Aberdeen from across its river estuary or Perth and its river frontage viewed from a high point above its opposite bank. This view, of a thriving port seen from the Tay estuary, would become Dundee's favourite image of itself. It had already appeared as an inset on Crawford's map of 1777 (*see* Introduction, fig. 13). Yet, like other iconic townscape views, it flattered to deceive. In the same vein as William Mosman's view of Aberdeen across its estuary, which exaggerated the steeples of both its parish church and tolbooth (*see* 2), this picture places Dundee Law – the most distinctive natural feature of the town's landscape – behind and to the left of its most prestigious new building, the Townhouse. In fact, Dundee Law was well to the west (or left) of the picture. The desire for artistic inclusiveness overcame reality.

The painting nevertheless conveyed a remarkable story of profound difficulties and overweening ambition, which saw a wholesale reconstruction of streets, civic buildings, shoreline and harbour. The new Townhouse was the first sign of Dundee's ambition to recover its position as one of Scotland's leading ports. It had experienced a severe

23. Anon., *Dundee from the Harbour*, 1780s

downturn in its fortunes in the years following the sacking of the town by Cromwellian forces in 1651. For the next fifty years or more, trade had stagnated. By 1700 the burgh was virtually bankrupt. Worse was to come. The tolbooth, built in 1562, was by 1730 in danger of falling down. Its replacement was a remarkable classical townhouse which dwarfed its predecessor in both size and quality. Its spire was over 138 feet (42 metres) high and it housed shops on the ground floor and a council house and gaol on the upper floors. Ironically, its interior was not finished for a further quarter of a century because funds had run out.[3]

Dundee's recovery crucially depended on its trade and harbour. Over the centuries, and certainly from 1500 onwards, land was reclaimed and the shoreline pushed further and further out into the estuary. One result of this process was anachronistic street names. The street called the Seagate is today far removed from the waterside but even in the 1780s it had already been cut off from direct contact with the shore. The 'New Shore' was built on reclaimed land in the seventeenth century but had to be renamed Butcher Row in the following century as the shoreline moved outwards.[4] The pack houses and fish market seen in the painting were all on recently reclaimed land. Yet there were hazards connected to reclamation. In 1755 a severe storm badly damaged the eastern part of the harbour and flooded the shore lands. The remedy was to raise the level of the streets and buildings in and around the shore to that seen in the picture.

The harbour, despite repeated reconstruction works from the 1670s onwards, remained vulnerable to silting. It was a problem not solved until the nineteenth century. The other obstacle to economic recovery lay in improving access to the harbour, which was bedevilled by the narrow medieval streets and wynds leading off the High Street. Improvement came in the last quarter of the eighteenth century, with new, more direct routes to the port. The motives behind 'Improvement' were reflected in the street names: the 'New Shore' evoked a sense of an escape from a difficult past; 'Shore Walk', later renamed 'Lime Tree Walk', suggested a new desire for civic order and space. The combined investment took time to take effect but the second half of the eighteenth century, bolstered by a sharp increase in the linen trade, saw shipping out of the harbour grow from a mere 3,500 tons in 1745 to over 21,000 tons by 1791. By 1788, the population had increased to 19,000.[5]

Sadly, a great deal of Dundee's classical period of Improvement – as significant in its way as Edinburgh's New Town period – has disappeared in comparatively modern times. The most significant loss was the demolition of Adam's Townhouse in 1932, despite a widespread public outcry. The council disingenuously maintained that it 'was of no historical value and of doubtful origin so far as real architecture was concerned'.[6] It made way for a new city square and new city chambers – a civic square so alien to the Scottish townscape that it has been used more than once in film to depict a Soviet parade ground.

Endnotes

1 For the two maps of Dundee in 1776–7 and 1793, *see* www.dundeecity.gov.uk/maps/dundee.htm.

2 C. McKean and P. Whatley, *Lost Dundee: Dundee's Lost Architectural Heritage* (Edinburgh, 2008), 12–14.

3 *Tolbooths and Town-houses*, 202; McKean and Whatley, *Lost Dundee*, 55–8.

4 S. J. Stevenson and E. P. D. Torrie, *Historic Dundee: The Archaeological Implications of Development* (Scottish Burgh Survey, 1988), 25, 29–30; McKean and Whatley, *Lost Dundee*, 29.

5 Stevenson and Torrie, *Historic Dundee*, 34–5, 48.

6 McKean and Whatley, *Lost Dundee*, 187–9. *The Scotsman*, 5 December 1931. To trace the peremptory decision to demolish the Townhouse, *see The Scotsman*, 29, 30, 31 December 1931 and 1 January 1932, when actual demolition began, and various fruitless protests made by the Ancient Monuments Board and others, between 1 and 12 January 1932. The provost from 1929 to 1932 was George Anderson Johnston, a grocer, but the key figure may have been another member of the council, who was a demolition contractor.

24   Dundee, 1821: *The Executive*

Henry Harwood (1803–1868) was about eighteen when he painted this picture of Dundee worthies – some of the most prominent men in the city in *c.* 1821. It is a lampoon, possibly intended to criticise a municipal administration badly in need of reform. If so, Dundee was not alone. His work may be compared with Thomas Sinclair's devastating cartoons ridiculing the establishment in Edinburgh and Canongate (*see* 12). Rules governing council practice had changed little since the fifteenth century and many Scottish councils were self-perpetuating bodies where nepotism and self-interest were the norm. In 1878 Dundee Council described the administration pictured here as 'a mode of municipal government called "self-election" – those having the good fortune to be "in" tacitly agreeing to withstand every attempt to introduce "new blood".'[1]

A good example was Alexander Riddoch (1745–1822), successful merchant and property speculator, who joined Dundee Council in 1776. For the next forty-three years, until his retirement two years before this picture was painted, he more or less ran the town. By then he faced accusations of malpractice by a growing lobby for reform which forced him to appear before a select committee of the House of Commons. Not included in this picture, Riddoch still cast a long shadow over municipal affairs.[2]

Provost Patrick Anderson (1783–1839), standing right of centre with a cane over one shoulder, was Riddoch's chosen successor. Another successful merchant, Anderson went straight onto the council when admitted a burgess in 1804. He served almost continuously until 1823, including four terms as provost.[3] Although council elections were held annually, voting was limited to serving councillors. This management of municipal affairs was not always to the town's detriment. Anderson was a particularly generous benefactor of the local infirmary and worked hard towards the establishment of a Board of Health in Dundee.[4] The town also benefited from the commercial success enjoyed by these men. Dundee's transformation into a major manufacturing town owed much to their ambition and enterprise.

To join the council, it was necessary to be a burgess, a position achieved by means of family connection, apprenticeship to a burgess and/or payment of a fee. Councillor David Brown (1769–1845), pointing with outstretched arm in the centre of the picture, was a clothier who became a burgess by marrying Margaret Peddie, whose father and brother both served on the council. During his twenty-five years on the council, Brown was also

24. Henry Harwood, *The Executive*, 1821

provost four times.[5] Facing Brown is Thomas Bell (1759–1844), who joined the council after serving as Riddoch's apprentice and paying his £40 fee to Riddoch, then town treasurer. Bell also sat in the provost's chair.[6]

In 1780 Bell co-founded the firm of Bell & Balfour, merchants and flax spinners. By 1821 there were no fewer than seventeen steam-driven, flax spinning mills in Dundee.[7] Jute, which would largely replace flax and hemp, was still in the experimental stage. Though not pictured, Bell's business partner, Alexander Balfour (1755–1865), also served on the council and became provost.

Robert Mudie (1777–1842), standing behind Brown in a light-coloured hat, was the odd man out in this picture, being both a councillor and a champion of reform. A talented satirist, he wrote articles in the *Dundee Advertiser* attacking the municipal administration.

THE EXECUTIVE.

TO THE MEMBERS OF THE GUILDRY, NINE INCORPORATED TRADES, AND BURGESSES OF DUNDEE,

This Print is Humbly Dedicated by their Most Obedient Servant, HENRY HARWOOD.

1. D. BLAIR, Esq. of Cookstone.
2. Provost BELL.
3. Provost ANDERSON.
4. Provost BROWN.
5. ALEXR. REID, Merchant.
6. GEORGE ROUGH, Glover.
7. Rev. J. THOMSON.
8. ROBT. CHRISTIE.
9. Deacon CATHRO, Dyer.
10. SAM. ADDISON, Butcher.
11. JAS. HOWIE, Shoemaker.
12. T. SPALDING, Manufacturer.
13. JOHN BAXTER, Writer.
14. WALTER THOMSON, Auctioneer.
15. ROBERT MUDIE, Teacher.
16. GEORGE CLARK, Shipowner.

24a. Key to *The Executive*

Its reformist editor, Robert Rintoul (1787–1858), would later move to London and found *The Spectator*.[8] As Mudie's principal income came from teaching, it was easy for his council colleagues to put him out of work. He lost his teaching post as drawing master in 1821.[9]

The group are standing in front of the Trades Hall, built in 1776 on the site of the medieval shambles, a public slaughter-house moved to the shores of the Tay for sanitary reasons. Designed by the town architect, Samuel Bell (*c.* 1739–1813),[10] for the Incorporation of Nine Trades, this ornate Hall signalled their increasing prosperity and also Dundee's growing urban ambition. It stood at the east end of the High Street between the Murraygate and the Seagate and was a favourite meeting place. Below the great hall on the first floor were several shops, one belonging to the erstwhile provost, Alexander Riddoch.

George Rough, the only hatless man in the picture, also had a shop on the High Street. He was a member of the glover trade. The Incorporated Trades still held a monopoly, strictly enforced, ensuring all tradesmen were paid up members of a craft. Third from the left is Deacon Cathro, a dyer to trade, which explains his blue hand.

The lampoon was a popular political weapon, ruthlessly used against George IV while Prince Regent (1811–19). In Dundee, Mudie had produced an amusing one against Riddoch, called *The Guildry Cow*. The lampoon was not only safer from prosecution than text, it also had lasting value as this picture and the many copies made of it demonstrate. Another explanation is that this was simply a local joke. Each man has been given a derogatory nickname like 'Man of Breeches', 'Solicitors' Jackal', even 'Judas', and the depictions are equally unflattering. Samuel Addison, deacon of the flesher trade, who stands second from the right, was said to have offered money to Harwood to give him a more dignified pose.

In 1821 Mudie moved to London where he died penniless. In 1822 Provost Riddoch died in Dundee, a wealthy man. The firm of Bell & Balfour went on to become part of the great Jute Industries Ltd and Henry Harwood, one-time satirist, became a successful portrait painter in Dundee. Ironically, many of his subjects were themselves Dundee worthies.

Endnotes

1 Magistrates and Town Council of Dundee, *The Municipal History of the Royal Burgh of Dundee* (Dundee, 1878), 149.

2 *See* E. Gauldie, *One Artful and Ambitious Individual: Alexander Riddoch (1745–1822) (Provost of Dundee 1787–1819)*, (Abertay Historical Society, no. 28, 1989).

3 *Roll of Eminent Burgesses of Dundee, 1513–1886* (Dundee, 1887), 242.

4 *Ibid.*, 242.

5 *Ibid.*, 241.

6 *Ibid.*, 230.

7 D. Bremner, *Industries of Scotland: Their Rise, Progress and Present Condition* (1869; reprinted in a new edition, Trowbridge, 1969), 249.

8 *DNB*, Robert Rintoul.

9 W. Norrie, *Dundee Celebrities of the Nineteenth Century* (Dundee, 1873), 73–9.

10 We are grateful to Dundee City Archives for information on Samuel Bell.

25   Dunfermline, *c.* 1860

This view of Dunfermline from the south appeared in MacDonald's *Tourists'*
Guide to Aberdeen, Dundee and Central Scotland (*c.* 1860). Such guides had become
a new form of literature in the opening decades of the nineteenth century,
designed for the intrepid traveller. The genre was given a fresh impetus by the
coming of the railways and mass tourism. It offered to the growing number of travellers a
'taster' and encouragement to visit; but usually these cheaper guides were hastily illustrated
rather than a 'work of art' and should be distinguished from earlier elaborate and expensive
works such as Nattes's *Scotia Depicta* (1804) or David Octavius Hill's *Land of Burns* (1846)
(*see* 19a, 77). The artist is unknown, and there is conflicting evidence about the date that
it was painted. It seems to pre-date 1865 when the Bothwell Works were founded, but are
not shown in this illustration.[1] However, the most westerly tall chimney, below the abbey,
was part of the Abbey Garden Works, erected in 1860, so this gives some sort of time-frame.
The two chimneys in the centre right of the picture confuse the dating, the nearer being
the Castleblair Works which was not founded until 1868.[2] The partially concealed chimney
behind, which is not working, could possibly be the commencement of the building of
the St Margaret's Works or represent the completed works, which opened in 1870.[3] The
unsmoking chimney below the building with a flag could have been the linen warehouse
of Erskine Beveridge, extant in Priory Lane in 1833 and possibly used for manufacturing,
before the building of St Leonard's Works. Overall, it might be deduced that this is a
conflation of views drawn by the artist for effect so as to highlight the importance of
weaving in Dunfermline.[4]

Dunfermline was at the beginning of its heyday of steam-powered weaving factories,
having undergone a depressed time at the partial change-over from hand-loom weaving
to power-loom manufacture, resulting in so much rioting and looting of shops by weavers
that soldiers were brought in from Edinburgh in 1842 to restore order.[5] The 1850s saw an
upturn, with six firms or individuals displaying their work at the Great Exhibition of 1851
in London. The first steam-powered damask weaving mill, the Pilmuir Works, opened
in 1849 and was the first of eleven in the town. *Campbell's Almanac* in 1875 commented
that 'amid the numerous tall stacks, belching forth their clouds of smoke, the clanking
of engines, and the noise of the power loom, were an emigrant to return who had been
absent only a few years . . . he would not know his own town'.[6]

25. Anon., *Dunfermline, c.* 1860

The artist, however, is at some pains to highlight the closeness of the rural to the urban. The harrowing equipment in the foreground is a reminder of a generations-old agricultural practice (*see also* 14). The harrowed land in the bottom right-hand corner would suggest the task was partially completed and that seed had been scattered, already attracting the attention of birds. A fisherman is seen making his way to the Nethertown, the houses seen in the foreground. He had probably been seeking his catch at nearby Limekilns, once the favoured port for land-locked Dunfermline.

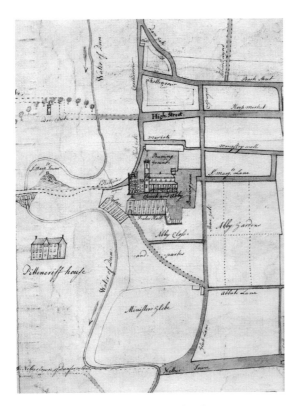

25a. Anon., *Map of Dunfermline*, 1766

Green areas stretch up towards the town to the left of the picture; these represent the glebe of the parish minister and the site of the old Bow Butts, where burgesses once met to practise their (bow and arrow) shooting and attend the 'wappinschaws'. At the foot of these green areas is a reminder that the town, while becoming industrialised, retained much of its more rural past: the old dovecot is clearly visible.

The wooded area behind walls to the left of the view is part of the policies of Pittencrieff. These estate lands had been known as such for centuries: as early as 1291 the monks of Dunfermline Abbey were given the right to obtain coal from 'the lands of Pittencrieff'.[7] By the 1860s the owners of the policies of Pittencrieff (the Hunt family) were not only assiduous at keeping their estate private but also at extending it, even laying claim to the palace ruins. After lengthy litigation, however, the House of Lords decided in 1871 that the ruins belonged to the crown, and not to James Hunt.[8] Set amid these trees may possibly be seen Pittencrieff House. It was constructed around 1610 (or possibly as late as 1635) for Sir Alexander Clerk of Penicuik.[9] His armorial insignia and initials may still be seen above the entrance. In 1740 a third storey was added to the house – reportedly with stones from the palace and abbey ruins.[10] It would be this storey that may be seen in this view. Within forty years, however, all was to change. In 1902 Andrew Carnegie purchased the Pittencrieff estate for the townspeople. On 30 November 1903, by disposition, the Pittencrieff policies were transferred to the newly formed Carnegie Dunfermline Trust for safekeeping on behalf of the people of Dunfermline. A recently discovered map of 1766 shows graphically the Pittencrieff policies, the glebe and the abbey.

Clearly seen, with a flag atop, is Dunfermline's Music Hall, which stood between Music Hall Lane and Guildhall Street. Life was not solely one of toil. Most prominent, as would be expected for historical reasons in its elevated site, is the medieval abbey nave and the New Abbey Church to the east. The nave was the old parish or 'utyr' church of the abbey complex. It was here that the townspeople worshipped in pre-Reformation times. They were afforded no access to the conventual, 'inner' church to the east. Some damage at the Reformation of 1560 and subsequent neglect led to the ultimate demolition of the conventual church. In 1818 the foundation stone was laid of the New Abbey Church, with its prominent square tower proclaiming 'King Robert the Bruce' above his resting place. Just visible to the west of the abbey are the ruins of the old Benedictine guest-house and royal palace. Dunfermline had changed much from the one-time seat and burial ground of royalty into a burgeoning industrial town by the 1860s.

Endnotes

1 H. Walker, *The History of Hay and Robertson Ltd and the Robertson Family of Dunfermline* (Carnegie Dunfermline Trust, 1996), 5.

2 *Ibid.*, 5.

3 *Ibid.*, 3, 7.

4 We have benefited greatly from conversations with Bert McEwan of Dunfermline Heritage Community Projects.

5 H. Walker, *The Story of Erskine Beveridge and St Leonard's Works, 1833–1989* (Carnegie Dunfermline Trust, 1991), 9–10.

6 Walker, *History of Hay and Robertson*, 5, 7.

7 *Registrum de Dunfermlyn* (Bannatyne Club, 1842), no. 323.

8 E. P. Dennison and S. Stronach, *Historic Dunfermline: Archaeology and Development* (Scottish Burgh Survey, 2007), 58.

9 P. Chalmers, *Historical and Statistical Account of Dunfermline* (Edinburgh, 1884), i, 325. Others, such as G. Pride in *The Kingdom of Fife: An Illustrated Archaeological Guide* (Royal Incorporation of Architects in Scotland, 1990), 13, suggest a later date of *c.* 1635.

10 E. Henderson, *Annals of Dunfermline and Vicinity* (Glasgow, 1879), 436.

26   Dunkeld, 1783 and 1693

Published in London in 1783 as a vignette on James Stobie's map of the *The Counties of Perth and Clackmannan*,[1] this prospect of the Perthshire town of Dunkeld captures it before a crucial development, the building of the Dunkeld Bridge in 1809. The mainly single-storey houses cluster around the medieval cathedral on a religious site that can be traced back to the ninth century, when it emerged as a key centre of the early Celtic Church. Ruined during the Reformation, the building's choir was restored as the parish church. Few of the other buildings are as old, as in 1689 there was a short but extremely violent battle between the Jacobites and the Cameronians when most of the town was burned to the ground. One of the houses said to have survived was the Dean's House, which was subsequently remodelled into its present form.

Immediately to the north of the cathedral the elegant seat of the dukes of Atholl, Dunkeld House, with its associated buildings and gardens, can be seen. A landscaped avenue runs behind the house and is terminated by an obelisk, temple or other feature. The original house was blown up by Commonwealth troops in 1653 but was rebuilt in 1679. It was eventually demolished in the early nineteenth century, although the stable block and court of offices remained until after 1858. Construction of a new house was started to the west but was never completed. John Slezer's engraving of the town in 1693 shows a house of more elaborate and imposing appearance but this may not have been an accurate depiction in both scale and detail.[2]

Thomas Telford's bridge, one of his most outstanding monuments, was built in 1809 as a toll bridge which led (as at Kelso) to toll riots before charges were removed.[3] With the opening of the fixed river crossing, the town was re-planned with new two- and three-storey buildings along Bridge Street and Atholl Street leading from the bridge to Inverness and the north and along the High Street, passing through the Cross to the gates to the cathedral precinct. Straggling lines of thatched roofed cottages were replaced by New Town terraces in local whin and slate and, as recorded on John Wood's plan, the gardens between the High Street and the river were formed on 'ground recovered from the Tay',[4] works which were presumably undertaken at the time of the bridge construction. In the mid-twentieth century the National Trust for Scotland undertook a pioneering and influential scheme to conserve the special architectural interest of the town, based on a

26. James Stobie, *Dunkeld. A Seat of His Grace the Duke of A'holl*, 1783

26a. John Slezer, *The Prospect of the Town of Dunkeld*, 1693

survey of 1936 by Ian Lindsay and a special study of the town's evolution commissioned by NTS from Ronald Cant in 1950s. This project, and the work done at Culross, was an important part of the 'national awakening' of interest in effective urban conservation in Scotland.[5]

The landscape setting as depicted was created through a long-term project involving several of the dukes of Atholl and the town was an integral part of this. The 2nd duke (1690–1764) laid out an informal landscape to the east bank of the Tay, just beyond the cathedral and house. This wooded place with grass walks and terraces overlooked the river. Ornamental planting was introduced on the opposite west bank, where the military road ran to the West Ferry, and the picturesque qualities of the valley of the river Braan which falls to the Tay there were exploited. The 3rd duke (1729–74) continued this work until his death, as did his successor, the 4th duke (1755–1830), who was known as 'Planter John'.[6]

Foreground activity shows men net-fishing for salmon while one stands waiting with landing gear. Women are undertaking laundry by boiling, washing by feet in a tub and rinsing in the river. Curiously, there is no evidence of a ferry. Immediately across the river from Dunkeld is the hamlet of Birnam. In the distance, on the same bank the village of Inver can be seen, location of the important ferry crossing, an inn and a centre for weaving, meal, waulk and saw-milling. The twin-arched stone bridge over the River Braan can be picked out among the trees. The picturesque character of this improved landscape and the 'Highland' hospitality of its inhabitants was well known and many travellers would pass time here on their way to the north of Scotland. At the time of the engraving, Inver was noted as the home of the fiddler Niel Gow, who was something of a quaint local celebrity.[7]

Arriving here, tourists and travellers were aware they were at both a geographical and a cultural interface: 'Dunkeld is, indeed, the portal of the Grampian barrier, and its environs offer an exquisite blending of all that is most admired in the Highlands with one of the richest margins of the Lowlands.'[8] Visitors, including a number of artists,[9] would also stop to view the wooded Hermitage pleasure ground laid out from 1757 and make the journey to Ossian's Hall, both of which were the creations of John, 4th Duke of Atholl. These can be seen on higher ground above the village. Other planting, in what has become known as Scotland's 'Big Tree Country', was still in its infancy.

Endnotes

1 J. Stobie, *The Counties of Perth and Clackmannan* (London, 1783). *See* also Stobie's 1783 portrayal and plan of Perth (86).

2 J. Slezer, *The Prospect of the Town of Dunkeld* (SL. 24), published in Cavers, *Slezer*, 41.

3 B. Walker and G. Ritchie, *Exploring Scotland's Heritage: Fife and Tayside* (Edinburgh, 1987), 43.

4 J. Wood, *Plan of Dunkeld and Environs* (1823).

5 D. Watters and M. Glendinning, *Little Houses* (The National Trust for Scotland's Improvement Scheme for Small Historic Homes, Edinburgh, 2006), 51–63.

6 C. Dingwall, *The Hermitage. A Historical Study* (Edinburgh, 1995).

7 H. Jackson, *Niel Gow's Inver* (Perth, 2000).

8 Groome, *Gazetteer*, ii, 435.

9 *See* J. Walker, *Dunkeld House: A Documentary Study* (2002). John Claude Nattes (*see* 77) visited and drew the town and the West Ferry (NLS, MS 5204).

27   Dysart, 1883 and *c.* 1854

Dysart was already a thriving port by the middle of the fifteenth century, exporting mainly salt and coal. A new harbour was constructed in the early seventeenth century, funded by the town council and Lord Sinclair, who had been the leading heritor in the burgh for over a century.[1] Trade with the Low Countries, particularly the port of Campvere (now Veere), gained the town the name 'Little Holland'. However, the burgh experienced a severe downturn in its assessments for national taxation in the seventeenth century. In the 1690s it was paying a twelfth of what it had done in the 1590s and it was still complaining of being 'altogether without trade' and in 'a poor and distressed conditione' as a result of the lingering effects of the Marquis of Montrose's campaigns of 1644–5, in which most of the local skippers and traders had been killed.[2]

Flax was imported from Europe, and there was hand-loom weaving with 130 looms maintaining 'a brisk trade in checks, tykes, and napkins' by the 1770s.[3] Robert Stevenson was commissioned to report on the harbour's state in 1819 when coal became again a major export, and in 1829 a new inner dock was completed.[4] This was closed by gates which allowed ships to load at all stages of the tide and was said to have been the first harbour on the east coast of Scotland to have such a facility. Coal was wheeled down to the port and loaded via chutes before transportation abroad and to the Carron Iron Works at Falkirk, Glasgow and other Scottish ports. The town was a centre for nail-making, and shipbuilding and repair was practised from 1764 at a yard and 'Patent Slip' within the harbour.

This view of the town was painted on a plaque by Karel Nekola (1857–1915), one of a number of Bohemian craftworkers brought to Fife in the 1880s by pottery owner Robert Methven Heron. Nekola was to become crucial in the successful development of Wemyss Ware pottery and is noted for his vibrant work from nature, including his rendering of roses and other flowers. On settling in Kirkcaldy, Nekola engaged in country walks to familiarise himself with the locality and undertook a number of sketches of scenes he encountered.[5] As an impressionable outsider, it is interesting to note that he gives equal, and accurate, prominence to the tower of the former St Serf's Church and the engine house, chimney and winding gear of the Lady Blanche colliery. This is in contrast with the work of other nineteenth-century artists, who tended to play down or ignore

27. Karel Nekola, *View of Dysart*, 1883

the colliery buildings in favour of a romanticised past centred on the maritime and fishing industries.

The wooded area between the tower and the colliery chimney was the site of the church nave and aisles. In 1800 the building was deemed beyond repair and inadequate for the size of the congregation, and a new parish church was built. The north aisle and much of the remaining structure of the old church was subsequently demolished to make a road from the colliery to the harbour.

The picturesque line of vernacular houses is the Pan Ha', or Pan Haugh, where salt was formerly won from seawater in coal-heated iron pans to be employed in the preservation of fish and export to the Low Countries (*cf.* Culross, 15). The houses date mostly from the seventeenth century and display the gabled fronts, harl, crow-steps, corbels and sweeping pan-tiled roofs typical of Fife coast villages.[6] The buildings are accurately depicted, the cottage with a projecting chimney in front of St Serf's tower being the sixteenth-century

27a. Sam Bough, *Dysart Harbour, c.* 1854

Bay Horse Inn, which was a rare survival of a medieval form containing a double height first-floor hall. Beyond, just beneath the colliery chimney, is The Anchorage, an L-plan house of 1582. There was a pier, and boats were also beached here prior to the construction of the burgh's harbour, which is to the left of the scene as painted.

In 1965 the National Trust for Scotland was invited to supervise, on behalf of the Crown Estates Commissioners, the restoration of the six early Pan Ha' houses and the erection of new ones in the gap sites. Along with their work at Culross, Dunkeld and elsewhere, the Dysart project helped demonstrate the value of burgh conservation in Scotland.[7] Notable among the other artists attracted by the picturesque qualities of old Dysart were the English painters John Wilson Carmichael (1799–1868), who specialised in seascapes,[8] and, most notably, the landscape painter, Sam Bough (1822–1878).[9]

Endnotes

1 Pryde, *Burghs*, no. 67.

2 'State and condition of the burghs of Scotland in 1692', in *SBRS Miscellany* (1881), 22–3.

3 Report by Board of Manufactures on Textile industries in Scotland (1778), quoted in J. Y. Lockhart, *Kirkcaldy 1838–1938. A Century of Progress* (Kirkcaldy, 1939), 11.

4 J. Swan and C. McNeill, *Dysart: A Royal Burgh.* (Dysart, 1997).

5 P. Davis and R. Rankine, *Wemyss Ware: A Decorative Scottish Pottery* (Edinburgh 1986), 55.

6 G. L. Pride, *The Kingdom of Fife: An Illustrated Architectural Guide* (Edinburgh, 1990). 60–2.

7 D. Watters and M. Glendinning, *Little Houses* (The National Trust for Scotland's Improvement Scheme for Small Historic Homes, Edinburgh, 2006), 106–13.

8 For example, *A View of Dysart on the Northern Shore of the Firth of Forth* (in sale at Sotheby's, London, 4 October 2005, lot 136). There is also a pencil sketch, *Dysart*, in the collection of Tyne and Wear Archives and Museums.

9 For example, *Dysart Harbour (Fife Council Museums); Fishing Boats entering Dysart Harbour, 1854* (NGS); and *Dysart on the Fife Coast, Sunrise* (in sale at Sotheby's, Gleneagles, 29 August 2007); *Dysart 1868* (in sale at Bonham's, 16 October 2008).

28   Edinburgh, 1550 and 1573

These are two of the first three views extant of Edinburgh. The third, which is generally better known, is a sketch of the burghs of Edinburgh and the Canongate made by an English captain in the raid of 1544 led by the Earl of Hertford. Although the English army attacked and burned part of the Palace of Holyroodhouse and the south side of Edinburgh in the area of the Cowgate, it was repulsed at the main east gate of the capital, at the Netherbow (*see* Introduction, fig. 29). These two views, of 1550 and 1573, could scarcely be more contrasting. One is a highly impressionistic view map of a capital city, made by a refugee from memory. The other, despite its crudities of style, is a highly accurate pictorial essay, made by a qualified military engineer of the spot at the time of its composition.

The view of 1550 is the first printed 'map' of Edinburgh. Entitled *A Description of Edinburgh, Royal City of the Kingdom of the Scots*, it was published in Sebastian Münster's *Cosmographia universalis* (1550), which went through a number of reprints.[1] A rival, obvious case for being the first map or view of Edinburgh can be made for the English sketch of 1544, also presumably map on the spot or shortly after. The claim that this is the first glimpse of sixteenth-century Edinburgh is based on the fact that its compiler had last seen his native town in 1531. The author was Alexander Allan (1500–1565), one of the hundred or more Protestant exiles who fled Scotland in the 1530s or early 1540s, most of them never to return. Allan had been a student at the new St Leonard's College (f. 1512) and a canon of the Augustinian Priory at St Andrews. He fled Scotland in 1531 and enrolled as a student at the Lutheran University of Wittenberg. His friend and colleague there, Philip Melanchton dubbed him 'Alesius', the 'wanderer'. True to type, Alesius taught at Cambridge (1535–9, Frankfurt (1540–2) and Leipzig (1542–65) but he and his wife, Katherine Mayne, also from Edinburgh, never returned to Scotland.[2]

The picture is Alesius's remembrance of his home town after an absence of almost twenty years. The 'view map' is in a thoroughly medieval genre, demonstrating that a city is judged by its prestigious buildings and especially by its churches. Despite his long-held Protestant beliefs, Alesius thought of his home town as dominated by its churches, chapels and religious houses. There are nine buildings marked and named in an accompanying key. One is the king's palace, another the royal castle, but seven of the nine are religious houses, churches or chapels. They include the collegiate churches of St Giles', though its crown

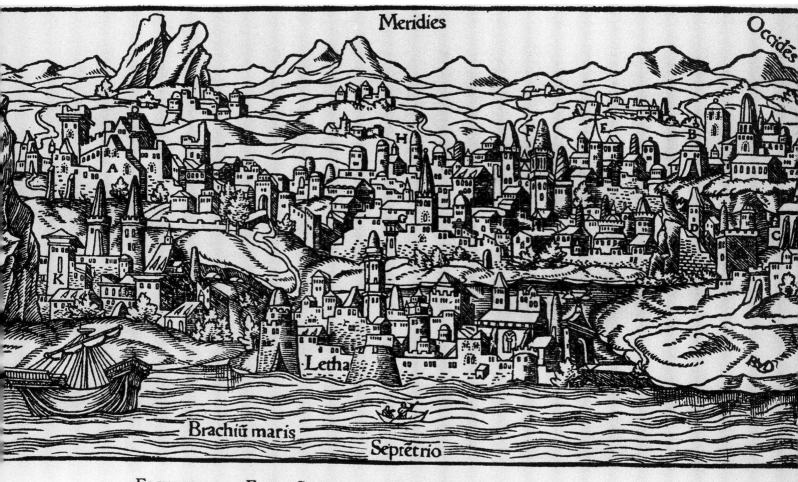

Meridies

Occidēs

Letha

Brachiū maris

Sepr̄etrio

EDINBURGH. FROM SEBASTIAN MUNSTER'S COSMOGRAPHY, 1550.

Palatium Regis. B. *Arx puellarum.* C. *Ecclesia S. Cutberti.* D. *Ecclesia S. Egidü.* E. *Minoritæ.*
Ecclesia beatæ Mariæ in cäpo. G. *Collegia reginæ.* H. *Prædicatores.* K. *Monasterium S. Crucis.*

28. Alexander Allan ('Alesius'), *A Description of Edinburgh, Royal City of the Kingdom of the Scots*, 1550

steeple was still uncompleted when Alesius left; 'beata Maria in ca[m]po', St Mary in the Fields or Kirk o' Field; the 'collegium reginae' (literally the 'college of the Queen') or Trinity College, the collegiate church established under the auspices of Marie de Gueldres, wife of James III (1460–1488). Out of shot, unnoticed or forgotten by Alesius, would have been the companion collegiate church, at Restalrig, founded by James III in 1470.

The 'Minoritae' is the Observant Franciscan friary or Greyfriars, founded in 1463. The 'Predicatores' is the house of the Friars Preachers or Dominicans, founded in 1230. By 1500 the Blackfriars comprised a substantial complex of buildings, with a great hall as well as a sizeable church. It performed various functions – for both the crown and burgh. It was frequently a place for the witnessing of both royal and private charters; it acted as a guest house for visiting ecclesiastics and royal visitors (including the English pretender Perkin Warbeck in 1495–7); it was the venue for the annual exchequer audit when its great hall saw a throng of sheriffs, chamberlains and stewards come to render their accounts; and it was a regular meeting place for the burgh's largest craft guild, the hammermen, up to the 1540s, when they acquired the recently built Magdalen Chapel, which is not portrayed in the view since Alesius had never seen it. As a result of its many uses, the destruction of the Blackfriars in 1559 had serious consequences, not least being the lack of accommodation in the Palace of Holyroodhouse.

Four of these ecclesiastical buildings survived the Reformation of 1560. The collegiate church of St Giles' became the main parish church of Protestant Edinburgh but was subdivided into three. Trinity College also survived, as an overflow for the north-east quarter, the smallest of Edinburgh's four quarters. And St Cuthbert's, the original parish out of which the parish of St Giles' had been carved in the twelfth century, continued as the church for Edinburgh's suburbs. The structure of the Kirk o' Field church survived, as can be seen in the well-known sketch portraying the murder of Darnley in an adjoining house in 1567. It eventually found a new role in 1583, as the base for the new 'tounis college'.

Edinburgh's port of Leith (*Letha*) is shown with far more impressive town walls and sea defences than it actually had when Allan had last seen it, although by 1550 work was underway by French military engineers to turn it into a citadel in *trace italienne* style.[3] The distance and road between Leith and Edinburgh's Netherbow gate is foreshortened and a rudimentary attempt is made to portray Edinburgh's own walls, which were crenellated, as befitted a capital. After skewing the view of Edinburgh with Leith in the foreground from east to north, the map makes a rudimentary attempt at geographical accuracy. St Cuthbert's is shown on the right (or west) of the picture and the place and monastery at Holyrood on the left (or east) and the Castle, Greyfriars, Kirk o' Field and Blackfriars are in correct alignment. Yet, otherwise, this might be any city in Europe.

The second view of Edinburgh shows the Castle under siege in May 1573, in the closing days of the civil war between rival supporters of the deposed Mary, Queen of Scots (1542–1567) and her infant son, James VI (1567–1625). Despite the matchstick appearance of the figures in the sketch, it is in other respects a highly accurate representation of

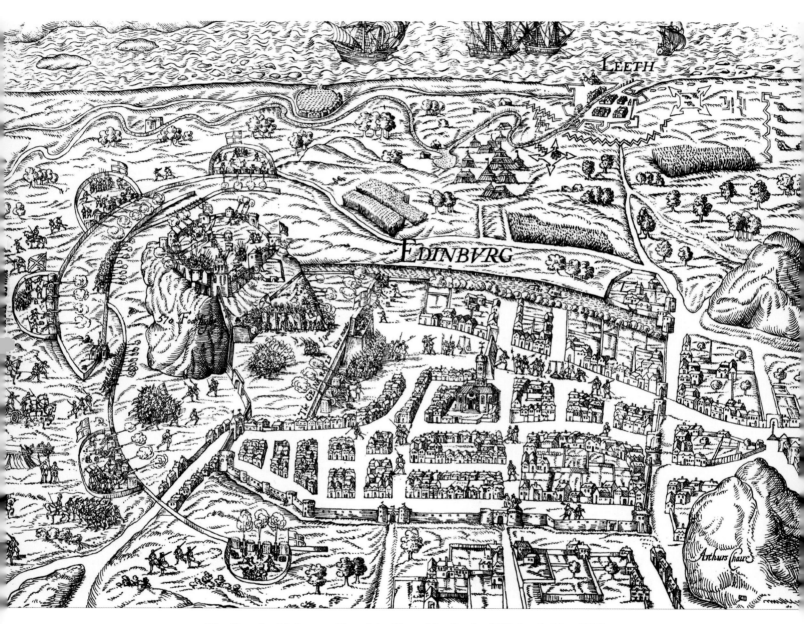

28a. Rowland Johnson, *Plan of the Siege of the Castle of Edinburgh*, May 1573

both the siege and the layout of the adjacent burghs of Edinburgh and Canongate. The reason for this is that it was the work of an English military engineer, Rowland Johnson, Surveyor of Works at Berwick-on-Tweed (fl. 1547–84).[4] The significance of the fall of the Castle, which brought to an end the bitter civil war between the queen's men and king's men (1568–73), was underlined by the publication of this rough sketch in Holinshed's Chronicles some fifteen years later.

Since the spring of 1571 the conflict had centred on the capital, where the Marians held out against the supporters of James VI, who were based in Leith. These were the so-called 'wars between Leith and Edinburgh'. By the end of 1572, the siege of the capital had taken the form of an economic blockade but, with only erratic military support for the king's party, it had become a war of attrition. The stalemate was broken in July 1572, when the king's men marched into the burgh in violation of a truce. The king's party regained control of the burgh but Marian forces remained in control of the Castle. A different form of stalemate resulted.

In it, considerable damage was suffered in the upper parts of the town which were most vulnerable, both to cannon fire from the Castle and to raids by the Castilians in which property and food supplies were plundered or destroyed. The main problem for the king's men was a lack of fire power. The shortfall was remedied from an unexpected quarter. In the spring of 1573, Elizabethan England, which had watched bemused as its former Protestant allies fought on both sides of the civil war, finally took action. A force with an heavy artillery train and pioneers under the command of Sir William Drury (1527–1579) was sent to finish off the Castilians.

The picture shows English gun emplacements ringing the Castle on three sides. The reference to 'The Generals two monts' probably refers to the great ordnance cast at Mons in Flanders, 'like the famous 'Mons Meg' (or 'Mounts Meg') housed in the Castle itself. Cannon are even placed in the steeple of St Giles' to give greater elevation and to add protection to a bulwark built across the High Street near the Overbow, the old west port of the burgh, at the head of the Lawnmarket. Bearing in mind that this picture was devised

28b. *The Spur*

for propaganda purposes with an English readership as its target, English pikemen and harquebusiers, under the banner of St George, are shown breaching the Spur, the Castle's outer defences. The Spur was not a medieval remnant; it had been constructed in 1548 by the Italian military engineer, Migiliorino Ubaldini, as part of the dramatic strengthening of Scotland's military defences by the French in the late 1540s and 1550s. The ease with which the picture, conceived in part as a 'cartoon' story, depicts the fall of the Spur is highly misleading. According to Johnson, it was twenty-two feet high and 'vamured with turfe and baskets furnished with

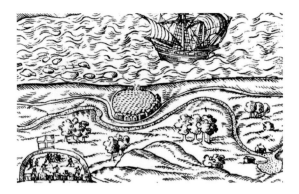

28c. *Newhaven Dry Dock, 1573*

ordinance' on a broad platform. It was a formidable obstacle which, more than any other factor, delayed the taking of the Castle, which took fully eleven days.[5]

The twin burghs are crudely depicted, though most of the key features are included, such as St Giles' (with a main entrance implausibly moved to the south), the tron (weigh beam), and its main ports. The drawing of the Canongate stops short of the Palace of Holyroodhouse but accurately depicts the Watergate port and the closeness of the Girth (or sanctuary) Cross to Holyrood's precinct wall. Leith is shown with a hint of its *trace italienne* fortifications constructed by the French garrison in the 1550s still intact (*see* no. 74) despite the provision in the Treaty of Edinburgh (1560) that they should be taken down. Interestingly, the large dry dock at Newhaven where the flagship of James IV's fleet, the 'great' *Michael*, was built between 1506–11, is depicted – the only known image of it.[6] First and last, this picture is the product of a military mind.

Endnotes

1 The view and accompanying Latin text are printed in 'Edinburgh regiae Scotorum urbis descriptio, per Alexandrum Alesium Scotum', *The Bannatyne Miscellany*, vol. i, pt. 2 (Bannatyne Club, 1827).

2 For Alesius's life and career, see *DNB*, under Alesius; and M. Sanderson (ed.), *Early Scottish Protestants, 1407–1560* (SRS, 2010), 38, under Allan.

3 M. H. Merriman, *The Rough Wooings of Mary, Queen of Scots, 1542–1551* (East Linton, 2000), 335, prints a Plan of Leith in 1560.

4 *A Biographical Dictionary of Civil Engineers in Great Britain, 1550–1830*, ed. A. W. Skempton (London, 2002), 377.

5 M. H. Merriman, *The Rough Wooings: Mary Queen of Scots, 1542–1551* (East Linton, 2000), 323–5, 356.

6 *The Michael* was described by the chronicler Pitscottie as being 240 feet long and 35 feet broad (73m × 10.66m), and capable of carrying 300 of a crew, 120 gunners and 1,000 troops. See N. Macdougall, '"The greatest scheip that ewer saillit in Ingland or France"', in *idem, Scotland and War, AD 79–1918* (Edinburgh, 1991), 38, 58n. The construction of the New Haven of Leith, which had much deeper water than the old royal dockyard in Leith, began in 1504: *ibid.*, 42–3. The *Michael* was more than twice as long as Henry VII's *Mary Rose*, which was 105 ft (32m) long and 38 ft (10.66m) broad.

29   Edinburgh, composed ?1641;
published 1670

This large-scale view map, *Edynburgum*, was the work of Wenceslaus Hollar (1607–1677), a Bohemian artist and engraver better known for his detailed depictions of London. The date and circumstances of its composition are unknown.[1] There are a number of false trails in the pursuit of its provenance, not least of which is the fact that there are at least three versions of the map produced and other derivative part copies.[2] The three versions have different titles, different dedications and one has an ornamental cartouche.[3] The most elaborate of the three – *The Citie of Edenbvrgh from the South* – bears a representation of the city arms, with the motto 'Nisi Dominus Frustra', and a separate dedication to the 'city councillors' by John Ogilby (1600–1676), a London-based engraver. The simplest, *Edynburgum*, which is illustrated here, has only a small lion rampant surmounted by a closed imperial crown.[4] The date of production as an engraving is known only for the *Citie of Edenbvrgh* version, which has the etched signature 'W Hollar 1670' in its right-hand bottom corner. The date of composition, however, must have been much earlier than 1670.[5]

There is also considerable variation in content in the different versions: the map entitled *Edynburgum* has a number of omissions, including from west to east (left to right) Heriot's Hospital, St Cuthbert's, the West Port, the Magdalen Chapel, the University and Parliament House. The *Citie* also has figures drawn near the castle and in the courtyard of Holyroodhouse, along with a carriage. The only staffage that *Edynburgum* has are two unconvincing horsemen in the foreground. There are, as a result, various conundrums to address and different drafts with which to contend. It is clear that *Edynburgum* is a crude, early draft, to which more detail and a key was later added. Its title, in Latin, may suggest a wider audience in mind than *The Citie*.[6]

Hollar was a native of Prague but became a refugee from the chaos of the Thirty Years' War, escaping first to Germany and then the Netherlands. He first came to England in 1636, following his patron, the Earl of Arundel, a celebrated collector of art and artists, whom he had met in Cologne. He stayed in London for much of the next eight years; he was employed for a time as a teacher of drawing to the children of Charles I (1625–1449), including the future Charles II and his younger brother, the Duke of York, the future James VII & II. After Arundel's flight into exile in 1642, Hollar became a 'serviteur domestique' in York's household.

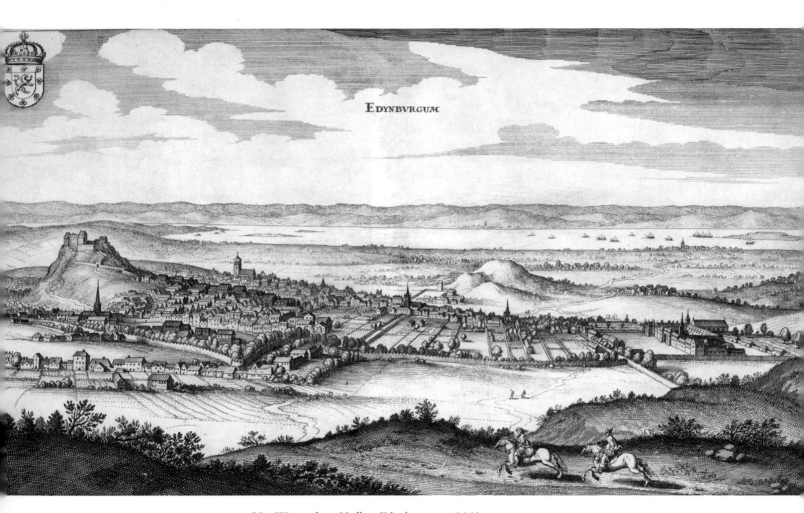

29. Wenceslaus Hollar, *Edynburgum, c.* 1641

His close connections with the royalist cause were probably why, in 1644 in the wake of a series of military defeats for the king, he escaped to Antwerp. Hollar remained there until 1652, when he returned to England. Given the huge output of his work in the 1650s and the fact that he had converted to Catholicism, a visit to Scotland in this period seems unlikely. There are other reasons to reject the claim that the map can be dated to 1649 or later. Internal evidence within the picture strongly suggests that its composition was earlier than the 1650s. Hollar's drawing of Edinburgh Castle shows the outer defences of the Spur, which were demolished in 1648.[7] His depiction of the Palace of Holyroodhouse is strongly reminiscent of Gordon of Rothiemay's picture of it in 1650, before the fire started by Cromwellian troops and before the restoration and heightening of the west range in 1658–9.[8] In 1669, Hollar was in Tangier, making even more likely that the date on the *Citie* map referred to its engraving and not its composition.[9]

It may be deduced that the picture was initially composed sometime between 1640 and 1644.[10] Hollar's connections with the royal household may suggest the date of a visit to Scotland: possibly, he was in the entourage accompanying Charles I on his prolonged, fruitless visit to Edinburgh between August and November 1641, although he may have had to abandon his new wife, a servant of the Countess of Arundel whom he married in July of that year, to do so.[11] It is, however, also possible that Hollar never visited Edinburgh at all, for by 1670, in his relentless pursuit of funds, he had drawn maps of places as far afield as China, Denmark, Italy and Candia (Heraklion) in Crete as well as his better-known work on London.[12] Nevertheless, the detail conveyed in the map confirms that, whether the source was an informant or Hollar himself, its origin must pre-date 1648.

Hollar had clear views on the attributes of capital cities, seen here as well as in his work on London and Prague. The order of listing of key buildings in the accompanying key of the *Citie*, which had twenty-seven place names, gives a strong clue:

> 1 The Castle; 2 The Weigh Beam [Tron]; 3 St Giles'; 4 Parliament House; 5 The Tron Church; 6 Netherbow Gate; 7 The Canongate

At this point, after a straight run down the Royal Mile, Hollar turns back:

> 8 The University; 9 The Mint House; 10 Palace of Holyroodhouse

Here are the key ingredients of what for Hollar made Edinburgh a capital city. It was a term first explicitly used in 1606 by the town council (*see* 33).[13] These then are the attributes of civic humanism, what distinguished the city dweller from his rural neighbours: the tolbooth, schools and university. There is a further difference between Hollar's view and the better-known bird's-eye view map of James Gordon of Rothiemay (1617–1686) which can firmly be dated to 1647. For Rothiemay, beyond the broad High Street are close-packed closes and wynds and tight clusters of houses. For Hollar, part of the value of urban living is about order and symmetry – so space in his view map is significant.

There was a final contrast to be made between the Hollar and Rothiemay maps. Rothiemay was paid 500 merks (£333 13s 4d Scots) by the town council for his work – a prodigious sum – and was made a burgess and guild brother. Despite a dedication on the map to Edinburgh's town council, Hollar was not commissioned; evidently, he relied on sales of his map. Despite his prodigious output – a catalogue of his works extends to 2,717 entries – Hollar died, aged seventy, in virtual penury. His goods were valued at a mere £22 sterling (£264 Scots).

Endnotes

1 The original map is large: 24.4 in wide × 16 in high. Rothiemay's map was larger still: 39.6 in × 16 in.

2 We are grateful to Chris Fleet of the NLS Map Room for his views and advice on the circumstances of the composition and production of Hollar's maps of Edinburgh.

3 R. Pennington, *A Descriptive Catalogue of the Etched Work of Wenceslaus Hollar* (Cambridge, 1982) lists three versions of Hollar's map: *see* p. 162, nos 973, 973a and 973b. Nos 973 and 973a have a key. 973b, *Edynburgum*, does not. Another version, printed by Frederick de Wit in his *Theatrum Praecipuarum Totius Europae* (1695), noted by Pennington as a postscript under 973, is a red herring. One of his two views of Edinburgh, from south and north, is clearly heavily dependent on Hollar, but his dedication, to Archibald Todd and four bailies, does not offer a clue to dating. It was lifted from his engraved version of Gordon of Rothiemay's 1647 map of Edinburgh, despite the passage of almost forty years; *see* Introduction.

4 The dedication by John Ogilby, who had a colourful and crowded career, adds nothing to the provenance of the composition of the map. He worked with Hollar on a number of projects in the 1660s and 1670s. See *DNB*, John Ogilby; C. Delano-Smith and R. J. P. Kain, *English Maps: A History* (Toronto, 1999), 188–9.

5 The NLS website, Town Plans/Views, 1580–1919, *Edynburgum*, dates the map as *c.* 1649, but this is unlikely in the light of Hollar's movements.

6 The NLS website has the *Edynburgum* version (973b) online. The BM has the more elaborate *Citie of Edenbvrgh* version (973) online. The possibility of more than one audience was also the case with Rothiemay's map of 1647, which had a key in both Latin and the vernacular, although it was not in the event included in Blaeu's *Atlas Novus* of 1654 (*see* Introduction).

7 For the Spur or 'French Spur', constructed in 1548, *see* the map of the siege of 1573 (29).

8 J. Gifford *et al.* (eds), *Edinburgh: The Buildings of Scotland* (London, 1984), 86, 126, 130. James Gordon of Rothiemay, *Palatium Regivm Edinense* (1650).

9 *DNB*, Wenceslaus Hollar; *Oxford Art Online*.

10 The depiction of the Tron Kirk, where building work began in 1636 and was completed only in 1647, argues for a later date. However, Hollar may have wanted to ensure that his map did not quickly become out of date and included the church although it was not yet finished.

11 D. Stevenson, *The Scottish Revolution, 1637–1644: the Triumph of the Covenanters* (Newton Abbot, 1973), 233–42. *DNB*, Hollar. None of the standard accounts of Hollar's career mentions a visit to Scotland. Most, indeed, ignore his map of Edinburgh.

12 *See* L. Worms and A. Baynton-Williams, *British Map Engravers: A Dictionary of Engravers, Lithographers and their Principal Employers to 1850* (London, 2011), 325–7, lists Hollar's main works, beginning with *Oxforde 1643*. See also G. Tindall, *The Man who drew London: Wenceslaus Hollar in Reality and Imagination* (London, 2002)

13 *See The Taking Down of the Netherbow* (33).

30   Edinburgh, Bruntsfield Links, 1750

Paul Sandby (1731-1809), a draughtsman on the Military Survey of North Britain in 1747-52, could be a satirist or even cartoonist as well as a landscape artist. This colourful and humourous impression, *Horse Fair on Bruntsfield Links, Edinburgh* (1750), has both aspects of Sandby the artist.[1] The vista allowed him to lay out a meticulous panorama of Edinburgh from west to east: in the west (on the left of the painting), the Wrights House, a striking baronial-style tower of the prominent lairdly family, the Napiers of Wrichthouses, mostly dating from the fifteenth century, is picked out in meticulous detail. So, too, is the unusual prospect of the geometry of the Castle rock, and the city itself stretched out from the Castlehill to the churches of St Giles and the Tron.

There are imaginative or even fictitious elements in this painting. Horse fairs were normally held in the Grassmarket rather than at the open spaces of Bruntsfield, as was the sale of cattle, despite the presence of horned Highland beasts in the painting. There is much drunkenness and revelry. The redcoats of British army uniforms are prominent in the painting, intermingling with all classes of Edinburgh society – a message which had a clear but subtle political resonance. Soldiers are more ready to converse with the natives than the gentleman in the foreground, shunning a beggar. Yet the figure of an army officer in red coat and Highland dress, presumably hinting that loyal Scots as well as English soldiery were involved in the putting down of the last Jacobite rising, stretches credulity: tartan was banned after the '45 rising and permitted again only in 1782. The ample figure in the right foreground suggests the satirist at work. Is this an Edinburgh counterpart of John Bull, ironically the creation of a Scot, John Arbuthnot (1667-1735)? By the 1750s, the edge had gone from the sharpness of the original satire: do the bluff, bovine characteristics of this Edinburgh caricature suggest that some Scots are natural cousins of John Bull, the very embodiment of the English people and personality? Bull's sister, Peg, after all, had originally been used to represent the Scots.[2]

Endnotes

1 J. Bonehill and S. Daniels, *Paul Sandby: Picturing Britain* (London, 2009), 128-9.
2 *DNB*, John Arbuthnot; *DNB*, John Bull.

30. Paul Sandby, *Horse Fair on Bruntsfield Links, Edinburgh*, 1750

31   Edinburgh, Grassmarket, 1750

Much of the work of Paul Sandby (1731-1809) lay unpublished, in the form of a series of sketch books discovered after his death. His *Scene at the Execution of John Young* is set in Edinburgh's Grassmarket in December 1750. Young, a long-serving sergeant in the regiment of foot of the Earl of Ancrum, had been convicted of handling forged Royal Bank of Scotland banknotes, although the actual forgers had escaped the hangman's rope by turning king's evidence against him. The case was a *cause célèbre*, which was reported in the London press. The actual execution, according to one newspaper report, was an unseemly affair, delayed for more than two hours by the extreme reluctance of the prisoner; he was dragged to the scaffold by the City Guard 'amidst Thousands of amaz'd Spectators' in the semi-darkness of a late winter's afternoon.[1]

In Sandby's sketch, the focus is on the street scene rather than the execution. The scaffold is shown only in outline in the background; in the foreground soldiers mix and converse with the ordinary men and women of the city and children peer eagerly from a rooftop. Here is a very different social mix from that portrayed at Bruntsfield Links (30). The Grassmarket was still the poorest area of the city as well as the traditional place of execution. The women are either dressed in shawls drawn over their heads or seem to be maidservants, in maid's cap and exaggerated finery, perhaps cast-offs from their mistresses. The men are mostly anonymous. The underlying message is clear. The British army is depicted as a force for civility as well as law and order. It was prepared to discipline its own miscreants as well as Jacobite rebels or Highland barbarians.

In a memoir published after his death, Sandby's son, Thomas Paul Sandby, claimed that his father 'made many drawings of figures in the costume, and of the habits and employment of the inhabitants of Edinburgh, that are particularly interesting and which mark a fertility of genius'.[2] That 'fertility', seen here and in the portrait of Bruntsfield Links, may suggest something else. In the self-proclaimed capital of North Britain there is squalor but no trace of 'barbarity'. Edinburgh's people, collectively, could be the nondescript inhabitants of any provincial town in the Hanoverian empire.

Endnotes

1 *Read's Weekly Journal or British Gazetteer*, 5 January 1751.
2 P. Oppé, 'The Memoir of Paul Sandby by his son', *Burlington Magazine*, 88 (1946), 143-7.

31. Paul Sandby, *The Execution of John Young, Grassmarket, Edinburgh*, 1751

32   Edinburgh Castle, 1750 and 1780

Paul Sandby (1731–1809) was described in a number of his obituaries as the father of English landscape painting. Born in Nottingham in humble circumstances as the son of a framework knitter, Paul followed his elder brother Thomas (1723–1798) into a post at the Board of Ordnance in the Tower of London in 1747. Later in that year, in the wake of the defeat of the last Jacobite rising, he became a draughtsman in the newly established 'compleat and accurate survey of Scotland', based in the 'drawing room' of Edinburgh Castle. As part of his application for this post, he drew – or, more likely, copied – a small-scale view of the castle from the east, with the buildings which housed the Board of Ordnance prominently and even exaggeratedly displayed.[1] The two brothers became key agents in the military occupation of North Britain: Thomas was on the staff of the Duke of Cumberland, butcher or hero of the victory at Culloden, and Paul was 'the chief Draftsman of the fair Plan' to survey the conquest.[2]

During the five years he spent in Scotland, Paul travelled extensively, in difficult and often dangerous territory, especially in the Highlands. One unofficial result of his travels was a series of landscape views of castles, including Edinburgh, Stirling, Bothwell and Dumbarton as well as views of Fort William (42) and the city of Edinburgh.[3] These landscapes were characterised by their meticulous accuracy and attention to detail. Nonetheless, his watercolour, *View of Edinburgh Castle* (1750), provides a dramatic perspective of the Castle rock and a rare view of the Nor' Loch before it was drained. In the distance, the elegant spire of St Cuthbert's Church provides both balance and perspective, as do the buildings in and around Cannonball House and the Castle Esplanade. In one sense, the sharpness and sparseness of Sandby's view is to be contrasted with the richer, more atmospheric version of the same scene, *Edinburgh Castle and Nor' Loch* (*c.* 1780), painted by Alexander Nasmyth (1758–1840), with the castle framed by a stormy sky. In another sense, this depiction of the castle was by far the most colourful of various views of the fortress which Sandby drew. The richness of the colour and the luminous quality of the scene, reminiscent of Sandby's later work such as the series, also painted in bodycolour, portraying Windsor Castle (*c.* 1765), may suggest that the final version of this painting of Edinburgh Castle was completed some years after Sandby's period in Scotland. It is certainly the case that others in the series of Scottish views which he published in 1751 were subsequently altered or retouched in some of their detail (*see* 67).[4]

32. Paul Sandby, *View of Edinburgh Castle*, 1750

32a. Alexander Nasmyth, *Edinburgh Castle and Nor' Loch, c.* 1780

Sandby was an agent of a militarised British state. His years in Scotland were spent making designs for bridges and fortifications and drawing relief maps of mountains and coastlines in hostile territory. In these maps the king's roads were marked out in red – the same colour as the uniform of the British army of occupation.[5] Yet a hint of a different Sandby is to be gleaned from another of his early works held in the National Galleries of Scotland: a watercolour entitled *Castle Duart, Isle of Mull*, even though it was part of an official survey made in 1748 of fortified sites in Argyll including Tioram and Duart.[6] Done in pen and wash over a graphite outline, the figures in the foreground, the ship and the mountains behind combine to lend a sense of scale to the castle and its strategic position. The blue and grey patches in the water add a softness to the painting not present in Sandby's other works on strategic strongholds in Scotland, save for his depiction of Edinburgh Castle, first composed in 1750.

Nasmyth was born in the Grassmarket, in the shadow of the castle. His depiction of it here is one of his earliest landscapes, done before he left Edinburgh for an eighteen-month extensive tour of Italy in 1782 and well before he began to describe himself as both a landscape and portrait painter.[7] His view is probably less accurate, in terms of the buildings, than that of the topographer, but he adds more human perspective to the scene as well as some artistic licence, so as to mask the walling clinically recorded by Sandby. On the other hand, there is very little of the meticulous detail with which Nasmyth, in his mature period in the 1820s, would record the life and architecture of his native city. His watercolour, *Edinburgh from Arthur's Seat* (NGS), painted in 1789, is a more skilful and better-framed view of the castle, no doubt influenced by his experiences in landscape painting in Italy and elsewhere on the Continent. In it, Nasmyth places the castle in an urban environment. In his earlier painting of 1780, without the context of either the houses to the east of the Esplanade or the distant prospect of St Cuthbert's, it is as if Edinburgh's castle is in a rural, isolated setting – a fortress in a wilderness.

Endnotes

1 J. Bonehill and S. Daniels, *Paul Sandby: Picturing Britain* (London, 2009), 76–7, which reproduces the drawing.

2 *DNB*, Paul Sandby: *DNB*, Thomas Sandby.

3 Bonehill and Daniels, *Paul Sandby*, 90–1, 95–7, 124–7.

4 L. Herrman, 'Paul Sandby in Scotland', *Burlington Magazine*, vol. 106, no. 736 (1964), 340.

5 L. Colley, 'Paul Sandby: Picturing Britain', *The Guardian*, 7 November 2009.

6 Bonehill and Daniels, *Paul Sandby*, 94.

7 *DNB*, Nasmyth; D. Macmillan, *Scottish Art, 1460–1990* (1990), 139.

33 Edinburgh, Netherbow, 1764

The Netherbow port, the main gateway to Edinburgh for over three centuries, had stood in the same place since the late fourteenth century when the burgh's boundary was extended farther east. Images of the Netherbow are familiar, though they almost invariably show the round towers, battlements and clock on its external frontage.[1] This etching, *The Taking Down of the Netherbow Port* drawn by the history painter John Runciman (1744–1769) at the time of its demolition in 1764, depicts the inside of the gateway, with workmen beginning to remove stones from the stone-built spire.[2] The picture tells a remarkable story, both for what it displays and what is missing from it.[3]

Ever since the reign of James III (1460–1488), Edinburgh had become increasingly conscious of its identity as a capital. The key icons of its position as a royal burgh and as one of the crown's chief vassals, were its market cross, literally the centre of the kingdom, its tolbooth and ports. Royal entries from the reign of James IV (1488–1513) onwards began at its western gate at the Overbow, where monarchs were conventionally gifted the keys of the burgh, proceeded past a series of pageant stations and ended at the Netherbow, where the most elaborate of the set-piece tableaux was staged. In 1590, to mark the marriage and coronation of Anne of Denmark, bride of James VI (1567–1625), a stage was built to portray the queen as Sheba, a fitting queen for a king already hailed as Solomon.

The gate itself was more than a mere emblem. It had been damaged, repaired and strengthened a number of times in the reigns of successive Stewart monarchs. In 1544 it had withstood the assault of the English army under the command of the Earl of Hertford. In 1571, at the height of the bitter civil war between supporters of Mary, Queen of Scots and her infant son, a full-scale assault by the king's men was repulsed at the Netherbow. (*see* 29). It was a mark of the changing expectations of the times that, when the gateway was next extensively repaired – in 1606 – its battlements and gun loops looked *inwards*, as depicted in Runciman's sketch, rather than outwards to face an external menace. The picture also shows, above the burgh coat of arms, an empty statue niche.

The work of 1606 was refurbishment rather than a wholesale new construction. This is evidenced by the mixture of styles which included medieval Gothic and

33. John Runciman *The Taking Down of the Netherbow Port, 1764*

190

French-influenced Renaissance elaborations. The external towers were rounded; the internal tower was square. The ornamental gun loops were set off by crenellation, both of the gateway and the walls around the town. Crenellation was usually reserved for royal castles or the tower houses of royal favourites, such as those built for the Setons at Fyvie and for the Gordons at Huntly in the 1590s.

Part of the refurbishment of the port in 1606 involved the commissioning by the burgh council of a statue of James VI and I: 'it is the custome of maist renownit cities to have the effigie or statue of their prince set up upon the maist potent part of the citie'.[4] This had a double significance: it was a visual demonstration of the capital's loyalty to an absentee king; but it was also the first time that Edinburgh had implied that it thought of itself as a city. In fact, the statue had only one known forerunner – a statue erected for Henry IV of France (1589–1610) in Paris in the 1590s – and it took the relationship of king and capital one stage further. Following a serious riot in Edinburgh in 1596, James VI had threatened to move his capital elsewhere. In the orgy of reconciliation which followed, the king made a toast in the tolbooth to Edinburgh's council as 'his looving gessoyiks'.[5] The goshawk – a bird without any bite used by James in his favourite pastime of hunting – was a useful metaphor for a creature of the crown whose political teeth had been pulled.

Three final ironies remain to be explained. Characteristically, the capital took over ten years to put its plan into operation: the statue was completed only months before the king's next visit to his capital, in 1617. The toothless capital would provide the spark for the revolt against James VI's son, Charles I (1625–1649) with the riot in St Giles' Cathedral in 1637. As for the statue, Oliver Cromwell's invading army would complete its capture of the king's capital by 'defacing and dinging doun' the statue, along with the royal arms on the market cross, in 1652, leaving an empty niche.[6]

33a. Daniel Wilson, *Netherbow Port*

Endnotes

1 The image of the external, eastern side of the gate, drawn by Daniel Wilson, was published in his *Memorials of Edinburgh in the Olden Time* (1872), 272. It and the Runciman image of the internal side of the port were published in R. S. Mylne, 'The Netherbow Port', *PSAS*, 46 (1911–12), 383–4.

2 The image was part of the contribution made by the Edinburgh antiquarian, George Paton, to Richard Gough's *British Topography* (1780), published after Runciman's early death. This edition did not include the Latin inscription below the statue, which can be translated as: 'Watch towers and thundering walls vain fences prove/No guards to monarchs like their people's love./Jacobus VI Rex, Anna Regina, 1606.'

3 For other images of both sides of the port, *see* H. F. Kerr, 'Notes on the Nether Bow Port, Edinburgh', *PSAS*, 67 (1933), 298–301.

4 *Edin. Recs, 1604–1626*, 1 May 1607; *see* pp. 28, 131, 147; Mylne, 'Netherbow Port', 385–6.

5 The modern printed edition of Calderwood's work renders James's toast to the Edinburgh council on 23 March 1597 as to his 'gossops', meaning 'godfathers' or 'friends': D. Calderwood, *History of the Kirk of Scotland*, 8 vols (Wodrow Society, 1842–9), v, 625. The episode, which followed a ritual humiliation of the council involving numerous political and financial concessions, suggests that the alternative rendering is more likely.

6 *Diary of John Nicoll* (Bannatyne Club, 1836), 81; J. Drummond, 'Notice of some stone crosses, with especial reference to the market crosses of Scotland', *PSAS*, 4 (1860–2), 110–11.

34   Edinburgh, Princes Street, 1825

This canvas is one of four important paintings of the city by Alexander Nasmyth (1758–1840). It was painted in the early 1820s and is commonly accepted as a visual celebration of the relationship between Edinburgh's Old and New Towns and of the continuity of Scottish identity from older times to the modern period. The foreground right features the construction of the Royal Institution building which, like the North Bridge in the distance, provides a symbolic as well as a physical link between the two towns, the future and the past. Its architect, William H. Playfair (1790–1857), can be seen on site (in top hat) directing the construction. While highly skilled masons dress stone and raise columns, the seemingly randomly scattered recumbent stones waiting to be finished suggest the new rising from the ruins of some ancient civilisation.

In commemorating this project the artist also celebrates the cultural optimism of the time. By 1822, the Board of Manufactures and Fisheries, a government body concerned with the promotion of industry, was turning its attention to the improvement of design. As a consequence, it commissioned Playfair to erect this facility which was to accommodate the Royal Institution for the Encouragement of the Fine Arts in Scotland, the Royal Society of Edinburgh, the Society of Antiquaries of Scotland and the Royal Scottish Academy. The institution was a privately funded and predominantly aristocratic organisation modelled on the British Institution in London. It was granted a royal charter in 1824, and membership grew rapidly with prominent Scottish artists as associates. Exhibitions of modern Scottish painting had been held in the city for some years previously but would in due course be housed in the new building. As with so many other new government buildings, an appropriately 'rational', austere Greek Doric architecture was favoured.[1]

On Princes Street we see that originally simple Georgian terraced houses have already been greatly adapted or replaced as commercial premises with flats above. Some shop fronts are quite sophisticated affairs and business signs are applied to upper façades broadcasting their services and wares to fashionable promenaders, carriage passengers and across the valley of the still untamed Nor' Loch. Nasmyth's depiction may contain a degree of suggested or projected architecture. Most notably, he shows a four-storey structure with corner shop, architrave windows, balustraded parapet and wallhead chimney on the corner with Hanover Street along the lines of what exists today but at odds with the lower gabled

34. Alexander Nasmyth, *Princes Street with the Commencement of the Building of the Royal Institution*, Edinburgh 1825

building as it was originally built and as seen in several illustrations that post-dated his painting.[2]

From the less ordered and perhaps crumbling Old Town, with its crown spire of St Giles' Cathedral and the old tower of the Tron Kirk, the scene is looked down upon by the cliff-faced City Chambers and the Bank of Scotland, one of the few new buildings there. In the distance, the landscape is manipulated by the artist to bring familiar features into the view. Arthur's Seat is moved to provide the backdrop and Calton Hill is realigned perfectly with Princes Street. Upon it the Nelson Monument is less clear, perhaps, as is sometimes said, because the artist had failed in a competition to design the building.

In a companion painting of the same year, *Edinburgh from Calton Hill*,[3] Nasmyth balances the concern with art, design and commerce in the modern Edinburgh and Scotland expressed here with concurrent interest in matters of progress in law and order. He does this by giving prominent position to Robert Adam's Bridewell, around which

34a. Princes Street shopfronts

34b. Old Town skyline

everyday city life flourishes. Again, there is a composition achieved by manipulation to include old and new parts of the city but in the mist of the middle distance we see a completed Royal Institution building which *has* already taken its place in the city scene.

Endnotes

1 M. Glendinning *The Architecture of Scottish Government: From Kingship to Parliamentary Democracy* (Dundee, 2004), 197. *See* also H. Smailes *Andrew Geddes, 1783–1844: Painter-Printmaker: 'A Man of Pure Taste'* (Edinburgh, 2001), 47–8: J. Morrison *Painting the Nation* (Edinburgh, 2003), 67–71; D. Macmillan, *Scottish Art, 1460–2000* (Edinburgh, 2000), 140–3.

2 *Princes Street Heritage Framework* (Edinburgh, May 2008), 59. We are grateful to Nick Haynes for drawing this to our attention.

3 In the collection of the Clydesdale Bank plc. *See* M. Glendinning, R. MacInnes and A. Mackechnie *A History of Scottish Architecture* (Edinburgh, 1996), 179.

35   Edinburgh, Grassmarket, *c.* 1830 and 1840

Horse Fair in the Grassmarket was painted by James Howe (1780–1836). He was a son of the manse who came to Edinburgh in 1795. Aged only fourteen, he began his artistic career as apprentice to a firm of coach painters in the Canongate. By the time of his death Howe was an acknowledged animal artist, possibly one of the greatest Scotland has ever produced.[1] This picture was likely to have been one of his last as it was found in his lodgings after his death. It and his earlier depiction of a horse fair in Haddington (52) amply demonstrate his talent but also highlight the importance of the horse before mechanised transport and the vital role of the horse fair.

This chaotic scene is set in the Grassmarket in Edinburgh which Howe knew well. Although there is archaeological evidence of industry and stabling in this area as early as the twelfth or thirteenth centuries, in the form of White Gritty Pottery and horseshoes, it is likely that the Grassmarket physically remained a suburb, outside the burgh walls, until the construction of the 'Flodden Wall' in and after 1513.[2] A large open space, the area 'under the wall fer west' was designated a horse and cattle market in 1477 by James III (1460–1488), stipulating that 'all qwyk bestis, ky oxon nocht to be brocht in the toune'.[3] Howe's picture graphically shows why, more than three centuries later, the authorities still would have wanted to keep such congestion out of town.

By contrast, the accompanying vignette by John Le Conte (1816–1887), painted in 1840, shows a more peaceful everyday scene with groups of traders meeting in this spacious market place. Le Conte, of French extraction, was born and died in Edinburgh.

For centuries, the Grassmarket had remained a suburb, first outwith the walls and later outwith polite society. In successive royal entries from 1503 until 1590, the keys of the burgh were presented at the Overbow, the original west gate to the town at the head of the High Street. It was only in 1633, with the entry of Charles I (1625–1649), that the ceremony of the keys took place at the West Port, which lay beyond and to one side of the large building on the left of the picture. The very word '*sub*urb', suggesting a lower form of civilisation is borne out by the low levels of rents in this, the south-west quarter of the burgh: in 1635, rents for stables, fleshers' yards and sub-standard dwellings in the

35. James Howe, *Horse Fair in the Grassmarket, c.* 1830

densely crowded vennels on the south side of Grassmarket were as low as £2 a year – a tiny fraction of average rents in the upper part of the burgh.[4]

Edinburgh's eccentric topography made it inevitable that the West Port became the main entry and exit point for horses, cattle and sheep. It is known that horse fairs continued to be held here because the area is called 'Horse Market Street' on Gordon of Rothiemay's 1647 *View of Edinburgh*. In William Edgar's plan of 1742 the name has changed to the Grassmarket, but this painting shows that it remained a traditional market place for horses well into the nineteenth century.

35a. John Le Conte, *Edinburgh Castle from the Grassmarket*, 1840

The Grassmarket also became a departure point for coaches and the headquarters of the carrier trade connecting Edinburgh with outlying districts. Printed over the archway of the tavern is an advertisement for a weekly carrier to Skirling, a particularly small village in Peebleshire but also the place where Howe was born. This was just the sort of joke Howe would have enjoyed, as is the precarious position of the man on the ladder putting a new sign up over the tavern. Add the mêlée of horses and the fight that has broken out on the stair below and it becomes the stuff of comedy.

The horse trading carried out at these fairs was a vital part of the nation's economy. The auctioneer in the centre is leading a great Clydesdale intended for the plough or the cart, but carriage horses, war horses, hunters, riding horses and ponies are all included, along with the diverse characters whose livelihoods depended on their ability to pick the right horse. We can see that it is crowded and chaotic, but Howe ensures that the smell and the noise of such fairs are tangible also. Behind the rows of horses is a colourful entertainment known as a menagerie. Early in his career Howe had been employed to paint panoramas. Like this menagerie and the one held in Glasgow during its annual fair (50), they displayed the unusual, the exotic or the imaginary for those prepared to pay. This one claims to show live tigers, elephants and lions, and Howe has included himself painting the side of it.

Another interesting feature of this painting is the corn market, the large arcaded building in the background topped with a central belfry and clock. William Edgar's plan of 1742 shows the corn market at the east end of the Grassmarket. Its move to this building at the west end in 1819 was short-lived; it moved again to a much grander building on the south side of the Grassmarket in 1849.

Howe's picture records a historically important site in the Old Town in the 1830s and one of the many markets that were the economic life-blood of the capital. In *The Heart of Midlothian*, Sir Walter Scott says of the Grassmarket that 'few of the houses which surround it were, even in early times, inhabited by persons of fashion'.[5] This may have been, as Scott notes, because the Grassmarket hosted public executions. It could also have been due to its being a centre of manufacture with all the pollution that entailed. What is certain is that, by the time this picture was painted, those who could afford to move were leaving for the cleaner air and more pleasant streets of the New Town, and the Grassmarket was descending into poverty and disrepair.

Endnotes

1 For the life of James Howe *see* A. D. Cameron *The Man who Loved to Draw Horses: James Howe 1780–1836* (Aberdeen, 1986).

2 J. McMeekin *et al.*, 'Early historic settlement beneath the Grassmarket of Edinburgh', *PSAS*, 140 (2010), 105–28.

3 *Edin. Recs.*, i (1403–1528), 34–6.

4 E. P. Dennison and M. Lynch, 'Crown, capital and metropolis. Edinburgh and Canongate: the rise of a capital and an urban court', *Journal of Urban History*, 32 (November 2005), 22–43, at 30, 38.

5 W. Scott, *The Heart of Midlothian*, 26.

36   Edzell, 1592

David Lindsay of Edzell (1550–1610) was the lord of a major barony. Along with many other lairds in Angus and the Mearns he had distinct sympathies with the reformed kirk, established in 1560. He was patron of his own parish church, held the tacks of teinds of several local ministers, and defended the rights of the kirk within his jurisdictions. Bibles, New Testaments and a copy of at least one work of the Swiss reformer, Oecolampadius, sat in his library, testifying to his strict Calvinist education at the universities of Cambridge and St Andrews.

Further evidence of both his learning and religious views may still be seen carved into the walls of the 'pleasance' or formal garden that he had constructed at Edzell in 1604. Sculptured panels represented the Seven Cardinal Virtues, including *Fides* holding a chalice and cross, the Seven Planetary Deities and the Seven Liberal Arts – all indicating the influence of both the Reformation and the Renaissance.[1] Yet two key changes were made to the conventional ordering of the Virtues: *Fides* is placed not first but fourth as Lindsay claimed that he had found true faith not in his childhood years in the 1550s but after he witnessed the carnage inflicted on fellow Protestants in the French Wars of Religion. And the Virtue which comes last is not Justice but Temperance, testimony to a family which had both suffered and inflicted considerable violence and murder.

There were, however, conservative and medieval aspects in the thinking of this educated man. In 1588 Edzell received the honour of being erected into a burgh of barony.[2] Lindsay himself planned the lay-out of the new burgh and produced a stylistic map of the proposed townscape entitled *Pourtraicte of ye new citie of Edzel, 4 Septb. 1592.*[3] This is one of the earliest proposed town plans in existence. It tells much about the man himself and his fascination with the past.

What he has drawn is, in effect, in many ways a classic medieval town plan. The town appears to be walled, although most medieval town walls were not substantial protective structures, but often merely wooden fences reinforced by a ditch, sometimes so weak that they might, as at Linlithgow, fall down in a high wind.[4] The four gates, or ports, are more distinctive, offering access and exit to the town. These ports would be closed at curfew at night-time and whenever danger was imminent, such as the arrival of plague. In pride of place at the centre of the open market place stands the town cross, where all transactions were

36. David Lindsay of Edzell, *Pourtraicte of ye new citie of Edzel, 4 Septb. 1592*

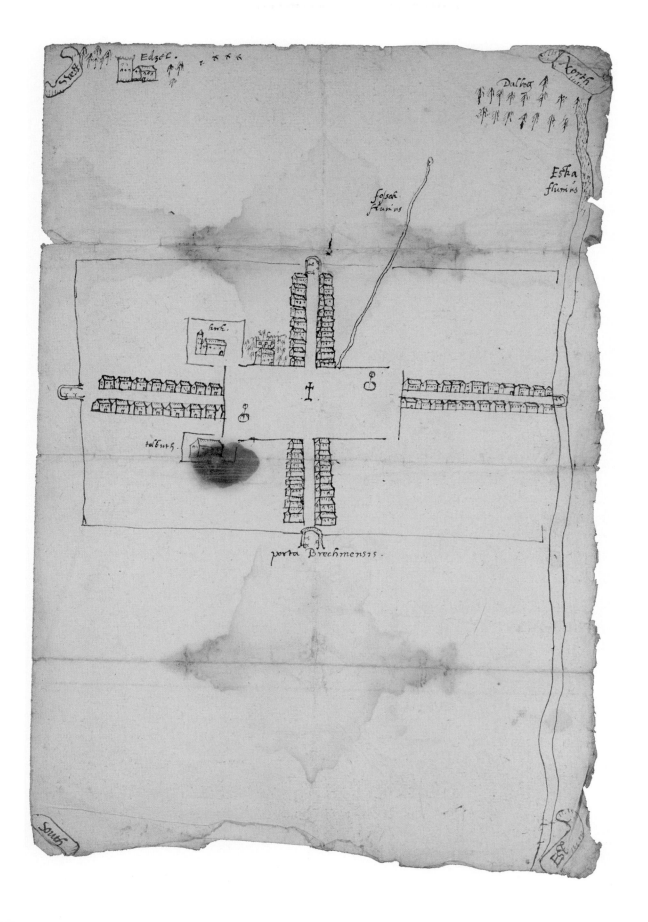

West

North

Edzel.

Dalbog

Eska
flumi's

fosch
flumi's

kirk

portis

tolbuth

porta Brechmensis.

South

Est

to be conducted openly so that market regulations were properly observed. Outsiders paid to come to the market by giving dues (tolls) for the privilege. These were collected usually at the tolbooth, but sometimes at the ports. As may be seen from this portrayal, the tolbooth was the most substantial building in the town, serving also often as the gaol and housing the town weights. All goods for sale had to be weighed at the official town-weighing machine, called the tron. It is unclear if one of the small symbols in the market square represents the tron. If so, the one nearest the tolbooth would be the most likely, being close also to the market cross. The other in the top right-hand corner might be a well.

36a. Edzell Parish Church

As would be expected from one with Reformist sympathies, the kirk and manse have prominent positions. Being proposed as a newly built kirk, its interior would have been intended to have been that of a 'preaching church', where attention was centred on the words of the minister rather than a pre-Reformation altar. It is interesting that Mr Alexander Norie is named as minister. He had previously been minister at Fern and felt sufficiently at ease with Lindsay to seek a loan in 1586.[5]

The houses are stylised, but it is worthy of note that the homes of the burgesses and indwellers are shown as two-storeyed, implying a relatively high standard of living.[6] Another interesting feature is that, just as in Dalkeith, Hamilton (*see* 16, 53), and elsewhere, Lindsay intended to set the new town away from his own policies. It is a further example

36b. Edzell Castle

of proposed urban clearance. The privacy of the aristocracy and gentry was of great importance, and while a new town, with all traditional features, was intended, it was held at arm's length. The first Edzell village, or Slateford, stood a mere 980 feet (300 metres) away from the castle to its south-east beside the old church. Its proximity was so disliked that the original main entrance to the castle, to the east, was superseded by one to the west in the 1550s.

In the event, this plan was never effected: the building of the 'new' burgh of Edzell did not begin until the early nineteenth century. The original plan, however, is reflected in the current main street running north to south and a small lane running eastwards to the ford over the river. But Lindsay's cruciform plan was abandoned. And the parish church that he had planned was erected in 1818 on a site to the north of the town.

Endnotes

1 F. D. Bardgett, *Scotland Reformed: The Reformation in Angus and the Mearns* (Edinburgh, 1989), 151–3.
2 *RMS*, v, 1579.
3 We are indebted to the Earl of Crawford and Balcarres for permission not only to view but also to obtain a copy of the map and to reproduce it (NLS, within the sub-series Acc.9769, Personal Papers, 4/1/80-145). We also appreciate the assistance given by Mr Kenneth Dunn, Senior Curator, NLS Manuscript and Map Collections.
4 *CDS*, iv, 459.
5 Bardgett, *Scotland Reformed*, 105–6, 107, 108.
6 Compare with some of the poorer houses of Stranraer; *see* 98.

37   Elgin and other Scottish towns: their urban defences, *c.* 1590s

The manuscript maps of Scottish towns drawn by Timothy Pont (*c.* 1565–*c.* 1615) are highly accurate and complement much of what may be learned from contemporary documentary sources.[1] He matriculated at St Andrews University in 1580 and graduated, with BA, in 1583, so Pont was at university while map-making and geography were being taught there between 1576 and 1586.[2] Why Pont was drawing together his meticulous views of towns, wooded areas, mountains, noble houses and other features of Scotland has never been totally established. The most likely incentive was probably royal patronage from James VI (1567–1625). As a result of the survival of much of this mammoth task, there are many aspects of Scottish life that may be gleaned from his work.[3]

Written accounts give interesting glimpses of the insubstantial nature of urban defences at the time of Pont's journeys around Scotland. Indeed, it is difficult to detect many references to town walls as such. Edinburgh, Stirling, Perth and Peebles were unusual in having strong stone walls, which were readily defended. Much more typical was the case of Linlithgow, where the townspeople erected a palisade and dug a ditch at the foot of their burgage plots. The palisade was of such slight construction that it blew down in high winds![4]

The main reason for the relatively insubstantial nature of these structures was that 'town walls' were not normally intended to be defensive but were, rather, psychological markers. They set the town apart from the countryside just as surely as the other physical manifestations of distancing and authority – the tolbooth, the market cross and the tron or public weigh-beam. Although burgesses often punctuated their 'heid dykes' with small gates leading to the town pastures beyond, entry to the town was through the official entrances – the town ports, or gates, which were closed at curfew, usually dusk, and opened at daybreak. At times of danger, such as the threat of plague or approaching enemies, the ports were permanently closed on the instructions of the burgh authorities. The ports held also a further significance. It was here, as well as at the tolbooth, that tolls to use the town market were collected.

Pont's depiction of Elgin is very fine, highlighting the cathedral in particular. But it is the low wall, punctuated by ports, that for the moment holds most interest. It is very much in the nature of 'heid dykes' at the foot of the burgage plots, which joined together to form

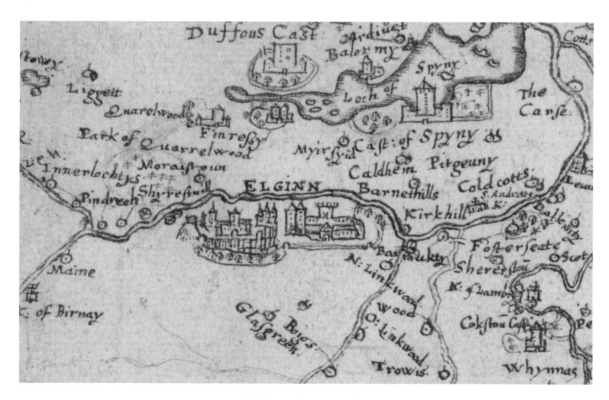

37. Timothy Pont, *Elgin*

37a. Timothy Pont, *Tain*

a 'town wall'. The West Port and South Port, standing until 1783 and 1795 respectively, are located precisely. The East Port is also in its accurate position, but probably farther east of its medieval site, having been moved outwards from the urban nucleus as the town expanded. The ports are formed in the shape of an arch, but may be somewhat stylised. This is true also of Hawick (Pont 35), Lanark (Pont 34), Hamilton (Pont 34), Glasgow (Pont 34) and Dumfries (Pont 35). Late sixteenth-century documentation gives no detail of the form of construction of town gates. According to Pont's delineation of Stirling's Barras-Yett (Pont 32), which is known to have been a massive structure, it was, in reality, a double archway. Similarly, Dundee's Murraygate Port (Pont 26), when enlarged, may be seen to also have been an impressive structure and possibly also double-arched.

It is perhaps Pont's depiction of town walls that

37b. Timothy Pont, *Stirling*

208

mostly reveals his skill as a chorographer. Single lines encircling a town seem to delineate either a ditch or a small wooden palisade, as at Dornoch (Gordon 20) and Sanquhar (Pont 35). Tain (Gordon 20) (*see* 37a) is similarly delineated – surrounded by a single line – with one little twist of the evidence. Pont clearly shows the two small rivers to the east and west of the burgh, which in themselves would offer a measure of protection and delineation.

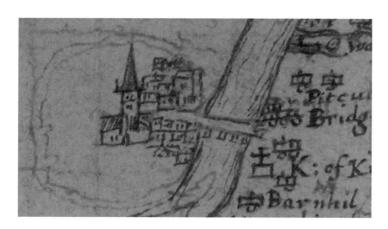

37c. Timothy Pont, *Perth*

But to the north, where the peninsula juts out into the firth, he draws a double line. Is he suggesting that this area is the most vulnerable to attack and is, therefore, protected by a stronger fortification?

Stirling's wall (*see* 37b), known to be of stone (Pont 32), is drawn clearly and boldly with a double line, a device he uses also on his first draft of Perth (*see* 37c), also encircled by a stone wall (Pont 26). Interestingly, Pont does not portray Stirling as totally encircled by the wall. This information coincides with a 1625 plan which suggests that to the north (where the town was least vulnerable to attack, the land being marshy) there was no wall and Stirling was protected probably merely by a ditch.[5] Whether a single line to the north of the town is intended to represent a ditch is unclear, but the highest degree of precision is being displayed.

Pont's views of towns are fascinating, telling us much more about them than merely their urban defences.[6] His depictions are an invaluable addition to the documentary and archaeological research being undertaken into Scotland's towns, as well as being a mine of information in their own right.

Endnotes

1 *See* NLS website, Pont's Maps of Scotland, 1580s–1590s.

2 C. Withers, 'Pont in context: chorography, mapmaking and national identity in the late sixteenth century', in I. C. Cunningham (ed.), *The Nation Survey'd* (Edinburgh, 2001), 148.

3 Cunningham (ed.), *The Nation Survey'd, passim.*

4 *CDS*, iv, 459.

5 *Stirlingshire; an Inventory of the Ancient Monuments*, 2 vols (RCAHMS, Edinburgh, 1963), 304.

6 E. P. Dennison, 'Timothy Pont's portrayal of towns', in Cunningham (ed.), *The Nation Survey'd*, 125–38.

38   Falkirk, 1824

This painting was one of a series of watercolours painted by John Clark between 1824 and 1828. Like other works by him – Dumbarton (18), Paisley (82), Peterhead (88), and Wigtown (100) – it would have been drawn on the spot and, as elsewhere, the town is subjected to detailed and clinical analysis from a well-chosen vantage point. However, what may have been the stimulus to the making of this prospect of the town of Falkirk is unseen, being located a distance behind the viewer. This was the newly opened Union Canal, which passes on high ground to the south of the town. As the major engineering work of its day, the engraving can be read as a calling card or advertisement for the town, promoting it as a good, clean place to live and do business. This same view may have been in the mind, if not on the walls, of the ministers of Falkirk and Grangemouth who wrote in the *Statistical Account* some years later:

> From the heights on the south a view may be obtained, scarcely enjoyed in Scotland for richness, variety and extent. In the north-west, and at the distance of thirty miles, are to be seen Ben Ledi and Ben Voirlich, raising their lofty heads in wild sublimity. Within a more contracted range, circumscribed by the high ground above Kilsyth and Denny, and by the Ochils and the Saline hills, many interesting objects meet the eye in a landscape studded with stately mansions, and with several towns and villages while the broad expanse of the Forth intersects, enlivens, and beautifies the scene.[1]

Clark's portraits of towns, it was claimed in the advertising literature, were subjected to scrutiny by local persons of quality, who frequently figured in the foreground of the paintings. Here, there is an extra, personal touch: the artist includes himself, surrounded by admiring, well-dressed, elegant women who stroll safely in the enclosed woods of Callendar Park. Deer graze in a nearby enclosure and, beyond the town to the north but far enough away not to pollute it, can be seen the Carron Ironworks (f. 1759) and associated industries belching out their smoke.

Falkirk is shown as neatly self-contained and laid out along a High Street occupying raised ground, with little suggestion of the 'ill-built town' recorded by Thomas Pennant in 1769.[2] It is well built with fine slate roof buildings and a good number of lesser pantiled

38. John Clark, *The Town of Falkirk*, 1824

38a. The artist at work

ones. The parish church, which gives the town its name, in origin a pre-Reformation structure, dominates the town centre, its spire recently added in 1811 to the tower rebuilt to designs by William Adam in 1738. The architect David Hamilton's elegant 1814 town spire, 'Falkirk's neo-classical assertion',[3] brings contrasting classical elegance; it was built on the foundations of an earlier seventeenth-century tower which was taken down in 1803 to provide a council chamber and municipal prison. On the south flank of the town is the distinctive rubble-built, octagonal 'Tattie Kirk' of 1806 that housed the town's Anti-Burgher congregation, a breakaway from the Erskine or Original Secession Church. There is little evidence of the lang rigs typical of other burghs, these having been long built over into the wynds and courts off the High Street. The surrounding agricultural land is plentiful and greatly improved.

As can be seen, there was little in the way of industry within the built-up area of the old town itself. This was restricted to some small-scale leather working, weaving and brewing, and it was largely supported by operations in the surrounding lands including the iron works, canals, collieries, nail making, agriculture and the commercial servicing of the great cattle markets or trysts held at Stenhousemuir. The Carron Iron Works was a major enterprise which employed 1,200 in 1840,[4] while the Falkirk Iron Works, half a mile to the north of the town, had 500 men and boys engaged in 'the manufacture of every description of small castings ... such as pans, pots, kettles. stoves, grates'.[5] Both manufactories led to the development of workers' communities close by and along the roads linking with the town, as can be seen behind the town steeple. Also important to the town was the Forth and Clyde Canal, which operated from 1773. Even before its arrival Pennant had noted how:

> There is also a great deal of money got here by the carriage of goods, landed at Carron wharf, to Glasgow. Such is the increase in trade in this country, that about twenty years ago, only three carts could be found in the town, and at present there are above a hundred that are supported by their intercourse with Glasgow.[6]

By 1839 the railways would arrive, linking Falkirk with Edinburgh, Glasgow, Stirling and beyond, and leading to the establishment of extensive suburbs and commercial and industrial operations closer to the town. During the third quarter of the century there were eleven large ironworks and foundries and commercial breweries and distilling in and around the burgh; its development as a 'conglomerate town'[7] was well underway.

Endnotes

1 *NSA*, viii, 2.
2 T. Pennant, *A Tour in Scotland* (London, 1769), 222.
3 J. Gifford and F. A. Walker, *Stirling and Central Scotland* (London, 2002), 473.
4 *NSA*, viii, 373–4.
5 *NSA*, viii, 17.
6 Pennant, *A Tour in Scotland*, 222.
7 Gifford and Walker, *Stirling and Central Scotland*, 461.

39   Falkland, *c.* 1639

Scotland's absentee monarch, Charles I (1625–49) made or tried to make three separate visits to his ancestral kingdom – in 1633, 1639 and 1641. Each brought in its wake a surge of artistic patronage and commissions. Within Scotland, elaborate arrangements had been in train ever since 1628, in the expectation of the king's first visit to his northern kingdom. The best known of these was the series of portraits made of the king's 109 forebears by George Jamesone (1589/90–1644), eventually used in Charles's formal entry into his capital in 1633.[1] Royal artistic patronage, in contrast, came after rather than before 1633, in large part as an attempt to recover prestige and impetus after the disastrous events of the visit, which had convinced many Scots that the king intended to intrude wholesale Anglican changes into an unwilling Kirk. One of the best known of these commissions took the familiar form of an engraving of an equestrian portrait, *Charles I at Edinburgh*, by a Dutch painter and draughtsman, Cornelis van Dalen the Elder (1602–1665), which can be dated to 1638. It shows the diminutive figure of the king with imperial crown, robes and sceptre astride a giant charger overweening his capital city.[2]

Less crude images of royal power and association appear in the two landscape paintings of *Falkland Palace and the Howe of Fife* and *Seton Palace and the Forth Estuary* by Alexander Keirincx (1600–1652), a Flemish artist from Antwerp. Their exact provenance is difficult to establish but both were probably completed in 1639–40. They were part of a set of ten views of 'the King's houses and townes in Scotland', which were sold in two lots by the Commonwealth regime in 1650 and 1651, part of the highly profitable raid by the revolutionary regime on the King's massive art collection after his execution in 1649.[3]

It seems likely that Keirincx accompanied Charles on his planned visit to Scotland in 1639, for another of these landscapes was *A Distant View of York*, through which the king passed at the end of March 1639 en route to Scotland.[4] Ironically, Charles did not manage to enter his Scottish kingdom. He was obliged to wait in Berwick while a peace treaty was concluded with his rebellious subjects. After his return to London late in July 1639, a propaganda campaign was launched to turn the inconclusive failure into a royal victory. Artistic commissions seem to have been part of that campaign.[5]

Keirincx was not one of the circle of a dozen painters from the Netherlands attached to the royal court, such as the portraitist Anthony van Dyck (1559–1641). He was in England for only a short time. Various references point to the length of his stay. He was

39. Alexander Keirincx, *Falkland Palace and the Howe of Fife*, c. 1639

invited to the royal court in 1637 and the King paid him a pension of £60 sterling and his rent of £50 for the year from March 1637 onwards.[6] He was granted a further pension of £60 a year in March 1638 and a house was rented for him in Westminster in July 1639.[7] A separate reference confirms that a further instalment of rent, amounting to £300, was paid for the period from July 1638 onwards.[8] He returned to Antwerp early in 1641.

Given the accuracy of detail of both buildings and landscape, it seems almost certain that he had travelled to Scotland, but the timing and circumstances of his visit are unknown. It is possible that Keirincx had a collaborator; all three landscapes of Falkland, Seton and York have small rustic figures depicted in the foreground or middle ground. It is likely that these are the work of another painter at the court of Charles I, who was also a near-neighbour, the Dutch artist Cornelis van Poelenburch (1594–1667). He specialised in painting small human figures, and it is known that he added small rustic figures to other landscapes painted by Keirincx.[9] If so, it seems likely that these additions would have been done as the paintings were in process of being finished in London and that van Poelenburch did not accompany Keirincx on his northern travels.

Both wishful thinking about the king's position in Scotland and personal loyalties probably underpinned these commissions: Charles had stayed at both houses during his state visit of 1633. Falkland was a royal palace, and Seton was the home of an ambitious family which had gained preferment and high office in the service of the crown over the course of almost a century. The current incumbent, George Seton, 3rd Earl of Winton (1586–1650) left his estates in East Lothian to join the king at Berwick in July 1639. His extensive properties were duly sequestrated by the Covenanting regime.

It is notable that both palaces are set in a wider landscape, which is depicted in detail and with accuracy. The small village of Seton, which had only eighty-six of a population in the 1790s, is shown alongside the palace. Falkland had become a royal palace in the reign of James II (1437–60), had been rebuilt into one of the *châteaux* of the Scottish Renaissance in the reign of James V (1513–42), and had undergone extensive refurbishment by the King's master mason, John Mylne, in preparation for the visit of 1633. All royal palaces were set within a specific jurisdiction, and this may be the reason why the acquisition of a hunting lodge at Falkland triggered the creation of a royal burgh during the same reign, in 1458. That charter was renewed in 1595, with the additional grant of a weekly market and four annual fairs. It was more than a parchment burgh but never a thriving market town: it never figured in the taxation rolls levied on royal burghs and its population in the 1790s was still under a thousand.[10]

The accuracy of Keirincx's depiction of the burgh may be judged by a comparison with John Slezer's engraving, *The Prospect of Falkland from the East*, composed in 1693, which was almost a carbon copy in its perspective and scale.[11] In both, the parish church, rebuilt in 1620 to the north of the palace, is prominent; the linear line of settlement traced is similar and the range of buildings behind the palace frontage and the precinct wall are virtually identical. In addition, Keirincx seems to have added another compelling detail:

Myers Castle, which had probably been built for John Scrymgeour, King's macer and James V's Master of Works at both Holyroodhouse and Falkland, appears to be depicted in the central band of trees on the far right of the picture.[12] The visual imagery in Keirincx's two surviving Scottish works is compelling, a tribute to the 'elysium of the arts' which Charles I tried to make his court and kingdoms.[13] They show that the landscape could be as much an image of regal power as any court portrait. Arguably, the king's next visit to Scotland, in the autumn of 1641, produced another compelling landscape of power – of his capital by Wenceslaus Hollar (*see* 30).

Endnotes

1 D. Macmillan, *Scottish Art, 1460–1990* (Edinburgh, 1992), 62–3.

2 BM, Prints and Drawings: 1894, 0611.70. The BM dates it to *c.* 1633. *See* Introduction, fig. 5.

3 O. Millar, 'The Inventories and Valuations of the King's Goods 1649–1651', *Walpole Society,* 43 (1970), 278; A. McGregor (ed.), *The Late King's Goods. Collections, Possessions and Patronage of Charles I in the Light of the Commonwealth Sale Inventories* (Oxford, 1989), 33. Two were sold in May 1650 and eight more in May 1651; all were bought by Remigius Van Leemput (1609–1675), an Antwerp dealer and copyist. It is possible that the cataloguers conflated landscapes of northern English and Scottish towns. If not, eight pictures of Scottish scenes have since been lost.

4 Tate Gallery, *Illustrated Catalogue of Acquisitions 1986–1988* (London, 1996).

5 R. P. Townsend, 'Alexander Keirincx 1600–1652' (Ph.D., Institute of Fine Arts, New York University, 1988), 22–35; *idem*, 'The one and only Alexander Keirincx: correcting the misconceptions', *Apollo Magazine*, 38 (October 1993), 220–23.

6 N. Sluijter-Seijffert and M. Wolters, 'Samenwerking tussen Alexander Kierencx en Cornelis Poelenburgh belicht', *Oud Holland*, 122 no. (2009), 14–42 at 15–17. We are grateful to Professor A. A. MacDonald for his help with this reference.

7 J. Wood, 'Orazio Gentileschi and some Netherlandish artists in London: the patronage of the Duke of Buckingham, Charles I and Henrietta Maria', *Simolius: Netherlands Quarterly for the History of Art*, 28, no. 3 (2000–1), 103–28. M. D. Whinney and O. Millar, *English Art 1625–1714* (Oxford, 1957), 261. *Cf.* Macmillan, *Scottish Art*, 68, who dates the painting to 1636–7.

8 Edinburgh University Laing MSS, I, 255, 256. The same payment included van Poelenburgh, though seemingly for a different dwelling. We are grateful to Dr Laura Stewart for pointing out this reference and to Dr Aaron Allen for further information regarding it.

9 *DNB*, Cornelis van Poelenburch.

10 Pryde, *Burghs*, no. 51; *OSA*, iv, 437–48.

11 Cavers, *Slezer*, 28.

12 J. Gifford, *Buildings of Scotland: Fife* (London, 1988), 328; MacGibbon and Ross, *Castellated Architecture*, v, 330–3. We are grateful to Robin D. A. Evetts for drawing the likely depiction of Myers Castle to our attention.

13 D. Howarth, *Images of Rule: Art and Politics in the English Renaissance, 1485–1649* (Berkeley, 1997), 217.

40   Forfar, *c.* 1821–5, 1590s and 1797

This early nineteenth-century view of Forfar was one of many views of towns in Angus and the Mearns, including Arbroath, Brechin and Montrose, composed by James Paterson in the early 1820s. Paterson was a drawing master at Montrose Academy and his pictures of towns betray a distinct similarity in their setting; each is viewed from a distance and is usually framed, as is this view across Forfar Loch, by verdant scenery and human figures in the foreground. The figures in this scene, however, are more specific than his usual agricultural labourers taking their ease and one may well be the artist himself at work. The other, wearing a top hat, may be the person who commissioned the picture for Paterson, conscious of selling his wares, was willing to depict his clients in his work, as in his view of the newly built Rossie Castle, in which the owner and his wife take centre stage.

Even so, Paterson's topographical details are usually accurate, as they are here. The view highlights two important factors in the history of the town. In the foreground can be clearly seen an island in a loch. This was traditionally known as the Isle of St Margaret, Queen of Scots. It was to this inch at the north end of Forfar Loch that Margaret, wife of Malcolm Canmore III (1058–1093), reputedly came for solitary contemplation. Certainly, it has been shown that there was once a chapel on the island dedicated to the Holy Trinity, which from at least 1234 was ministered to by two Cistercian monks from Coupar Angus, but its association with Queen Margaret is more difficult to confirm. Two artefacts were discovered on the inch – one a carved bone playing piece, now in the keeping of the National Museums Scotland, and the other a piece of oak with an image of Malcolm Canmore on it, now deposited in the Skaill House, Orkney.

What the picture does correctly hint at is that Forfar had a long and privileged association with royalty. Malcolm II (1005–1034) reputedly granted a charter to the bishop of Mortlach from Forfar in 1011[1] and it is said that Malcolm Canmore held a parliament in the town in the first year of his reign.[2] It was claimed, at the end of the seventeenth century, that Forfar was:

> a very ancient toune and we find in historie the first parliament that was ryden in Scotland, was kept ther also King Malcome Canmore had a house and lived frequently there, the ruines of the house are yet to be seen in a place called the Castlehill. At litle

40. James S. Paterson. *Town of Forfar, c.* 1821–5

40a. Timothy Pont, *Forfar*, 1590s

distance is ane other litle mott where the Queens lodgings were, called to this day Queen's Manore.[3]

A measure of how the crown favoured Forfar from its castle on Castlehill came in the reign of William I (1165–1214), when twelve acts were dated at Dunfermline, thirty-four at Edinburgh, forty-four at Stirling and forty-five at Perth. Forfar matched Perth and trounced the other burghs with forty-five acts.[4]

40b. James Wright, Halfpenny Trade Token, 1797

The loch was originally considerably larger than that viewed in this picture and depicted in the half-penny trade token, designed by James Wright, Dundee, and issued in 1797. In the last decades of the eighteenth century the loch had been drained of about eighteen feet depth of water. This gave access to rich marl on the drained bed and also by machine in the submerged areas. This marl was used to fertilise the surrounding fields, a great boon to a market town. Another immediate advantage was that peat could be extracted from the edges of the drained loch bed. This was used as fuel, a scarcity in the Forfar area, coal having to be imported from Dundee or Arbroath at great expense.[5] Coal from Dundee had not always been welcome; there was great rivalry between little Forfar and her larger and more wealthy neighbour, the latter resenting Forfar's historic position as head of the sheriffdom. A local rhyme sums up Forfar's view:

Bonnie Munross will be a moss,
And Brechin a braw burgh toon,
But Forfar will be Forfar still
When Dundee's a' dung doon.

The town's windmill may be seen at the extreme left of the picture.[6] The most obvious building is the tall spire of Forfar parish church. A chapel, dedicated in 1241 to St James the Great, stood on a small raised hill to the south of the High Street. At this time, Forfar did not have its own parish church, but shared worship at Restenneth, approximately a mile and a half to the east of the town. But in 1568, after the Reformation, a new church was built on the site of the medieval St James' Chapel. By May 1586, in the *Booke of the Universal Kirk*, Forfar and Restenneth were entered as separate parishes; they were clearly to be recognised as distinct. And in 1591, it was agreed that the church at Forfar should replace that at Restenneth as the parish church. In 1791, the parish church was replaced on the same site to a design of Samuel Bell (1739–1813), who later became burgh architect in Dundee. It is this church that is seen on Paterson's view, although it was soon to benefit from a new spire and further remodelling later in the century. We do not know the design of the 1568 church. Our only extant illustration, drawn in the 1590s by Timothy Pont (*see* 40a) suggests an aisled building. It is possible that some remnants are embedded within the 1791 successor. Whether or not archaeology will ever be able to answer this remains to be seen; but, clearly, Forfar's parish church was one of the very first Protestant churches to be built, if not *the* first – a distinction often accorded to Burntisland.

Endnotes

1 A. Lawrie (ed.), *Early Scottish Charters, prior to 1153* (Glasgow, 1905), 5.

2 A. Reid, *The Royal Burgh of Forfar: A Local History* (Paisley, 1902), 7–8, quoting Hector Boece, *Scotorum Historia*.

3 W. Macfarlane, *Geographical Collections Relating to Scotland*, 3 vols, ed. A. Mitchell (SHS, 1906–8), ii, 25.

4 E. P. Dennison and R. Coleman, *Historic Forfar: The Archaeological Implications of Development* (Scottish Burgh Survey, 2000), 14; *RRS*, ii, 28.

5 Dennison and Coleman, *Historic Forfar*, 28–9.

6 We are indebted to Mr Norman Atkinson for his helpful comments on the text.

41   Fort Augustus, 1746

This impressive army encampment set in a rugged Highland landscape was painted by Thomas Sandby (1723–1798).[1] Sent north to defeat the Jacobites, this had become an army of occupation. Dominating the camp are the ruins of Fort Augustus, once envisaged as the centrepiece of a 'utopian' town,[2] but here depicted, with greater accuracy, as the headquarters of a military campaign led by William Augustus (1721–1765), Duke of Cumberland, 'Butcher' of Culloden and Captain General of his father's forces at home and in the field.

After the first Jacobite rising in 1715, the government had taken a more measured approach. General George Wade (1673–1748) had established a chain of forts along the Great Glen from Fort George in the east to Fort William in the west. Linking the two, at a midway point, was Fort Augustus. The three forts, named for the dynasties they served, housed garrisons to police the Highlands while an ambitious programme of road building began to open up the region.

Hand in hand with military strategy went a civilian proposal 'to build a Town after the English Manner, and procure for it all the Privileges and Immunities of a royal borough in Scotland.'[3] The thinking was broadly similar to that behind the original foundation of Scotland's burghs. Foreigners, in this case English and Lowland Scots, were to be induced to settle in Fort Augustus, establishing it as a commercial centre and the main market in the Highlands. Highlanders coming to trade were to enjoy the civilising influences of a way of life radically different from their own. The scheme came to nothing because nearby Inverness not only enjoyed the privileges of a royal burgh but also all the advantages of its ancient history and natural geography.

These companion pieces (*see* 41a) painted by Thomas Sandby in 1746, remained in Sandby's possession so were not used as political propaganda,[4] though the artist's Hanoverian loyalties are clear and leave little room for any opposing view on Highland suppression. Sandby was working as a draughtsman with the Board of Ordnance in the Tower of London when the rebellion began in 1745 and joined the Duke of Cumberland's staff the following year. Further proof that Sandby was a staunch Hanoverian comes from the patronage he enjoyed throughout his life from the duke and other members of the royal family.

41. Thomas Sandby, *Fort Augustus*, 1746

41a. Thomas Sandby, *Fort Augustus*, 1746

The minute detail of this camp and its surroundings are proof also of Sandby's skills as a military draughtsman. Although the camp appears large, the companion piece, taken from a wider angle, shows the full extent of a military presence claimed to be the largest ever seen in Scotland. Sandby's portrayal of a professional British army firmly in control of this mountainous land was more a statement of intent than of fact. Behind this disciplined façade, soldiers from the camp were still working to crush rebellion in a region that had long defied government control. With the aid of a network of spies and informers, some of whom had old scores to settle, these soldiers were able to punish rebel Highlanders in the knowledge that questionable brutality would be condoned as excessive 'Zeal for His Majesty's Service'.[5]

The 'market' established in Fort Augustus in 1746 bore little resemblance to that envisaged thirty years before. As described by an English volunteer, it offered a chilling insight into the subjugation of the Highlands. A soldier claimed to have seen 'near twenty Thousand Head of Cattle brought in, such as Oxen, Horses, Sheep, and Goats, taken from the Rebels (whose houses we also frequently plundered and burnt)'. It was, in effect, a distribution point for forfeited livestock. He also states that 'great Numbers of our Men grew rich by their Shares in the Spoil'. This was a calculated device to avoid the pitfall which had undermined the Cromwellian regime in Scotland in the 1650s (*see* 7): expropriation from the natives solved the problem of the exorbitant cost of an army of occupation. These markets attracted buyers from as far away as Yorkshire.[6] Prices must have been low indeed to have made such a journey worthwhile.

Despite this, the army had to work hard to keep up morale. Real reward and promotion lay in Flanders, not in Scotland. When the Duke of Cumberland marched south to a hero's welcome and a return to continental campaigning, his successor, the Duke of Albemarle (1702–1754), declared: 'I find my Doom is decreed and that I am upon ye brink of ruin.'[7] The ordinary soldiers were no more comfortable in a mountainous landscape they found as foreign and fearful as the Highlanders themselves.

It has been suggested that these two pictures may be early examples of collaboration between Thomas Sandby and his younger, better-known brother Paul (1731–1809).[8] Given the latter's talent for characterisation, he may have been responsible for the more overt propaganda of the figures in the foreground. Looking at the elegantly relaxed group,

playing a ball game, it is hard to believe the widespread allegations made at the time that soldiers from this camp were committing murder, rape, pillage and arson.[9] It is easier to believe the counter-claim that these soldiers were the saviours of the common Highlander, rescuing him from the feudal bondage of his chief. The confused Highlander watching them could well be their interpreter. One of the many differences between them was that Highlanders and soldiers did not speak the same language.

In the companion piece, the soldiers and their prisoners look relaxed as they walk towards the fort. In reality many prisoners faced death or transportation. The woman and child pleading with the soldiers personify a commonly held conviction in the rest of Britain that Highlanders, in their attempts at king-making, had failed in their duty to their families.

Fort Augustus was built to combat the Jacobite threat in the Highlands. As that threat abated, so did the rationale behind this military presence. In 1857 the fort was sold to the Lovat family, their Jacobite affiliations apparently forgiven. The township that had grown beside the fort changed its military association for a religious one when a Benedictine college, monastery and hospice were established on the site.

Endnotes

1 We are indebted to Hugh Cheape for his advice.

2 *Burt's Letters from the North of Scotland* (London, 1754, reprinted Edinburgh, 1974), ii, 337.

3 *Ibid.*, ii, 336.

4 J. Bonehill and S. Daniels, *Paul Sandby: Picturing Britain* (London, 2009), 79.

5 C. S. Terry (ed.), *The Albemarle Papers: Correspondence of William Anne, Second Earl of Albemarle, Commander in Chief in Scotland, 1746–7* (New Spalding Club, 902), i, 87.

6 Volunteer, *Journey through part of England and Scotland, Along with the Army under the Command of His Royal Highness the Duke of Cumberland etc* (London, 1746), 95.

7 Terry (ed.), *Albemarle Papers*, i, 6.

8 Bonehill and Daniels, *Paul Sandby*, 79.

9 A. I. Macinnes, 'Scottish Gaeldom and the aftermath of the '45: the creation of silence?', in M. Lynch (ed.), *Jacobitism and the '45* (London, 1995), 71–83.

42   Fort William, *c*. 1747 and 1736

This is a print of Fort William, sometime in the aftermath of the 1745 Jacobite rebellion.[1] The cluster of houses in the foreground, that would one day become the town of Fort William, was then called Maryburgh. This picture has been attributed to Paul Sandby (1731–1809),[2] a young Englishman who came to Scotland in 1747 to work as draughtsman on the military survey of the Highlands being carried out by the Board of Ordnance.[3] The clarity with which the fort is depicted suggests that it and its occupants were of greater importance to Sandby than the dark houses in front or the local inhabitants. The fort has the air of a colonial outpost, a view shared by many from the south, especially the soldiers who were stationed there. The fortunes of Maryburgh, a garrison town, were inextricably linked to the power struggles of the age and the tensions existing between the inhabitants of the fort and the local people in the surrounding countryside.

The original fort was built by General George Monck (1608–1670) in the mid-1650s. Monck needed a base from which to pacify Lochaber, a region controlled by Clan Cameron which was hostile to the Cromwellian regime. With overland communications almost non-existent, this narrow strip of land on the shore of Loch Linnhe, a sea loch, had the advantage of being accessible by boat.

As with Fort Augustus (41), it was inevitable that a township would grow round the fort which lay near the thirteenth-century castle of Inverlochy, visible in the background to the right.[4] Known as the fort at Inverlochy, Monck's fort again became strategically important in 1689 when James VII (1685–1689) fled to France and the throne passed to William of Orange (1689–1702) and his wife, Queen Mary. With Lochaber once more up in arms, General Hugh Mackay of Scourie strengthened the fort and renamed it Fort William in honour of the new king. The town that had grown beside it was christened Maryburgh, in honour of the Queen.

The Jacobites, supporters of the exiled Stuarts, mounted a rebellion in 1715, and Fort William withstood a full-scale attack before the rebellion was defeated. One result of the rebellion was an influx of officials from the south as part of government policy to bring law and order to the Highlands. To this end, surveyors, draughtsmen and engineers, like the well-dressed men relaxing on the right of the picture, designed and built a great

42. Paul Sandby, *South West View of Fort William and Inver Lochy Fort, c.* 1747

number of new roads and bridges. Leading this operation was General George Wade (1673–1748), who began mapping the region.

One of Wade's maps, dated 1736 and reproduced here, shows that much of the town was separated from the fort by a large open area.[5] Rows of houses line this on three sides, indicating the town's growth and the possible use of this site as a market place. Traditional west-coast houses were single storey but two of those illustrated in the picture have upper windows in the gable ends. The roofs were thatched with a variety of material such as rushes, straw, grass or bracken and may have had an additional layer of turf beneath. Some houses in the town have central chimney stacks suggesting paired central hearths below, a feature of housing in Lochaber.[6] These houses are in sharp contrast to the substantial stone buildings and tiled roofs of the fort.

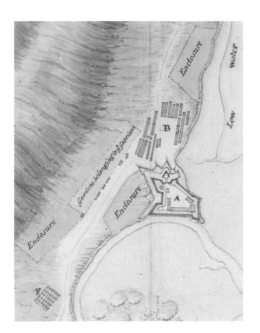

42a. General George Wade, *A Plan of Fort William in the Shire of Inverness*, 1736

The map may have a connection with an action brought by the inhabitants of Maryburgh in 1736 against the governor of the fort and General Wade.[7] The townsfolk accused the military authorities of ignoring their rights and privileges, and also of treating their houses as belonging to the crown rather than the superior, the Duke of Gordon. The issue was security of tenure, but the action indicates a unity of purpose and a belief in the status of their town. The Court of Session found in favour of the townspeople.[8]

Spinning, weaving, fishing and trading occupied the town until the Jacobites mounted their last and most determined rebellion in 1745. In 1746, with a large Jacobite force marching on the fort, the governor ordered Maryburgh to be burned to avoid giving cover to the insurgents. The rebels failed to take the fort, but many of the inhabitants of Maryburgh were said to have been ruined. The houses in the foreground may have survived this destruction or they may have been rebuilt. Research shows that creel houses like these could be erected speedily by skilled hands.[9] Rapid reconstruction of this trading post linked to the sea would also have been in the best interests of all concerned. In the summer of 1746, the Duke of Cumberland ordered the construction of additional barracks of timber to accommodate a further 160 soldiers at Fort William.[10] The presence of these barracks in this picture confirms a date post-1746.

In 1753 the town was renamed Gordonsburgh after the superior. A map prepared for the duke shows parallel rows of new houses along the shore, numbered to match a list of tenants. The esplanade that formed the nucleus of the old town still had a 'brurie', court house and church beside it. An attached description of Gordonsburgh has harsh words to say about the poor inhabitants of Maryburgh, accusing them of being 'people of poor Character' and 'extremely indolent', who begged and stole to survive. However, their old gardens, like those in the picture, produced 'exceeding good crops of kitchen stuffs'. The long list of fruit and vegetables contradicts the notion that these people were feckless and lazy.[11]

Each change of name reflected power or the desire for power but they are not straightforward. Gordonsburgh is first recorded as a burgh of barony in 1618,[12] but may never have been built. Remodelled in the 1770s and 1790s, it was said to have been established under an Act of 1597.[13] In the *Statistical Account* of the parish in 1792, the minister claimed that the town was known either as Maryburgh or as Gordonsburgh.[14] A further complication arose when Sir Duncan Cameron of Fassifern became heritable proprietor in 1834 and attempted to introduce the name Duncansburgh.[15] In 1846 the town appears as Fort William in a *Topographical Dictionary of Scotland*,[16] some eighteen years before the fort was dismantled in 1864. A constant in this succession of names is *An Gearasdan* or 'The Garrison', the traditional name of Fort William in the Gaelic of the district. It remains the Gaelic name for the town to this day.

Endnotes

1 We are indebted to Hugh Cheape for his helpful comments on the text.

2 Personal comment, A. V. Gunn, School of Art History, University of St Andrews.

3 *DNB*, Paul Sandby.

4 MacGibbon and Ross, *Castellated and Domestic Architecture of Scotland*, i, 78.

5 NLS, *A Plan of Fort William in the Shire of Inverness, no. 12* (1736).

6 E. Beaton, *Some Patterns in Highland Building* (Highland Vernacular Buildings Working Group, Edinburgh, 1989), 7–8.

7 NAS, CS16/1/66, Court of Session Minute Book, 15 January 1736.

8 W. T. Kilgour, *Lochaber in War and Peace, being a Record of Historical Incidents, Legends, Traditions and Folk-Lore* (Paisley, 1903), 34–6.

9 We are grateful to Hugh Cheape for his research on this subject. For further information on wattlework and creel houses, *see* H. Cheape, 'Currachs to coffins – Wickerwork and basketry as cultural and historical indicators', a talk given to The Woven Communities Symposium, 30 August 2012. *See* http://wovencommunities.org/.

10 NLS, *Plan, Elevation and sections of additional Barracks of Timber, Ordered by The Duke of Cumberland to be built at Fort William . . .* MS1646 Z.02/30a (1746).

11 NLS, *General Survey of the Town of Gordon's Burgh with the Houses, Gardens and other Lands contiguous thereto, the Property of his Grace Allexr: Duke of Gordon*, by PM, 1753.

12 Pryde, *Burghs*, no. 303.

13 N. Allen, *Highland Planned Villages* (Highland Vernacular Buildings Working Group, Edinburgh, 1989), 42.

14 *OSA, Kilmallie*, viii, 138.

15 Kilgour, *Lochaber in War and Peace*, 63.

16 S. Lewis, *A Topographical Dictionary of Scotland* (London, 1846), i, 446.

43 Fraserburgh, 1815

In 1813 William Daniell (1769–1837), a celebrated topographical artist and engraver, set out from Land's End 'minutely to describe the whole coast round Great Britain' including 'the grandeur of its natural scenery, the manners and employment of people, and modes of life in the wildest parts'.[1] By the time he painted this picture of Fraserburgh in 1815, Daniell had travelled the length of the west coast, including the Outer Isles, and was heading south again, painting during the summer months and returning to work on his plates in winter. Given the difficulties of travel at the time, this voyage of discovery was a remarkable achievement. The brief notes that Daniell wrote to accompany each plate are informative, but it is his pictures that give them depth and meaning. This view of Fraserburgh is typical, capturing as it does the very essence of this town in the far north-east for a public that was increasingly curious but less adventurous than he.[2]

In the centre of the picture are the remains of Kinnaird Head Castle, built by Sir Alexander Fraser (1536–1623), 8th laird of Philorth and founder of Fraserburgh. All that is left of Fraser's sixteenth-century castle is the central tower, converted into a lighthouse in 1787. The building alongside was the lighthouse keeper's living quarters. Kinnaird Head lighthouse was the first to be lit following the establishment of the Commissioners of Northern Lighthouses in Edinburgh in 1786. It was designed and built by Thomas Smith (c. 1752–1815), the Board's first engineer, who went on to construct many of the much-needed lighthouses round Scotland's coast.[3]

Like the lighthouse itself, the two towers to the right can be seen more clearly in the accompanying vignette, painted by Daniell at the same time. The smaller structure, with crow step gables, was a doocot, since demolished. The larger was known as the Wine Tower. It was built on rock over a great cave to which it may once have been connected. The history of this strange tower is uncertain. It is three storeys high with a vaulted chamber in each, connected by trap ladders. The top floor would appear to have been a Roman Catholic chapel but theories differ as to the building's original purpose. One suggests that it was built by Sir Alexander Fraser (c. 1495–1569), 7th laird of Philorth, as a local base from which to oversee improvements to his hamlet of Faithlie, erected a burgh of barony in 1546, which would become Fraser's Burgh.[4]

A more recent theory is based on its use as a covert Catholic chapel by the 8th laird, another Alexander Fraser, and his family after the Reformation of 1560.[5] Protestantism

43. William Daniell, *Fraserburgh, Aberdeenshire*, 1815

43a. William Daniell, *Kinnaird Head, Aberdeenshire*, 1815

was slow to establish itself in the north-east of Scotland, and Alexander Fraser may have needed to establish his Protestant credentials for political reasons. Perhaps this is one reason why he obtained a charter from the crown in 1592 to establish a college and university in Fraserburgh for which the General Assembly recommended a staunch Protestant, the Revd Charles Ferme, as principal. Nothing came of the university, but Ferme reluctantly became minister of Fraserburgh, ensuring that the town and its laird were seen to be following a politically correct path whatever the personal ambivalence of the laird's religious convictions.[5] No theory quite fits the facts so the Wine Tower remains a mystery.

Daniell has placed the harbour, the most important element in the development of Fraserburgh, in the centre of his picture. The first harbour, built in 1546, was replaced as early as 1576 putting Fraserburgh amongst the leading ports on the east coast.[6] Further redevelopment was underway at the time this picture was painted. The north pier which curves round to form one side of the harbour entrance had been completed only three years before. The old pier which goes out to meet it was about to be removed and a new south pier constructed in the foreground. These proposals were sketched out in 1818 by the famous engineer Robert Stevenson (1772–1850), stepson of Thomas Smith who had designed the lighthouse.[7] By the time a new middle pier had been built, the total cost of ensuring Fraserburgh's pre-eminence as a port was £30,000.[8]

A major reason for enlarging the harbour was the rapidly expanding herring industry. As Daniell points out in his notes, Fraserburgh is 'well situated for the herring fishery, which is here carried on with great spirit'.[9] Writing in 1840, the Revd John Cumming pinpointed 1815 as the year herring fishing 'began to be prosecuted upon an extensive scale'.[10] To emphasise the point, Daniell has placed two fishing boats in a prominent position. As at Wick (*see* 99), the herring fishing season ran from July to September, when this picture was painted.

Another local industry highlighted by Daniell was already in decline. The figures on the beach with creels on their backs are harvesting seaweed for the kelp industry. The seaweed was burned to produce an ash rich in soda and potash which was sold to glass and soap manufacturers. Recent removal of government duty on barilla, a cheaper Spanish alternative, was having a catastrophic effect on the industry. Having spent so much time on the west coast where the kelp industry was largely based, Daniell would have understood the crisis this industry was facing. The shore at Fraserburgh, which previously had been let for as much as £150, would fetch only £15 by 1840.[11]

Evidence of an industry that Fraserburgh was keen to exploit can also be seen in the sandy bay in the foreground and the long low building out on the point. With tourism and the therapeutic value of salt water becoming ever more popular, this building was the Fraserburgh baths. They were still a new phenomenon in 1807, when a writer commented that 'scarcely can anything be imagined neater than the Warm and Cold Baths and the dressing places for either'. For those of a weak constitution, there was also the local mineral water which was 'light and not unpleasant'.[12]

Endnotes

1 W. Daniell, *Daniell's Scotland: A Voyage Round the Coast of Scotland and the Adjacent Isles 1815–1822* (Edinburgh, 2006), i, p. xxviii.

2 We are indebted to Dr David Bertie, Curatorial Officer, Documentation and Conservation (Aberdeenshire) for his advice.

3 *DNB*, Thomas Smith.

4 MacGibbon and Ross, *Castellated and Domestic Architecture of Scotland*, ii, 31.

5 I. B. D. Bryce, 'The Wine Tower, Fraserburgh', *The Double Tressure: Journal of the Heraldry Society of Scotland* (1989), no. 11, 9–10.

6 J. Cranna, *Fraserburgh Past and Present* (Aberdeen, 1914), 18.

7 R. Stevenson, *Sketch Plan of the Harbour of Fraserburgh with sections shewing the New Southern Pier etc.* 1818, NLS, MS5850 No. 60.

8 *NSA*, xii, 255.

9 *Daniell's Scotland*, i, 282.

10 *NSA*, xii, 252.

11 *NSA*, xii, 256.

12 Cranna, *Fraserburgh Past and Present*, 436.

44   Galashiels, 1845 and 1824

This panoramic view of Galashiels from Buckholm Hill is given the date 1845, just before the arrival of the railway; it received greater prominence when it was used as the frontispiece in R. Hall's *The History of Galashiels* in 1898.[1] It highlights admirably the settlement nestled in a narrow valley, partially in both Selkirkshire and Roxburghshire. The town developed here mainly because of the Gala Water, which provided a source of power for the many mills that sprang up. This source was supplemented in the late sixteenth century by the construction of the Galashiels Dam, a lade which followed the contours of the valley. The town was granted burghal status in 1599, which opened the way to greater trading prospects with its weekly markets.[2] This and the ready supply of wool from nearby farms gave Galashiels an important headstart in becoming a leading textile-producing town.

This view emphasises the valley, set within rolling hills, and the importance of mills to Galashiels. Indeed, little of the emerging town is portrayed – to the middle left is Old Gala House, the old parish church, peeping above trees, the Corn Mill and the Glasite Church with two very distinctive windows. Trees conceal what became known as the 'old town' and no attempt is made to portray the emerging town in the valley near the Gala Water, so vividly shown in John Wood's map of 1824. This is essentially a view of textile mills. A clump of trees takes the place of the old town, and has in front an over-scaled Glasite church (1842, the two windows beside the minister's house) and behind it the towers of Old Gala House (as if it were a tower house) and the parish church.

By the early 1580s at least two waulk mills, or fulling mills, are known to have existed. Fulling was the first of the processes in the preparation of woollen cloth to be mechanised, with the use of water power from the Middle Ages onwards. At the fulling mill cloth was beaten and cleaned with the use of either soap or fuller's earth; it was thus the technological infrastructure for later expansion.[3] These two mills were said to have been sited on the positions of the later Mid and Waulkmillhead Mills.

By 1797 four mills had been set up for teasing, scribbling and carding yarn. Wilderhaugh Mill was built in 1790 by George Mercer to accommodate the new machinery involved in the emerging textile industry – a scribbler or carding machine. It was the first mill for machine carding in Galashiels.[4] The tenting grounds of the

44. Anon., *Galashiels from Buckholm Hill*, 1845

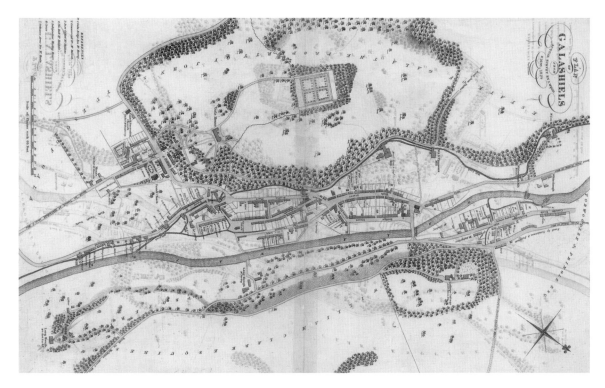

44a.   John Wood, *Plan of Galashiels*, 1824

mill are depicted clearly in the right-hand foreground of the picture. These are lines of frames with 'tenter hooks', on which cloth was stretched and dried in the open air after fulling.

Mid Mill was built in 1792 on the site of one of the fulling mills belonging to the Gala estate in the 1580s.[5] It was originally called the Mid Waulkmill and is portrayed towards the middle left of this view, with twin gables. Ladhope Mill, founded in 1793, on Low Buckholmside dam, is seen to the left of this view near the stone-arched bridge, with a chimney indicating that this had, from 1836, the first steam engine in the town. Following in 1797 was Botany Mill, a fulling mill known initially as Weirhaugh Mill, seen to the right of the Glasite church.[6]

Prominent in this illustration is a suspension bridge. While the Gala Water provided for Galashiels' nineteenth-century prosperity with its motive power for the mills, there were also disadvantages. It created a barrier that needed bridging. In times of drought almost all of the water was drawn off by the factories, many of which are shown in this view, but when the river was full it frequently flooded the town.[7] In an attempt to prevent flooding, a type of construction described in 1833 as 'puts' embanked the river:

These are masses of stones loosely piled in the interior, but finished on the surface after the manner of a pavement, and shaped like the fore half of a shoemaker's last, pointing up the stream, and forming with the bank an angle of 45 degrees . . . The main thing is to guard the base with piles well driven, for if one stone suffered to give away, the whole scheme is futile.[8]

Such masonry still forms the base of the river embankment at Galashiels.

To cross these waters the first modern suspension bridge in Britain was erected in 1816 by the woollen manufacturer Richard Lees. Its purpose was to provide access between the workers' houses at Buckholmside and the Galabank Mill, seen in the right of this view. It was inspired by reports from America of James Finley's bridges, and was a replica in wire of one of those over the Schuylkill at Philadelphia. The *Edinburgh Evening Courant* announced on 2 December 1816 that:

A wire bridge for foot passengers, after the model of those constructed in America, which are so serviceable in crossing ravines, small lakes, etc. in that country, has just been erected across the Gala at Galashiels . . . to every appearance [it] may last for a number of years at little or no expense.

In fact, it was destroyed by flood in 1839, which, interestingly, dates the production of this view to earlier than 1845. Or is it an attempt to recall the significance of this suspension bridge – a landmark in the long history of mastering and manipulating the Gala Water? And is that the late Sir Walter Scott (1771–1832), tireless champion of the textile industry in the Borders, and his favourite deerhound surveying the scene?

Endnotes

1 We are grateful to Mark Watson, Historic Scotland, for his advice on Galashiels. We searched, in vain, for what we thought might exist – an original painting, from which this illustration was copied. However, at the eleventh hour a coloured image was located at RCAHMS, for the use of which we are very grateful. Many people helped. We would like to thank Mark Watson, Elizabeth Hume of Scottish Borders Council Museum and Gallery Service and the staffs of the Heritage Hub, Hawick; Old Gala House, Galashiels; and Melrose Library.

2 Pryde, *Burghs*, no. 264; *RMS*, vi, no. 988.

3 C. Giles and I. H. Goodall, *Yorkshire Textile Mills: The Building of the Yorkshire Textile Industry, 1770–1930* (London, 1992), 12; M. Rorke, D. Gallacher, C. McKean, E. P. Dennison and G. Ewart, *Historic Galashiels: Archaeology and Development* (Scottish Burgh Survey, 2011), 18.

4 W. Rutherford, *Galashiels in History* (Galashiels, 1930), 28; M. C. Lawson, *Guid Auld Galashiels* (Galashiels, 1997), 1–2; Groome, *Gazetteer*, iii, 67–8.

5 W. Rutherford, *Galashiels in History* (Galashiels, 1930), 28; J. R. Hume, *The Industrial Archaeology of Scotland: II, The Lowlands and Borders* (London, 1976), 239.

6 Rorke *et al.*, *Historic Galashiels*, 32.

7 Groome, *Gazetteer*, iii, 67; R. Hall, *The History of Galashiels* (Galashiels, 1898), 88–9, 105, 578–9.

8 *NSA*, iii, 13.

45   Glasgow, Saltmarket, 1630 and 1844

This anonymous picture of the Saltmarket in Glasgow, purportedly in 1630, shows a street in a medieval town which was bursting at its seams.[1] Strictly, this street was still called Waulkergate, meaning 'the way to the place of the waulkers' (or fullers) until 1650, when a new salt market was established. Waulkergait had led to the original south port of the burgh, but much of the story of Glasgow in the sixteenth century was of an urban settlement overspilling its bounds in all directions. As the picture of the Saltmarket shows, the timber-framed buildings are built close together and the upper storeys often overhang the street. Overcrowding, insanitary conditions and the risk of fire were the inevitable result.

The precise rate of expansion of the town is difficult to pin down with precision, but there were many indicators of growth. In 1596 Glasgow created a second parish, with its own church, thereby ending the centuries-old tradition of a single parish church for the whole burgh. This was the Tron Kirk, built beside the public weigh-beam or tron in 1599. With urban growth went further civic ambition. A new tolbooth was built in 1626, a remarkable five storeys high and five bays wide, though only its steeple remains today. The High Street was broadened in 1628; new wells were dug in the 1620s and 1630s; and the steeple on the Tron Kirk was built between 1630 and 1636. The speed of change from a medieval bishop's burgh to what was in a very real sense a new town, anxious to forge a new image of itself, quickened with each decade in the first half of the seventeenth century.

In 1652, the almost inevitable result of unchecked growth, defying the strictures on planning of the Dean of Guild court, was a severe fire. It might well be claimed that it was Glasgow's equivalent of the Great Fire of London in 1666 for it too heralded a new civic vision. Contemporary accounts bemoaned the loss of 'foir scoir closes all burnt, estimate to about a thousand families' and eighty warehouses.[2] Settlement had been characterised by the close-packed lay-out of housing, the use of timber as the main construction material and the combustible nature of the contents of warehouses, which probably included miniature mountains of hay and malt in the spider's web of alleys and closes off the Saltmarket and Trongate. In the aftermath of the 1652 fire, the largely unplanned shambles which had grown up along the medieval town's main roadway to its bridge was replaced. A new quarter of houses and warehouses grew up. They were

45. Anon., *Old Glasgow Saltmarket in 1630*, n.d.

45a. Thomas Fairbairn, *Old Wooden House in Close, Saltmarket*, 1844

built partly of stone rather than wholly of wood as before; instructions were laid down to establish a more carefully planned street pattern, without overhanging upper storeys and garrets. All houses on both sides of the Saltmarket were to be built to 'conforme to ane straicht lyne, and none to come fader then another'. But the 'new town' took time to become a reality. A further fire in 1669 destroyed 136 houses and shops in the Saltmarket and its adjoining streets.[3] In 1654 and again in 1679 candlemakers were forced to move to 'such remote places from houses as the filthy, stinking and nosiesome smell may be avoided'; they moved to nearby Candleriggs. In 1711, baxters became the next target because of danger posed by their wood fires. And breweries were banned from closes in 1725 because of the threat posed by their furnaces to thatched dwellings.[4]

This new precinct lasted until it, in turn, became a slum. Evidence of a reversion to type comes in many images drawn from the middle decades of the nineteenth century when the area around the Saltmarket became a ghetto, fuelled by successive waves of migrants and Irish immigrants which forced the population of the city up by 5,000 a year throughout the 1820s and 1830s. A revealing image of number 77, The Saltmarket by Thomas Fairbairn (1820–1885), first drawn in 1844, shows overcrowded and cramped housing which might have predated the fires of the seventeenth century – only the lower walls were built of stone; the upper storeys had projecting wooden walls and unglazed windows had wooden shutters.[5] Most of these dwellings were finally demolished in the late nineteenth century after the City Improvement Act of 1866. With the strictly contemporary image drawn by Fairbairn in mind, this anonymous impression of a street in the 1630s seems more like picturesque but ill-informed conjecture – in effect, a Victorian recreation of a late medieval slum.

Endnotes

1 SCRAN, Glasgow City Council Libraries and Archives, Early Views of Glasgow project, which dates the picture as 1630.

2 J. Gibson, *The History of Glasgow* (Glasgow, 1777), Appendix xxii, pp. 314–17.

3 A. Gibb, *Glasgow: The Making of a City* (London, 1983), 25, 27.

4 T. M. Devine and G. Jackson (eds), *Glasgow, Volume One: Beginnings to 1830* (Manchester, 1995), 35–6, 85–6.

5 Thomas Fairbairn, *Relics of Ancient Architecture and other Picturesque Scenes in Glasgow* (Glasgow, 1849). For the original drawing of 1844, *see* Glasgow University Library, Bh11-x.14 Item fol. 12.

46   Glasgow, 1693

The first glimpses of Glasgow are to be seen in three of the maps of Timothy Pont (*c*. 1565–*c*.1615), dating to about 1596. Common to all three maps is the exaggerated focus on its bridge over the Clyde.[1] Almost exactly a century later, the army officer and topographical draughtsman John Slezer (*c*. 1650–1717) assembled an apparently meticulous view map, *The Prospect of the Town of Glasgow from the South*, which took the bridge as its starting-point. It was one of three views he drew of Glasgow, its cathedral and university. It is, in fact, a view from the south-east, so as to allow a more comprehensive capture of the town's most iconic buildings. The trio of views accurately reflects Slezer's two main themes: distant or panoramic townscapes and key buildings or sets of buildings.[2]

Unusually, a preliminary drawing of this landscape survives, in the Ashmolean Museum in Oxford; it reveals part of the process by which the drawing was transferred to copper plate by being divided into squares and gridlines.[3] But it also reveals a series of minor differences of detail between the preliminary sketch and the eventual engraving. Most of these are contextual but they underline some of the aims of Slezer's townscapes. There is a focus in both scenes on the eight-arched bridge leading to the Brigport and in both the perspective is exaggerated. In the end product, the figures on the bridge have been augmented and the cart on the bridge has become a gentleman's coach; extra figures have been drawn on the shore, a skiff with prow and mast has been added, as have four small boats, two in mid-stream, the others moored on the far bank.

Slezer was the first in Scotland to use a camera obscura to give more accuracy to his drawings. Despite this, artistic licence was practised at two stages: in the original drawing, with its packman and his dog in the foreground; and perhaps at 'touch-up' stage, when Jan Wyck (*c*. 1645–1700), a jobbing artist who was paid ten shillings a time to add 'little figures' to the fifty-seven drawings published in *Theatrum Scotiae* (1693), got to work.[4] But the same double process tended to lend extra regularity and order to a townscape: the houses immediately to the right of the bridge are depicted as much more evenly spaced, with more windows and symmetry, than those farther east (right) crowded together amidst steeples and spires. Moving left to right (west to east) in the picture, the first very distinctive steeple is immediately recognisable as that of the Merchants' House or Guild Hall, completed in 1665. The next is a reasonable facsimile of the squat structure of the Tron Church

46. John Slezer, *The Prospect of the Town of Glasgow from the South*, 1693

(1599) with its clock. Next should be the tolbooth (1626), a seven-storey-high structure surmounted by a crown spire, which has been described as the finest Renaissance tolbooth in Scotland. Given a rather anonymous shape in the original drawing, it has been mistaken at a later stage for an ecclesiastical building and anachronistically surmounted by a large cruciform symbol. Beyond it are a cluster of spires representing the Old College (1656), the Church of the Blackfriars and the cathedral.

In reality, as can be seen in Slezer's detailed engraving, *The Colledge of Glasgow*, it and the Blackfriars' adjoined each other. But the cathedral was some considerable distance further away, as Slezer's 'prospect' from the north-east demonstrates. The cathedral was presumably included for the sake of completeness rather than accuracy. Much discussion has taken place about the relationship between Pont's original sketches and the eventual publication by Blaeu. Similarly, the chance survival of a handful of Slezer's original drawings offers a glimpse of the partial 'make-over' which his work underwent before publication.

It may be concluded that Slezer, like Wenceslas Hollar (1607–1677) before him (*see* 30), saw symmetry, order and civility as the marks of urban settlement. But for Slezer, unlike Hollar, cities were also about human activity. Hence figures were scattered about his townscapes, often larger than life. The combined effect is why Slezer's *Theatrum Scotiae* (1693) provides the first comprehensive pictorial record of Scotland. But it is also a record which should be viewed with some considerable scepticism as to the veracity of all its detail.

Endnotes

1 *See* NLS website, Pont maps, nos 32, 33, 34.
2 Cavers, *Slezer*, 6.
3 *Ibid.*, 5; Ashmolean Museum Drawings Catalogue, vol. iv, nos 234–6.
4 Cavers, *Slezer*, 9.

47   Glasgow from the south-east, *c.* 1762

Until the three depictions of Glasgow made by John Slezer in the 1690s (*see* 46), no contemporary impressions of its townscape are known to have existed. Yet, despite Slezer's work, much of the lay-out and topography of the city is educated guesswork for no detailed contemporary map existed before 1734. Even then, much has to be deduced or inferred from later evidence, since John Watt's map of that date was drawn on such a small scale as to give only an outline of the main streets and buildings. All of this changed dramatically in the last four decades of the eighteenth century. Robert Collier's *Plan of Glasgow* (1776) was the first detailed view of Glasgow's core and the plan drawn by John McArthur (1778) extended wider, to include the Gorbals, Calton and beyond.[1]

In the case of Glasgow, unusually, art came before cartography. In the 1760s and early 1770s, a whole series of views of the city were drawn by pupils of the Foulis Academy of Fine Arts. The Academy was the creation of Robert Foulis (1707–1776) and his brother Andrew (1712–1775), sons of a Glasgow maltman. In the years after 1744, the partnership of the two brothers published 584 volumes, ranging from classical texts to English literature and academic works. The Academy acquired a collection of continental works of art, sourced by the brothers during their visits to mainland Europe to sell their printed books. Landscapes were not the first priority of the Academy, which was firmly focused on mainstream art and sculpture. Amongst the better known of its pupils were David Allan (1744–1796) and Robert Paul (1739–1770), who drew a fine view of Glasgow from the south-west (1764).

Most of the views of Glasgow which originated in the Foulis Academy, however, were by unknown pupils. Two views of the city of *c.* 1762, both described as being from the south-east but from noticeably different angles, can, if taken together, provide a revealing insight into the development of the other side of the city from that which has usually drawn most attention in this period. Much has been written about Glasgow's steady, westward expansion in the quarter of a century after 1750, mostly based on the laying out of a dozen new streets, such as Virginia Street (1753), Queen Street and Buchanan Street (both 1765).[2] Much less attention has been devoted to development to the east along Gallowgate, parallel to the river, and Drygate, immediately south of the cathedral.

47. Foulis Academy, *Glasgow from the South-East, c.* 1762

The first view, which can be firmly dated to 1762, takes the vista between the cathedral and the Tron Church as its canvas. In its centre is the Old College (1656) and its extensive gardens. Some encroaching settlement along the Drygate is obvious in the far right of the picture but otherwise fields are being seeded and ploughed. In contrast to the geometrical grid of westward planned expansion, the older town twists and turns, closely following the natural contours of the land. Long, narrow rigs extend outwards from the back of buildings along the curving High Street, towards agricultural land. Some development is apparent along Gallowgate on the left of the picture, but much of it is hidden by the slope of the Dowhill, which, by 1807, according to a plan drawn up by Peter Fleming (1783–1851), had been turned into residential suburbs and gardens.[3]

47a. Foulis Academy, *Glasgow from the South-East, c.* 1762

The other view, taken from the south-east, shows, to the south of the Dowhill, the High and Low Green, separated by the Camlachie Burn. It is also much more inclusive in its distant vista of the city. No fewer than eight spires and steeples are depicted, from the Merchant Trades Hall on the left to the cathedral on the right. The familiar eight spans of the old bridge are shown, as is the low-lying ground on the north side of the river, where the two streams – the Camlachie and the Molendinar – met, making much more understandable another Foulis Academy drawing of the 1760s, depicting the whole street of the Bridgegate under water (*see* Introduction, fig. 9). Here, too, there is much more human activity than a single ploughman and seedsman. There is fishing and washing of clothes along the riverbank, even though the old washing house – the squat building in the foreground – is nearby; a dog is being exercised on the Calton Hill and militia is drilling in the fields.

These two views provide a brief snapshot in time. Within ten years, this panorama no longer existed. By 1765 the old bridge was in so dangerous a condition that it had to be closed to carts. Charles Ross's plan of 1773, an inset in his county map of Lanarkshire,[4] and Collier's map of 1776 both described the land between the north bank of the river and the Gallowgate as 'laid out for building'. By 1808, much of the land beyond the flood plain between the Camlachie Burn and the river had been parcelled and feued. The stage was set for the wholesale industrialisation of Bridgeton and much of the north bank of the river all the way to Dalmarnock, with tanneries, cotton mills and dye works.

Endnotes

1 T. A. Markus *et al.*, 'The shape of the city in space and stone', in T. M. Devine and G. Jackson (eds), *Glasgow Volume I: Beginnings to 1830* (Manchester, 1995), 107, 118–20, 136n. For McArthur's map, *see* the online version at 'The Glasgow Story, 1778'.

2 *See* J. R. Kellett, 'Glasgow', in M. D. Lobel (ed.), *Historic Towns: Maps and Plans of Towns and Cities in the British Isles*, vol. i (Oxford, 1969), 6; A Gibb, 'New horizons', in *Glasgow: The Making of a City* (London, 1983), 69–78.

3 Markus, 'Shape of the city', 123–4. *See* NLS website, Town Plans/Views, Glasgow (1807), for Fleming's map of that date.

4 *See* Introduction, fig. 17, for Ross's inset map of 1773.

48   Glasgow, 1817

This enormous oil painting of Glasgow's Old Bridge, *Panorama of the City of Glasgow*, by the Paisley-born artist John Knox (1778–1845), was a celebration of a city on the point of social and economic transformation. It and his even larger painting of Glasgow's Trongate (1826) subjected both the townscape and Glasgow society to almost encyclopaedic scrutiny. As well as showing an enviable mastery of light and structure, Knox, as with Alexander Nasmyth's (1758–1840) depiction of Edinburgh's Princes Street (*see* 34), moulded architecture, landscape and people into a harmonious whole.

Knox's career began as a portrait painter before he moved on to painting landscapes. His *Landscape with Tourists at Loch Katrine* was only one of a series of large-scale oil paintings by him of Highland scenery. Closer to home were a number of studies of the Clyde, including *The First Steamboat on the Clyde* (*c.* 1820), sometimes hailed as his best-known work.[1] It, like his urban landscapes, revealed Knox as a social chronicler of his times.

The original bridge – the so-called Old Bridge – across the Clyde, which may have dated to *c.* 1350, has featured in views, maps and artwork across the centuries. Never before had it and its surrounds been subjected to such forensic scrutiny as in Knox's panorama. The view was a familiar one, from the south-east and the Gorbals, looking across to the north bank of the Clyde. In his sweeping panorama, a fraction short of four feet (1.2 metres) in width, Knox spans the distance of half a mile between three bridges: the wooden pedestrian bridge up-river (right), which replaced the Hutchesontown Bridge swept away by a flood in 1795; the Old Bridge itself; and down-river (left) to the bridge at the Broomielaw (1772), the first bridge across the river to be built since medieval times.[2] Beyond the Broomielaw Bridge, Knox frames the distinctive cone of the Jamaica Street Glassworks centre-stage, amidst the cluster of factory chimneys of new industries which had recently engulfed the village of Anderston.[3]

Knox carefully picks out the details of the buildings between the Broomielaw and the Old Bridge: the almost white stone of the newly built St Andrew's Roman Catholic Chapel (1817) is the building closest to the Broomielaw Bridge. Behind it is the spire of St Enoch's Church (1770). Near to it on the riverbank stands the distinctive triple frontage of the Town's Hospital, built in 1733 as a catch-all solution to the problems of the city's

48. John Knox, *Panorama of the City of Glasgow*, 1817

poor, indigent, infirm and orphans.[4] The Palladian mansions built by the tobacco lords in the classical style which predominated in the third quarter of the eighteenth century, including one built for Allan Dreghorn (1706–1764), completes the line of prestigious buildings between the two bridges.

To the east of the Old Bridge, behind a large, newly built tenement, the familiar Gothic steeple of the Merchants' House or Guild Hall (1665) dominates the skyline. Another monument to the city's ambition, again easily picked out in Knox's painting by the pristine whiteness of the stonework, is the Justiciary Buildings, built in 1814 at

St Andrew's Roman Catholic Chapel

the foot of the Saltmarket, close to the makeshift wooden bridge. Underneath it, the mouth of the Molendinar Burns discharges into the river. Beyond that lies the open space of Glasgow Green and the tall column of Nelson's Monument, just visible in the far distance.

For Knox, the city and its river are a theatre of human activity. The urban experience is essentially ordered and humdrum, at one and the same time. People go about their everyday business; a pair of women are beating a carpet; a variety of small boats are on the river; and horses are being watered in the shallow water. Another picture of 1776 showed how shallow the river was: fords on both sides of the bridge were used to avoid the toll.[5] Knox shows the white toll gates standing open. It does not yet have lamps fitted to ease traffic at night. That would follow in 1821 – a detail which, along with the known completion of the new buildings depicted, confirms the date of the painting as 1817 or thereabouts.

Knox has not enjoyed the reputation enjoyed by Nasmyth. His range was almost as broad, but his work depicting Glasgow, while impressive in its detail, was slight in volume. His misfortune lay in what works survived him. He was one of the first and perhaps the most prominent of Scotland's painters of panoramas. The device of a 360-degree painting, viewed from a platform within a rotunda, was invented in 1787 by Robert Barker (1739–1806), an Irish-born artist living in Edinburgh. His first exhibition was a *View of Edinburgh* but subsequent displays of British victories in the Napoleonic wars at the Panorama on Edinburgh's Mound took advantage of the jingoism of the moment. Glasgow had more than one panorama theatre: in 1825 an exhibition of the Battle of Waterloo played at a rotunda in

Justiciary Buildings

Buchanan Street.[6] The enormous pieces of work by Knox involved in making a panorama – some extending to thousands of square feet of canvas – have not survived. All that remains are a few sketches, works such as this *Panorama of Glasgow* and two even larger studies of the landscape from the summit of Ben Lomond, and a small collection of some of his work, in much reduced format, *Scotland's Scenery Drawn from Nature upon Stone* (Glasgow, 1823).

Endnotes

1 D. Macmillan, *Scottish Art, 1460–1990* (Edinburgh, 1990), 145, 147.

2 *See* www.theglasgowstory.com/ under 'panorama'.

3 A. Gibb, *Glasgow: The Making of a City* (London, 1983), 91–2.

4 T. A. Markus *et al.*, 'The shape of the city in space and stone', in T. M. Devine and G. Jackson (eds), *Glasgow, Volume I; Beginnings to 1830* (Manchester, 1995), 118.

5 *See* S. Mullen, *It Wisnae Us: The Truth about Glasgow and Slavery* (Glasgow, 2009), 57, for James Brown's picture of the bridge in 1776.

6 Cartoon of Buchanan Street rotunda, *Glasgow Looking Glass* (25 June 1825), GUL Special Collections, Bh14-x.8. *See* Introduction, figs 21, 22.

49   Glasgow Fair, 1825

The annual Glasgow Fair, held in July, was established under the burgh's charter, like those illustrated in Haddington (52), Oldhamstocks (81) and Pitlessie (89), primarily for the trading of livestock, produce and the hiring of labour. The event was held in various locations over the centuries but from the early 1800s it was found at the foot of the Saltmarket between the city and the river. Inevitably, food and drink stalls and popular entertainment were provided for fair-goers, and as dedicated produce markets were established in different places and residents came to enjoy regular, if regulated, holiday periods, the fair shifted focus to become a major event in the public calendar. It began to attract amusements such as theatres, circuses, drinking booths and all kinds of shows and side-shows, especially for the working classes. In 1815 a ground rent was introduced for stall-holders, the proceeds going initially to the cost of maintaining the city's wells.

This hand-coloured cartoon drawing records the annual event as viewed from the roof of the recently completed Court of Justiciary, with the stalls of the fair laid out as an extension of the Saltmarket and along the western flanks of Glasgow Green. Drawn by the prolific caricaturist William Heath (c. 1794–1840) of London, it was published in an 1825 edition of *The Glasgow Looking Glass*, a satirical and irreverent broadsheet on the city and the life it contained.[1]

In the town can be seen the tower of St Andrew's Parish Church (built 1739–57) and the rear elevations, with tripartite Venetian windows, of the elegant terraced houses that surround it. The small, Palladian St Andrew's by the Green Episcopal chapel of 1750 faces the open park before the developing backdrop of industrial buildings and chimneys of Calton. The steeple of the seventeenth-century tolbooth marks Glasgow Cross, from where the hordes are descending. And there is a glimpse of the soon-to-be-lost Old College tower, its Low Countries-derived design adopted from the church of Holyrood Abbey, like those at Linlithgow, Dumfries, Stirling, and Edinburgh's Tron church.

The Saltmarket consists mainly of four-storey tenements although there is at least one older two-storey vernacular building with small windows and crow-stepped gable and perhaps a court behind. Another building with a gable facing the street is also a survivor from early times as timber-fronted houses of this type were recorded in this street in the nineteenth century (*see* 45).

49. William Heath, *Glasgow Fair*, 1825

Despite the initial impression of disorder, the fair comprises highly organised and commercialised entertainment offered in specially built stands and theatres. Although there are some lettered signs, most stalls and shows are advertised through large canvasses painted to depict the delights on offer and via callers, drums and loud music. In addition to the paid attractions, 'walk-ups' or 'penny geggies', there are table stalls, some of which are covered. Within the crowd there are militia (some of whom are apprehending a drunk) and the inevitable soldiers from Highland regiments. The customers appear to come from a wide demographic base including women and children, some elegantly dressed.

The viewpoint of the artist of this work is clearly one of detached observation. There is little feeling of engagement by the observer who looks down, perhaps condescendingly, from a symbol of law and order, and the subjects are largely anonymous and caricatured. Yet it captures the spirit of the mêlée[2] better than John Knox's 1832 painting of the fair, where his primary aim of artistic effect suggests a more restrained and ordered affair.[3] This approach also reflects the descriptions of the gathering found in vernacular verse such as the chapbook song, *The Humours of Glasgow Fair*, which depicts the attractions:

> 'Twas there was the funning and sporting,
> Eh, Lord, what a swarm o' braw folk;
> Rowly-powly, wild beasts, wheels o' fortune,
> Sweety stans', Mr Puch and Black Jock.

and reports on the ad hoc drinking establishments:

> Then hie tae the tents at the pailing,
> Weel theekit wi blankets and mats,
> And deals seated round like a tap-room,
> Supported on stools and on pats.[4]

Another street song, *Glasgow Fair on the Banks o' the Clyde*,[5] mentions talking animals, a giant and giantess, panoramas with special effects, a camera obscura and describes how:

> Large booths are arranged to the eye,
> There's horsemanship, theatres and tumbling;
> With all sorts of games to rely,
> Where losers are always a grumbling.

A report from the 1840s also talks of Toby, the dog with spectacles on his nose, a denuded athlete balancing weights upon his chin, groups of 'Tyrolese peasants' dancing, a dwarf at the miniature window of a miniature mansion, a gentleman lying with his legs in the air dancing a hornpipe and at the same time balancing a pole on his toes, swings, roundabouts, peep shows, shooting ranges, statuary groups, the skeleton of a whale, a stuffed mermaid, a horse with six legs and a pig with two heads, eight feet and 'et ceteras too many to mention'.[6] The drawing clearly shows a large number of animal attractions, and it is known that the principal travelling menageries attended the fair without fail, with newspaper reports praising the quality and educational value of such attractions.[7] Horse trials or sales also appear to be underway on the distant side of the green, suggesting comparisons to be made with the entertainments which accompanied Leith races (*see* 68).

By the 1850s the magic of the fair was wearing off; most holidaymakers preferred to head out of the city by rail or steamboat for the holiday period. Inevitably, the quality of the attractions, and their customers, deteriorated, and there was concern at the 'stately brick erections and cardboard and canvas edifices which have a sort of permanent location at the western limit of Glasgow's beautiful green'.[8] In response, the fair was moved in the 1870s to Crownpoint in the east and then to Vinegar Hill, north of Camlachie, where it continued as a carnival. The name of the original fair survives in the annual trades' holiday or Glasgow Fair Fortnight in July.

Endnotes

1 *Glasgow Looking Glass*, 1, no. 4 (Glasgow, 1825) 4.

2 There is another cartoon illustration of the fair reproduced in C. A. Oakley, *The Second City* (Glasgow, 1967), 104, which shows the characters more clearly, including a disabled ballad singer, fist fighters and a piper.

3 Mitchell Library, G 941.435 EYR. Accessed at http://www.theglasgowstory.com/imageview.php?inum=TGSA 01121.

4 From a broadsheet, published by The Poets Box (Glasgow, 1850). Contained in a scrapbook of Glasgow songs. Mitchell Library, GC 398.5. The collection also includes broadsheet ballads, *The Sights of Glasgow Fair* (1850), *Jock Clarkstone's Description of Glasgow Fair* (1851) and *Glasgow Fair* (1857).

5 From a broadsheet in the Murray Collection, Glasgow University Special Collections, Mu23-y.1. Bound volumes, p. 22.

6 Article in *Hogg's Weekly Instructor* (1847), quoted in 'Glasgow Fair, a Picture of 75 Years Ago', *Glasgow Herald* (8 July 1922), 4.

7 'Glasgow Fair', *Glasgow Herald* (21 July 1858), 5.

8 *Glasgow Herald* (8 July 1922), 4. Aspects of the fair at Glasgow are discussed in J. Burnett, 'Carnival and other festivities in Scotland in the nineteenth century', *Scottish Studies*, 35 (2007–10), 36–58.

50   Glasgow and Garnkirk Railway, 1831

This is one of four images by David Octavius Hill (1802–1870) published by Alexander Hill of Edinburgh, the artist's older brother (1800–1866) in 1832, to commemorate the opening of the Glasgow and Garnkirk Railway.[1] Passengers were carried between Garnkirk and Townhead by steam train for the first time on 27 September 1831. In the preface to the publication, the artist notes that, while on a sketching excursion in the West of Scotland in the autumn of 1831, he was requested by a friend connected with the railway to provide one or two drawings 'of objects on the line' to be engraved on a small scale for the company directors and stakeholders. This was developed into a more substantial project of larger lithographs 'without any pretensions as works of art', while 'professing to give, not only a tolerably correct picture of the localities of the railway in question, but a characteristic and unexaggerated view of the generally important subject of railway travel'. In an attached essay on the railways in Lanarkshire, civil engineer George Buchanan described the works as conveying 'a very accurate and striking representation' of the subject.

The view, titled *Opening of the Glasgow and Garnkirk Railway. View at St Rollox Looking South East*, shows two of the system's Stephenson steam locomotives, the *St Rollox* and the *George Stephenson*, passing at the eastern depot at St Rollox, although this precise conjuncture of trains is unlikely to have occurred if they left from the different ends of the line at the same time. The *St Rollox*, on the right, carries passengers, mainly the company directors, their friends and families, while the other train pulls a large demonstration load of coal, iron, lime and grain as well as passengers who had worked on the engineering project. The buildings behind include Charles Tennant & Company's St Rollox Chemical Works, with a 200-foot (61 metres) chimney, and a branch railway for delivering coal to the furnaces. To the left are the tonnage office, the spinning and weaving factory of Couper, Maitland & Company, and the St Rollox Foundry. Further down the line the signal-house and porter's lodge can be seen. The spire of Glasgow Cathedral, the Knox Monument at the Necropolis and another city tower, perhaps the Tron Steeple, can be seen in the distance to the south, on the right of the painting behind the mass of chimney stacks and roofs of the Tennant works.

The construction of the line was financed by Charles Tennant & Company with the intention of importing coal for its own use and onward distribution, as the Monkland

50. David Octavius Hill, *Opening of the Glasgow and Garnkirk Railway.
View at St Rollox Looking South East*, 1831

Canal was unable to transport sufficient amounts to meet demand. It began operating from May 1831 as a goods-only service between the coalfield and Townhead station, and, although passengers had been carried on other lines before this date, the opening of this facility as commemorated is seen as the start of the passenger rail transport system in Scotland. It is also seen as the start of an association with the railway industry which was to make north Glasgow the largest manufacturer of locomotives in Europe.

Charles Tennant (1768–1838), originally a weaver, was the chemist who is famous for having patented in 1788 the process of using lime and chlorine gas to bleach linen. Charles Tennant & Company was first registered in Glasgow in 1797 and became one of the largest industrial complexes in Scotland. The St Rollox chemical works grew to be the largest in the world during the 1830s and 1840s and its 435½-foot (133 metres) high chimney, known as 'Tennant's Stalk', dominated the Glasgow landscape from 1842 until 1922, when it was struck by lightning and had to be demolished. This burgeoning of industrial development led to the construction of associated mass housing in this part of the city.

Despite claims to the importance of the railway in the development of passenger transport in Scotland, the facilities, as can be seen, were primitive. In praising the new line, George Buchanan, an engineer, had nothing specific to say on the opportunities for the general public stressing instead its commercial potential:

> This railway promises to be of incalculable benefit, by raising the value of its mineral and other produce, and also with it the value of every kind of property, as well as in many other ways opening up and improving the country.[2]

It is no surprise, therefore, that the public service was severely criticised, especially after more advanced provisions, such as used by the Edinburgh and Glasgow Railway, were being established.[3]

Hill's images contain old-fashioned elements, which may have been deliberately chosen to contrast the old Scotland with the cutting-edge technology and opportunities of the new railways and industry. The characters in kilts, plaids and tam o' shanter bonnets, sitting with their sheep dogs drinking in the left foreground, could have come directly from the late eighteenth-century paintings of Scottish life and society by David Allan or the poetry of Robert Burns (who was a friend of the family of Alloway-born Charles Tennant).

In another of the four images published together, *View near Provan Mill Bridge Looking West*, the trains pass through the 'artificial valley'. Milton farm steading is on the left, while to the right Hill records a row of thatched cottages complete with 'hingin lums', which he notes as the temporary accommodation of the construction workers. On the opposite side of the tracks a group of neo-Jacobite Highlanders hold aloft a banner in a heroic grouping which would not be out of place in one of the of the artist's famous historical paintings.

50a. David Octavius Hill, *View near Provan Mill Bridge Looking West*, 1831

Hill's 'friend connected with the railway' was the engineer John Miller, of engineers Grainger & Miller, and the artist was to go on to produce a number of other works associated with the company's projects, particularly the Edinburgh and Glasgow Railway.[4] The handsome folio of prints, of which this illustration forms part, was part of the response to the emerging market for commemorative images, both printed and photographic, within which members of the Hill family were to play a number of highly important roles.[5]

Endnotes

1 D. O. Hill, *Views of the Opening of the Glasgow and Garnkirk Railway. Also an Account of That and Other Railways in Lanarkshire drawn up by George Buchanan* (Edinburgh, 1832).

2 *Ibid.*, 10.

3 F. Whishaw, *The Railways of Great Britain and Ireland* (London, 1840), mentioned in J. Hume, *The Industrial Archaeology of Glasgow* (Glasgow, 1974), 10.

4 R. Simpson, *Hill and Adamson's Photographs of Linlithgow* (Linlithgow, 2002).

5 Alexander Hill's obituary in *The Scotsman* (16 June 1866) stressed his role in developing print-selling and publishing in Scotland, and his son carried on the trade.

51   Greenock, 1854 and 1820

L ooking at this picture of Greenock from the east in 1854, it is hard to believe that
as late as 1700 this industrial boom town was a fishing village on the south bank
of the Clyde, its population little more than 1,600. By 1835, it had increased more
than fifteen-fold to over 29,500.[1] Several factors behind Greenock's remarkable
growth are included in this oil painting by Thomas Carsell (1810–1860), who lived and
worked there as a portrait painter.[2]

One reason for Greenock's expansion was its location. It offered a sheltered
anchorage on the Clyde, as the picture shows, within easy reach of the Atlantic Ocean.
In the eighteenth century, the town was also quick to take advantage of the opportunities
created by the lack of a navigable channel preventing ocean-going vessels from sailing
up to Glasgow. Greenock's success, achieved despite the nearby rival harbour of Port
Glasgow, financed by Glasgow merchants, owed much to the willingness of local people
to invest in its harbours and docks. Sir John Schaw, the superior, paid for the first harbour,
completed in 1710 at a cost of £5,000, recouping his investment with a levy on every sack
of malt brewed into ale within the town.[3] Increasing trade produced a growing income
from tariffs, but harbour extensions and maintenance costs meant another levy had to be
imposed in 1751. A group of local trustees was appointed to carry out these and other
public works.[4] Refused government grants, the town fought a constant battle to ensure
that its harbours and ship-maintenance facilities were the best on the Clyde.

Victoria Harbour, the larger of the two in the picture, was a tidal harbour completed
in 1850 at a cost of £120,000. It was a demanding feat of engineering which needed nine
shiploads of timber to construct the coffer-dam alone. When finished, the harbour covered
an area in excess of six acres. It also met new demands from owners that required even
the biggest ships stay afloat while being fitted. The crane built beside the harbour could
lift seventy tons.[5]

The top-hatted man in the foreground, surveying the town, represents another of
Greenock's great assets, the local businessmen. A fine example was Robert Steele (1791–
1879), shipbuilder, town councillor, magistrate and justice of the peace, whose energy and
foresight lay behind the construction of Victoria Harbour. Steele's company made paddle
steamers for Samuel Cunard and fast tea clippers for the China trade that were often
the first to bring the new season's tea to London. Committed to quality, men like Steele

51. Thomas Carsell, *Greenock*, 1854

kept abreast of rapidly changing technology to stay ahead of their rivals, many of whom were their neighbours on the Clyde.[6] Another of these enterprising men was Abram Lyle (1820–1891), shipowner, cooper, company director and provost of the town. Lyle purchased a sugar refinery which became the largest in Greenock and later, faced with a collapse in the price of raw sugar, found success with golden syrup, a by-product of the refining process.[7] Between 1700 and 1868, the amount of sugar used in Britain rose from 10,000 tons to an astonishing 700,000 tons. By then, fourteen of the twenty refineries in Scotland were in Greenock, and Clyde sugars were considered the best in Britain.[8]

Sugar production required plenty of good clean water, so sugarhouses often had flat roofs, like the one on the left of the picture, which probably belonged to Robert MacFie & Sons, where water was stored in rooftop tanks. This was useful if the building went on fire, which they sometimes did. In the mid-1820s another major feat of engineering and local investment, known as 'Shaw's Water Scheme', ensured that Greenock had plenty of this vital commodity. Under the direction of Robert Thom (1774–1847), a talented engineer from Rothesay, water was gathered in the hills south of the town and channelled down through a series of sluices and filters for domestic and industrial use. Many of Greenock's industrial plants ran on water-power, a cheaper alternative to steam.[9]

The railway running through the centre of the picture was built as the Glasgow, Paisley, Greenock Railway, which opened in 1841. It was a Greenock-based initiative that rekindled old rivalries as the town made a bid to seize river traffic to Glasgow by offering a quicker, cheaper service by rail for passengers and goods. Glasgow money lay behind the Glasgow to Ayr line, linking Glasgow to the smaller harbours of Ayr and Ardrossan, which hoped to become alternative ports to Greenock.[10] In the event, cheaper, quicker travel greatly increased demand and the amount of business available. In 1851, the Glasgow, Paisley, Greenock Railway was officially amalgamated with the Caledonian Railway Co.

The vignette of the Greenock Customhouse, was painted by the English maritime artist Robert Salmon (1775–1845) in 1820, just two years after its completion. Designed by William Burn, it included the Excise Department, entered by a second great portico on the left-hand side. The position of the Customhouse can also be seen in Carsell's picture. It is the large building on the river at the far end of the smaller East India harbour. Greenock had every reason to celebrate its success with this magnificent piece of civic architecture. Between 1728 and 1822 gross receipts of customs at the port had risen from £15,000 to £263,000. Six years later this figure had jumped to a staggering £455,000.[11]

Carsell's painting presents the ideal of industrial success – a picture of order, space and prosperity. It gives no hint of the rather different picture set out by a local minister in his description of the town in 1840: a huge influx of immigrants from the Highlands and Ireland, who came in search of work, led to a high density of low-grade housing, chronic overcrowding, unsanitary conditions and disease. His portrait of this port town, one of the longest reports in the whole of the *New Statistical Account*, much of it a diatribe lamenting the 'moral contagion' which this influx of immigrants brought with them, echoed the

51a. Robert W. Salmon, *The Custom House, Greenock*, 1822

stinging comment of the radical journalist William Cobbett (1763–1835), though without his humanity: 'pigs in England were better lodged … than the poor in Ireland' – or in parts of Greenock.[12]

Endnotes

1 *NSA*, vii, 426–7.

2 We are indebted to George Woods, Assistant Curator, McLean Museum and Art Gallery, Inverclyde Council, for his advice.

3 R. Murray Smith, *History of Greenock* (Greenock, 1828), 120.

4 *Ibid.*, 23

5 G. Williamson, *Old Greenock from Earliest Times to the Early Part of the 19th Century* (Paisley, 1886), 200–1.

6 *DNB*, Robert Steele.

7 *DNB*, Abram Lyle.

8 D. Bremner, *Industries of Scotland: Their Rise, Progress and Present Condition* (1869; reprinted in a new edition, Trowbridge, 1969), 459–60.

9 *NSA*, vii, 433–8.

10 C. J. A. Robertson, *The Origins of the Scottish Railway System 1722–1844* (Edinburgh, 1983), 142.

11 D. Weir, *History of the Town of Greenock* (Glasgow, 1828), 42.

12 *NSA*, vii, 429–30.

52   Haddington, *c.* 1830s

The name Haddington is of Anglian origin meaning the 'farm associated with Hada', which suggests that there was a habitation there during the period of Anglian settlement in the Lothians around the seventh and eighth centuries AD.[1] The town received burgh status, one of the earliest to do so, during the reign of David I (1124–1153).[2] The historic core of the town comprises two almost parallel streets running east to west, the principal being the High Street, the other now being known as Market Street. It is highly likely that the town was originally laid out around one single public space with rig gardens running behind the houses and that the terraces which separate the High Street and Market Street are a later addition, as found in the mid rows of other burghs. This painting by James Howe (1780–1836) looks west down the tapering Market Street, the view terminated by the townhouse steeple of 1830.[3]

Being at the main centre of a large agricultural hinterland, it is to be expected that Haddington had a lively market and fair. James V (1513–1542) sanctioned a weekly market, and another was subsequently added under Charles I (1625–1649) but this did not last. Most early market activity was held in the High Street with shoes, vegetables, eggs and poultry sold near the market cross located there. However, it is noted that in 1543 trading in salt and meat was forced to move to the 'frier wall', where the fish market was held.[4] Different positions in the west part of the High Street, now Court Street, were set aside for the sale of wheat and beans and of oats and barley.[5] By the 1770s there was a dedicated flesh market to the north, on Newton Port, and this moved to Hardgate before 1820.

The earliest reference to a market cross is in 1425, and it is known that it was of a pre-Reformation form until 1693, when stones were bought for the erection of a new secular one which had a square base with four steps, surmounted by a unicorn. The current monument, with its finial of a grape-eating goat from the burgh arms, was gifted in 1881. In the eighteenth century a tron stood close to the cross,[6] and in the nineteenth century there was a steelyard straight-beam balance in the west end of the High Street.[7] From information contained on maps, it would appear that Market Street received its formal name, and therefore its function, in the relatively recent past, as it is known as Back Street on plans before the Ordnance Survey map of 1853.[8]

In the 1790s it was reported that there were 'two fairs held annually, one in July, and one in October but neither of them are much frequented' although the Friday market was

52. James Howe, *Fair, Haddington, c.* 1830s

'reckoned the greatest in Scotland for all kinds of grain'.[9] It was originally proposed that the townhouse building of 1788 would, 'owing to the great increase of the barley and oat market', contain a purpose-built grain market on its ground floor but this was subsequently abandoned in favour of rooms for sheriff, court and town uses.[10] Haddington's prosperity was reflected in the new architecture of the main streets and wynds of its town centre from 1750 onwards:

> But there is plenty of evidence of the wealth brought in by more efficient farming; not only in the good-quality tenements which are the surest indication that an eighteenth-century burgh was doing well, but in the palace-fronted merchant's houses built alongside them in the narrowest streets – a distinctive Haddington type of which 'Carlyle House' is the oldest and most famous.[11]

While Haddington's grain market was famous, the livestock trade seems to have been more evident in surrounding towns such as Gifford, where a typical market of the late eighteenth century would handle around 500 horses and as many cows.[12]

Although commonly thought to depict the corn market, this painting may actually show another public agricultural event focused in the town, the annual hiring fair. Agricultural improvement, which in Scotland was largely pioneered in East Lothian, involved a reduction in the number of independent farmers and the emergence of a new, mobile agricultural labour force, which was obliged to seek fresh employment each season. Haddington's hiring fair, which was held in early February, saw prospective farm workers gather in Market Street to meet and negotiate terms with employing farmers. The foreground shows a bonneted man with a horse striking a deal with a gentleman, as well as a young man in light clothing being led away by uniformed militia.

Agreements were reached in terms of remuneration, length of engagement, accommodation and the number of 'bondagers' they might bring. Farms rarely employed single men unless they could bring one or more bondagers – women who would help with the spring planting, harvest and other duties. Having no wife or daughters, the single male employees had to engage bondagers out of their own pockets. Understandably, this source of great dissatisfaction and resentment with the system came to a head in the middle of the nineteenth century when the workers met on the East Haugh before marching en masse to Market Street. A large number of contracts were not concluded on that day, and in 1866 the system was abandoned.[13]

During the fair the streets would be very lively indeed. Stalls were set up to provide essentials and the inns, such as the Bay Horse, Rising Sun, Black Bull, Gardeners' Arms and Crown, would be the scene of many a negotiation, transaction, complaint, meeting or farewell. Horse-drawn carts awaited in large numbers to carry the workers and their furniture and wooden kists of personal and household goods to the places which would be their homes for the duration of their employment.[14]

The town enjoyed a number of civic improvements in the second quarter of the nineteenth century. Forestairs and projecting shopfronts were removed and pavements laid from 1826, and the town had its own gas works providing lighting by 1836.[15] In 1831 Haddington was the first place in Scotland to be affected by the cholera asphyxia, resulting in fifty-seven deaths. This was a stimulus to enhanced management of the town centre, including cleansing and, no doubt, more rigorous regulation of markets.

The Haddington hiring fair continued well into the twentieth century, by which time it was a popular event attracting fairground rides, market stalls and live musical shows. The last fair was held in 1925.[16]

Endnotes

1 R. Gourlay and A. Turner, *Historic Haddington: The Archaeological Implications of Development* (Scottish Burgh Survey, 1977), 1.

2 Pryde, *Burghs*, no. 9.

3 For the life of James Howe *see* A. D. Cameron, *The Man who Loved to Draw Horses: James Howe 1780–1836* (Aberdeen, 1986).

4 Gourlay and Turner, *Historic Haddington*, 6.

5 J. Martin, *Reminiscences of the Royal Burgh of Haddington and Old East Lothian Agriculturalists* (Edinburgh, 1883), 70.

6 A. Andrew and A. Mostyn, *Map of the Three Lothians* (Edinburgh, 1773).

7 J. Wood, *Plan of Haddington and Nungate* (Edinburgh, 1819).

8 OS, *Town Plan of Haddington* (1853, Sheet 1).

9 *OSA*, vii, 535.

10 *Tolbooths and Town-houses*, 105.

11 C. McWilliam, *Scottish Townscape* (Glasgow, 1975), 68.

12 *OSA*, vii, 172.

13 Haddington Historical Society, *Haddington Royal Burgh: A History and a Guide* (East Linton, 1997), 56.

14 B. D. Cotton, *Scottish Vernacular Furniture* (London, 2008), 59–65; *Haddington Royal Burgh*, 55–6.

15 Martin, *Reminiscences*, 8–9; *NSA*, vii, 4–5.

16 There are photographs from Haddington hiring fair in the collection of East Lothian Council, viewable via SCRAN at: www.scran.ac.uk/000-000-471-329-C, www.scran.ac.uk/000-000-471-330-C and www.scran.ac.uk/000-000-471-331-C. One view of the fair in Market Street shows that over the decades the event had changed little from that shown in Howe's painting.

53   Hamilton, 1824 and *c.* 1600

Amap is a statement in time. It can tell us neither what has gone before nor what will come in the future. John Wood (*c.* 1780–1847) made a series of such statements between 1819 and 1846. This 1824 plan of Hamilton reveals much. Hamilton Palace, standing in splendid isolation, surrounded by parkland and gardens, is remote from urban settlement and potential squalor. A curving Castle Street/ Wynd and Muir Wynd are lined with occupied burgage plots and a 'Jail' stands prominently in an open area at the junction of the two streets. Leading in a south-westerly direction from the jail is New Wynd, which gives access to Church Street, a thoroughfare scarcely occupied on its more easterly side, culminating, however, at the parish church. Such is the Hamilton of 1824.

Two earlier plans offer challenges to an understanding of the town. Thomas Barns's view of 1781 reveals the main features of Wood's plan, but shows a road called High Toun leading from the open site of the jail towards the palace. An unnamed and regrettably partially destroyed mid-eighteenth-century plan shows this High Toun, or 'Hietoun', as a clearly occupied routeway leading towards the palace and possibly, had it not been damaged, beyond to the Clyde.[1] Possibly a further and the most telling depiction of Hamilton is that executed by Timothy Pont (Pont 34; III.102–3) at the turn of the sixteenth and seventeenth centuries. It shows the High Street passing in front of the palace and the collegiate church, through an east port and beyond to a ferry crossing the Clyde.

From documentary and other sources it becomes clear that from the time that Anne, Duchess of Hamilton (1632–1716) instituted her 'grand design' for the palace and its policies, the town could not but be affected. The common green of the town, where the burgesses grazed their horses, was situated between the palace and the Clyde.[2] There must have been considerable hustle and bustle in front of the palace; and it was perhaps for this reason that the duchess and her husband 'for enlarging of their yeards, and for other conveniences about the palace of Hamilton had taken in the common green of the burgh of Hamilton, extending to two acres thereby'.[3]

Hamilton's collegiate church also stood between the palace and the Clyde. It was to this church that the townspeople came to worship and it was the local school beside it that those children who were lucky enough to be educated attended. The duchess came to an agreement with the town council that, as long as she replaced the school, the old

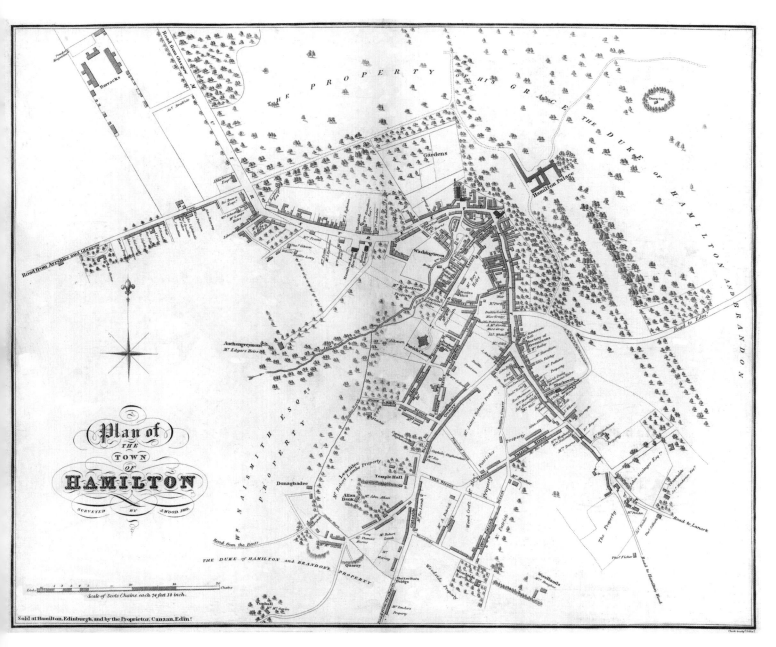

53. John Wood, *Plan of Hamilton*, 1824

one might be demolished 'for her conveniency' since it was 'near to her grace's gardens'.[4] Wood's map shows the site of the new school, at the end of New Wynd, where the pupils doubtless proved less of an irritant to the palace occupants.

Duchess Anne's grandson succeeded her as 5th Duke of Hamilton (1703–1743). It was clear that he intended to follow his grandmother's policy of purchasing land and properties near to the palace and clearing the environs. In 1732 a new parish church (still standing) was built to a design of William Adam (1689–1748). It stood outwith the settlement and was initially approached by a path only a yard wide. The old collegiate church was demolished, although one transept was left standing until the nineteenth century (when the present mausoleum was built) as it was the burial place of the dukes of Hamilton.

53a. Timothy Pont, *Hamilton*, 1590s

The death knell for the Hamilton ferry passage was the building of the Clyde Bridge, and in 1781 the last ferry boats were put up to roup.[5] So ended one of the town's early *raisons d'être* and an important historic phase in its life. Further major changes came with the arrival of John Burrell, the agriculturist, placed in charge of the Hamilton estates. Burrell's journal in 1788 tells of ongoing 'trenching and digging out the founds of the seats of the old houses'. In 1795 it records much fencing, a young plantation at the old boathouse and the following year potatoes being grown in the now disused boathouse. The most telling entry was dated 2 June 1797: posts, boards and lettering were obtained for three notices 'against trespassing within the policy'.[6] The policy of successive dukes of Hamilton of consolidating their estates and removing townspeople from their doorstep had proved highly effective.

The townspeople were persuaded in 1812 to accept a new, improved, albeit longer, route to the bridge. The 9th duke thus became the proprietor of the old public way to the ferry. The few remaining buildings left in the Hietoun were demolished and a gate was placed across it, barring access. All that was left was the old tolbooth, or jail, as Wood calls it.[7] As a postscript to Wood's map, even the rump of this would be sold in 1846 to the current duke since the council had 'always been desirous of accommodating his grace'.[8] The doors and windows of Muir Wynd and Castle Wynd were blocked with stone. Only the old entrance to the Hietoun remained as a reminder of this important old township. One morning the townspeople woke to find that that, too, was walled up. The 'Hietoun' had gone.[9]

Endnotes

1 Both the possessions of His Grace the Duke of Hamilton.

2 MS Charter, 23 October 1475, in the keeping of Hamilton District Museum.

3 MS Hamilton Burgh Records, 1642–1699, 22 August 1695; E. P. Dennison Torrie and R. Coleman, *Historic Hamilton: The Archaeological Implications of Development* (Scottish Burgh Survey, 1996), 25–6.

4 Typescript. Hamilton Burgh Records by A. G. Miller (R108.L352, Hamilton District Library), 17–18.

5 A. G. Miller, *Municipal Hamilton* (n.p., n.d.), 13.

6 Duchy of Hamilton Estate Papers on Loan to Hamilton District Library, Journal of John Burrell, 1787–90, 5; 1793–96, 13; 1787–90, 125; 1793–96, 108, 1796–7, 34, 141.

7 Dennison Torrie and Coleman, *Historic Hamilton*, 56–7, 62.

8 *Ibid.*, 35.

9 Miller, *Municipal Hamilton*, 30–1. Remnants of the 'Hietoun' were to survive into the twentieth century, partly because the palace complex site had become the town's rubbish dump in the post-war years after 1945. This partially protected the remnants, in spite of nineteenth-century landscaping and the insertion of modern roads, especially the M74 motorway. Some medieval remains were found by archaeological excavation and test pits in 1995.

54   Inveraray, *c.* 1747 and 1747–55

The first settlement of Inveraray comprised a few fishermen's huts at the convenient crossing point and mouth of the River Aray where it enters Loch Fyne. There was safe anchorage and the Aray Glen acted as a trade route with the hinterland. The site attracted a fortified house around 1432, which became the seat of Colin Campbell, 2nd Lord Campbell (*c.* 1433–1493), created 1st Earl of Argyll in 1457. Further growth came as the town developed as a ferry point.[1] The town was made a burgh of barony in 1474 and a royal burgh in 1648.[2] It developed as a base for the herring fishing which operated from July to January and attracted a considerable number of boats. Writing in 1769, Thomas Pennant (1726–1798) noted:

> But the busy scene of the herring fishery gave no small improvement to the magnificent environs of Inveraray. Every evening some hundreds of boats in a manner, covered the surface of Loch Fyne an arm of the sea, which, from its narrowness and from the winding of its shores, has all the beauties of a fresh water lake; on the week-days, the cheerful noise of the bagpipe and dance echoes from on board; on the Sabbath, each boat approaches the land, and psalmody and devotion divide the day.[3]

The town was laid waste by the Marquis of Montrose, scourge of the Campbells, in 1644 when houses were burned and the church partially destroyed, after which it was largely rebuilt along the lines drawn here. The view by Paul Sandby (1731–1809) must have been drawn shortly after he took up a post with the Board of Ordnance as a surveyor in the military survey of Scotland. It shows the central core of the town, which consisted of a market square adjacent to which were the principal buildings, including the castle which comprised two towers with a courtyard, offices, stable and coach houses. This is backed by Roy's map of much the same date and by estate plans which show the core surrounded by a huddle of buildings.[4] The most important and substantial, slate-roofed houses were by the cross and bridge over the river; the lower, thatched ones associated with the fisher community were by the river mouth and along the shore. The buildings as depicted, and the gentry gracing the scene, are clearly carefully selected by the artist to make a good impression, as they contrast sharply with contemporary descriptions of the town.

The three central features of Old Inveraray were the castle, tolbooth and market cross. The duke had tried to improve the outlook to and from the castle: in 1722 he

54. Paul Sandby, *Prospect of Duniquich and Old Castle of Inveraray from the Market Place*, c. 1747

ordered all houses 'above Widow Clerk's' to be demolished to make an avenue to improve its view.[5] This was urban clearance as yet on a minor scale compared with that inflicted on Dalkeith (15) and Hamilton (53). The castle, however, proved to be beyond repair and, within a few years, was used only for storage and housing servants. The duke used the pavilion, built *c.* 1720–1, as a temporary residence. The foundation stone for a new castle was laid in 1746. The old town is also recorded in a painting by John Clerk of Eldin, completed *c.* 1760. It shows both the old castle (with the pavilion) and the new one, by now completed.[6]

The tolbooth, built *c.* 1650, comprised a wing attached to the parish church and was used as a court and prison, although it was long deemed inadequate as major trials were held in the parish church.[7] The town cross, of much the same date and erected on a pilastered stone plinth, was a recycled monolith of ecclesiastical origin which had originally been the monument of nobleman Duncan MacCowan or MacGille-Chomgáin. Although tradition said it came from Iona or Southend, Kintyre, it almost certainly came from the collection of late medieval stones at the churchyard of Kilmalieu.[8] The carving suffered post-Reformation mutilation, removing a crucifix and other figures, one of which may have depicted St Michael the Archangel, one of the two saints whose feast days were celebrated by fairs. There was a public well close to the cross, and there was a midden between the cross and the tolbooth, which from time to time required to be made 'clean and redd' and overlaid with sand and gravel.[9] It escaped Sandby's attention.

54a. William Roy, *Inveraray Town, Military Survey of Scotland, 1747–55*

With selective urban clearance having failed, the more drastic concept of a replacement new town emerged in the mind of Archibald, 3rd Duke of Argyll (1688–1761) in the 1740s. In 1750 the common town muir was brought into the duke's policies, forcing residents to pasture their cattle at the farm of Auchenbreck. Houses were allowed to fall into disrepair, and summons for removal were raised against a number of inhabitants. Progress in removing residents was slow, and orders had to be enforced throughout the 1750s. There was considerable demolition during the 1770s, and most houses had been taken down and the market cross removed by 1776.[10] As might be expected, there was a drop in population of a third between 1750 and 1800.[11] Inveraray was therefore one of a small number of Scottish 'transplanted towns', whereby an existing burgh was moved to a new site; others included Cullen, Fochabers, Scone and Preston in East Lothian.[12] Sandby's view, as a result, is a valuable record of a historic town immediately before its planned destruction.[13]

The new Inveraray was slow to emerge. Pennant was unsympathetic as to the plight of the displaced inhabitants of the Old Inveraray:

> Near the new castle are some remains of the old. This place will in time be very magnificent: but at present the space between the front and the water is disgraced with the old town, composed of the most wretched hovels that can be imagined. The founder of the castle designed to have built a new town on the west side of the little bay the house stands on: he finished a few houses, a custom-house and an excellent inn: his death interrupted the completion of the plan, which, when brought to perfection will give the place a very different appearance to what it now bears.[14]

The power of the dukes of Argyll gave the new town fame greater than its modest size would otherwise have deserved.[15] This, combined with the undoubted beauty of its setting, attracted other artists. Jean Claude Nattes (*c.* 1765–1839) drew the *Port of Inverary* in 1799 and noted that 'the Old Town is now nearly deserted, and the inhabitants have removed to a new one'.[16] And it was two years later that Alexander Nasmyth (1758–1840) produced his exquisite *Inverary from the Sea* (1801), which eschewed the old town and placed the new within a wider cultural landscape.

Endnotes

1 A. Fraser, *The Royal Burgh of Inveraray* (Edinburgh, 1997).

2 Pryde, *Burghs*, nos 79, 151.

3 T. Pennant, *A Tour of Scotland, 1769* (London, 1771), 239.

4 *Military Survey of Scotland, 1747–1755*; I. G. Lindsay and M. Cosh, *Inveraray and the Dukes of Argyll* (Edinburgh, 1973), 23; *see ibid.*, 28, for a *Plan of Policies and Old Town of Inveraray* (*c.* 1722).

5 Letter from John Campbell to John Campbell, younger, of Barcaldine, 1722, NAS, GD 70/1013/1 (Canmore 23349: Old Inverary Castle).

6 Clerk of Eldin's painting is reproduced in Lindsay and Cosh, *Inveraray*, 182, 258, and 389, n. 1.

7 *Tolbooths and Town-houses*, 106.

8 A. Steer and J. W. M. Bannerman, *Late Medieval Monumental Sculpture in the West Highlands* (Edinburgh, 1977), 35, 141.

9 Fraser, *Inveraray*, 26.

10 *Ibid.*, 41.

11 *OSA*, v, 292–3.

12 C. McWilliam, *Scottish Townscape* (London, 1975), 91.

13 A reconstructed plan of Old Inveraray, a 'compact classical small town', has been devised in R. J. Naismith, *The Story of Scotland's Towns* (Edinburgh, 1989), 92.

14 Pennant, *Tour of Scotland*, 238–9.

15 E. A. Beaton and S. W. MacIntyre, *The Burgesses of Inveraray, 1665–1963* (SRS, 1990), p. i.

16 J. Nattes, *Scotia Depicta* (London, 1804), plate 18.

55   Inverkeithing, 1870

Inverkeithing was founded between 1153 and 1162 as a market, its strategically positioned and sheltered harbour in a bay on the north bank of River Forth having been recognised as highly suited to trade. The painting by a local artist, David Buchan Young (1830–1920), shows part of the principal public space, a long, wide and almost rectangular area, with the High Street running north away from the viewer into Church Street. To the right, Bank Street leads down to the harbour and it is to here that the fine market cross was moved from an earlier position outside the tolbooth. As with other burghs of the east coast, the main town was laid out separately from the working harbour: 'Inverkeithing is pleasantly situated on a rising ground above the bay of the harbour; it consists of one street, with another smaller turning off near the middle, besides some wynds.'[1] As in the burgh of Crail in east Fife, the original central market place was vast. This indicates the commercial status of the burgh, which enjoyed exclusive trading rights between the waters of the Leven and Devon, granted by William the Lion (1165–1214) and ratified by his successors in 1223 and 1259, although in reality overlapping jurisdictions often lead to dispute.[2]

The tolbooth, which today is separate from the market square, is located behind the group of buildings in the centre of the painting. This was the result of 'market repletion', whereby parts of such public open space were appropriated to make space for building blocks. The same may be found in other burghs, such as Dunbar (20), Haddington (52), and Montrose (73).

The original route to the harbour was directly from the market square, and the commercial importance of Inverkeithing and its vulnerability to attack by sea led to the ordinance that it be walled for protection. In 1503 a law was enacted which required 'that all tounis and portis on the sey side, sik as Leth, Inverkethin, Kinghorne, Disert, Crail and otheris, was spend their commone gudis one the wallis of thair toune to the sey side with portis of lyme and stane'.[3] Also, in February 1557, the inhabitants of the town were charged 'to big dikes and fowseis and to have stafe slungis in the reddiness to the portis thairof'.[4] Although the town's walls and four ports were removed in the sixteenth century,[5] elements were still apparent in the early eighteenth century as Defoe described Inverkeithing, probably during his tour of 1706, as 'an ancient walled town'. Sir Thomas Cave, who made a tour through Scotland in 1763, wrote of the 'little town

55. David Buchan Young, *Inverkeithing High Street*, 1870

of Inverkeithing, once walled round (gates still standing) as all these coast-towns have anciently been'.[6] Some existing fragments of early wall are, in all probability, surviving portions from the early defences.[7]

The tall building in the foreground left is Gala Tower or Gala Hall. Built on the site of a 'large and ruinous tenement' acquired by Henry Kinglassie in 1611, it carried a gable dated 1612, the year of its restoration.[8] The house shows the common arrangement of a projecting stair tower, the upper storey of which contained a room approached by a small corbelled turret. Also, there was an arcade running along its front, as evidenced by remains of an arch surviving against the wall of the tower.[9] In an angle of the tower, above the door, was a small niche for a figure, which, it has been suggested, would point to the building being of pre-Reformation date.[10]

The low building adjacent displays a balustraded forestair and first-floor entrance, a common feature in Inverkeithing and other Fife coastal towns. Just beyond are the first manifestations of the late nineteenth-century redevelopment of the town in the new ashlar tenement providing spacious flatted accommodation and purpose-built shops.

On the right is the harled and pantiled Providence House of 1688 which takes its name from the inscription on the moulding above the door, 'GODS PROVIDENCE IS MY INHERITANCE'. This was built for Isobel Bairdie, who had been granted permission from the town council to project the west wall into the street nine feet beyond the original line of frontage.[11] The merchant's house to its right has an arched entrance accessed by a forestair and a projecting slated gable front of timber construction. Built in 1664, it contained a fine stone staircase and Dutch overmantel paintings.[12] In the distance is the squat fourteenth-century tower (and sixteenth-century century parapets) of the parish church, with its spire added in 1835.

The late Georgian or early Victorian house which is the central focus of the painting is clearly of some importance on account of its elegant façade, solid construction, architectural door surround and dressed stone quoins. All other buildings are shown as neatly, if modestly, constructed. Most façades appear to be harled and lime-washed in the Fife manner, and all roofs are of pantile or slate, the once common thatch long abandoned. Inverkeithing's status was reflected in many other good buildings not shown, including its friary, tolbooth, town-houses and residences of burgesses.

The view shows a clear separation between carriageway and the generous pavements. Trees have been recently planted and there are iron streetlights on stone bases. These were subsequently adapted to carry gas supply pipes before new cast-iron columns lit by gas were introduced in the late nineteenth century. In comparison to the elaborate facilities shown in other paintings, the nineteenth-century public water supply was by modest standpipes. Most burghs had at least one principal public well and it is possible that there was another not shown in this picture.

Unlike Alexander Milne's painting of Montrose (73), the inhabitants are anonymous and are recorded simply going about their daily business. However, the ambience of the town as painted is reflected in the words of 1870 that describe it as 'an old-fashioned, sleepy looking place with quaint gables and red-tiled houses'.[13]

Endnotes

1   *OSA*, x, 501.

2   Pryde, *Burghs*, nos 19, 92.

3   *APS*, ii, 243; quoted in C. McWilliam, *Scottish Townscape* (Glasgow, 1975), 36.

4   *TA*, x, 336. 'Stafe slungis' were a kind of catapult.

5   G. L. Pride, *The Kingdom of Fife: An Illustrated Architectural Guide* (2nd edn, Edinburgh, 1999), 34.

6   T. Cave, 'A diary of a journey from Stanford Hall to the North of Scotland and back in the year 1763', in C. Holme (ed.), *A History of the Midland Counties* (Rugby, 1891), 183–241.

7   A. T. Simpson and S. Stevenson, *Historic Inverkeithing: The Archaeological Implications of Development* (Scottish Burgh Survey, 1981), 6–7, 18.

8   W. Stephen, *History of Inverkeithing and Rosyth* (Aberdeen, 1921), 36–7, which has an illustration of Gala Tower.

9   MacGibbon and Ross, *Castellated and Domestic Architecture*, v, 29. Fig. 1129 shows a public well outside the building.

10 *Ibid.*, v, 30–1.

11 Stephen, *Inverkeithing*, 38.

12 *Ibid.*, 39, 40. *See also* MacGibbon and Ross, *Castellated and Domestic Architecture*, v, 31, fig. 1134. The building was demolished in 1888.

13 Groome, *Gazetteer*, iv, 298.

56   Inverness or Fort William, *c.* 1747

This scene of a Highland market is taken from one of a pair of sketchbooks acquired by the National Galleries of Scotland in the 1990s.[1] They have been attributed to Paul Sandby (1731–1809), although others are also thought to have contributed.[2] What makes these sketchbooks and this market scene so valuable is the scarcity of pictures of Highland life up to this period.

One of the few written accounts in a dearth of such sources is *Burt's Letters from the North of Scotland*. Though published anonymously in book form in London in 1754, the writer, Captain Edmund Burt (d. 1755), was revealed as the author after his death.[3] Burt, an officer of engineers, was sent north following the defeat of an earlier Jacobite revolt in 1715. He may have been involved in the construction of Wade's Roads, an operation led by General George Wade (1673–1748) to open up the Highlands by building some of the first roads and bridges seen in the region. Mostly written between 1727 and 1728 to satisfy the curiosity of a London friend and to while away his free time, Burt's letters offer a wealth of previously unrecorded detail. His illustrations, though few, are informative but crude compared to Sandby's.

The twenty-six-year-old Sandby was sent to Scotland as official draughtsman to the military survey being carried out by the Board of Ordnance. Following the defeat of the Jacobite rebellion in 1746, mapping the Highlands and gathering much-needed strategic information were seen as crucial to effective government. In charge of the military survey was Lieutenant-Colonel David Watson (*c.* 1713–1761), an ambitious Lowland Scot whose pro-Union background and anti-Highland prejudices may well have influenced the young Sandby. It is remarkable that this valuable material on Highland life in the mid-eighteenth century should have been supplied by two Englishmen to whom the region was primitive, dangerous and like an alien land; at best, an anachronism perched on the edge of an otherwise civilised and rapidly modernising British state.

From what is known of Sandby's movements, this market scene can reasonably be placed in either Inverness or Fort William, which had been renamed after William III & II (1689–1702) in the 1690s, and was also known as Maryburgh.[4] Both were towns serving a wild hinterland in a region where few urban settlements existed. Both were sea ports where goods, including luxury items, could be found and both were garrison towns for the army of occupation, here represented by the soldier in the background. Sandby

56. Paul Sandby, *Highland market scene, c.* 1747.
Attributed to Paul Sandby, 'Sketchbook of Drawings Made in the Highlands'

and Burt were known to have spent time in each location. Like all towns, regular markets would have been held for the sale of local produce, mostly foodstuffs. Inverness also held several fairs throughout the year. All such trading had to be transacted within the town and was subject to local taxes and strict rules. These were enforced by magistrates and burgesses, but discord was not uncommon.

Here, the woman with her back to us appears to be making an accusation against the man beside her. She has a lamb, or perhaps a kid, strapped to her back. It is stretched on a gamrel, a wooden spar used to separate the legs of a carcass for butchering. The barefoot woman would not have been an unusual sight; many Highlanders went barefoot in all weathers. Men who wore brogues, a sort of flat pump, often had holes cut in them to allow water to drain out.[5] The highlander in the accompnaying vignette from Sandby's sketchbook is also barefoot. The artist has written 'Gillee wet feit' or 'Errand-Runner' beneath. This comes from the Gaelic term gille cas-fliuch, the chief's personal messenger who was not only expected to be a fast runner but also to carry his master across rivers when necessary.[6]

56a. Paul Sandby, *Gillie wet feit*.
Attributed to Paul Sandby, 'Sketchbook of Drawings Made in the Highlands'

The scene in the market shows creels, woven baskets of varying shapes, being used to carry goods and also as containers from which to sell them. One man has a creel strapped to his back while a woman is bent almost double under the weight of another. People, particularly women according to Burt, were forced to carry large loads because of the difficult terrain. Even the smallest wheeled carts were uncommon. Goods that were not carried were attached to two poles that could be pulled by people or horses.

Hay for horses was often in short supply. Burt records buying a few pence worth at the haymarket in Fort William from women who had made it 'from Grass cut with a Knife by the Way-side'. These women filled their creels with horse dung before returning home to spread it on the fields by hand.[7] He also tells us that, when wet, flat bonnets like that being worn by the man with the creel, were 'frequently taken off, and wrung like a Dish-Clout, and then put on again'.[8] Burt also gives a detailed description of the plaid worn by many Highlanders, presumably because of its novelty. When it comes to the 'Gentlemen, Magistrates, Merchants, and Shop-keepers', he says simply that they were 'dressed after the English Manner'.[9] Perhaps the burly man trying to sort out the dispute is a town magistrate and the other a merchant or shopkeeper.

'Shopkeeper' is an interesting term because there were no shops as would now be understood, and retailing, once illegal, was still viewed with suspicion. Burt writes about 'the Warehouse' in Inverness: 'a Shop up a Pair of Stairs, which is kept by three or four Merchants in Partnership, and that is pretty well stored with various Sorts of small Goods and Wares, mostly from London'.[10] Ships left Inverness carrying exports such as fish, meat and skins and returned with goods such as timber, iron, window glass, soap, writing-paper, cloves, tea, sugar, lemons, wine and coffee.[11]

Sandby's market scene gives a sense of the poverty and barbarity that are recurring themes in Burt's letters. The 'meanest' soldier, according to Burt, was not used to the conditions they faced quartered in the houses of Inverness which 'would hardly be thought good enough for a favourite Dog'.[12] The soldier in this scene is a reminder of the military presence that dominated life in the Highlands after the Jacobite Risings. A more positive note on this aspect of Highland life is recorded in the *Statistical Account* for Inverness in the 1790s in which the local minister claimed that the money circulated by the soldiers revitalised a stagnant economy and brought prosperity to the region.[13]

Endnotes

1 We are indebted to Hugh Cheape for his helpful comments on the text.

2 J. Bonehill and S. Daniels, *Paul Sandby: Picturing Britain* (London, 2009), 79.

3 *DNB*, Edmund Burt.

4 Pryde, *Burghs*, no. 303. Fort William or Maryburgh had originally been called Gordonsburgh when erected as a burgh of barony in 1618.

5 *Burt's Letters from the North of Scotland* (London 1754; reprinted Edinburgh, 1974), ii, 135.

6 H. Cheape, *Notes on Sketch Books*, 18 September 1992.

7 Burt, *Letters*, ii, 152–3.

8 *Ibid.*, ii, 121.

9 *Ibid.*, i, 86.

10 *Ibid.*, i, 66.

11 W. Mackay (ed.), *Selections from the Letter Books of John Steuart, Baillie of Inverness, 1715–52* (SHS, 1915), pp. xvi–xxii.

12 Burt, *Letters*, i, 172.

13 *OSA*, ix, 617.

57   Inverness, *c.* 1840

Nothing is known of William Fraser, the artist of this charming view of Inverness. It is so appealing that it might have come out of an 1840s' tourist brochure of the town. Hotel guest lists show that Inverness, the acknowledged capital of the Highlands, had become a popular base for those touring the region.[1] Indeed, a contemporary travel guide claimed that 'for elegance and comfort' the town's inns were 'nowhere surpassed in Scotland'.[2] The long, pink building on the riverbank, with high arches, housed the stables of the Caledonian Hotel. The man standing in the river near the end of the slipway could well have come from there to wash down a pair of travel-stained horses.

Tourism was a recent phenomenon for Inverness. As early as the fourteenth century the Lowland historian, John of Fordun, described Highlanders as those 'wild caterans across the mountains'.[3] It was a widely held view of the Highlander that was encouraged by distance, culture and the power struggles that beset the region. Much of this fighting had centred on Inverness, culminating in the final defeat of the Jacobite forces in 1746 at Culloden, on the outskirts of the town. It was only after this major rebellion had been crushed that the government set about pacifying this remote corner of Britain once and for all. The tranquillity of this scene illustrates that this policy, though brutal, had been effective. The artist shows us an Inverness that has been transformed from rebel base to peaceful British market town.

One legacy of the rebellion was the destruction of the castle at Inverness, so it was a gala day in 1834 when a grand masonic procession marched up the hill to lay the foundation stone of the new castle in the centre of the picture. It was not the fort its predecessors had been, but a new County Buildings and Court House. The domed white building to the right, built at the same time, was the United Charities School, dedicated to the welfare of women and young children. The fact that it included an observatory and was also a place where clothes and blankets were distributed to the poor underlines its combined educational and charitable aims.[4] These institutions marked a new era in local government in Inverness, similar to other regional centres in Britain.

The handsome toll bridge in the centre of the picture was built in 1685. It contained a small, dark vault between two of the arches for criminals awaiting trial. Later, it was used to confine lunatics. Conditions in the replacement jail below the spire to the left of the

57. William Fraser, *A View of Inverness, c.* 1840

bridge were such that one prisoner complained: 'he was so ill-fed, and that the prison was so weak ... That if he did not get more meat he would not stay in another hour'. He carried out his threat but was recaptured.[5] By the time this picture was painted, plans had already been approved for a new prison that would incorporate the latest ideas on prison reform. A space had been left for it adjoining the County Court buildings. In 1849, shortly after the new prison was completed, the bridge and its dark vault were swept away in a great flood when the River Ness burst its banks.

57a. Felice Piccioni, *Roman Catholic Church, Inverness, c.* 1834

The accompanying vignette of the Roman Catholic church in Huntly Street, drawn by Felice Piccioni (fl. 1831–1870s) (*see* 60), shows that the river normally provided a living for salmon fishermen, here seen dragging a net stretched between the men on the bank and a rowing boat on the water. The same technique is being used in the main picture.

The two soldiers talking on the quayside are further evidence of integration and patriotism. A century earlier, government forces in Inverness had been part of an army of occupation, punishing rebellious Highlanders and subduing the region. By 1840, Highland regiments had come to be seen as some of the best in the British army. Raising Highland regiments was one way local lairds could demonstrate their loyalty to the crown. Of the 9,000 people living in Inverness in 1841, nearly 5,000 were women while less than 4,000 were men, a disparity that can be explained by men absent on military service. It is interesting to note that one of these soldiers is wearing tartan. From 1747 till 1782 tartan had been proscribed because it was seen as a Jacobite 'uniform'. Now it could be worn again without being considered a threat.

The fortified house between the two steeples is difficult to identify. Apart from its great height, it resembles Abertarff House, once a townhouse of the local lairds, the Frasers of Lovat. Condemned as one of the ringleaders of the 1745 Jacobite rebellion, the last Lord Lovat (1667/8–1747) had been executed for treason and his estates forfeited. Having raised the Fraser Highlanders, who rendered great service to the crown in North America, Major General Simon Fraser (1726–1782), master of Lovat, was granted his father's estates in 1774, although he had to pay nearly £21,000 for the privilege and the title was not revived until 1837.[6] The artist, William Fraser, may have practised artistic licence to emphasise the Fraser family's position in this peaceful, patriotic town.

The great changes that had taken place in the town were summed up in 1834 by George and Peter Anderson of Inverness, who wrote a popular guide to the Highlands at this time. In it, they recalled that:

> so late as the period of the Disarming Act (1746), men in all parts of the Highlands appeared on Sundays as if fully accoutred for war; and, seventy years ago, only three ladies with straw bonnets were to be seen in the High Church of Inverness.

However, they go on to say that 'now, no distinctions can be perceived in the dress, manners, or modes of living of the inhabitants of the burgh from those of other towns in Scotland'.[7] As in William Fraser's portrayal of it in art, they perceived the new Inverness to be a model regional capital.

Endnotes

1 *Inverness Courier*, published weekly.

2 G. and P. Anderson, *Guide to the Highlands and Islands of Scotland including Orkney and Zetland* (3rd edn, Edinburgh, 1851), 220.

3 D. E. R. Watt (ed.), W. Bower, *Scotichronicon* (Edinburgh, 1996), vii, 359.

4 *NSA*, xiv, 16.

5 J. G. Fyfe, *Scottish Dairies and Memoirs, 1746–1843* (Stirling, 1942), 382.

6 *DNB*, Simon Fraser.

7 G. and P. Anderson, *Guide to the Highlands and Islands of Scotland* (1st edn, Edinburgh, 1834), 219.

58   Inverurie, *c.* 1850s, 1810 and 1796

Tucked between the rivers Don and Urie, the twelfth-century burgh of Inverurie emerged from relative obscurity at the turn of the nineteenth century to become one of Aberdeenshire's leading towns.[1] The building that dominates this lithograph by James Cassie (1818–1879) is the town hall, built in 1807 to mark the town's recent growth and newly acquired commercial success. Progress was such, however, that this rather charming building was demolished within sixty years to be replaced by a much larger, more impressive town hall, one more in keeping with the numerous 'fine shops and private houses'[2] that by then enhanced the burgh.

The town's first purpose-built tolbooth, with a prison on the ground floor and a council chamber above, was built about 1600.[3] There is no record of any other townhouse until 1804 when the 'decayed state and small accommodation' of the old thatched building prompted the construction of this townhouse. The site chosen 'on the Green or Market Place' was at the opposite end of the High Street from the old tolbooth, which still stood beside the church and the cross.[4] Clearly the nucleus was shifting to this larger open square as the town grew.

The growth of Inverurie began with the bridging of the Don in 1791. At that time the population was 360.[5] By 1841 it had jumped to 1,619,[6] an increase that can also be linked to other changes in the local infrastructure. A turnpike road from Aberdeen reached Inverurie in 1800, and the stretch from Inverurie to Huntly was finished in 1804, the year that Inverurie decided to build this new townhouse. Three years later, the opening of the townhouse coincided with the completion of the Aberdeen to Inverurie canal, which put the seal on the town as a centre of trade and distribution at the heart of the Garioch, a region rapidly embracing all the latest agricultural techniques.

The canal, which cost £44,000, was not an unqualified success but did offer the means to transport heavy goods to and from Aberdeen. Cargoes included building materials, fertilisers, grain, coal, wood and, of course, granite. To avoid the problem of crossing the Don, the canal stopped just short of Inverurie at Port Elphinstone, named after Sir Robert Elphinstone, an enthusiastic supporter of the project. 'The Inverury Port', as the local minister described it in 1841, was 'a scene not unlike the quays at Aberdeen', with cart numbers daily running into the hundreds.[7]

58. James Cassie, *Inverurie Town Hall*, c. 1850s

In the vignette, two horses are pulling a barge along the canal with the twin spires of St Machar's Cathedral, Aberdeen, behind. When canal mania gave way to railway mania, the canal was sold to the Great North of Scotland Railway for £36,000. The first turf of the Aberdeen to Huntly line was cut with great ceremony in 1852 on the estate of Great North chairman, Sir James Elphinstone. As far as Inverurie the track followed much the same course as the old canal, in places even on top of it. From the start, The Great North of Scotland Railway was fully fitted with electric telegraph, putting it ahead of its rivals.[8]

58a. Canal barge being puled along the Aberdeenshire Canal

It is difficult to be precise about the particular event captured in Cassie's picture but it provides a unique glimpse of the townhouse built in 1807, which is otherwise unrecorded. What is certain is that the people of Inverurie knew how to celebrate each landmark in their town's rise to prominence. This scene with the fluttering flags, the large crowd of smartly dressed onlookers and the immaculately turned-out schoolchildren, girls on one side, boys on the other, is all about that civic pride, though less about reality. The only urchin in sight is the little dog escaping to find fun elsewhere.

Such occasions were regularly the subject of graphic reports in *The Aberdeen Journal*. Had photography been further advanced, the paper could have saved numerous column inches by catching the spirit of such events in an image like this.

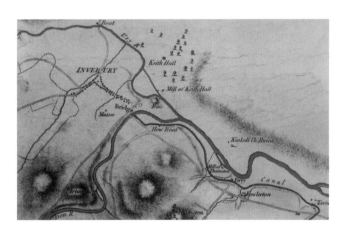

58b. *The Extended Navigable Channel from the Harbour of Aberdeen to the Bridge over the River Don at Inverury, 1796*

Although these articles were headed 'Inverury', it was no misprint. The present spelling, adopted to avoid regular misdirection of mail to Inveraray, did not come into effect until 1866.[9]

When Queen Victoria visited Inverurie in 1857, two triumphal arches were constructed to celebrate the occasion. The Queen was greeted outside the Kintore Arms, where a change of horses had been arranged. Here a particularly 'handsome portico' of 'flowers and evergreens' had been designed,[10] not unlike the one decorating the door of the town hall in the picture.

The carriage at the foot of the steps may be carrying local dignitaries, such as the Earl of Kintore, especially after his marriage to his cousin, Madeline Hawkins, in 1851 and the birth of a son and heir, given the title of Lord Inverury. Their popularity owed much to their family's support for the town and its improvements. It was on their estate of Keithhall, just outside Inverurie, that James Cassie was born and brought up. This scene, an unusual subject for Cassie, most of whose work lay in portraits, seascapes and animal painting, may have been specially commissioned because of his local connection. Cassie, a pupil of James Giles (*see* 17a) went on to become an associate of the Royal Scottish Academy and moved to Edinburgh.[11]

The attached plan by J. Cary is dated 1796. It was drawn to show the proposed route of the canal from 'The Harbour of Aberdeen to the Bridge of the River Don at Inverury'. The section reproduced here shows the town nestled between its two rivers, the bridge that marked the end of the canal where Port Elphinstone would develop and the triangular market place in the town centre where the new town hall would be built

This town hall hosted many civic banquets to celebrate Inverurie's new and improved services and amenities. In the fashion of the day, they included numerous toasts to the council and burgesses of Inverurie, landowners, local MPs and the 'agricultural interest' around the town.[12] Yet what sounds like an over-abundance of mutual congratulation was arguably well deserved. Like other successful towns at that time, it was local people, not government, who battled to raise the necessary funds and risked their money to improve the commercial viability and infrastructure of Inverurie.[13]

Endnotes

1 Pryde, *Burghs*, nos 30, 93.

2 *The Aberdeen Journal*, 15 July 1863.

3 *Tolbooths and Town-houses*, 204.

4 *The Aberdeen Journal*, 15 July 1863.

5 *OSA*, vii, 334.

6 *NSA*, xii, 683.

7 *Ibid.*, xii, 683.

8 M. Barclay-Harvey, *A History of the Great North of Scotland Railway* (London, 1998), 16.

9 S. Wood, *The Shaping of Nineteenth-century Aberdeenshire* (Gateshead, 1985), 283 n. 1.

10 *The Aberdeen Journal*, 14 and 21 October 1857.

11 *DNB*, James Cassie.

12 *The Aberdeen Journal*, 15 July 1863.

13 We are indebted to Dr David Bertie, Curatorial Officer, Documentation and Conservation (Aberdeenshire) for his advice.

59 Jedburgh, 1800

The origins of this town are to be found in the settlements by the Jed Water established by Bishop Ecgred of Lindisfarne around 830 AD. In 1138 King David I (1124–53) invited Augustinian canons from Beauvais in France to settle in the town, and by 1154 the status of the priory had been raised to that of an abbey.[1] The town had become a burgh by about 1165.[2] By the Middle Ages it was known as Jedworth and it is still known locally as Jeddart.

Its location close to the border with England gave it a strategic significance but also ensured that it was subject to repeated attack, capture and deliberate damage, which limited its development and affected its lay-out and appearance. In this painting by Thomas Girtin (1775–1802), the image gives the view of the visitor to the town arriving from the south. It is painted from the location of the former royal castle, which had existed since at least the twelfth century and had helped to protect the town from southern attack and provide a base for exerting control over southern Scotland. This complex was demolished early in the fifteenth century and, by the time of the painting, the site was a mound of grass and trees with some residual masonry, which served as the site of the town gallows.[3] One of the town ports had also been here.

The earlier houses were almost certainly of wood and thatch which explains why their walls had to be rebuilt in 1288, after a winter storm, and why the place was so easily burned in 1410, 1416, 1464 and 1523. In 1523 it was claimed that its size rivalled that of Berwick-upon-Tweed, but six good towers had been taken down and the town was 'so burnt that it must be rebuilt before new garrisons are lodged there'. The town recovered only to be burned again by the English in 1544.[4] The abbey, which also suffered, was ruinous by the mid-sixteenth century and its associated activities withered away after the Reformation of 1560.

While the Union of the Crowns in 1603 brought stability and some increase in trade, the economy of the town suffered after the Union of the Parliaments in 1707, when punitive taxes saw a decline in traditional local industries such as tanning and brewing. By the middle of the eighteenth century it was in a state of poverty, and financial assistance had to be sought. In the mid-1780s the population of the town was recorded as 2,000 but falling, a situation which still prevailed at the time of painting and contributed to its neglected appearance:

59. Thomas Girtin, *The Village of Jedburgh, Roxburgh,* 1800

The vestiges of uninhabited houses are to be seen both in the town and country. This decrease is partly to be attributed to the Union between the two kingdoms, by which the trade of Jedburgh was, in a great measure, ruined, and the population of the town diminished of consequence; and partly to the union of farms, which has depopulated the country.[5]

Along with Paul Sandby (*see* 31, 32, 42, 54, 56, 67) and others, Thomas Girtin (1775–1802) was a central player in the early development of English watercolour painting. With his friend and rival, William Turner (1775–1851) (*see* 71), he helped to move the genre away from tinting towards painting, thus establishing watercolour as an independent and reputable art form which could rival work in oils. He received initial training from the topographical artist Edward Dayes (1763–1804) in the traditional approach of outlining in pencil and laying in shades in greys before adding local, mainly pastel, colours. He then undertook architectural subjects and, with Turner, copied drawings on commission. From 1796 he undertook sketching tours, after which he developed his compositions of more distant views of buildings set within their wider settings and developed greater use of strong colour, including the greater use of blues and browns. He visited a variety of locations in northern England and southern Scotland and was particularly attracted by the artistic potential of Jedburgh with its old streets, ruined abbey and riverside mills within an attractive surrounding landscape.[6]

Girtin looks down over the principal single street comprising the Lawnmarket (now Castlegate) to the market cross before it continues as the Highgate (High Street). The principal road appears to be in poor condition and animals roam freely along it. In the foreground are a tollgate and associated buildings.[7] The houses are separated from the main thoroughfare by rough common areas that are known in some Scottish towns, such as Linlithgow, as 'loanings'. Smoke rises from the chimneys of backland development in the toft gardens of the main street houses. The only substantial, and modern, building is the recently completed steeple of the Newgate (1791), which was built to replace the older tolbooth in 1756. Immediately to its right, the Canongate, the principal entry into the town, leads away from the cross and down to a port and bridge crossing over the River Jed. The centre of this street had, as at Inverkeithing (55), Montrose (73) and Musselburgh (75), a 'mid row', a linear group of buildings running down its length, known here as 'The Tongue'. The ruined abbey and its precincts are immediately out of view, although it is included by Girtin in different versions of the prospect and in other pictures where it is the principal subject.

Girtin's view gives the townscape a strongly homogeneous character, although it is not known whether this is a true reflection of local vernacular building or a deliberate artistic effect. The walls appear to be of light-coloured masonry, which may be lime-washed. All the roofs of the town are in thatch or turf, which is generally in poor but picturesque condition. It is known that these were the local roofing methods until at least

1817, turf having been brought in from Ulston Moor to the east of the town.[8] All houses have very small windows and some have dormer openings set into the thatch.

Attempts to introduce woollen manufacture, as in other Border towns, were not successful until well into the nineteenth century when there was output of blankets, flannels, tartans, shawls, plaids and lambs' wool yarn. This new prosperity allowed the redevelopment of most of the older houses depicted, and by the 1830s it could be said, at last, that 'the streets are wide and clean, and the houses are well built'.[9]

Endnotes

1 Scottish Borders Council, *Jedburgh Town Trail* (Newtown St Boswells, n.d.), 2.

2 Pryde, *Burghs*, no. 17.

3 A. T. Simpson and S. Stevenson, *Historic Jedburgh: The Archaeological Implications of Development* (Scottish Burgh Survey, 1981), 34. The site can be seen on John Ainslie's map of 1780, *Jedburgh and its Environs* (Edinburgh, 1780).

4 Simpson and Stevenson, *Historic Jedburgh*, 4.

5 *OSA*, i, 6.

6 *Oxford Art Online*, Thomas Girtin.

7 Anon., *A Plan of the Town of Jedburgh* (1775). *See* NLS Town Plans/Views, 1580–1919.

8 C. A. Strang, *Borders and Berwick: Illustrated Architectural Guide to the Scottish Borders and Tweed Valley* (Edinburgh, 1994), 128; Simpson and Stevenson, *Historic Jedburgh*, 30.

9 *NSA*, iii, 18.

60   Keith, *c.* 1834

The old town of Keith developed along the banks of the Isla river as a centre for agriculture and textiles but in 1750 the improving landlord, James Ogilvy, 6th Earl of Findlater and 3rd Earl of Seafield (1714–1770), replanned the settlement as a New Town based on a grid-iron plan devised by a land surveyor Peter May (d. 1795).[1] This had, as its centrepiece, the 'enormous, continentally-proportioned' Reidhaven Square, through which pass the principal streets.[2] The resulting New Keith was 'a clean thriving-like village, on rising ground sloping towards the east, with three parallel streets running due south and north, intersected by a narrow lane between each alternate feu'.[3] The severe neatness of the original town plan of three parallel streets was compromised by the building of three new churches between 1808 and 1832 in response to a surge in population and migration into the town. In 1755 the population of the whole parish was 2,683, with only thirty Catholics among them. By 1831, by which time the economy of New Keith had diversified from its original dependence on textile manufacture into a distillery and a variety of mills for corn and flour as well as carding and wool, it was 4,464. The rise in population was also reflected in the size of the newly built churches: St Rufus (Church of Scotland, 1819) could accommodate 1,661 and the Roman Catholic chapel of St Thomas could seat 450.[4]

This pencil drawing of the new Roman Catholic church at Keith is one of a series of views of such buildings in north-east Scotland by the artist Felice Piccioni (fl. 1831–1870s). St Thomas was built in 1831–2 to designs by the architect William Robertson of Elgin, in conjunction with its priest Father Walter Lovi (1798–1878). It was the successor to the 1785 chapel and cottage at Kempcairn,[5] which lay outside the town and, from 1827, a small chapel in Land Street. The church was built on a prominent site on the axis of Reidshaven Square.

Father Lovi was Edinburgh-born of Italian-Scottish parentage and had trained at the Scots College in Rome before his appointment to Keith in 1825. He travelled extensively to raise funds for the church throughout Scotland, England, Ireland and France. While in Paris he approached Charles X (1824–30), who had been given sanctuary at Holyrood in the 1790s during his long period of exile, for a contribution to the proposed new church. In addition to financial assistance, Charles commissioned the successful painter François

60. Felice Piccioni, *Roman Catholic Church, Keith, c.* 183⁴

Dubois to provide an altar-piece on the subject of 'The Incredulity of Saint Thomas'. This was painted around 1828 and is housed in the church.[6]

The façade is clearly based on that of the church of Santa Maria della Vittoria, Rome, an important early Baroque work by Giovanni Battista Soria (1581–1651) under the influence of Carlo Maderno (1556–1629). Sitting high above the modest vernacular architecture of the town, it can be read as a confident symbol of the reinstatement of Catholic culture in a former heartland following Catholic emancipation in 1793 and the establishment of a new national seminary at Blairs, near Aberdeen, in 1829 to replace the separate seminaries of the old Lowland and Highland districts. Fr Lovi's efforts did not end with Keith, where he served until 1837. He also raised funds for new churches at Wick (1836) and Braemar (1839).[7]

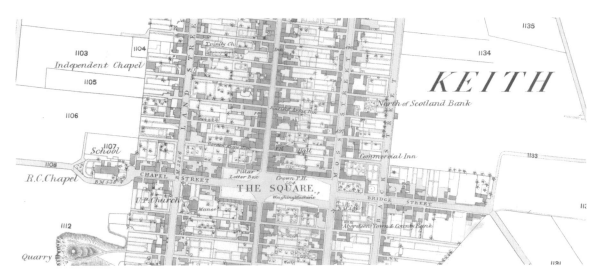

60a. Ordnance Survey Banff Sheet XIV.4 (Keith) 1868

The drawing shows a building higher than actually constructed, and it is possible that it was undertaken prior to completion of the façade. Photographs show that there was an open bell tower and statues of saints flanking the pediment, but these differed from those in the drawing, having been added in 1837, and were of different forms from those sketched. These features have since been removed and a 'bulbous, imposing dome' added to the church.[8]

Little is known of Piccioni, who may have been something of a journeyman artist. There is a record of his marriage at Edinburgh to Jean Renton, daughter of a smith in Ormiston on 23 July 1838,[9] in which he is noted as a landscape painter residing at Haddington Place. Could the artist have been drawn to the north-east of Scotland in search of opportunities on account of the programme of Catholic church building being pursued there? It is also known that Piccioni was in the area in March 1834, as he wrote from Elgin to Bishop James Kyle (1788–1869), who had been appointed Vicar Apostolic of the new Northern District in 1827. The matter concerned two bas-relief sculptures of the Virgin and St Luke being stored there by a local merchant. These were offered to the bishop, no doubt for this or one of the other new church projects.[10]

Piccioni appears also in Ireland, having been brought there by Marcus Ward, the Belfast printer and publisher. He did portraits in chalk and in oil and is said to have had a good practice in Belfast and the north of Ireland. In 1834 he exhibited a *Portrait of Professor Bertinchamp* at the Royal Hibernian Academy and subsequently drew portraits in Cork and Fermoy.[11] In 1844 he undertook the celebrated altarpiece in St Malachy's, Belfast, which is said to incorporate figures of both himself and a son.[12] Belfast street directories record a Felix Piccione, artist, and an artist photographer, F. A. Piccione, in the 1870s.[13]

Endnotes

1 *Papers on Peter May, Land Surveyor*, ed. I. D. Adams (SHS, 1979), pp. xvii–xxv, 58–60, 269; R. J. Naismith, *The Story of Scotland's Towns* (Edinburgh, 1989), 92–4.

2 C. McKean, *The District of Moray: An Architectural Guide* (Edinburgh, 1987), 139.

3 *NSA*, xiii, 390–1.

4 *OSA*, v, 417–18, 420; *NSA*, xiii, 389–90.

5 Illustrated in J. F. S. Gordon, *The Book of the Chronicles of Keith* (Glasgow, 1880). 5.

6 *DSCHT*, 498.

7 C. Johnson, 'Scottish secular clergy, 1830–1878: the Northern and Eastern Districts', *Innes Review*, 40 (1989), 42; M. Dilworth, 'The building of the Roman Catholic chapel in Wick, 1832–39', *ROSC*, 5 (1990), 67–75. *See DSCHT*, 499, for Lovi.

8 McKean, *Moray*, 142–3. The alterations were carried out in 1916 to designs by the architect Charles Menart.

9 Register of Marriages, St Cuthbert's Church, Edinburgh 1838.

10 Letter from Elgin, 7 March 1834, to Bishop Kyle offering two bas-reliefs. Scottish Catholic Archives BL6/101/15. *See DSCHT*, 467, for Kyle.

11 W. Strickland, *A Dictionary of Irish Artists*, ii, (Dublin, 1913).

12 E. Black, *Art in Belfast 1760–1880. Art Lovers or Philistines?* (Dublin, 2006), 107; J. O'Laverty, *An Historical Account of the Diocese of Down and Connor, Ancient and Modern* (Dublin, 1878–84), ii, 424–7; and C. E. B. Brett, *Buildings of Belfast, 1700–1914* (Belfast, 1985), 23. According to O'Laverty, the Piccioni family were 'refugees to Belfast from Austrian Italy'.

13 Belfast Street Directories, accessible at: www.proni.gov.uk/index/search_the_archives/street_directories.htm.

61 Kelso, *c.* 1780

The picturesque town of Kelso has proved a popular subject for artists and engravers over the centuries. John Slezer (*c.* 1650–1717) provided two views of the town in the 1690s.[1] There are also fine topographical prints by Charles Catton (1728–1798) of 1793 and William Daniell (1769–1837) of 1804,[2] and a painting showing the old bridge after damage, which may be by Alexander Nasmyth (1758–1840).[3] This anonymous painting portrays the town's principal public space around the time Walter Scott (1771–1832) attended school there; he later described it as 'the most beautiful if not the most romantic village in Scotland'.[4]

Kelso developed around the abbey founded by David I (1124–53) and was first mentioned as a burgh in 1237.[5] The town suffered severe fire damage in both 1686 and 1742, after which building in timber and thatch was abandoned in favour of reconstruction in masonry, tile and slate. Kelso grew in prosperity during the eighteenth century; farmers and labourers from the surrounding area moved to the town as the land was improved and new agricultural practices introduced. It developed as a centre for retail, leather goods, agricultural machinery, coach building, cabinet working, woollen cloth and other service industries, reaching a population of around 3,500 in 1792, some ten years after the time depicted in the painting.[6] In time, salmon fishing, horse racing and tourism added to the local economy, and the erection of Kelso Bridge meant the town became an important stop for the Edinburgh to London coach, encouraging the provision of inns and associated services.

According to tradition, the town square, or Market Place, was built on the garden of the abbey. Whether true or not, the square is one of the most attractive public spaces in Scotland due to the elegantly detailed tenements that surround it. The square was the site of the St James' Fair, held each August until the 1930s, when the Border Union Show took over. The square is now the site of the annual Civic Week celebrations, introduced in 1937 by John Scott, baker and Provost, so that Kelso could have a Common Riding similar to the other Border towns. The painting clearly shows the bull ring where animals were once tethered and proudly displays a good public water supply (with a second well just off the square) and a machine for weighing goods. None of the gable-fronted tenements shown in the painting survives today and the pantile roofs with their catslide dormers, too, are now gone.

61. Anon., *Market Place, Kelso*

The townhouse shown, which may be the termination of a 'mid row' dividing an originally wider space, was replaced in 1816 with funding from James, 5th Earl of Roxburghe. This building was in turn remodelled in the early twentieth century into its present form. Redevelopment of the old town hall or tolbooth was promoted, as its arcade had become the haunt of drinkers and ruffians.[7]

61a. Public well and bull ring

The Georgian house in the centre of the painting, at 3–6 Woodmarket, with its render, rusticated quoins, piended roof and first-floor Venetian windows still makes a significant contribution to the street scene. The Swan Inn, one of several establishments with painted signs, can be seen to its left. A few houses appear to have been rendered or finished in a distinct and attractive ochre lime wash. Most buildings in the vicinity have since been redeveloped or refaced but some set back at Abbey Place survive. The presence of elegant shops, integrated into the street façades from the start rather than adaptations of earlier buildings, confirm the importance of the town as a retail centre. Many fine shop fronts survive, contributing to the town's reputation as 'the most architectural of all Border burghs'.[8] Bridge Street, which can be seen heading south and away from the viewer, connected the town centre with the Kelso Bridge of 1754 and its replacement of 1804. The first bridge, which had six arches, replaced a ferry but was destroyed by floods in 1797. The new crossing, built in 1800–3, was designed by John Rennie (1761–1821), who used the bridge as a model for his design of Waterloo Bridge and provided the town with 'one of the most splendid entries in Scotland'.[9]

61b. Weighing machine

Looking down the thoroughfare, a street is shown lined by elegant houses, some of which still exist. The tenements on the left are most likely coaching and other inns, while the gap to the right, flanked by two-storey structures, frames Ednam House (originally Havanah House) of 1761, which is set back from view. The view is closed by Abbey House, which serves the same townscape role today. The first public gas light in Scotland was introduced by an enterprising coppersmith outside his premises there in 1818.[10]

Endnotes

1 Cavers, *Slezer*, 64–5, 66.

2 Both in the British Library.

3 SCRAN 000-000-554-417-C.

4 Groome, *Gazetteer*, iv, 343.

5 Cowan and Easson, *Medieval Religious Houses*, 68–9; Pryde, *Burghs*, no. 100.

6 *OSA*, x, 586.

7 *Tolbooths and Town-houses*, 112.

8 C.A. Strang, *Borders and Berwick: Illustrated Architectural Guide to the Scottish Borders and Tweed Valley* (Edinburgh, 1994), 101.

9 *OSA*, x, 579; C. McWilliam, *Scottish Townscape* (Glasgow, 1975), 100.

10 *Ibid.*, 149.

62   Kilmarnock, 1840

This picture of the central market area – the Cross – in Kilmarnock, which was the work of the painter and photographer David Octavius Hill (1802–1870), appeared in *The Land of Burns* (1846), an illustrated compendium of places associated with Robert Burns which benefited from the new, cheaper production which came with steel-plate engraving. It was only natural that Kilmarnock, the place where the first edition of his poems was published in 1786, featured prominently in the volume.

The location is carefully recorded. A number of streets branched off from the Cross. The one on the right of the picture, Cheapside, widened into Bank Street, which was where the Laigh Church, one of the two Church of Scotland parish churches in the burgh, was situated. It had been rebuilt in 1802, and its steeple is prominently depicted by Hill. The main street – King Street, which was more than a mile in length – pushes southward, with the octagonal belfry and spire of the new two-storey Town House shown on the east (left) side of the street.[1] In the far distance, on the west (right) side of King Street is the tall spire of the Relief Synod Church (later the United Presbyterian Church), built in 1836.[2]

Hill's picture, as is often the case with his artistic work, is an artful composite. There is quaintness in it, but he is also depicting some of the best features of what was, in effect, a new town.[3] The street plan was described in the *Statistical Account* of the 1790s as 'extremely irregular'. A private act of parliament of 1802 paved the way to clear away some of the old, narrow streets and lay out new ones, 'adorned with many elegant buildings and shops'.[4] Unlike Aberdeen, where the new main street took almost half a century to be laid out (*see* 3), there was little delay in Kilmarnock's town plan being implemented. King Street was first laid out in 1804 and the new Town House was finished in 1805. The names of the other new streets superimposed on the old shambles were self-evident – Portland Street, Waterloo Street, Wellington Street, Bank Street. The nearest buildings in the picture are obviously new, built in the typical Georgian style of the 1810s and 1820s. Most were demolished in a fit of civic vandalism in the 1970s.

By 1841, Kilmarnock's population, as distinct from that of the parish, stood at 17,846. It had long been a manufacturing town, but the main supporting struts of its economy had changed drastically in the 1820s, when the declining industry of muslin-weaving had

62. David Octavius Hill, *Kilmarnock Cross*, 1846

been largely replaced by the manufacture of worsted printed shawls. By the 1830s the new industry employed over 1,200 weavers and 200 print workers, and its annual production of shawls was well over a million. The shawls in distinctive 'Ayrshire plaid'

proliferate amongst the town's women and children in Hill's picture. Also noticeable is Kilmarnock's other symbol of mass production – some of the 18,000 dozen bonnets produced annually in the town.[5] One wonders why Hill chose to depict a military pipe band, probably of Volunteers, unless it underlines the extent to which Kilmarnock supplied the army with bonnets and caps.

In the picture taken as a whole, there is an odd mixture of old and new, careful observation and likely invention for the sake of adding local colour. The railway came late to Kilmarnock, not until 1843, so the stagecoach – improbably overloaded with passengers on its roof – is probably one of the four a day which connected the burgh to Glasgow. Kilmarnock was a police burgh, which allowed it to implement improvement early and rapidly. Gas lighting was installed in some of the new main streets as early as 1822 yet, curiously, Hill's picture, drawn almost twenty years later, shows no sign of it. A constable occupies centre stage, near the stagecoach, as if to prove the claim

made by the minister who composed the *New Statistical Account* that property and persons were 'more secure' than in any other town in Britain of comparable size.[6] But a man with a peg-leg stands unsteadily near him, begging, presumably one of the 500 or so on parish support. The dress of many of the inhabitants is a curious mixture of old and new fashions. A man in a tricorn hat and knee breeches, typical of the 1810s, stands beside another wearing a dress coat and top hat, garb which typically belongs to the 1830s or 1840s.[7] On one side of the street, ale is being sold from a barrel at an open market stall, with an old-fashioned measuring jug beside it. On the other side, a fashionable coffee house stands on the corner, but what looks like drunken revelry is taking place outside it. Kilmarnock, as depicted by Hill, is a market town with one foot in its past – Burns's past.

Endnotes

1 *Tolbooths and Town-Houses*, 211.

2 *NSA*, v, 535.

3 Apart from an outline glimpse in Roy's military survey of the Lowlands (1752–5), there is no extant town plan of Kilmarnock before the wholesale changes to its street pattern after 1802.

4 *OSA*, ii, 84–96; *NSA*, v, 542.

5 *Great Reform Act Plans and Reports (1832)*, Kilmarnock.

6 *NSA*, v, 553.

7 J. F. McCaffrey, *Scotland in the Nineteenth Century* (London, 1998), 17.

63   Kinghorn, 1840

This image of the harbour and burgh of Kinghorn appeared in a three-volume gazetteer, *Fife Illustrated or History of the County of Fife* (Glasgow, 1840).[1] The text gives a potted history of the burgh, largely culled from the *Statistical Accounts* of the 1790s and the 1830s, but it does not provide a commentary on the picture, which has elements of the fanciful about it.

Any image of Kinghorn before the railway cut it in two in 1847, demolishing in the process a number of old houses in the south-east part of the burgh (to the left of the picture), poses problems of interpretation.[2] By 1840 Kinghorn had two harbours: the older, sometimes called the 'Kirk Harbour', had long since been ruinous; the other, at Pettycur Bay half a mile to the south, had seen investment in it since the 1760s and was used by ferries along the Fife coast and across the Forth to Newhaven. This is a view of the Kirk Harbour and the layered streets of the older part of the town above it. Some of the two- and three-storey houses on the foreshore are identifiable as being in St James Place.

Kinghorn had been a royal burgh since 1165 x 1172.[3] Most of the difficulties in recreating its past originated before the arrival of the railway. By 1840, as a result of what its parish minister in 1843 called a 'rage for modern improvement', many of the older buildings in the town had already been demolished. Here already, according to its parish minister, was a historic burgh without a built heritage. Or, as he put it, 'history and not stone walls must tell us what Kinghorn formerly was'.[4] This may have partly been the jaundiced view of a contemporary, unhappy with rapid economic and social change. In fact, there is, in the historic core of the burgh, mostly to the north and east of the Town Hall, still a significant number of eighteenth- and early nineteenth-century buildings, although most are modest in size and proportions and vernacular in style.[5] The most significant exception to this stricture was the parish church itself, which stood on a hill above the headland to the immediate north of the old harbour. It had been refurbished in 1774, and its crow-stepped gable, porch and manse behind are visible immediately to the north-east (right) of St James Place, although it was in reality on a more elevated site than depicted here.[6]

By the 1830s, as the *New Statistical Account* was at pains to point out, few comparable places had 'undergone such a transformation' in the previous thirty years.[7] The population,

63. James Stewart, *Kinghorn, Fife Shire*, 1840

which had been in decline in the second half of the eighteenth century, had sharply increased after 1820 with the extension of flax-spinning mills to a total of 2,594 in 1841, with 1,555 living in the burgh itself. The three spinning mills and the bleach-field which provided most of the employment in the town in 1840 – some 537 – are all clearly depicted in the engraving. The farthest away is the Nethergate Mill. The middle of the three chimneys is the largest of the three complexes, the St Leonard's Mill, which adjoined the new Town Hall, constructed in 1829–30, replacing the St Leonard's Tower, a pre-Reformation structure which since 1560 had served as both tolbooth and prison.[8] By 1840 the mill employed 287, most of them women. The positioning of the bleach-field, on the hill to the south-east of the burgh, is probably to be taken as symbolic of the burgh's economy rather than an accurate representation of its location. The main bleach-field, owned by the St Leonard's Mill, which employed seventy workers as part of the process of preparation of the thread and yarn, was fully a mile and a half out of town to the north.

The author of the historical descriptions in *Fife Illustrated* was John M. Leighton (fl. 1828–40); the engraver was Joseph Swan (1796–1872); and the artist was James Stewart (1791–1863). *Fife Illustrated* was typical of a number of works which were published in the late 1820s and 1830s, the era immediately preceding photography, combining description, historical jottings and illustrations to attract a new readership interested in well-known or historically evocative places in Scotland. The advent of steel-plate engraving allowed costs to be kept down. No one was more productive in this sphere of publishing than David Octavius Hill (*see* 19a, 62), but Leighton and Swan, a Glasgow landscape engraver and publisher, were highly active in the same market. At first, they seemed to have stayed close to home; a series of illustrated works on the Clyde appeared, including *Select Views of Glasgow and its Environs* (1828) and *Strath-clutha; or Beauties of the Clyde* (1839). They then branched out into an even more lucrative market: their *Views of the Lakes of Scotland* (1834) went through numerous reprints and new editions, including one in separate parts (1839).

For most of their works on Glasgow and the Clyde, Leighton and Swan had used local artists such as John Fleming of Greenock (1794–1845) (*see* Introduction fig. 30) and the better-known John Knox (1778–1845; *see* 48).[9] For *Fife Illustrated*, they turned to James Stewart, an Edinburgh-born artist and line engraver and a founder member of the Royal Scottish Academy in 1826, to produce an original set of drawings. Stewart had executed engravings of some of the most iconic paintings by Sir William Allan and David Wilkie, including the latter's *The Penny Wedding*.[10] It may be that the sketch artist with a fashionably dressed lady alongside, depicted in this engraving in the right foreground, is Stewart himself. If so, they viewed the harbour scene from the basalt rock formations at the headland formed by Carlinhead Rocks, still a favourite vantage point, a mile south of the harbour. Oddly, Stewart never worked again for Leighton and Swann.

Endnotes

1 J. M. Leighton, *Fife Illustrated or History of the County of Fife* (Glasgow, 1840), 206–10. *See* CANMORE, ID 52760.

2 A. Reid, 'Old houses and wood-work panelling at Kinghorn', *PSAS*, 44 (1909–10), 313–18.

3 Pryde, *Burghs*, no. 21.

4 *NSA*, ix, 808.

5 *See Kinghorn Conservation Area Appraisal and Management Plan* (n.d.), pp. 18–23, Appendices 2 and 3, for the listed buildings in the burgh's conservation area. This generally follows the recommendations set out in A.T. Simpson and S. Stevenson, *Historic Kinghorn: The Archaeological Implications of Development* (Scottish Burgh Survey, 1981).

6 *OSA*, xii, 229–45.

7 *NSA*, ix, 800–21. *See* Simpson and Stevenson, *Historic Kinghorn*, esp. 13–20.

8 *Tolbooths and Town-Houses*, 116–17. *See* MacGibbon and Ross, *Castellated and Domestic Architecture*, v, 116–17, for a picture of St Leonard's Tower before its demolition in 1822. The B-listed Town Hall, which had been derelict for twenty years, was restored by the Fife Historic Buildings Trust in 2009, to provide offices for the Trust and holiday accommodation above.

9 For John Fleming of Greenock, *see* www.inverclyde.gov.uk/community-life-and-leisure/mclean-museum-and-art-gallery/museum-collections/fine-art/scottish-painting-john-fleming-ii.

10 *DNB*, James Stewart. The details of Stewart's career, however, suggest that his work on Kinghorn must have been made earlier, before 1833, when he emigrated to South Africa.

64   Kirkcaldy, 1838

There is documentary reference to the shire of Kirkcaldy in the reign of Malcolm III (1058–93) and, in 1183, the first evidence of the place as a town. Rights to a market and annual fair were granted in the early 1300s, and it was subsequently elevated to a burgh, dependent on the abbey of Dunfermline, with the further trading privileges this entailed. Over time, it assumed greater responsibility for its own administration and in 1644 it was confirmed as a royal burgh.[1]

By the 1450s the town had a harbour, which by the mid-sixteenth century was noted as a 'very good landing', and a new pier was in place by 1600. Timber and textiles were imported with salt, fish, tallow and yarn, hides, wool and coal sent abroad. At the end of the seventeenth century there were fourteen vessels engaged in exporting coal[2] and coarse cloth and nails were being made in and around the town.

The town first developed close to where East Burn enters the Forth. It grew as a single long street between the sands and the foot of the sloping raised beach, giving the place its popular name, 'The Lang Toun'. The rigs of the houses on the inland side, with high walls and wynds between them, ran up the slope upon which a back lane was created. The parish church of St Bryce was established on the higher ground, with a wynd linking to the High Street, close to the tolbooth.[3] On the sea side the rigs had private access points onto the sands. Ports, or gates, controlled access at the north and south ends of the town and at the head of the Kirk Wynd.

Wealth from foreign trade supported the development of substantial townhouses, many of which, as in other burghs, were built with gables facing the street. As level ground for expansion was at a premium, properties were extended into the thoroughfare by booths, galleries and forestairs and by excavating into the lower restricting slope of the raised beach.

Sea-borne trade suffered badly during the seventeenth and eighteenth centuries and the harbour became neglected; the pier was 'dung through and through' by violent storms in 1717 and 1794.[4] It has been estimated that around 1640 the town had a population of no more than 3,200. This rose by only a few hundred more over the next fifty years and may have fallen again by 1750. However, linen weaving was being established and a reinvigorated sea trade included whaling and shipbuilding. By the time of this painting, Kirkcaldy had already entered a period of rapid industrial and urban development and was on its way to becoming 'the most thriving town on the north coast of the Firth of Forth'.[5]

64. Anon., *Kirkcaldy from the North*, 1838

This anonymous work shows an improving High Street with new bank buildings and stone-fronted tenements contrasting with the older vernacular buildings, merchants' houses and inns by the harbour.[6] Constrained by the sea to the east, new development was beginning to eat into the lower slopes of the raised beach. St Bryce's, the parish church of 1807, its sandstone still untainted by industrial pollution, looms over the centre of the town. The scale of the building is exaggerated by the artist, and its gable masks the incorporated older medieval tower which was viewed at the time as something 'not only itself devoid of beauty, but … destitute of historical interest and even of the common attraction of a ruin'.[7] The gabled tower to the right is probably the old burgh school in Brycedale Avenue, founded in 1582 but largely demolished in its old form in 1843.[8] New villas were beginning to 'adorn the upper and country parts of the town' and there were 'newer streets now leading upwards from the shore'.[9]

By this time, the harbour had become unsafe and inconvenient, and this was having an adverse effect on trade. This led to calls in the 1830s and early 1840s for improvement, as the revenue from the harbour was the principal income of the town. In response, the facility was improved in 1843 through works to form the outer harbour, inner harbour and wharves.

There is a slate-roofed warehouse on the quay (including the office of the Leith & Kirkcaldy Shipping Co.), for the handling of high-value goods, and there are warehouses, cooperage and whale-oil processing buildings close by. The steamship indicates passenger communication with other Forth ports, a service between Leith, Grangemouth and Kirkcaldy having been introduced in the 1820s.[10]

Further along the shore, we *see* the outcrop known as the 'Bucket Pats' or 'Bucket Pans', a basin in the rocks from which salt water was drawn for the adjacent salt pans. It later became a popular bathing place before being lost, like the rest of the foreshore, under the modern esplanade.

> Weel dae I mind when a wee ragged laddie,
> I scamper'd about on the sands o' Kircaldie,
> And howkit sand eels till I reekit and swat,
> Or sail'd paper boats in the Auld Bucket Pat.[11]

Flax-spinning by machinery had been introduced in 1792, closely followed by steam-powered weaving; such work becoming the principal employment in the town.[12]

There were factories for the making of sailcloth canvas and linen, for net making and for dyeing and yarn bleaching. There were also iron and engineering works, including those of millwrights, makers of steam engines and flax-spinning machines, as well as foundries, such as can be seen just to the west of the parish church. Kirkcaldy was also becoming the world's largest centre for the manufacture of wax floor-cloth and was thus ideally prepared to become, from 1877, a principal player in linoleum production. The

64a. Anon., *Kirkcaldy from the South*, 1838

manufacture of ceramics, including field and roof tiles as well as domestic ware, was long established, taking advantage of excellent clay deposits and the ready availability of salt and coal. The Links Pottery can be seen in the middle distance of the painting, close to the shore. Much of the industry was established to the west of the town, where the chimneys mark works for spinning, chemicals, dyeing and brewing. The West Mills had been operating before the 1830s and a considerable community grew around this and other manufactories. Residents here were served by the newly constructed plain box of Inverteil Parish Church with its squat spire, as can been seen in the painting.

Endnotes

1 E. P. Dennison Torrie and R. Coleman, *Historic Kirkcaldy: The Archaeological Implications of Development* (Edinburgh, 1995), 9–21; Pryde, *Burghs*, nos 78, 113.

2 J. Y. Lockhart, *Kirkcaldy 1838–1938: A Century of Progress* (Kirkcaldy, 1939), 5.

3 J. Wood, *Plan of the Town of Kirkcaldy* (Edinburgh, 1824).

4 Lockhart, *Kirkcaldy*, 4.

5 *Report on the Burgh of Kirkcaldy, Fifeshire, to Accompany the Reform Act of 1832* (Crewe, n.d.), quoted in Dennison Torrie and Coleman, *Historic Kirkcaldy*, 19.

6 There is a fine, now restored merchant's house at 339–43 High Street, near the Port Brae. The house was built in the 1590s for a member of the merchant and shipowning family named Law.

7 *NSA*, ix, 761.

8 Groome, *Gazetteer*, iv, 412.

9 *Ibid.*, iv, 413.

10 *Cassell's Old and New Edinburgh* (London, *c*. 1880), vi, 212.

11 P. K. Livingstone, *A History of Kirkcaldy* (Kirkcaldy, 1955), 77–8.

12 Nairn's first canvas factory had been established in Coal Wynd in 1828; Lockhart *Kirkcaldy*, opposite p. 10.

65   Kirkwall, 1805 and 1766

This lithograph of Kirkwall was engraved by Robert Scott (1771–1841), one of the greatest Scottish engravers of the day. It comes from a history of Orkney, published in 1805, written by the Revd George Barry (1748–1805), minister of Kirkwall and later of Shapinsay.[1] The first mention of Kirkwall comes from the colourful *Orkneyinga Saga*, an early Icelandic history of the Earls of Orkney. It claims that Earl Rognvald was wintering in *Kirkiuvag* in the year he was slain.[2]

Kirkiuvag is Old Norse for 'church on the bay', which refers to the small eleventh-century church of St Olaf, predecessor of the great cathedral in this picture. The building of the Cathedral of St Magnus was begun in 1137 by another Earl Rognvald in memory of his murdered uncle, Earl Magnus the Good (*c.* 1075–*c.* 1116). The canonisation of Magnus, who became the patron saint of Orkney, put the earldom on a par with other Scandinavian kingdoms creating royal saints at that time.[3] The decision to move Magnus's remains from Birsay to Kirkwall not only bolstered the power and prestige of the earldom but also that of the town.

Kirkwall, the capital of the Orkney Islands, developed beside the natural harbour in the picture. Earl Rognvald's decision to winter there with his longships shows that it had long been a favoured anchorage. The large sailing ship on the left is anchored in the 'Road of Kirkwall' which led to the open sea. On the right is the Oyce or Peerie Sea, an inlet almost landlocked except for the opening behind the upturned boat in the foreground. Protecting the Oyce from the open sea is the Ayre, a gravelly beach stretching out from the shore, useful for beaching or tying up boats as the artist shows. The mouth of the Oyce was kept open by the inhabitants of Kirkwall who would regularly come 'with Speads, Shovells, and other Instruments' to clear it.[4]

Building on the Ayre seems to have gone unopposed until an application to build a windmill sparked a furious protest. Evidently, the people of Kirkwall had a fondness for the Ayre as a place for walking, letting their children play and even drying washing.[5] The building at the end of the Ayre was the girnel, a large seventeenth-century granary where rents to the king were paid. A nearby jetty called the Corn-slip was a reminder that these rents were often paid in kind.[6]

At the end of the eighteenth century Kirkwall had still not grown beyond the confines of a narrow street, about a mile long, with many of its houses standing gable

65. Robert Scott, *View of Kirkwall from the West*, 1805

end onto the road.[7] The oldest part of town on the shore was known as the burgh, the earl's domain. Extending south from the Cathedral was the Laverock, the bishop's domain. Between the burgh and the Laverock a third section evolved which was known as Mid-town. This became the commercial heart of Kirkwall.[8] The town's defences, the Ramparts, can be seen along the shore of the Oyce with several slipways clearly marked where the Oyce lapped up to the gardens of the houses.

Behind the Ramparts, to the right of the cathedral, are the remains of Kirkwall's two great palaces. Most of the ancient Bishop's Palace, where King Haakon of Norway died in 1263, was already ruinous though its round tower is still prominent. This was built by Bishop Robert Reid (d. 1558), humanist, lawyer, diplomat and pluralist. Unusually, the rooms within were square.[9]

Behind are the roofless remains of Earl Patrick's seventeenth-century palace, 'one of the finest specimens of domestic architecture in Scotland'.[10] Patrick Stewart (c. 1566–1615), 2nd Earl of Orkney, was the son of Robert Stewart (1533–1593), 1st Earl and illegitimate son of James V (1513–42). William Thomson describes Patrick as having a 'compulsive need to sustain a lifestyle which proclaimed his royal origins, at whatever cost

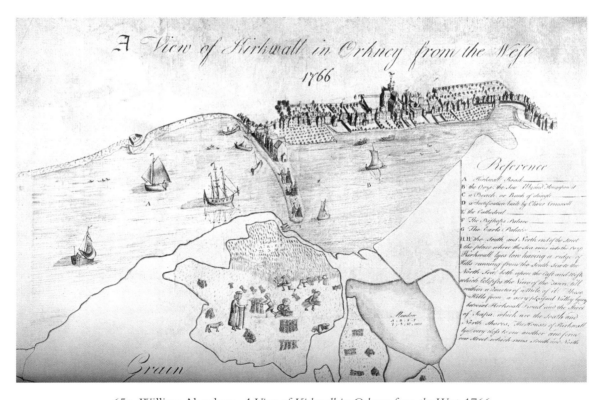

65a. William Aberdeen, *A View of Kirkwall in Orkney from the West*, 1766

to himself and to others'.[11] Patrick, who built his fine palace on the proceeds of ruthless exploitation of his tenants and neighbours, was finally accused of treason and executed by the maiden, a type of guillotine, at the market cross in Edinburgh.

In 1766 Sir Lawrence Dundas (1712–1786), self-made businessman and war profiteer, bought the estate of the earldom of Orkney and the lordship of Shetland for £63,000. This made him one of the major landowners in the United Kingdom and explains his nickname, the 'Nabob of the North'.[12] It was for Dundas that William Aberdeen produced a map called *A View of Kirkwall in Orkney from the West*, the year of the Orkney purchase.[13] It shows Kirkwall's long street and the extent of building that had already taken place on the Ayre. It also seems to show the Ayre as a place of recreation.

The Revd Barry dedicated his history of Orkney to Dundas's son, Thomas (1741–1820), Baron Dundas of Aske, landowner, politician and lord lieutenant of Orkney, whose principal family seat was in Yorkshire.[14] The book attempted to persuade Lord Dundas, a noted improver and man of considerable means, to invest in the island's economy. The cheerful fishermen relaxing in the picture, with the decaying symbols of the island's former greatness behind them, are there to support Barry's theory that a lack of capital and skill was all that stopped these men turning the 'multitude and variety of excellent fish' in the waters around them into a profitable business.[15] Barry also linked the newly acquired titles and fortune of the Dundas family to the ancient earldom of Orkney and the long line of illustrious families who had held the title. Thomas Dundas's son, another Lawrence (1766–1839) did become an earl, but not of Orkney. He was created 1st Earl of Zetland in 1838.

Endnotes

1 G. Barry, *The History of the Orkney Islands* (Edinburgh, 1805), 24.

2 J. Anderson (ed.), *The Orkneyinga Saga* (Edinburgh, 1873), 37.

3 *DNB*, Magnus Erlendsson, Earl of Orkney (St Magnus).

4 B. H. Hossack, *Kirkwall in the Orkney* (Kirkwall, 1900), 375.

5 *Ibid.*, 374.

6 *Ibid.*, 127.

7 *OSA*, vii, 529–30.

8 R. Gourlay and A. Turner, *Historic Kirkwall: The Archaeological Implications of Development* (Scottish Burgh Survey, 1977), 4.

9 *DNB*, Robert Reid.

10 MacGibbon and Ross, *Castellated and Domestic Architecture of Scotland*, ii, 337.

11 W. P. L. Thomson, *The New History of Orkney* (Edinburgh, 1987), 299.

12 *DNB*, Dundas Family of Fingask and Kerse.

13 J. Storer Clouston, *A History of Orkney* (Kirkwall, 1932), 354.

14 *DNB*, Thomas Dundas of Kerse.

15 Barry, *Orkney Islands*, 373.

66   Largs, 1636–8

The Skelmorlie Aisle was built in 1636 as a funerary monument by Sir Robert Montgomery of Skelmorlie (d. 1651) to mark the death of his wife, Lady Margaret Douglas, in a tragic accident involving her horse in 1624. Although attached to the parish church of St Columba in Largs, the aisle had a separate entrance. The monument took the form of a highly elaborate Renaissance canopied tomb. In 1638 a painted timber ceiling was completed by James Stalker (fl. 1632–8), an Edinburgh artist who signed and dated his work 'fecit Stalker'.[1] The monument was completed in 1639. The ceiling decoration has no fewer than forty-one separate compartments, a dazzling myriad of heraldic, emblematic and historical subjects. Alongside the armorial bearings of Montgomery and Eglinton, impaled with those of Douglas and Mar, are representations of the Cardinal Virtues and the four seasons, and appropriate texts from the Geneva Bible.[2] It may be that Skelmorlie Castle also had similar decoration; certainly, there were Renaissance buildings within it dating to this same period.[3]

Of particular interest here, at the edges of the ceiling, are four landscapes associated with the seasons, which are the crudest part of the whole decoration. One, under the heading of 'Aestas' (summer), shows children playing, on both sides of a river with Skelmorlie Castle on one side and Largs church on the other, and has twin mottoes underneath. 'Trust ye in the Lord for euer, for in the Lord God is strength for ever more' (Isaiah 26:4) is juxtaposed against an unassigned, crude version of one of the beatitudes: 'Blessed are the children that inlargeth the Kingdom of Heaven and cursed are the children that inlargeth the Kingdom of Hell.'

This was a landscape of the mind, as was the whole ceiling, rather than a geographical representation for the castle was fully eight miles distant from the parish church in Largs. Another panel, representing 'Ver' (spring), is also centred on a river, which may be the Skelmorlie Water, with a bridge over it and a windmill in the background; it shows men fishing and boating and has the quotations below the castle: 'Blessed are those that mourne for they shall be comforted' (Matthew 5:4), an orthodox rendition of one of the beatitudes, and 'But the day of the Lord will come as a thiefe in the night, in the which the heavens shall passe away with a great noise' (2 Peter 3:10). Interestingly, these passages were taken from the Authorised Version of 1611 rather than the Geneva Bible.

66. James Stalker, *Summer*, Skelmorlie Aisle, 1636–8

The underlying messages conveyed by and in the monument and ceiling are complex and multi-layered. On the face of it, here is uncompromising Calvinist predestination theology, particularly in some of the Biblical mottoes. Yet there is also, with both the tomb and the ceiling, Catholic iconography and the use of Continental models, probably taken from Renaissance pattern books. Family ambition, even Mannerist vanity in extreme form, is everywhere: the device of a Tempera decorative ceiling is unusual in a religious setting and much of the detail is copied from the work of a goldsmith at the French court, Etienne Delaune, and the overall design of the marble, Baroque-style construct was based on the pair of elaborate neo-classical monuments erected in Westminster Abbey by James VI & I (1567–1625) between 1605 and 1613 for Queen Elizabeth and his own mother, Mary, Queen of Scots.[4] This was a conceit of breathtaking proportions for a family which

66a. James Stalker, *Spring*, Skelmorlie Aisle, 1636–8

324

had risen from a knighthood granted by James VI to a baronetcy gifted by Charles I (1625–49) in 1628.

How should such conspicuous piety in the theatre of death be viewed in early seventeenth-century Presbyterian Scotland? It was later claimed that Montgomery visited the tomb each night for fifteen years, in preparation for his own burial.[5] The progress from life to death becomes more obvious in the scene depicting the autumn of his days, again poised between castle and church spire: Montgomery, descendant of the 'first Adam', is the 'last Adam made a quickening spirit' (1 Corinthians 15:45), confident in the exhortation in the matching Biblical quotation: 'Precious in the sight of the Lord is the death of His saints' (Psalms 116:15). In effect, Skelmorlie was used by its founder as a Protestant version of a Catholic chantry chapel. Prayers for the dead and the belief in purgatory may officially have gone, as some Presbyterian historians insist even to this day,[6] but the same underlying fears of death persisted. Status, godliness, righteousness and piety intermingled in Montgomery's mind and in the fabric of his divine creation.

The century before the Reformation of 1560 had seen the foundation of a score or more rural churches upgraded to collegiate status in the century after 1450, such as Crichton, Lincluden or Rosslyn, a process linked to the emergence in the 1450s of a new class of landed power, the lords of parliament. Rosslyn was not only a pilgrimage church; it was also a burial vault and family chapel, designed to allow worship in private. The same desire for exclusion and privacy lay behind the resort of many post-Reformation nobles – old and new – to family lofts, burial aisles, sepulchres and mausoleums. These circumvented the reformers' desire for public worship but also continued in the tradition of the collegiate church, often intended as a *private* chapel. For the living elite, it was a new version of the rood screen; for the dead elite it was a new variant of the old prestigious place for burial within the nave of the church. It also fed the desire of new noble *arrivistes* to devise for themselves a past and a lineage. Skelmorlie was unique only in the scale of its devout pretentiousness.

Endnotes

1 D. Macmillan, *Scottish Art, 1460–1990* (Edinburgh, 1992), 58, 61.

2 A. W. Lyons, 'The painted ceiling in the Montgomery Aisle of the Old Church at Largs, Ayrshire', *PSAS*, 35 (1900–1), 109–11.

3 A. McKechnie, 'Evidence of a post-1603 court architecture in Scotland?', *Architectural History*, 46c (2003), 115.

4 M. Bath, *Renaissance Decorative Painting in Scotland* (Edinburgh, 2003), 128–45; A. White, 'Westminster Abbey in the early seventeenth century: a powerhouse of ideas', *Church Monuments*, 4 (1989), 19–29; D. Howard, *Scottish Architecture: Reformation to Restoration, 1560–1660* (Edinburgh, 1995), 203.

5 *OSA*, vi, 427–8.

6 J. Kirk, *Patterns of Reform: Continuity and Change in the Reformation Kirk* (Edinburgh, 1989), p. xvi.

67   Leith, 1747 and 1751

Paul Sandby (1731–1809) arrived in Scotland in 1747 to take up an appointment as a draughtsman in the military survey of Scotland carried out in the wake of the defeat of the Jacobite rising of 1745–6. He was based in Edinburgh Castle, although he travelled far and wide, especially in the Highlands, in the next five years in the course of his official work. His early period in Scotland produced a significant corpus of work, although much of it is still only in the form of rough sketches in notebooks.

Another facet of his art was landscape. Before his posting to Scotland, Sandby had spent almost all of his life in the textile town of Nottingham where he was born, save for a brief period working for the Board of Ordnance in London. The impact of exposure to an alien culture, a strange, mangled tongue and the varied, dramatic landscapes of what was for most Englishmen a *terra incognita* must have been considerable. Sandby's art found opportunities to display a sharp sense of social observation and even satire, seen in his notebook studies of life – often low life – in Edinburgh. But the striking setting of Scotland's capital city and its port of Leith offered a different kind of opportunity for the artist who would be described in a number of his obituaries as the father of English landscape painting.

Two of his early works in Scotland were distant views of Leith. They reveal a talent for the atmospheric, reminiscent of Dutch landscape painting rather than the dry precision of most of his Scottish work. In *A Distant View of Leith* (1747), done in watercolour and pencil, the panorama of Leith in the middle ground, bathed in the bright light of sunset, is framed by the trees and humble dwellings in the foreground, cast in grey shadow. Some half-completed figures and a horse appear in the right foreground.[1] The aspect is atmospheric rather than delineable; the only readily recognisable buildings in Leith itself are the square tower and nave of the parish church and, nearby, the distinctive cone shape of a glassworks with smoke rising out of it, and a hint in miniature of a windmill to the right (east) of it.

His *South Prospect of Leith* is also a portrait of the town from the south, but the vantage point is farther to the west, so allowing focus on a more easterly vista. It is signed and dated *Paul Sandby Delint et fecit Edin*^r. 1749, and was one of a series of views of Scotland published in 1751. Then, with some alterations made to the staffage of figures and coach in the foreground and a ship in the distance, it was entitled *View of Leith from the East*

67. Paul Sandby, *A Distant View of Leith*, 1747

67a. Paul Sandby, *View of Leith from the East Road*, 1751

Road (virtually on the same line as present-day Easter Road) and inscribed and dated *Paul Sandby Delin^t et sculpt Windsor Augt. 1751*, indicating that he was also involved in its etching on copperplate.[2] In both versions, the houses and church are more clearly delineated than in the view of 1747.

To the east of the town, etched here much more sharply, are the same cone of a glassworks and a windmill as before and, behind them, the island of Inchkeith. Here there is both Sandby's characteristic attention to detail and some artifice. Both the glassworks and sawmill are noted on a detailed map of 1759, and a contemporary sasine describes the glassworks as being 'on the sands adjacent to the links of Leith', thus just to the west of Leith Links, near where Salamander Street is now situated.[3] And both the glassworks and windmill feature again in Sandby's enormous panorama of Edinburgh (1750), although with no trace of an island to the north of the glassworks.[4] In *South Prospect*, the distance between the church and the glassworks seems exaggerated and the view of Inchkeith, fully five miles north of the shore, foreshortened.

The framing of the townscape is artful, with a tree partly overhanging the scene, much vegetation, a collection of individual figures and a packhorse prominent in the foreground and others at work on the harvest. The figures bringing in the harvest may be suggestive. They might come from any rural scene of the English countryside. They are very far from some of his caricatures of Highlanders (*see* 42, 56). They might be the embodiment of 'improvement' and industry which the Hanoverian regime preached as the surest route out of 'barbarity' and 'idleness'.[5] (*See* Introduction.) In sum, the view shows a port town in an attractive setting and it also carries positive messages about industry and agriculture. In that sense, it is a part collage. Neither view – of 1747 or 1749 – is detailed enough to be of any military value but both testify to a young talent – Sandby was only twenty-six when he arrived in Edinburgh – which chose to follow a different path after he left Scotland in 1752.

Endnotes

1 L. Herrman, 'Paul Sandby in Scotland', *Burlington Magazine*, vol. 106, no. 736 (1964), 339–40. Both of these views of Leith are in the Sutherland collection, Ashmolean Museum, Oxford. The painting is also reproduced in J. Bonehill and S. Daniels, *Paul Sandby: Picturing Britain* (London, 2009), 59.

2 Herman, 'Paul Sandby', 340, 344 (image). The version without a coach is reproduced in Bonehill and Daniels, *Paul Sandby*, 14, where it is dated as 1747.

3 J. Turnbull, *The Scottish Glass Industry, 1610–1750: 'To serve the whole nation with glass'*, 168–72. We are grateful to Dr Turnbull for her valuable advice.

4 Bonehill and Daniels, *Paul Sandby*, 95, 96–7, reproduces this watercolour panorama.

5 P. Langford, *A Polite and Commercial People: England, 1727–1783* (Oxford, 1989), 216–17; Bonehill and Daniels, *Paul Sandby*, 14.

68   Leith Races, 1859

This animated scene, painted by an amateur artist William Thomas Reed (*c.* 1842–*c.* 1883), immortalises the centuries-old carnival of horse racing on Leith Sands. It records the final race day on 22 September 1859. Reed, a philosophical instrument maker, was a 'Leither' whose family was well known locally for its musical and artistic talent.[1] This intriguing glimpse of mid-nineteenth century Leith is the only recorded picture of a Scottish scene by Reed to have survived.

Horse racing, a popular sport in Scotland for centuries, is mentioned in the *Treasurer's Accounts* of James IV (1488–1513), whose interest in 'hors rynnyng' is recorded as early as 1504.[2] The history of organised racing on Leith Sands could already be described as one of the locals' 'accustomed recreations' in 1661 after the restoration of Charles II (1649–85), when races took place each Saturday. Charles's brother, the Duke of Albany and York, later James VII (1685–89), was known to have patronised these races when king's high commissioner at Holyrood between 1679 and 1682.[3] Reed's painting illustrates how popular the sport was at all levels of society.

Leith Sands was where the Edinburgh race meeting was held for a week each summer under the auspices of the city magistrates. The day began with a procession from the City Chambers led by a dignitary holding aloft the beribboned City Purse, worth £50, which was one of the prizes. Along with a drummer and members of the city guard, known as 'the toun rats',[4] the procession was joined by numerous racegoers en route. By the time it reached Leith it was a veritable mob. Races consisted of three heats run over a distance of 400 yards (366 metres) from a starting post to a distance marker and back. Racing began as soon as the tide went out but had to finish when it returned.[5]

Robert Fergusson (1750–1774), himself fatally addicted to the pursuit of both merriment and alcohol, wrote a poem that captures the carnival atmosphere of the races but also the possible consequences. The man in the foreground, with his hands in his pockets, would seem to be saying that he has lost all his money, something many of these racegoers could ill afford:

> Whan on Leith-Sands the racers rare,
> Wi Jocky louns are met,
> Their orra pennies there to ware,

68. William Thomas Reed, *Leith Races*, 1859

And drown themsels in debt
Fu deep that day.[6]

In 1816 the Edinburgh Race Meeting was moved to the links at Musselburgh. The advantages of turf over the wet sands at Leith had become more critical as owners were increasingly loathe to risk fine horses on a heavy course, where success often went to the strongest rather than the fastest. Leith achieved a measure of independence from Edinburgh in 1833 by becoming a parliamentary burgh, and three years later the old race meeting was revived as the Leith Annual Subscription Races. Unlike the races at Musselburgh, these were as riotous as they had always been.

In his *Glimpses of Old Leith*, William Hudson claims that the figures in Reed's painting are not only well executed but also true to his own boyhood memories.[7] Reed can have been little more than a boy himself when he painted it, being about seventeen when these last races were run at Leith. All the fun of the fair is included, enough to rival the festivities at Glasgow's annual fair (50): the tents and booths in the background, the peepshows, shies, roley-poleys, hobby-horses and swing boats. The grandstand was built above the high water mark, but the course and many of the tented booths could be set up only after the tide had receded.[8] In the foreground is the inevitable Punch and Judy show along with gingerbread sellers, fortune tellers and Old Malabar, a famous conjuror and acrobat who sits by a table talking to some children.[9]

68a. Old Malabar

Also shown is the drunkenness for which the races were notorious. The constable on the left is pouring a large drink for himself, while a man in the centre lies with a flask to his mouth and another, slumped on the ground, is being lifted by a friend. Scenes such as this resulted in an appeal to Leith Dock Commission, which banned the sale of drink on the beach in 1856. Hudson describes how a tug boat, which was legally allowed to sell alcohol on the Forth, got round this rule by becoming temporarily stranded by the outgoing tide. A ladder over the side enabled customers to climb aboard and buy drink from the well-stocked vessel. The beached fishing boat by the shore was an annual attraction. It sold food in the form of freshly cooked partans, Old Scots for crabs, which came from nearby Newhaven.[10] Perceptions of this merry-making and the brawling that followed were changing, and a growing body of opinion wanted to see the races stopped. Descriptions of the over-use of whips and the wearing of heavy spurs show that attitudes towards animal cruelty were also changing.[11] The day's events included a Carters' Procession. A prize-winning

Leith carter can be seen on his beribboned horse watching the race over the heads of the spectators.[12]

Reed also provides a view of the wide sandy shore at Leith, a popular recreation ground before it disappeared beneath land reclamation, industrial buildings, housing, roads, bridges and docks. The racing is set against a backdrop of the trade and industry that drove this expansion and would soon claim the sands. The three great, smoking cones are furnaces where glass production, almost continuous in Leith from the end of the seventeenth century, was still in operation, predominantly with bottle production. In the centre is the old Signal Tower, originally a windmill, above which a flag is flying. Out to sea is Leith's Martello Tower, built during the Napoleonic Wars to protect the docks. Left empty for many years, it was renovated in 1850 but would be abandoned in 1869 and become landlocked as the shore was developed.[13] Behind the crowds is a great store of timber. The area is still known as Timber Bush, a reference to the town's occupation by the French during the mid-sixteenth century from which 'bourse', the French for market, gradually evolved to bush.

Covering the events in this picture, *The Scotsman* reported that the annual races on Leith Sands had taken place in fine weather and that 'every spot on the beach from which a view of the races could be obtained was covered with spectators'.[14] The crowds, carriages and carts pictured here confirm that horse racing on Leith Sands remained popular with many to the last.

Endnotes

1 W. Hudson, *Glimpses of Old Leith: The Races, The Games, Sundays of Long Ago* (Leith, 1910), 26.

2 *TA*, ii, 430.

3 J. Grant, *Cassell's Old and New Edinburgh, its History, its People and its Places* (Edinburgh, 1883), iii, 268–9.

4 J. C. Irons, *Leith and its Antiquities from Earliest Times to the Close of the Nineteenth Century* (Edinburgh, 1897), ii, 416.

5 J. S. Marshall, *The Life and Times of Leith* (Edinburgh, 1986), 59–60.

6 J. Robertson (ed.), *Robert Fergusson: Selected Poems* (Edinburgh, 2000), 154.

7 W. Hudson, *Glimpses of Old Leith* (Leith, 1910), 19.

8 *Ibid.*, 19.

9 *Ibid.*, 21.

10 *Ibid.*, 24–5.

11 *Ibid.*, 23.

12 *Ibid.*, 26.

13 S. Mowat, *The Port of Leith, its History and its People* (Edinburgh, 1980), 298.

14 *The Scotsman*, 23 September 1859.

69   Lerwick, 1850s and 1828

This view of Lerwick, the capital of the Shetland Islands, was drawn by John Irvine (1805–1888), son of a local merchant and Shetland's best-known portrait painter.[1] It was drawn in the 1850s from the vantage point of the Old Battery, near a promontory known as the Knab.

Erected a burgh of barony in 1818, Lerwick is a surprisingly young town.[2] It grew beside the west shore in Bressay Sound, a natural haven capable of holding a great number of ships. Sheltered by Bressay Island to the east, it offered a safe anchorage all year round that could be entered from the north, as this picture shows, but more commonly from the south. Yet as late as 1633, Captain Smith, a frequent visitor to Bressay Sound, made no mention of a town.[3] The first recorded public building was a fort, built in the 1650s to protect this important anchorage.[4] A century later, during the American War of Independence, a new pentagonal fort was built on the site, named Fort Charlotte in honour of the Queen (1744–1818). The flag flying high above the town shows the position of this fort.

Lerwick's status as a town was established in the late seventeenth century when a tolbooth and parish church were built. In 1767 this first tolbooth was replaced by a new, much larger tolbooth, showing how much the town had grown. The clock-tower of this tolbooth can be seen near the shore in front of the ships.[5] Although Lerwick did not become a parish until 1701, it had already outgrown two parish churches and built a third by the time this picture was painted. The back of this third church, still in use, is visible just right of centre, a large white building with two tall windows. The whole church can be seen in the accompanying vignette, painted by Thomas Woore (1804–1878) around the time it was built in 1828. It is easy to see why this neo-classical church, which could hold 1,000 people, was described as 'Da muckle kirk' shortly after completion.

Woore was a naval surveyor who worked on the first complete hydrographic survey of Britain. The Royal Navy's first purpose-built survey vessel, *Investigator*, was a regular visitor to Bressay Sound between 1825 and 1834 while work was underway. Sunday services were usually held on board, but after 1829 the crew went ashore to worship because the town's new parish church was large enough to accommodate them.[6]

Irvine's view of Lerwick is dominated by new buildings like the Big Kirk, the recently completed United Free Church, now St Olaf's Hall, to the left, and Prospect

69. John Irvine, *Lerwick from the Old Battery*, 1850s

69a. Thomas Woore, *The Presbyterian Church, Lerwick, c.* 1828

House, Sheriff Duncan's imposing three-storey mansion, built in 1818, on the far left. A visiting Free Church minister described Lerwick in 1845 as 'different from anything to be seen in the mainland of Britain and interesting from its novelty'.[7] It was a theme echoed by many visitors. One reason is that the majority of people arrived in Lerwick by boat so the view painted by Irving would not have been their first impression of the town. They would have stepped ashore in the old town, hidden behind the houses in this picture. With its narrow lanes, known as 'closses', and its overcrowded houses, the old town was haphazardly squeezed in around the shore. The pathway along the shore, where most of the shops and businesses grew, was named Commercial Street, its width so irregular that it was 'at one place ten yards wide, and at another only two'.[8] The layout of the buildings was so random that an eminent scientist compared them to the participants in a dance.[9]

Another difference in Lerwick was its Norse background. The Shetland Islands remained under Norse rule until 1468 when they were annexed to Scotland following the marriage of Margaret of Denmark (1456–1486) to James III (1460–88). Norse influences will have contributed to the novelty noted by the Free Church minister, the very name Lerwick coming from *leir-vik*, Old Norse for 'muddy bay'.

The buildings in this picture were the result of a burgeoning economy derived from fishing and the sea. The town played host to vast numbers of ships, such as Dutch herring busses, the Greenland whaling fleet and the Royal Navy. In addition to the provision and repair of ships, money was earned from visiting crews and the hire of Shetlanders as additional crew, valued both for their seamanship and their willingness to accept lower wages. In 1814, as many as 1,400 islanders were said to have joined the whalers which, with the agent's commission and the money spent by their crews, injected an estimated £22,500 into the island's economy that season.[10]

Another factor was the emergence of a new merchant class, their businesses often founded on smuggling. These men bought their own ships and built themselves lodberries. This, taken from Old Norse *hladberg*, a 'loading rock', was a type of eighteenth-century building with its foundations in the sea, combining pier, courtyard, store and dwelling house. One successful merchant, James Hay, built a fine house beside the Big Kirk, part of which is visible on the left of the vignette. In 1839 Christian Ployen, Danish governor of the Faroe Islands, visited another enterprising Shetland merchant and was clearly impressed by the luxurious standard of living enjoyed by these men.[11]

From the Old Battery, a former gun position, Shetland's first road can be seen entering Lerwick between the Big Kirk and the United Free church. Built by the naval authorities to transport guns between the battery and the fort, for many years this was the only road in Shetland.

John Irvine, the artist, left the islands shortly after this picture was completed and settled in New Zealand.[12] Thomas Woore, who painted the vignette, resigned from the navy in 1834 and emigrated to Australia.[13]

Endnotes

1 We are indebted to Mr Douglas Sinclair for his advice.

2 Pryde, *Burghs*, no. 478.

3 A. Edmondston, *A View of the Ancient and Present State of the Shetland Islands* (Edinburgh, 1809), ii, 25.

4 C. H. Firth, *Scotland and the Protectorate* (SHS, 1899), 64.

5 *Tolbooths and Town-houses*, 134.

6 D. Flinn, *Travellers in a Bygone Shetland: An Anthology* (Edinburgh, 1989), 109–13.

7 *Notes of a Tour in Shetland and Orkney September 1845, by a Free Church Minister* (Inverness, 1846), 6.

8 Flinn, *Bygone Shetland*, 80.

9 S. Hibbert, *A Description of the Shetland Islands, comprising an Account of their Scenery, Antiquities, and Superstitions* (Edinburgh, 1822), 126.

10 Flinn, *Bygone Shetland*, 75.

11 *Ibid.*, 195.

12 M. S. Robertson, *Sons and Daughters of Shetland: 1800–1900* (Lerwick, 1991), 89.

13 I. Tait, *Sketches in the Zetland Islands, 1828: Thomas Woore (1804–1878)* (Shetland Museum and Archives), 1.

70   Linlithgow, 1693

These two views of Linlithgow were probably drawn by John Slezer in the 1670s and form part of a series of illustrations of town life which give invaluable insights into the late seventeenth century. Captain John Slezer (*c.* 1650–1717), a German-speaking military engineer, came to Scotland in 1669. While travelling around the country on his military duty of surveying Scotland's fortifications and defences, he produced views of the many places he visited. These included a number of towns and cities. Later engraved, his resultant work – the *Theatrum Scotiae* – was published in 1693 (*see* 15, 22, 46).

The first view is of the Palace of Linlithgow, but it shows us very much more. The palace stands to the north of The Peel (the left of the picture), almost completely surrounded by the waters of Linlithgow Loch – a highly defensive position. Given the site of Linlithgow, at a mid-point between Edinburgh and Stirling and near the only possible fording point of the River Avon for many miles, this became a key point for travellers, royal and others, between the two settlements. As early as the reign of David I (1124–53) there was a royal castle and manor, or grange, nearby.[1] It is uncertain where the royal castle was sited, but, in all probability, the royal residence was on the secure site now occupied by the palace. Archaeological excavations around the palace in 2002 recorded foundations for a timber palisade and buildings, which have been dated to no later than the twelfth century. These could well have been the defences and outer buildings of the royal residence.[2]

Over the centuries the castle and its appurtenances underwent renovation and destruction, parts being demolished in the early fourteenth century by instruction of Edward I of England (1272–1307) and then by Robert I (1306–29). Fire also took its toll in the fifteenth century. But the fifteenth and sixteenth centuries were to see a transformation. The fact that from 1429 the castle was termed a 'palace' attests to growing sumptuousness. In 1650, however, the palace received an unwelcome visitor – Oliver Cromwell installed himself, with his troops encamped on The Peel. Whether any damage was done to the fabric of the palace is unclear, but John Lauder, Lord Fountainhall, commented in 1668 that it was 'for the most part ruinous', as did Thomas Kirk in 1677.[3] Both of Slezer's views, however, show the palace as still roofed, and it is known from their graffiti that cooks were still using the kitchens in 1685 and 1687.[4] James, Duke of Albany

70. John Slezer, *The Prospect of Their Maj'ties Palace of Linlithgow*, 1693

70a. John Slezer, *The Prospect and Town of Linlithgow*, 1693

and York, later James VII (1685–88), also felt Linlithgow Palace a fit place in which to reside in 1679 and from 1680 to 1682.

Close by the palace may be seen the parish church of St Michael. A church had existed, probably on this site, from the reign of David I (1124–53), if not before. Rebuilding and embellishments, particularly in the fifteenth to sixteenth centuries, made this a magnificent building with its twenty exterior niches filled with statues of saints and a tower topped with a stone imperial crown, as seen in this view. The main entrance was by a southerly doorway and, stressing the closeness of church and palace, there was a smaller entrance to the north, now blocked up. St Michael's Church was to serve a number of functions: in 1620 it was used as a wood store and twenty-five years later it acted as the home of Edinburgh University when the plague-stricken capital was abandoned.[5] Both the Reformation of 1559–60 and occupation by Cromwellian troops also took their toll; in the 1650s horses were stabled in the nave and troops were housed in the triforium.[6]

At the foot of The Peel is the steeple of the tolbooth. It is seen in more detail in Slezer's second view. The medieval tolbooth had been demolished on Cromwell's instructions to serve as building materials for defences of The Peel. After the restoration of Charles II (1649–85) in 1660 much repair work awaited the townspeople. Around 1661, the burgh council petitioned the privy council that the town was 'destitut of a prison house … ever since the year 1651 at which tyme not only was the prison house destroyed by the Inglish usurpers bot their toune and inhabitants were harazed and undone so that they are not yet in a capacity to rebuild any prison house by themselves without supply'.[7] The new tolbooth was constructed between 1668 and 1670, to a design of John Mylne, the king's master mason, with a double staircase to the first floor, as may be seen, and a spire added about 1673.[8] The interior was embellished with paintings by a Dutchman who was paid £6 7s 7d.[9]

Major reparations were effected throughout the town: a new grammar school, repair of the Cross Well, a shambles and a meal market, as well as private housing all needed upgrading or rebuilding. Slezer's view portrays an orderly town, with a low, apparently stone, wall replacing the ditch and the flimsy wooden palisading which blew down in high winds.[10] But just as with its predecessor, this was no highly defensive structure, but rather a demarcation of the burgh (*see* 37). One feature that may be seen to the near left is an old dovecot, still extant to this day. Cromwell's occupation did not destroy everything in the town.

Endnotes

1 Groome, *Gazetteer*, v, 515.

2 S. Stronach, J. Franklin and C. Wallace, 'Linlithgow before the palace: new evidence for the early royal residence' (unpublished Headland Archaeology report for Historic Scotland, 2007).

3 R. D. Pringle, *Linlithgow Palace. A Historical Guide to the Royal Palace and Peel* (Historic Scotland, 1995), 21; P. Hume Brown (ed.), *Tours in Scotland, 1671 & 1681 by Thomas Kirk and Ralph Thoresby* (Edinburgh, 1892), 43.

4 E. P. Dennison and R. Coleman, *Historic Linlithgow: The Archaeological Implications of Development* (Scottish Burgh Survey, 2000), 62.

5 B. Jamieson, *The Church of St Michael of Linlithgow* (Kirkcaldy, n.d.), 12–14; *Extracts from the Records of the Burgh of Edinburgh*, eds J. D. Marwick *et al.* (SBRS, 1869–), viii, 78, 84.

6 Dennison and Coleman, *Historic Linlithgow*, 34, 64–5.

7 NRS, B48/18/108, Town Council petition to Privy Council, *c.* 1661.

8 P. Cadell (ed.), *The Third Statistical Account of Scotland: The County of West Lothian* (Edinburgh, 1992), xxi, 144; *Tolbooths and Town-houses*, 135–8.

9 NRS, B48/9/4, Linlithgow Town Council Minute Book, 1673–94, 14 March 1674.

10 *CDS*, iv, 459.

71 Linlithgow, 1806–7

Joseph Mallord William Turner (1775–1851) filled eight sketchbooks during a three-week tour of Scotland in the summer of 1801. In these he rapidly captured views and outlined compositions that he occasionally worked up with watercolour. While concerned mainly with landscapes, his pages also contained a number of townscape views including Dunkeld, Edinburgh Old Town, Glasgow Cathedral, Inveraray, Queensferry and Stirling.[1]

By the time the artist visited Linlithgow, the town had around 3,500 inhabitants with the principal trades being wool, tanning, shoemaking and distilling. It had lost its former importance and had become a quiet, yet highly picturesque backwater, its atmosphere enhanced by degrees of neglect and decay. It was noted that 'while Linlithgow wants the elegance and regularity which distinguishes modern towns, it possesses a variety of objects which cannot fail to impress the mind of an attentive observer with an idea of ancient grandeur'.[2] Another wrote that:

> Many of the houses have, it must be owned, a mean aspect, and exhibit striking symptoms of decay. Several, however, have been recently rebuilt, and other operations of a similar kind are now going forward; so that, in process of time, the whole may be expected to assume a modern and more elegant appearance. … Even the old houses have their effect on a contemplative mind. As many of these, during the Royal residence at Linlithgow, belonged to persons of the first rank, they mark the simplicity of simpler times, contrasted with the luxury of the present; and, by their decayed condition, show the natural tendency of all human things.

The writer, the local minister, stressed the artistic potential of the place recognised by Turner: 'Few places, indeed, would afford a finer subject for the pencil.'[3]

As clearly demonstrated in Slezer's prospects of the town (70), Linlithgow enjoys an exceptional townscape on account of its landscape setting and the dramatic positioning of its palace and parish kirk on a promontory on the south shore of the loch. From the late thirteenth century, this was the site of an important noble residence that developed in scale, strategic and symbolic significance. In 1440 the palace was rebuilt and, from then until 1603, when James VI (1567–1625) ascended the throne of England, it was a seat of the Scottish court. Linlithgow was a favourite residence of James V (1513–1542) and his

71. J. M. W. Turner, *Linlithgow Palace*, 1806–7

daughter Mary, Queen of Scots (1542–1567) was born there in December 1542. By 1688 it was in a ruinous state, and it was further damaged in 1746 when soldiers of the Duke of Cumberland's army, who were stationed in the palace, accidentally burned it down.

The adjacent church of St Michael is one of the grandest parish churches in Scotland and was once graced by a crown spire, symbolising the royal associations – one of only a few buildings with such a feature – but removed in 1821 because of its threatened collapse. The townhouse is also one of the finest in the country and reflects the former importance of the town. At the time of the painting, it still retained its timber upper steeple, although lost in a fire of 1847, which, like those at Stirling, Dumfries, Glasgow University and the Tron Kirk in Edinburgh, was based on the tower of Holyrood Abbey Church.[4] In some views, particularly from the south, the three buildings – palace, church and townhouse – read as an ensemble that gives the centre of the town a critical focus and picturesque profile. Separately, they represent each of the Three Estates, the representatives of the nobility, church and burghs which made up the parliament of Scotland prior to 1690. This is reinforced by the fact that the Scottish parliament met at Linlithgow on several occasions and the palace was the setting at Christmas 1540 for a performance of *Ane Pleasant Satyre of the Thrie Estaitis*, the Scots morality play by Sir David Lyndsay (*c.* 1486–1555), before James V and Mary of Guise.

Turner's painting, done in oil on canvas, suggests the work of Poussin, but with a medieval Scottish rather than a classical backdrop, in which the buildings are adjusted and repositioned for artistic effect. Knowing the history and symbolism of the buildings it contains, one could interpret the painting as a representation of the innocence, beauty and youth surviving beneath the overshadowing, crumbling symbols of the town's and the nation's troubled historic past. However, this was almost certainly not Turner's intention; he simply recognised and exploited the possibilities of the buildings and their setting for convenient artistic effect, employing their exceptional profile as a time-weathered backdrop to a scene in Arcadia, the Gothic replacing classical ruins.

The composition can be traced to one of two sketches of the town now in the Fogg Art Museum at Harvard.[5] The oil painting is dateable to around 1806–7, having been first shown at the one-man exhibition that Turner staged in his own gallery at his home in the summer of 1810. It is one of three works mentioned in John Taylor's newspaper, *The Sun* (12 June 1810), as displaying 'all the higher qualities of the art'.[6] David Wilkie noted in his diary for 7 and 8 May 1810 that he thought it 'one of his best pictures'.[7] The painting was shown in Manchester in 1829 when the critic of the *Manchester Guardian*, clearly dissatisfied with the artist's then more advanced style, called on him to return to the concern for 'nature' it displayed.[8]

Turner was similarly attracted to the dramatic landscapes of Europe including France, Switzerland and later the Rhine valley with its romantic ruins of castles. His artistic response to such scenes was central to the development of the thoughts and writings of his defender William Ruskin (1819–1900), who privileged the idea of the picturesque as a combination of beauty and the sublime, given nobility by the effects of time.[9]

The roofless shell of the palace which captivated Turner has remained as a picturesque ruin since he sketched and painted it, although deliberately preserved as such in accordance with accepted best practice in relation to national monuments. How appropriate is the fact such monuments and aspects of the historic built environment are sustained through state care and legislation, which is guided by a philosophy of conservation that has its roots in the thinking of Turner's champion, Ruskin, and his followers.

Turner had further associations with Scotland in which he drew its towns. In 1818 he sketched Linlithgow once more while in visiting Edinburgh in connection with making illustrations for Walter Scott's *The Provincial Antiquities of Scotland* (1818–26).[10] He was in Edinburgh in 1822 for George IV's state visit, and returned in 1831 and 1834, when he stayed at Abbotsford in connection with his illustrations for *The Poetical Works of Sir Walter Scott* (1834),[11] and the later prose works and an edition of Waverley novels (1839).[12]

Endnotes

1 In particular, the *Scotch Lakes Sketchbook* in the Turner Bequest, Tate, London.

2 R. Heron, *Scotland Described: or, a Topographical Description of all the Counties of Scotland* (Edinburgh, 1797), 95.

3 *OSA*, xiv, 549.

4 D. Howard, 'Dutch influence on Scottish architecture in the sixteenth, seventeenth and early eighteenth centuries' in J. L. Williams, *Dutch Art and Scotland. A Reflection of Taste* (Edinburgh, 1992), 40–2; J. Gifford, C. McWilliam and D. Walker, *The Buildings of Scotland. Edinburgh* (Harmondsworth, 1984), 137–8.

5 *Linlithgow Palace and Church* (1801, Fogg Art Museum, Harvard, Cambridge, MA, USA). Another watercolour of 1801 in the National Gallery of Victoria, Melbourne, Australia, shows the palace with the kirk tower and some town buildings behind, viewed across the loch from the south-east. Also framed by trees, the buildings are largely in silhouette but the drawing effectively captures the landscape setting of the Peel. A watercolour sketch in the Indianapolis Museum of Art views the scene from the opposite side.

6 H. F. Finberg, 'Turner's Gallery in 1810', *The Burlington Magazine*, vol. 93, no. 585 (December, 1951), 383–7.

7 Quoted online at Walker Art Gallery, Liverpool website: www.liverpoolmuseums.org.uk/walker/collections/19c/turner.aspx.

8 *Manchester Guardian,* 29 August 1829.

9 J. Jokilehto, *A History of Architectural Conservation* (Oxford, 1999), 179.

10 W. Scott, *The Provincial Antiquities of Scotland* (Edinburgh, 1818–26). This includes the engraving *Edinburgh from the Calton Hill.*

11 This includes the engraving *Edinburgh from Blackford Hill.*

12 A. Wilton, *Turner in the British Museum. Drawings and Watercolours* (London, 1975), 110–12.

72   Melrose, 1830 and 1821

This lively view of Melrose was drawn by Thomas Shepherd (1793–1864), a topographical draughtsman and drawing master who specialised in city scenes.[1] Much of his work comprised views of London, where he lived, but this print of the market square in Melrose, dated 1830, shows that he was also skilled at capturing rural life.

Melrose grew in the shadow of its famous abbey. Much of the town's early history, as a settlement at one of the abbey gates, is conjectural, supported by occasional references in the much better documented history of the abbey itself. In 1303, for example, during an English invasion, an English knight escaped from the abbey but was captured in a house outside one of the abbey gates, which suggests that some form of settlement, however small, existed then.[2] Formal recognition of the town's status did not come until 1609, when Melrose was erected a burgh of barony for John Ramsay, 1st Viscount Haddington (c. 1580–1626), and favourite of James VI (1567–1625), who also granted Ramsay the title of Lord Ramsay of Melrose.[3]

Dominating this view of Melrose is the town cross. The *New Statistical Account*, written a few years after this picture was drawn, tells us that it stood 'near the south entrance of the monastery'[4] (also the likely site of the original settlement).[5] It is possible that a cross had stood on or near this site for centuries, a decree of excommunication by the abbot being proclaimed 'at the cross before the gate' as early as 1422. This early cross may have been a sanctuary cross, marking the abbey boundary.[6] It was not unusual for the religious character of such crosses to become secularised over time to reflect a growing municipal importance and many came to be used as market crosses. After the Reformation, this process was accelerated, and, in many cases, every vestige of religious association was removed.

The *NSA* claims that the 'popish emblem' on top of the Melrose cross was replaced by the arms of the Earl of Haddington in 1604.[7] As John Ramsay did not acquire the Earldom of Haddington until 1606 and that of Lord Melrose until 1609,[8] the date 1604 is unlikely to be correct. The date actually carved at the top of the shaft is 1645 but whether the cross was altered, repaired or even replaced that year is not known.[9] That some secularisation of the cross took place would accord with a claim in the earlier *Statistical Account* that sixty-eight religious statues from the abbey ruins were destroyed about that time.[10]

Shepherd appears to have painted a religious cross but the sketch made by Sir David Erskine (1772–1837), nine years earlier, clearly shows an animal on top of the shaft.[11] A

72. Thomas Shepherd, *The Market Square with Cross and Fant Well*, 1830

72a. Sir David Erskine, *Melrose Cross, June 17th, 1821*

description published in 1900 supports this, stating that the cross had a shield with a carved mell (or mallet) and rose, the date 1645 and a sundial on its squared head. Above was a 'very much-weathered and decayed unicorn'.[12] This would not have been unusual. The unicorn rampant was very common on such crosses.

One possible explanation is that Shepherd drew his picture en route between London and Edinburgh, where he went to prepare illustrations for a book. Melrose lay on the main road between Jedburgh and Edinburgh, and Shepherd may have stopped to admire the magnificent ruins of the former abbey. His sketches complete, Shepherd returned to London to prepare the plates. *Modern Athens*, a celebration of the city of Edinburgh, was published in 1828. This print is dated 1830, so Shepherd could have been working on it as many as three years after the original sketch was made. If the sketch was unclear because the unicorn was already much 'decayed' and, given the religious associations of the abbey, Shepherd may simply have made a mistake.

The unusual domed structure beside the cross is the town well. A woman can be seen drawing water to fill her bucket while a boy drinks from cupped hands or washes his face. Known as the Pant Well, it was built about 1813 as part of a private initiative to improve the town's water supply. Some twenty years after this print was made, it was replaced by an 'elegant fountain', more in keeping with Melrose's growing popularity as a tourist destination.[13]

It is ironic that the once wealthy and politically important abbey, that had played such a significant role in the early life of the town, should remain one of its greatest assets long after its destruction by the English in 1545. Still described at the end of the eighteenth century as 'one of the most magnificent in the kingdom',[14] Melrose Abbey was the area's most famous tourist attraction to which the highly popular novels of Sir Walter Scott (1771–1832) added romance. It was the spirited Scott, who lived just outside Melrose, who organised much needed conservation work on the abbey ruins in 1822.[15]

Melrose did not embrace the industrial revolution in the way that the nearby manufacturing town of Galashiels did (*see* 44). Yet Shepherd's print shows that Melrose had achieved a certain sophistication. Although thatched, the houses in this picture are well proportioned, with good masonry chimneys, elegant astragaled windows and good ceiling heights, the sort of buildings that would typically have been reroofed in slate before the large-scale redevelopment of the nineteenth century. One house in East Port even boasted a sundial, built onto a window sill.[16]

At the time this picture was drawn, Melrose had a population of about 500 and among the new houses being built were some substantial villas. By 1861 the population had more than doubled through 'an influx of the middle and higher classes'.[17] Set on the banks of the Tweed, with the Eildon Hills behind, as the picture shows, Melrose had become a highly attractive residential town.

Endnotes

1 *DNB*, Thomas Hosmer Shepherd.

2 E. P. Dennison and R. Coleman, *Historic Melrose: The Archaeological Implications of Development* (Scottish Burgh Survey, 1998), 27.

3 *Ibid.*, 35; Pryde, *Burghs*, no. 276.

4 *NSA*, iii, 61.

5 Dennison and Coleman, *Historic Melrose*, 27.

6 *Ibid.*, 32.

7 *NSA*, iii, 61.

8 *DNB*, John Ramsay, Viscount Haddington.

9 Dennison and Coleman, *Historic Melrose*, 36.

10 *OSA*, ix, 90.

11 *DNB*, Sir David Erskine; *see also* K. Cruft, J. Dunbar and R. Fawcett, *The Buildings of Scotland: Borders* (New Haven and London, 2006), 552–3.

12 J. W. Small, *Scottish Market Crosses* (Stirling, 1900), plate 18.

13 Dennison and Coleman, *Historic Melrose*, 45–8.

14 *OSA*, ix, 89.

15 Dennison and Coleman, *Historic Melrose*, 43.

16 *Ibid.*, 99

17 *Ibid.*, 45.

73   Montrose, 1826

Montrose was probably founded in the reign of David I (1124–53), and its achievement of burgh status may arguably be narrowed to the period 1134–46.[1] It occupies an exposed peninsula bounded on the west by a tidal basin, on the east by the North Sea, and on the south by the river South Esk which connects the two. The town developed as a single, wide street along the highest ground with rig gardens running from it. By the seventeenth century, it was described as 'a very handsome, well-built toune, of considerable trade in all places abroad, good homes, all of stone, excellent large streets, a good tolbuith and church, and shipping of their own, a good shore at the toune'.[2] The good harbour and rich hinterland were the basis of thriving trade and economic activity, including the export of grain and the import of flax and timber which were worked locally.[3] This encouraged construction at the shore of 'malthouses and kilns and granaries for cornes, of three storeys high and some more, and are increased in such number that in a short time it is thought they will equal if not exceed the town in greatness'.[4]

This portrait by Alexander Milne or Mill (fl. 1820–42) of the principal public place shows a neat, ordered burgh with modestly prosperous residents. Pavements and public lighting are in place and there are well-cleaned street surfaces. The spacious High Street, 'one of the finest town spaces in Scotland',[5] owes its character to 'improvement' works undertaken in 1748, when a 'mid row' block which ran up its centre (itself an addition dividing the original medieval space) was demolished, as at Musselburgh (75), to combine Murray Street and High Street into one. After it was 'ca'd down', owners were allowed to form new frontages fourteen feet nearer the street, resulting in further change. The drama of the demolition is recorded in a verse, which also contains information on how the demolished buildings had been constructed:

> Auld Willy Grubb gied round the town,
> And rang his merry bell;
> And cried, 'Ilk man and mither's son
> Take heed to what I tell.
>
> 'Come a' ye masons, wi' your pikes,
> Your hammers and your shools;
> And a' ye wright's. wi' files and saws,
> And sic mischievous tools.'

73. Alexander Milne, *Montrose High Street*, 1826

'For I proclaim the Rotten Raw,
I' the middle of the town,
Is ordered by the magistrates
This day to be ca'd down.'

...

Wi' pike and shool, wi' axe and saw,
Wi' swinging rope and hammer,
The wrights and masons struck the Raw,
Until the jeasts did stammer.

The roofs were made o' auld stob thack,
The waa's o' plastered fir,
So down they came wi mony a whack,
That ruddied wi' the virr.

The loons did gather up the strae,
Ilk broken door and rafter;
Though at their heels Rob Davidson,
The town's-keeper, ran after.[6]

The terrace of buildings shown between the church and the High Street was a remnant of the old row. Further realignment of streets was proposed, including extending the High Street in a straight line south to the river, but this was not done. In the distance is a series of gable ends presented to the street. James Boswell wrote in 1773 that 'many of the houses are built with their ends to the street, which looks awkward',[7] although such Dutch-inspired architecture was common throughout the Scottish burghs. It was this building tradition which earned natives of the town the nickname 'gable-endies'.

The words of the local minister in 1835 echo the image of neat order portrayed in the painting:

> Montrose is justly accounted one of the first provincial towns for its size in Scotland, or perhaps in Great Britain. It receives, on account of its neat and cleanly appearance, many encomiums from visitors. The houses, if not elegant, are, on the whole, well built and regular; but, like those in Flanders, their gable ends are often pointed towards the street. With one or two exceptions they are now all of stone, and many of them covered with blue slates.[8]

The painting shows the west front of Montrose townhouse, which was built in 1762–4 and altered in 1819, to add assembly rooms and an extra storey and wing. It has an elegant arcaded loggia or *piazza* and is the most notable building in the scene. It was erected to replace the medieval tolbooth that remained in use as a prison until it was demolished in 1837.[9] With its council chambers, guildhall, court room, coffee-room and public library, it was a symbol of the town's status and prosperity, and it is now difficult to understand the criticism it once attracted as something which 'disfigures the High Street by encroaching too far upon it'.[10] The building was refronted in ashlar in 1908. The old church spire was replaced in 1832 by a new flying-buttressed one by Gillespie Graham, which developed his earlier work in Alloa (5). Milne painted another view, looking from the north, which confirms that the activity seen just beyond the townhouse in the painting under consideration here is the burgh's outdoor market.

The identities of many of the people in the image are known, including burgh officials such as the top-hatted Dean of Guild Court officer, the town keeper in a tail coat with red trim and white stockings, the town officer, church minister, the artist himself (outside the tinsmith's shop), the Provost's child being carried by a servant girl, as well as several other local worthies. Among the 'characters', we see a pickpocket in action, a tartan-clad blind fiddler led by his callant, a Highland soldier, a one-legged man and the local barber walking towards a man holding a salmon in the shadows of the right-most gable.[11]

The prosperity of Montrose continued throughout the nineteenth century, and this painting captures the town just prior to a wave of redevelopment in which many of the remaining vernacular buildings and details, such as boarded shop fronts and forestairs, were lost to grander Victorian structures. What this painting does not show is the town as a thriving commercial port with busy wharves and warehouses by the water on 'a stage set by nature for a Dutch town'.[12] Fortunately for posterity, the wider prospect of the town was captured by a number of artists including Slezer,[13] James S. Paterson[14] and Milne himself.[15] Each of these works shows a tight-knit urban fabric built in the tradition of the 'weather protected city', so typical of Scotland and elsewhere in northern Europe.[16]

Endnotes

1 Pryde, *Burghs*, no. 15.

2 Groome, *Gazetteer*, v, 53.

3 G. Jackson and S. G. E. Lythe (eds), *The Port of Montrose. A History of its Harbour, Trade and Shipping* (New York, 1993).

4 Groome, *Gazetteer*, v, 53.

5 C. McWilliam, *Scottish Townscape* (London, 1975), 243.

6 D. Mitchell, *The History of Montrose* (Montrose, 1866).

7 J. Boswell, *The Journal of a Tour to the Hebrides with Samuel Johnson, LL.D*, quoted in McWilliam, *Townscape*, 242.

8 *OSA*, v, 48–9.

9 *Tolbooths and Town-houses*, 144–8.

10 *NSA*, xi, 282.

11 There is another version of this painting, but without the *dramatic personae*, in Milne's *Montrose High Street, Steeple and Town House* (Angus Council).

12 McWilliam, *Townscape*, 242.

13 Cavers, *Slezer*, 40.

14 *Montrose from the South West* (Angus Council).

15 *Montrose from Ferryden* (Angus Council).

16 C. McKean, 'The evolution of the weather-protected city', in E. P. Dennison (ed.), *Conservation and Change in Historic Towns: Research Directions for the Future* (York, 1999), 24–38.

74   Musselburgh and Leith, 1547

In September 1547, the Duke of Somerset, Lord Protector since the death of Henry VIII (1509–47) eight months before, entered Scotland with a largely professional force of 15,000 men, the largest invasion army assembled since the reign of Edward I (1272–1307).[1] Three years before, while Earl of Hertford, he had staged a daring amphibious raid on Leith and Edinburgh, burned part of the Palace of Holyroodhouse but had been repulsed at the great Netherbow Port, the capital's eastern gate.[2] These were the two most dramatic episodes in the 'Rough Wooing', a phrase first coined by Sir Walter Scott to describe the series of attacks, invasions and occupation by English forces in the 1540s, to coerce the Scots into agreeing to a marriage between the infant Mary, Queen of Scots (1542–67) and Henry's young son and heir Edward. In the reign of the young Edward VI (1547–53), as in that of his father, maps were a key element in military strategy. Equally, battle plans were used to add lustre to the reputation of English armies and their military victories.

The campaign of 1547 produced a series of images. Some were of newly constructed English forts, strategically placed at the passes through the Scottish Borders and along the east coast as far north as Broughty at the mouth of the River Tay. Others were in the form of story-telling cartoons, including this account of the Battle of Pinkie, near Musselburgh.[3] It show the initial positions of the two armies, either side of the River Esk, the rash foray of the Scots across the river and their subsequent headlong flight to the gates of Edinburgh, pursued by murderously effective English cavalry. The Scottish losses were between 6,000 and 10,000 men, a significant proportion of them by drowning in the River Esk. The English claimed to have lost only 200 men, but probably suffered nearer to 800 dead.[4] The plan was published forty years later, by the London printer Raphael Holinshed (c.1520–c.1581) in his *Chronicles*,[5] even though by then the two realms were supposed to be bound together in a Protestant-inspired 'amity'.

Somerset's strategy was innovative in a number of ways. The tried and tested nostrum of invasion armies was that a military campaign could last for only thirty days, the maximum time that an army could provision itself. In 1544 Somerset had doubled the effective length of a campaign by having his army transported to the Forth by a fleet of

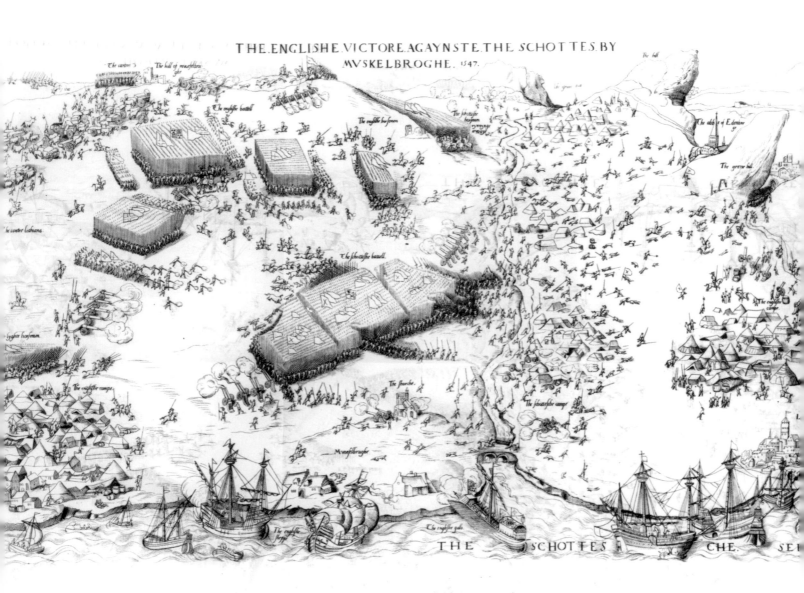

Within the illustration, the following labels appear:

THE.ENGLISHE.VICTORE.AGAYNSTE.THE.SCHOTTES.BY MVSKELBROGHE. 1547.

74. Raphael Holinshed, *The Englishe Victore against the Schottes by Muskelbroghe*, 1547

ships. In 1547 his force was too large to do other than travel by land, along the well-worn path through Berwick-upon-Tweed. But a large fleet accompanied the invasion, to form an effective supply line.

The image of the battle provides the first available glimpse of both Musselburgh and Leith. In the case of Musselburgh, a burgh since the fourteenth century, only a few houses are depicted.[6] The priorities of military mapping were clear: the two key elements were the bridge over the fast-flowing River Esk and the church at Inveresk, a strategic landmark at the top of a hill, overlooking both the burgh and the sharp defile through which the river passed en route to the sea. Inveresk had been the site of a key Roman fort, and there had been a bridge across the Esk since Roman times.[7] The key decision for Somerset was which of the two viable routes for an invasion army to take. In 1214 Edward II (1307–27), en route to Bannockburn, had chosen the shorter inland route from Coldstream northwards via Soutra, virtually on the line of the present A697 and A68 roads. In 1547 Somerset, with an accompanying fleet, chose the longer coastal route, which crucially depended on securing the bridge at Musselburgh.

74a. Leith, 1547

At the bottom right of the drawing, another bridge is highlighted, linking North and South Leith, with buildings portrayed on both sides of the Water of Leith, including the prominent tolbooth, but no town walls. By 1559, when an English fleet next attempted an assault on Leith, a complete citadel had been built with walls around it in the *trace italienne* style (*see* 7a).[8] That was the main reason why the English fleet was repulsed and why a siege of the town begun in the following April by an English army in support of the Protestant Lords of the Congregation failed to take the town. Ironically, *trace italienne* was the same novel and extremely expensive star-shaped design used by the English to build their chain of forts in Scotland in 1547–8.

In 1547, perhaps surprisingly, Somerset did not march on to take either Leith, which surely would not have withstood an assault, or Edinburgh, which might well have done so, as it had in 1544. Both are depicted at the edge of the drawing, beyond the 'Grene Hill' (or Greenside). He preferred instead to construct an English 'pale' or buffer zone across the Borders. The English headquarters were established at Haddington for the next three years. However, a combination of regional revolts in Cornwall and Norfolk, overstretched resources and bankruptcy led to the fall of Somerset as Protector in 1549 and an English withdrawal from Scotland in the following year.

Endnotes

1 For the English campaign of 1547, *see* M. H. Merriman, *The Rough Wooings: Mary, Queen of Scots, 1542–1551* (East Linton, 2000), 232–64; G. Phillips, *The Anglo-Scots Wars, 1513–1550: A Military History* (Woodbridge, 1999), 178–200; D. H. Caldwell, 'The battle of Pinkie', in N. Macdougall (ed.), *Scotland and War, AD 79–1918* (Edinburgh, 1991), 61–94.

2 For the campaign of 1544, *see* Merriman, *Rough Wooings*, 143–9.

3 A series of five drawings of the battle were discovered in the Bodleian Library, Oxford, by Sir Charles Oman in the 1930s. They were published in C. R. Oman, 'The battle of Pinkie, Sept. 10, 1547', *Archaeological Journal*, 90 (1933), 1–25. In another version, shown here, the five images were compacted into one. *See* C. de W. Crookshank, 'Military battle prints', *Journal Soc. Army Hist. Research*, 12 (1933), 102–3.

4 Caldwell, 'Battle of Pinkie', 86–7.

5 R. Holinshed, *Chronicles of England, Scotland and Ireland* (London, 1808), vol. iii, 872–3, 876; R. Holinshed, *Historie of Scotland* (London, 1805), 549–50.

6 Pryde, *Burghs*, no. 112.

7 E. P. Dennison and R. Coleman, *Historic Musselburgh: The Archaeological Implications of Development* (Scottish Burgh Survey, 1996), 14–15, 18.

8 For the French citadel at Leith, *see* F. W. Steer, 'A map illustrating the siege of Leith, 1560', *PSAS*, 95 (1961–2), 280–3; S. Harris, 'The fortifications and siege of Leith: a further study of the map of the siege in 1560', *PSAS*, 121 (1991), 359–68. Another view is to be found in G. Donaldson, 'Map of the siege of Leith, 1560', *BOEC*, 32 (1966), 1–7. The Petworth map is located in West Sussex Record Office, PHA 46/40 (1960).

75   Musselburgh, 1827

This view of Musselburgh is a watercolour on paper by William Carroll (fl. 1790s–1827)[1] who may have been an Irish artist living in London in the 1790s. The circumstances of its composition are unknown; no other Scottish subject by him has been found to date. It was painted in 1827, at a time when Musselburgh was experiencing relative prosperity, as may be seen by certain clues in this illustration.

The largeness of the market place was often an indication of the wealth of a burgh and the pull that market had on the local hinterland. Musselburgh's market place had been impressive from medieval times, but as pressure for space came in the town centre new roads were forced in. A Mid Row was built in post-medieval times in the centre of this open space, with the main thoroughfare passing to the south of it. Its removal some time in the eighteenth century, probably *c.* 1761, restored Musselburgh's market place to its former grandeur.[2]

The most important symbols of the power of a burgh's market were the tolbooth, the market cross and the tron. Musselburgh's tolbooth was largely destroyed in 1544 during the 'Rough Wooing' (*see* 74) but the steeple seen on the left of the lower section of the later tolbooth building survived. This probably dated to at least the first half of the sixteenth century and probably earlier as the town clock, seen on the tolbooth wall, dates to the fifteenth century. The clock was donated to the people of Musselburgh by the 'Dutch States', a sure indication of close trading links, and indeed the steeple itself portrays the influence of the Low Countries. Attached to the tolbooth is an elegant two-storeyed council chamber wing or town hall erected in 1762.[3]

Burghs were set up and organised for trade. All marketing had to be seen to be open and fair; strict market regulations monitored all trading transactions; and the weight and quality of goods were checked by the town authorities in the open near to the cross or at the tron, using the town's official weights and measures. The market cross may be seen to the right of the picture just in front of one of the hostelries. Musselburgh also benefited from its proximity to the capital. It often functioned as a satellite town, offering services, agricultural produce from the rich, local soil and manufactures from its industries, which depended greatly on good coal reserves nearby.

75. William Carroll, *Musselburgh Town House*, 1827

The prosperity of the town is also seen in the substantial houses, many built for wealthy Edinburgh-based merchants and their families. Built of stone and with slated roofs, they were considerably superior to many in the poorer parts of town that were still thatched. Significantly, too, coaching inns flank the sides of the market square. Musselburgh was the first stop for the Edinburgh coaches moving south. The air of prosperity is reinforced by the number of horse-drawn carriages in the market square; one might well have been the Edinburgh–London fly.[4] Only the wealthy could afford to travel in such style. Gentlemen in top hats trot though the square, in sharp contrast to the modest trader with his pack-horse passing by, possibly carrying a load of textiles. Here were no 'play areas' for children. The streets were the only playgrounds when little ones were lucky enough to have free time – they worked long hours. They took their chance to make fun wherever they could, even if it meant trying to avoid horses' hooves.

75a. Pinkie Pillar

In the right foreground is one of the two Pinkie Pillars, erected in 1770 at the eastern limit of the town. Topping the pillars are urns bearing the burgh arms. Some of the lower course stones indicate a previous use as they show the diagonal broaching of Roman masons, possibly once resident at nearby Inveresk.[5]

An open grid may be seen running along the central section of the market place. This was for the removal of rainwater and any effluence that might have resulted from market days. Burgh officials were constantly vigilant in monitoring the health of the town. Those who brought rancid meat into the town were prosecuted on a number of occasions. Regulations ordering the removal of dunghills and rubbish from thoroughfares and prohibiting butchers from slaughtering animals on the streets were routine and regularly repeated. And livestock was free to roam the town well into the nineteenth century.[6] This, then, is a somewhat idealised picture, portraying the very best of the town and not the full reality.[7]

Endnotes

1 W. G. Strickland, *Dictionary of Irish Artists*, 2 vols (Dublin and London, 1913), i, 201.

2 E. P. Dennison and R. Coleman, *Historic Musselburgh: The Archaeological Implications of Development* (Scottish Burgh Survey, 1996), 20, 39; NRS, MS Musselburgh Council Minute Book, 1762–86 (B52/3/3). 17 September 1774.

3 Dennison and Coleman, *Historic Musselburgh*, 86; *Tolbooths and Town-houses*, 149–51.

4 E. P. Dennison, *Holyrood and Canongate: A Thousand Years of History* (Edinburgh, 2005), 122.

5 Dennison and Coleman, *Historic Musselburgh*, 86.

6 NRS, MS Musselburgh Council Minute Book, 1679–1714 (B52/3/1), 8 and *passim*; J. Paterson, *The History of the Regality of Musselburgh* (Musselburgh, 1861), 32; NRS, B52/3/1, 248.

7 We appreciate the assistance of Craig Statham of the John Gray Centre (Library Museum Archive), Haddington, in locating this image.

76   Nairn, *c.* 1590 and 1832

This view of the coastline of the Moray Firth was drawn around 1590 by the map-maker Timothy Pont (*c.* 1565–*c.* 1615) who had graduated from St Leonard's College, University of St Andrews, probably in 1583.[1] There is no common agreement as to why Pont undertook this huge task of mapping Scotland in such detail. He was possibly commissioned by James VI (1567–1625).

Pont's attention to detailing human settlements and their related structures – cottouns, milltouns, kirktouns, churches, chapels, mills, as well as castles and large houses, with some bridges, standing stones, mines, roads or tracks and boundaries – is impressive. Less obvious but equally important are the depictions of natural features – woods, rivers, burns, hills, glens, lochs and islands. This view illustrates many of the above features, some settlements being so small as to receive merely a place name, but it may be seen as a well-populated and wooded area.

The burgh of Nairn is marked clearly, and in italicised capital letters as with many burghs. Today, one may walk through the town and still see some extant medieval features, such as the lie of the burgage plots or tofts (*see* 1) along the High Street. There is, however, no standing evidence of a castle built by at least 1196, when King William the Lion (1165–1214) stayed there in the autumn and received hostages from Harold, Earl of Caithness and Orkney. This fortress was part of the crown's master-plan to set aside land to build the castle, as well as to found a burgh called Invernairn (later, Nairn). Some have argued, however, that the king was merely re-establishing or enlarging an existing castle; the chronicler, the Revd James Fraser, writing in 1666, argued that the castle was standing in the reign of Alexander I (1107–24). Others contend that in the twelfth century it belonged to the bishops of Moray and some have argued for a still earlier provenance, being reputedly captured by the Danes in the reign of Malcolm I (943–54).[2] Whatever the origins of Nairn Castle, it certainly existed by the twelfth century.

What does not come through so clearly is that the coastline on which Nairn was founded is notoriously unstable. A map is a statement in time; and Pont delineated what he saw at that time, which could take no account of the appearance of the landscape and seascape before and after the 1590s. But documentary evidence gives a few clues: Robert Gordon of Straloch (1580–1661), writing some time before 1661, commented that 'time has changed the appearance of [Nairn] and the sea has

76. Timothy Pont, *Nairn*, 1590s

partly destroyed with sandbanks and partly washed away a good part of the highly productive land';[3] and in 1663 Alexander Brodie of Brodie wrote in his diary 'Nairn was in danger to be quitt lost by the sand and by the water'.[4] In 1694 the Culbin estate of 3,600 acres, a little to the east of Nairn, was completely covered with sand, and the township there was buried for ever.[5] To add to the insecurity of the site, the River Nairn, which runs though the town, moved its course dramatically to both east and west throughout the centuries as is shown in a map of 1832.[6]

76a. Timothy Pont, *Nairn*, 1590s

There are many reasons for the choice of site when a new burgh was founded, one of the more persuasive being the existence of a man-made pre-urban nucleus, such as a fortified residence, a castle, or an important ecclesiastical establishment. It is likely that Nairn Castle was such a pre-urban nucleus, offering a measure of protection

76b. Great Reform Act Plans and Reports, 1832: *Nairn*

to the small burghal settlement that clustered near its gates. But where exactly was this early fortification? Intriguingly, Pont's *Mapp of Murray* shows some ruins in the waters off-shore from the mainland, with, in the hand of Robert Gordon (who adapted and transcribed much of Pont's work) 'Ruins of the old Cast[le]'. Gordon, rightly or wrongly, identified Nairn with Ptolemy's *Alata Castra* (winged camp); but he is supported by the *Old Statistical Account* which recounts that the site was 'entirely covered with water', and by the reminiscences that some people remembered seeing 'some vestiges of the foundation at spring tide'.[7] Place-name specialists have likewise stressed the water associations of the name 'Nairn'. Some have argued that 'Nairn' means 'the mouth of the river of alders'; others that it derives from the Indo-European root 'ner' meaning dive, cave or submerge, from the river name Narenta in Illyria, as in the case of a number of European towns such as Narais in France and Narasa in Lithuania.[8]

Is there here evidence that the original castle and burgh stood farther north than the medieval remnants of Nairn that we now see? Is it likely that the early burgh was forced to move its site for geographic and geological factors, as was the case with so many early towns? Some excavations have already revealed evidence of prehistoric occupation beneath the sand dunes of Culbin and the potential for fieldwork to reveal much about coastal settlements has been established elsewhere in the north-east, notably at the deserted burgh of Rattray in Aberdeenshire. Perhaps only archaeology can answer this intriguing question for Nairn.

Endnotes

1 NLS, website, Pont's Maps of Scotland, 1580s–1590s.

2 J. Fraser, 'Polichronicon Seu Policratica Temporum', in W. MacKay (ed.), *Chronicles of the Frasers, 916–1674* (SHS, 1905), 43; G. Bain, *History of Nairnshire* (1st edn, Nairn, 1893), 119; L. Shaw, *History of the Province of Moray*, 3 vols (Glasgow, 1882), iii, 88.

3 A. Mitchell (ed.), *Macfarlane's Geographical Collections*, 3 vols (SHS, 1906–8), ii, 459.

4 D. Laing (ed.), *The Diary of Alexander of Brodie of Brodie and of His Son, James Brodie of Brodie, 1652–85* (Spalding Club, 1863), 293.

5 Bain, *History of Nairnshire*, 290.

6 E. P. Dennison and R. Coleman, *Historic Nairn: The Archaeological Implications of Development* (Scottish Burgh Survey, 1999), 26–7, 35.

7 C. Fleet, 'Writing and signs', in I. C. Cunningham (ed.), *The Nation Survey'd* (East Linton, 2001), 46; OSA, xii, 382–3; F. Petrie, 'Ptolomey's Geography of Albion', *PSAS*, 52 (1917–18), 12–26.

8 Bain, *History of Nairnshire*, 78; W. H. F. Nicolaisen, *Scottish Place-Names* (London, 1989), 188.

77   New Galloway, 1801

This image is one of forty-eight published in 1804 in *Scotia Depicta or The Antiquities, Castles, Public Buildings, Noblemen and Gentlemen's Seats, Cities, Towns and Picturesque Scenery of Scotland*. The illustrations were etched by the noted engraver James Fittler (1758–1835) from drawings 'made on the spot' by John Claude Nattes (*c.* 1765–1822).

Nattes worked throughout Great Britain and France and is recognised as an early champion of watercolour painting in England but one who 'worked mainly among the topographers, and did not get beyond their methods'.[1] He was an occasional exhibitor at the Royal Academy from 1782 to 1804 and a founder member of the Society of Painters in Water Colours, although he was expelled from the Society after he was accused of exhibiting the work of others as his own in 1807. He resumed exhibiting at the Royal Academy up to 1814 and died in London in 1822. In 1789 he was commissioned to record the buildings of Lincolnshire and this resulted in more than 700 drawings and watercolours. He then, like other English artists of his day, turned his attentions to Ireland (*Hibernia Depicta* was published in 1802) and Scotland, drawn by the artistic opportunities of their landscapes. Nattes made most of the Scottish drawings in the company of Dr John Stoddart (1773–1856), author of *Remarks on Local Scenery & Manners in Scotland during the Years 1799 and 1800* (1801). The text which accompanies the collection draws upon this, the *Statistical Account of Scotland* and other published works. Stoddart, an acquaintance of both Sir Walter Scott (1771–1832) and Lord Byron (1788–1824), was heavily influenced by the Romantic movement and its aesthetics of picturesque scenery. He made several journeys through Scotland, mostly on foot or by Shetland pony in the company of Nattes.

New Galloway was granted royal burgh status in 1630 but, on account of its relative remoteness, suffered from competition with Kirkcudbright, nineteen miles to the south.[2] It attracted very little trade or manufacture and remained little more than the small focus of a local agricultural community. At the time of Nattes's drawing, the population was only 300. Settlement in the area dates back much further, as witnessed by Kenmure Castle a mile to the south. The castle is on the flat summit of a perhaps artificial knoll, said to have been the site of the fortress of the Lords of Galloway and the birthplace, in 1249, of John Balliol. The property was a ruin at the time of the visit by Stoddart and Nattes.

77. John Claude Nattes, *View of New Galloway*, in *Scotia Depicta*, 1804

Nattes's image of New Galloway is a view from the north. The town nestles in the valley with the castle set above it and the water 'forming altogether a most charming landscape' in which 'the general features of the scenery around are both grand and picturesque'. The text accompanying the image suggests a bountiful land with pearls in the river, gold in the hills and an improved landscape of lime trees where the cultivated parts contrast with the 'rude but magnificent scene'.[3] The artist was clearly aiming to provide an overall impression but in doing so both the words and drawing over-play the scale of the landscape by making the hills disproportionately high, scenery more typical of the Highlands than Galloway.

The town is depicted as little more than a picturesque, incidental part of the wider landscape. There is little attempt to depict its features or details accurately and, as a consequence, nothing is conveyed of it, its inhabitants or what goes on there. What can be deduced is a village strung out along a single rutted road that passes through the town with some buildings at right angles to it and some set back. These are mainly single-storey, with primitive chimneys and few windows. Most appear to be thatched, which is in keeping with the record that 'the houses were, even at the beginning of the present century, low, ill built, straw-thatched, and often dilapidated'.[4] The steeple looks as if it were that of a church but is in fact part of the townhouse.[5] The text has little to say of the town but does devote some attention to the castle, no doubt on account of its romantic historical associations as much as its architecture. The building is inaccurately depicted by any standards, but particularly when compared with the near-contemporary engravings of Francis Grose (1731–91).[6]

These faults in Nattes's output were recognised in a review of the collection issued shortly after its publication. It judged that its contents were 'by no means sufficiently numerous and varied to justify the very comprehensive range of the title' and observed that 'Mr Nattes is more happy in architectural than in rural painting' and too often poor in his selection of viewpoints when compared to others.[7] In a similar vein, Elizabeth Grant of Rothiemurchus recalled aspects of Nattes's character and work, when he was a drawing tutor to her family circle in London and a visitor to their Highland estate:

> Mr. Nattes was a handsome Italian, elderly, most agreeable … and in some repute as an artist, though never high up among his brethren; he had been sketching in the Highlands when my father fell in with him and brought him to the Doune, where he filled a portfolio with beautifully-executed sketches most accurately drawn. Some of these he reproduced in water-colour, and we framed them and hung them up, and they were pretty enough, but no more like the scenes they were meant to represent than if they had been taken from any other place on the artist's tour; they were, indeed, mere fancy pieces with names below them fully as much travestied as the scenery.[8]

Viewed historically, *Scotia Depicta*, despite its flaws, is important for its place in the history of an emerging new market for illustrated travel literature, as extravagantly promoted in its preface:

> In possession of works like the present, the traveller can at his leisure, and without stirring from his fire side, revisit those scenes, he had some much pleasure in formerly passing through, and recall them to his recollection in a way, which the most laboured and finished descriptions are by themselves inadequate to effect: while to distant nations, and those persons who from business or other causes are either unable or unwilling to encounter the fatigues and expenses of travelling, these works give the most distinct and accurate impression.

Nattes made a speciality of this genre and followed it with collections dedicated to fashionable watering places in England, France and Wales.[9]

Endnotes

1 G. R. Redgrave, *A History of Water-Colour Painting in England* (London, 1905), 98.

2 Pryde, *Burghs*, no. 74.

3 *Scotia Depicta*, plate 30.

4 Groome, *Gazetteer*, iii, 72.

5 *Tolbooths and Town-houses*, 156–7.

6 F. Grose, *The Antiquities of Scotland* (London, 1797). A number of Grose's watercolours of Dumfries and Galloway are to be found in the nine-volume Riddell Collection in NMS.

7 *Scotia Depicta* (London, 1804) in the *Monthly Review*, vol. 46 (1805), 256.

8 E. Grant, *Memoirs of a Highland Lady*, Book 1 (1898). *See* the 1992 edition, 178.

9 *Select Views of Bath, Bristol, Malvern, Cheltenham, and Weymouth* (1805), *Bath Illustrated* (1806) and *Views of Versailles, Paris, and St. Denis* (1809). He also produced drawings for the *Beauties of England and Wales, Copperplate Magazine*, and Howlett's *Views in the County of Lincoln*.

78   New Lanark, *c.* 1818

New Lanark lies just over a mile south of the burgh of Lanark. The village was founded in 1783 by the philanthropic and enterprising David Dale (1739–1806), in conjunction with the industrial innovator Richard Arkwright (1732–1792) as a village of houses, mills and community buildings for cotton manufacture. Dale had previously attempted to establish an industrial enterprise at Blantyre but this had failed. The first mill was opened in 1785 (reduced from five to three storeys in 1945 but now restored as a hotel), the second in 1788 (destroyed by fire before completion and rebuilt in 1789), with a third (built 1790–2 but rebuilt in 1826–33 after burning down in 1819) and a fourth built around 1791–3 but lost to fire in 1883. The spinning machinery invented by Arkwright was powered at first by a supply from the River Clyde brought to the site via a 300-foot (81 metres) tunnel and a lade. Housing was provided in masonry-built tenements laid out along the contours of the slope of the river valley looking down over the mills.

In addition to offering bountiful water resources, the site must also have been selected on account of its picturesque beauty. The Carmichael family of Bonnington House, visible in the left distance, improved the landscape and in 1708 built the handsome viewing pavilion above the Corra Linn, also shown, for the entertainment of friends and guests. On the opposite bank, the Corehouse estate also exploited the topography in its landscape planning, including the densely wooded slope which provides the backdrop to the village. The fame of the wild Falls of Clyde attracted and inspired the work of J. M. W. Turner, Sir Walter Scott, Samuel Taylor Coleridge and the Wordsworths, among many other writers and artists.

In 1799 Dale sold the village to a partnership including his future son-in-law Robert Owen, a Welsh cotton-master who, as mill manager from 1800, was able to apply his theories of enlightened management in pursuit of an ideal industrial community. This he did through 'humane authoritarianism',[1] which saw education and personal development central to life in the community. Owen improved the housing accommodation by combining small flats, paved the streets and introduced management rules for life in the village. He built his reputation on two facilities in particular: the Institution for the Formation of Character, built 1809–16 and later known as the Institute; and the School, one of the first

78. John Winning, *New Lanark from the North-East, c.* 1818

for working-class children in Scotland, which opened in 1817 with fourteen teachers and 274 pupils. These buildings, which were used interchangeably, offered between them a suite of facilities not seen elsewhere, including a variety of classrooms and apartments, some of which had viewing galleries frequented by the many interested visitors who came to the town. There were spaces for lectures, dancing and musical participation, and the walls were dressed with zoological and geographical charts.[2] Both buildings were constructed as two storeys, with basements and central pediments. It was Owen who commissioned this painting, one of a series of watercolours of the village made around 1818 by John Winning (1780–1839), who taught painting at Owen's Institution, where his daughter Janet was also a teacher.[3]

The association of Owen, who was to become renowned as a social reformer, the part the project played in the industrial revolution and its contribution to modern town planning have assured the town of a place in history well beyond Scotland. The village had many visitors, including those interested in progressive education and social reform, those eager to observe how housing and industry could, where properly planned and managed, co-exist satisfactorily and those drawn by the idea of *urbs in rure*, an industrial community in a beautiful countryside setting.

The four large mills can clearly be seen, the buildings displaying Venetian windows to their stairs. The buildings to the far left are the village workshops and dye works and, furthest left, the classical building is the School. The Institution stands in from of one of the four mills. The house of mill manager Robert Owen is in the centre of the picture and that of David Dale is to the right, both being of 1790. Other buildings shown include the mill offices. The long rows of tenement housing, including the four-storey tenement block known as the Nursery Building (1809), where orphan children who worked in the mill were housed, are not shown in this view. Similarly, left out is the four-storey, plain New Buildings of around 1799, 'the same size as the north side of Charlotte Square' in Edinburgh with its pediment and a small bell-house.[4] However, the artist devotes much space to the village's landscape setting, and Dundaff Linn, one of the falls, can be seen in the background. Children and residents wander, play and go about their business in this self-contained, safe and pleasant environment.

Winning's images of the village also became well known in far-away places after he was commissioned by Owen to design a label with an illustration of the village to be affixed to consignments of yarn produced there. A principal destination for the goods was St Petersburg, where Owen and his agent Allan Stewart had managed to corner a market share after the defeat of Napoleon in 1812. In Russia these products became known as 'Picture Yarn' on account of the label illustrations.[5]

Owen left Britain in 1825 for the United States to found his new settlement at New Harmony, leaving the village with a family-owned company. The works were purchased in 1881 by the Lanark Spinning Company, which doubled their former size and introduced more modern machinery.[6] It was eventually closed in 1968.

The outstanding natural landscape setting, the picturesque juxtaposition of buildings and the limited palette of architectural styles and material gives the village a high degree of charm and visual integration. No wonder, therefore, that it attracted several artists. There are earlier illustrations of the village, most notably those by Robert Scott (1777–1841) who visited in 1799, which show the four great mills in place.[7] There is also a large watercolour *c.* 1810 by Hugh William Williams (1773–1829)[8] and, as might be expected, a prospect by John Clark (fl. 1824–8), dated 1825.[9]

The village has undergone considerable conservation and adaptation since the 1970s and now has new life as a tourist destination, with the independent charity, New Lanark Trust, and associated companies playing a major part in its management. The outstanding significance of the site has been recognised through its inclusion on UNESCO's list of World Heritage Sites.

Endnotes

1 C. McWilliam, *Scottish Townscape* (London, 1975), 106.

2 I. Donnachie and G. Hewitt, *Historic New Lanark* (Edinburgh, 1993), 53.

3 *Ibid.*, 88–9; N. Allen, *David Dale, Robert Owen and the Story of New Lanark* (Edinburgh, 1986), 14.

4 McWilliam, *Scottish Townscape*, 106.

5 Donnache and Hewitt, *Historic New Lanark*, 67, reproduced in Allen, *David Dale*, 13.

6 Groome, *Gazetteer*, iv, 456.

7 Allen, *David Dale*, 7; Donnachie and Hewitt, *Historic New Lanark*, 64.

8 Glasgow Museums, HS 34.

9 J. Clark, *Town of Lanark* (1825).

79   Newburgh (post-1815)

This picture of the townhouse in Newburgh has been painted inside the lid of a rectangular wooden chest, known as a kist. Kists were practical and versatile as furniture but their main purpose was storage. Anything from clothes, tools or food to documents were kept in them. The bracket feet on this kist lifted it enough to protect the contents from damp. A feature of Scottish kists was the lidded kist locker for valuables. This one has three drawers. The emblem on the front shows that it belonged to the Newburgh Friendly Society, which used it to store their records and cash. The Society was established in 1807 at much the same time as John Speed, a local mason, was drawing up plans for a new townhouse on the main street in Newburgh.[1]

Newburgh had had a tolbooth in the sixteenth century, the legacy of a complicated history. Originally dependent on the nearby Abbey of Lindores, it was granted a weekly market in 1266, and converted into a burgh of regality in 1600 and erected a royal burgh in 1631, although it was never represented in either the Convention of Royal Burghs or parliament.[2] Since 1755 the population had increased by almost a quarter, to 1,552 in the 1790s. With a rising population had come a measure of economic expansion and construction. As the kist's picture shows, single-storey thatched cottages had recently been replaced by two- or three-storey, stone-built, slated houses, giving its architecture 'some pretensions to neatness'.[3] The house on the right of the picture stands to this day, little changed, while that to the immediate left of the townhouse is much the same, save for inserted dormer windows. With a new-style town rising out of the footprint of the old, it was only to be expected that the old tolbooth would also need to be replaced.

Work on the townhouse began in 1808. By the time it was completed in 1815, it contained a large council chamber on the first floor with a gallery on one side. Below was a library and cells for debtors and criminals, but it was not long before two of these were converted to create space for a weekly stock market, which traded in local produce like barley, wheat, oats, beans and potatoes. It is hardly surprising that the Newburgh Friendly Society chose to decorate this kist with such an elegant piece of civic architecture and a symbol of their town's economic success.

Friendly societies offered protection to those who relied on their own labour to support themselves and their family. It was a form of insurance similar to that offered by individual trades such as tailors or skinners. Members of a friendly society were not tied

79. Anon., *Newburgh Townhouse*, post–1815

to one occupation but tended to live in the same town or its immediate area. Membership was open to anyone between fifteen and forty considered to be of good reputation and with the ability to pay the entry fee plus a quarterly subscription. In 1857 a young person paid two shillings and sixpence to join the Newburgh Friendly Society with a quarterly payment of two shillings thereafter.[4] This entitled members to financial support in sickness, infirmity and old age and provided a one-off payment for widows or other relatives when a member died. Financial security was not the only benefit. The members formed a tightly knit group who supported each other in the event of hardship and protected each other from the indignity and inadequacy of publicly funded aid.

In the early nineteenth century poor relief in Scotland was still the responsibility of individual parishes. It relied on voluntary contributions to make subsistence level payments to those in need but was seldom extended to the able-bodied poor or incomers from another parish. Not for nothing did The Gentle Shepherd's Friendly Society of Hamilton

79a. *Newburgh Box*

claim that it would protect its members from 'the cold hand of charity'. By the time this picture was painted, the system was breaking down under the pressure of rapid urban and industrial growth. The rules of the Newburgh Friendly Society were typical of most other societies. The governor kept this kist in his house, but, for security, all three keys were held by other office bearers. Members could apply for assistance after five days of sickness. Thereafter, a weekly allowance was paid at the discretion of two visiting stewards. A fraudulent claim led to immediate dismissal from the Society and no claim was paid if it resulted from intoxication.[5]

Between 1845 and 1850 the Newburgh Friendly Society had 172 members of whom eight died and another eight were struck off for non-payment. Along with grocers, bakers, tailors and barbers, there were boatmen, seamen and a port master, reflecting Newburgh's role as a trading outlet at the mouth of the River Tay.[6] Coal, salmon, wood and, of course, linen were all traded. But the majority of the Society's members were weavers, underlining the importance of the linen trade locally. It may be the reason why the artist has included a man wheeling a barrow of yarn or possibly wool down the High Street.

The Revd John Anderson, writing in the early 1830s, recorded 564 looms in the town, employing 343 people. Many were women.[7] Anderson describes a thriving town, largely rebuilt during the previous fifty years and containing a number of 'spirited individuals',[8] who might now be called entrepreneurs, such as the well-dressed man in the picture with the elegant lady on his arm walking towards the townhouse. The Newburgh Friendly Society was dissolved in 1881, but the townhouse of which they were so proud still looks very much the same now as it did then.

Endnotes

1 *Tolbooths and Town-houses*, 154–5.
2 *Ibid.*, 155; Pryde, *Burghs*, nos 75, 104, 158.
3 *OSA*, viii, 185–6, 179–80. *See also* R. J. Naismith, *The Story of Scotland's Towns* (Edinburgh, 1989), 149.
4 NAS, Friendly Benefit Society of Newburgh, 1807.
5 *Ibid.*
6 *Ibid.*
7 *NSA*, ix, 76.
8 *NSA*, ix, 75.

80   Oban, 1857

This anonymous painting captures the youthful town of Oban just prior to the explosion in transport, holiday, villa and tenement development which accompanied its expanding role as the tourist destination and travel hub it was to become and remains to this day.

The town grew very slowly during the eighteenth century, largely remaining a series of hamlets of a few thatched cottages of farm labourers and fisher folk. The shelter afforded by the bay was recognised by the herring fishery and a Renfrew company had established a trading station by 1720. In 1758 the land was surveyed for the Duke of Argyll and other landowners, leading to the relocation of the custom house from Fort William in 1760, and the foundations were laid for development. The Government Fishery Board established a fishing station in 1786 but this proved unproductive, partly due to poor road links, and was abandoned. Entrepreneurial general merchants, brothers Hugh and John Stevenson of Glasgow, had more success by operating trading boats between the town and the Clyde, with connections to Liverpool and the Irish ports. They also established a boat-building yard and a distillery in the town.[1] West Coast sea traffic became busier with the opening of the Crinan Canal in 1801 and the Caledonian Canal in 1822. By 1811 the town was a burgh of barony and it became a parliamentary burgh in 1833.[2] The population grew from 586 in 1791 to just under 3,000 at the time of the painting.[3] Given the limited extent of the street layout shown in a Hydrographic Office map of 1847, it is likely that much of the population increase came in the 1750s.

The first, and still principal, thoroughfares were established and plots feued at Shore Street, the rear of which can be seen in the near distance in the painting, and George Street which faces the bay. From 1812 steamships connected with Glasgow, stimulating construction of the first harbour buildings, including South Pier of around 1816 (hidden from view in the painting) and the pier master's house of 1814. In a short time the George Street development was extended northwards on a simple grid layout and the town had attracted a tannery, school, inns, hotel and its first church.

In 1845 it was reported that there were 'streets of good and commodious houses'.[4] The North Pier was established by 1846. In 1859, just after the painting of this view, the fashionable northern quarter of the town, known as the 'Corran', was feued from the proprietor of Dunollie and in the two following years Columba Terrace, including the

80. Anon., *Oban*, 1857

Great Western Hotel, was built. The Esplanade, which had been formed by 1860, was also extended north from the pier. Development then progressed farther around the bay and on the hills inland. To the right, on the face of the rising ground behind the town, stands

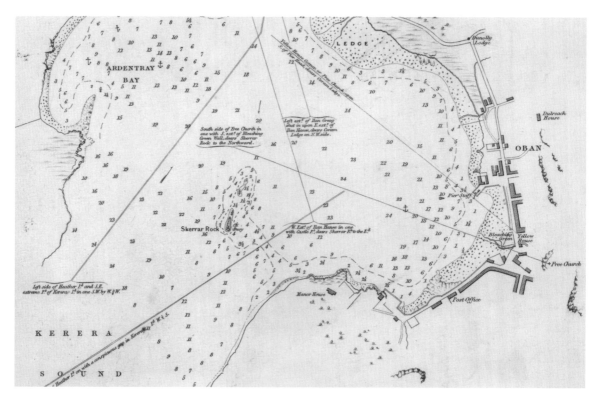

80a. Hydrographic Office, *Oban Bay, Troon Harbour*, 1847

the conspicuously located Free Church, of light early Gothic style with a low Norman tower and pointed spire, built in 1846 from a design by Pugin.[5]

Oban was long noted by writers and diarists whose words reinforced its romantic image and helped develop its status as a resort. In 1773 Mrs Grant of Laggan mentioned the town in the first of her *Letters from the Mountains*: 'Oban is now becoming a large and flourishing village'.[6] Visiting in the same year, James Boswell remarked with approval the accommodation which he and Dr Johnson received in the little clachan at Oban.[7] Sir Walter Scott visited the burgh in 1814, the year in which he published his *Lord of the Isles*, a book which did much to raise the profile of the West Coast. In August 1847 the town was visited by Queen Victoria, who recorded that it was 'one of the finest spots we have seen'. Her visit, via the Crinan Canal, prompted a succession of guidebooks to describe Oban as one of the most fashionable of Scotland's watering places and to dub her voyage as the 'Royal Route'.[8]

Illustrations such as this, particularly when reproduced in the developing popular press, also contributed to the attractiveness of such towns as resorts attracting urban visitors in search of comfortable 'wild' landscape and a proximity to a romantic past, despite the fact that the only genuine historic building in view is the roofless but conveniently romantically situated Dunollie Castle, on its promontory in the distance.[9] The establishment of a comprehensive Isles-wide ferry system and the arrival of the railway in 1880 sealed the town's fate and brought further change as land was reclaimed at Shore Street to create a bustling traffic interchange, which earned the town the nicknames of the 'Gateway to the Isles' and, more fancifully, the 'Charing Cross of Scotland'.

Endnotes

1 C. J. Uncles, *Oban and the Land of Lorn* (Ochiltree, 2001), 42.

2 Pryde, *Burghs*, no. 479.

3 *OSA*, xi, 131 (parish of Kilmore and Kilbride); Groome, *Gazetteer*, ii, 123–4.

4 *NSA*, vii, 532.

5 F. A. Walker, *Argyll and Bute* (London, 2000), 406.

6 A. MacVicar Grant, *Letters from the Mountains; being the real correspondence of a lady, between the years 1773 and 1807* (5th edn, London, 1813), 1.

7 J. Boswell, *Journal of a Tour to the Hebrides with Samuel Johnson* (London, 1785).

8 E. Bray, *The Discovery of the Hebrides* (Edinburgh, 1996), ch. 16.

9 Walker, *Argyll and Bute*, 422.

81   Oldhamstocks Fair, 1796

This painting by Alexander Carse (1770–1843) is of a bustling fair in a small village in East Lothian.[1] At the time of painting Oldhamstocks (Aldhamstoc: 'old dwelling-place') was little more than a single row of houses occupying a terrace on the top of the steep north bank of the Oldhamstocks Burn. The population of the parish was just over 500 but had declined due to agricultural change from small to larger farms and the closure of small-scale coal and salt works in the vicinity. Most residents were engaged in work associated with the agricultural hinterland and the village was noted for the quality of its cart bodies and wheels. It was to one local family of wrights that the famed piano maker John Broadwood (1732–1812) was born.

The centrepiece of the painting is the village cross, a tall affair which appears to have weighing scales attached to it that are being used in market activities. It is certainly more substantial than the cross shaft that stands in the green today and therefore may not be an accurate depiction of the original. It is recorded that the old cross was removed some time before 1890 and preserved in the garden of the manse until 1966 when it was re-erected, perhaps in a new position, with a ball finial. As painted, the column is terminated, as was once common in Scotland before secularisation during and after the Reformation, by a Christian cross, the arms of which are aligned by the artist to point towards the parish kirk in the centre distance.

The original church of Oldhamstocks was dedicated to St Michael, and dated from before 1127. The harled church, as featured here, was constructed in 1701, although medieval elements were incorporated into the new fabric. Clearly identifiable is the sandstone Hepburn Aisle, the lower level section with its traceried arched window and thistle finial on its gable. To the left of the church is a substantial two-storey, crow-stepped, gabled building – most likely the manse – which was built in 1677 and adapted over time to become a 'good house'. Also, its walled garden has since encroached on the green and the view towards the church.

The ruin to the right is the Black Castle of the Hepburns, which was almost certainly more dilapidated at the time of the painting than shown here, as in 1853 it was noted that:

> In the memory of the oldest inhabitants now living there existed a portion of the vaulted rooms of the ground flat, the walls of which were almost 3ft thick, but which

81. Alexander Carse, *Oldhamstocks Fair*, 1796

are now all removed and the ground ploughed over. It does not appear to have been a place of great strength or extent.[2]

Heraldic panels from the castle, dated 1581, are incorporated into the masonry of the church. There are few trees, and this is almost certainly an accurate recording of the setting of the old village, as in 1793 the parish minister, Revd John Cochrane, lamented the lack of enclosure of farm land which gave the landscape a bleak appearance. He noted, too, that 'the natural wood, with which it once abounded is, for want of care, almost entirely destroyed'.[3] Exceptions are those associated with the principal buildings including those by the church, which in the 1890s were noted as being at least 300 years old.[4]

The village was given the right to hold a weekly market in 1627 and fairs were held here twice a year. As the trees are in leaf and the fairgoers are lightly dressed this represents a summer fair. The event is well underway and all participants are preoccupied, save the young woman and children in the centre foreground who look enquiringly outwards and link the artist and observer to the activity.

There would appear to be a mêlée (perhaps involving fisticuffs) around the large building on the left and this is being overviewed by two gentlemen, one on horseback and the other standing on the plinth of the cross.[5] By its scale and painted sign this is almost certainly the village inn, an inevitable focus of activity during any fair. It is known that there was an inn in the village where, according to tradition, Oliver Cromwell once stayed. However, this is generally regarded as being in a different place, a tenement located to the east of the settlement and behind the viewer. The bold, external chimney stack, here with a single-storey outshot, is an architectural feature which appears in a number of illustrations of the buildings of pre-Improvement rural Scotland, including *Mauchline Holy Fair* and *The Village Ba' Game*, both also by Carse. This architectural form was found in the Lothians but also carries a symbolic suggestion of the ideas of antiquity, hearth and the convivial hospitality within.[6] With the exception of the church and perhaps the manse, all roofs are thatched, which was certainly a local roofing tradition. All traditional buildings in the village are now roofed in slate or pantile.

Beyond this group there is an animated figure with drawn-back arm, perhaps engaged in a fight or a tossing game. The picture includes two horses, both of which carry a pair of passengers. Leaving the fair, to the right, is a fiddler, undoubtedly blind as he is led by his callant who has a hand on his shoulder. We see shoes and crockery being sold, although cloth would appear to be the most common commodity. This is in keeping with a recollection made in the 1890s that 'when fairs, which fell on the first Tuesday of July and November, were held, the produce of the spinning wheels of the farmers' and shepherd's wives and daughters was exchanged here for the finished goods of the weavers'.[7] Livestock does not feature, other than the man struggling to separate a pig from some dogs. However, this may have material significance for just a few years before the painting it was noted that, in comparison with the village thirty years earlier, 'the mode of living is also much changed for the better, not only among the farmers, but even among the lower class of people; to which change, the feeding of swine. and the habits of eating pork, have contributed not a little'.[8]

Despite the high degree of artistic licence and possible inaccuracies in architectural detail, this painting does capture the spirit and detail of an important, if declining, part of the social and economic calendar in one of the older settlements, which were being eclipsed by the emerging ferm touns and rapidly developing industrialised settlements. In doing so, Carse undertook this with a charm, wit and sensitivity which drew on his training with David Allan (1744–1796). He also preceded the work of David Wilkie (1785–1841), including his *Pitlessie Fair* (89), which may have been inspired by this work and that of other Scottish realists. Furthermore, the painting links the artist directly to the verse of Fergusson and Burns, and to the oral tradition and confirms Carse's description of himself as 'a painter, chiefly of domestic, familiar and poetical subjects'.[9]

Endnotes

1 There are at least two other versions of the watercolour by Carse: they include one in Glasgow Art Gallery and Museums (L. Errington, *Alexander Carse c. 1770–1843* (Edinburgh, 1987), 31) and one of 1805 which includes 'a small troupe of circus performers drumming up business under an advertising board, as well as a fiddle and singer, game of dice and the inevitable drunken brawl' (F. Bruce, *Showfolk. An Oral History of a Fairground Dynasty* (Edinburgh, 2010), 31, 35).

2 *Name Books of the Ordnance Survey*, nos 16, 35.

3 *OSA*, vii, 403.

4 R. Martine, *Reminiscences and Notices of the Parishes of the County of Haddington* (East Lothian, 1999), 145.

5 It has been suggested (Errington, *Carse*, 9) that the painting may have followed on from a commission for a separate work from the scholar and local landowner, Sir James Hall of Dunglass. Could he be the gentleman on horseback?

6 A. Fenton and B. Walker, *The Rural Architecture of Scotland* (Edinburgh, 1981), 11, fig. 3.

7 Martine, *Reminiscences*, 145.

8 *OSA*, vii, 403.

9 Alexander Carse biography in National Galleries of Scotland web site, accessed at: www.nationalgalleries.org/collection/artists-a-z/C/4590/artistName/Alexander%20Carse/recordId/5813.

82   Paisley, 1825

This view, *Paisley from Saucel Hill*, was one of a series of townscapes painted by John Clark (fl. 1824–8). Taken from a promontory to the south of the town, the painting captures a period of considerable growth, as it developed to become a centre of industrial production. The foreground figures, typical of Clark's work, are gentlemen poring over a plan, no doubt included to reinforce this image of a place in transition.

The earliest settlement is thought to have occurred on the east side of the White Cart River by the fording point at Seedhill where St Mirrin established a religious seat. By the twelfth century there was a church, burial ground, mills and a monastic complex, with a secular community based on the opposite, west bank of the river. Abbey status was granted in 1245 and the place became an important pilgrimage destination. The church, 'once the greatest abbey in the West of Scotland',[1] suffered neglect and partial collapse after the Reformation and, although the remnants were adopted as the parish church in 1560, its locality changed little until the eighteenth century. The profile of the abbey, awaiting re-creation of its tower and choir, can be seen in the centre right of the view.

After burgh status was gained in 1488,[2] the town expanded west along its winding High Street from the cross, close to the river crossing-point where a stone bridge was first built in the fifteenth century, and onto the high ground of Oakshawhead where the narrow lanes and vennels still betray their medieval origins. Urban expansion also took place along the principal routes into the town from the surrounding countryside.

The town's modern development became tied to its roles as an administrative centre and the development of Renfrewshire, encouraged by the London market and capital, as a centre for the manufacture of quality textiles which contrasted with the coarse output of the rest of Scotland. By 1750 growth in both production and population was several times the Scottish rate as new skills and efficient water-powered technologies were adopted, centralised manufacturing became the norm and silk weaving was added to thread and linen production. By the last quarter of the eighteenth century it had become a 'a mature integrated textile manufacturing region',[3] dominated by established merchant families ready for the later transition to steam-powered cotton spinning. Continued population growth, including migrant labour, supported increased output, a boom in the manufacture

82. John Clark, *Paisley from Saucel Hill*, 1825

82a. John Slezer, *The Prospect of the Abbey and Town of Paisley*, 1693

of fashionable shawls and, by the time of Clark's illustration, a massive switch to cotton thread manufacture.

Clark expertly captures the general profile and essential character of the townscape while concentrating detailed attention on a few of the key buildings. John Slezer (*c.* 1650–1717) had used the same viewpoint for his prospect of the town in 1693, and comparison of the two images gives a valuable insight into the town's development in the early modern period. The lower steeple on the centre left of the skyline is that of the tolbooth, which was located at the cross. The original building which served as the tolbooth was rebuilt in 1610 (its steeple can be seen in Slezer's view) and again in 1757 as a three-storey block with the steeple illustrated by Clark. The main building was redeveloped again in 1821, although the steeple survived until 1870 when it was removed.[4]

As the Abbey Church struggled to cope with the burgeoning population, new buildings were erected including the Gothic Old Low Church or Laigh Kirk of 1738 (now the Paisley Arts Centre), close to the town centre but impossible to identify in the view. The second steeple, on higher ground to the left, was added in 1770 at the expense of the town council to another of the new churches, the High Kirk (now Oakshaw Trinity Church), built in 1750–6 to designs by John White, architect.[5] A third, the Middle Church, was built in 1781 and may be the large plain building on the skyline just downhill to the right of the High Kirk. Many other church buildings followed with several on and around the Oakshaw hill, although the only building which can be identified with any certainty is the 1819 St George's Church by William Reid, a 'good Grecian building',[6] on the left of the view which was located on the new George Street, laid out to link Paisley to the weaving village of Maxwellton in the late 1740s.

Other new residential suburbs developed, including a new town in the area of the Abbey garden,[7] and new public spaces were formed. Most significant was County Place with its baronial County Buildings of 1818–20 by Archibald Elliot and William Reid and, between it and the river, the severe, castellated jail. Both of these buildings, which can be seen beyond the old bridge over the river, were to give their architectural style to the new Gilmore Street Station that was subsequently added to the square. The classical façade immediately to the left is, presumably, the New Secession church, an 'elegant Grecian erection',[8] constructed around the time. The view shows that single-storey, thatched cottages, as shown in Slezer's prospect, still survived in places but substantial townhouses and tenement blocks were already becoming the norm.

In the right foreground are the Saucel Distillery and Brewery, both taking advantage of the adjacent Glasgow and Johnstone Canal which operated from 1810. Passenger traffic on the canal was heavy until the Glasgow and Paisley Joint Railway was opened and competition was ended by an agreement whereby the canal company gave up passengers' services in return for an annuity. The Glasgow and South Western Railway subsequently bought the largely derelict canal and converted it to a railway in the 1880s.[9] A boat on the canal can be glimpsed on the bottom right of the view and beyond it, across the river, the mills at Seedhill which would soon be the location of more and larger manufactories.

Within fifty years much of this scene would already have been transformed beyond recognition with the coming of the substantial steam-powered mills, factories, railways, commercial and public buildings of every kind serving a massively growing population.

Endnotes

1 J. Hume *Scotland's Best Churches* (Edinburgh, 2005), 25.

2 Pryde, *Burghs*, no. 156.

3 S. M. Nisbet, *The Rise of the Cotton Factory in Eighteenth-Century Renfrewshire* (Oxford, 2008), 123.

4 *Tolbooths and Town-houses*, 211.

5 Hume, *Churches*, 61. A view drawn by Robert Paul of the town from the east (1767) shows the High Kirk without its tower. The lower tower of the almshouse located on the High Street is also visible. Both the Old Abbey Church and the new High Kirk are portrayed, along with other public buildings, in a plan of the town drawn by William Semple, *A Plan of the Town of Paisley & Suburbs* (1781); *see* Introduction, fig. 12.

6 Groome, *Gazetteer*, v, 153.

7 A. Turner Simpson and S. Stevenson, *Historic Paisley: The Archaeological Implications of Development* (Edinburgh, 1982), 4–5.

8 *NSA*, vii, 199.

9 J. Hume, *The Industrial Archaeology of Glasgow* (Glasgow, 1974), 116.

83   Paisley Abbey, 1827 and 1828

This view of the west gable of Paisley Abbey in 1827 had not been seen for over half a century.[1] John Wood's plan of the town, published in 1828 but evidently composed a few years earlier, clearly shows a large building at the corner of Abbey Close, effectively obstructing the view of the Abbey from Causeyside, across the River Cart.[2] This was the Burgher Meeting House, erected in 1763 in Abbey Close to cater for a congregation of 300. It was demolished in June 1827, when its congregation, which had more than tripled in sixty years, moved to a new, purpose-built church across the river in George Street.

Although the history of the Secession Church (or Burghers) can be traced back to 1736, it had been in the 1760s and 1770s, in Paisley and in other fast-growing mill towns, that dissenting congregations burgeoned.[3] Often initially concentrated among small groups of tradesmen or textile workers, secession churches tended to seek out cheap premises, such as this site perilously close to the river, which had the additional advantage of compromising the view of what had been adopted as the parish church of the burgh in 1736 and was, in the 1820s, still the main place of worship of the Established Church of Scotland in Paisley.

If the Burgher Meeting House was a minor irritant, much else had happened in the fifty years prior to 1827 to challenge the situation of the abbey. Originally a Cluniac foundation, a semi-closed order of Benedictine monks, in the early twelfth century, it had been built at a distance from settlement.[4] In 1693, when Paisley's population amounted to only 2,200, the abbey was still, according to John Slezer's (c. 1650–1717) plan (82a), in almost splendid isolation from the main body of the old town across the river.[5] Another plan of 1781, by William Semple, shows the beginning of the lay-out of a regular street pattern of a new town, to the west of the river, channelled through the entry point across the river of a new bridge – the Abbey or Saucel Bridge, completed in 1763.[6] The abbey fell victim to the rage for 'Improvement' – or profit – which characterised many towns in the last decades of the eighteenth century. In this case, the improver was the 8th Earl of Abercorn, who supervised the creation of the new street lay-out and then, in 1781, maximised his return by selling off the stone of much of the old abbey precinct wall to the new feuars to build their houses.

83. John Cook, *A View of Paisley Abbey from Causeyside*, 1827

Initially residential, the new town quickly changed character with the dramatic increase in population and industrialisation of the textile sector of the economy (*see* 82). The *New Statistical Account* in 1837 claimed that the population had trebled since the 1780s and that Paisley was now the third largest town in Scotland. It exaggerated only slightly: the population in 1791 had been 10,792; by 1831 it was 31,460.[7] Paisley's new town and the surrounding industrial villages have been called 'Scotland's first industrial region'.[8] The streets around the abbey itself proclaimed their provenance – Cotton Street, Gauze Street, Thread Street.

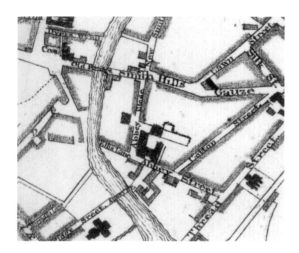

83a. John Wood, *Paisley*, 1828

Turning to the picture itself, it was produced by an otherwise little known local printer and publisher, John Cook, who was associated with a family firm which later produced *The Paisley and Renfrewshire Gazette* (f. 1864). It can be seen that the abbey was by 1827 hemmed in on three sides. A factory chimney, belching smoke on the right of the picture, is in Cotton Street, just behind the Abbey Church. A range of shops is illustrated. On the left of the picture is the 'Saucel Distillery and Spirit Cellar'. The *Statistical Account* complained bitterly of the number of taverns and licensed premises in the town: in 1829 there were 274 in the main burgh and 198 in the abbey parish and new town to cater for a population of 31,000.[9] On the right of the picture are the shop of John Lochead and the general store of Thomas Wright, selling a range of wares including tea, coffee, spices and fancy goods. Beside it is a warehouse of John Gibb, storing shawls, which testifies to the growing predominance, after 1820, of that sector of the textile trades.[10]

The example of Edinburgh's New Town encouraged grid-style new settlement and also a symmetrical distribution of new public buildings, often aligned in new public squares. Paisley fell into both patterns, with enthusiasm.[11] The erection in 1819 on an open green-field site beside the river of the 'County Buildings', in a new 'County Square', dubbed a municipal 'castle' in the *New Statistical Account*, testified to a new civic pride, characterised by 'wealth, refinement and public spirit'.[12] Unusually, in the case of Paisley, the notion of a new-style municipality also helped to foster a desire to preserve the best of its past, more than half a century before public legislation moved towards a policy of conservation of historic buildings and sites. The gap site immediately in front of the west side of the abbey was bought by means of public subscription to ensure the historic vista was preserved.[13] Ironically, that new-found sense of heritage did not extend to the dead.

As the picture shows, the clearance extended – as in many other towns of the period experiencing the pressures of population of both the living and the dead – to part of the historic graveyard in Abbey Close.

Endnotes

1 Paisley Museum and Art Galleries, *A View of Paisley Abbey from Causeyside*, 1827.

2 *See* NLS website, Town Plans/Views, Paisley (1828).

3 C. G. Brown, *Religion and Society in Scotland since 1707* (Edinburgh, 1997), 6, 19–20, 24.

4 Cowan and Easson, *Medieval Religious Houses*, 64–5.

5 *See* NLS website, Slezer, *The Prospect of the Abbey & Town of Paisley* (1693).

6 William Semple, *Town Plan of Paisley and Suburbs, 1781* (Paisley Museum and Art Galleries); *see* Introduction, fig. 12.

7 *NSA*, vii, 248–9, 252, 300–1; OSA, vii, 91.

8 S. M. Nisbet, 'The making of Scotland's first industrial region: the early cotton industry in Renfrewshire', *Journal of Scottish Historical Studies*, 29 (2009), 1–28.

9 *NSA*, vii, 190, 249.

10 *See* SCRAN, 000-000-497-499-C, for a commentary detailing the shops in the picture. *See also* NMS, Scottish Life Archive, for an invoice of 30 June 1835 detailing purchases from Thomas Wright's store.

11 M. Glendinning *et al.* (eds), *A History of Scottish Architecture* (Edinburgh, 1996), 281.

12 *NSA*, vii, 301.

13 Most of the buildings around the west end of the abbey remained until demolished in the 1930s, from which point the abbey regained some of its former splendid isolation.

84   Peebles, 1836

This work, *View of Peebles from Tweed Green*, was painted by Charles A. Blyth (fl. 1836–48), an Edinburgh-based landscape artist.[1] It shows the 'new town' of Peebles, the royal burgh founded during the reign of David I (1124–53), and built separately from the straggling 'old town' that had grown around an ecclesiastical seat across the Eddleston Water immediately to the west.[2] In common with other Scottish burghs, the new town was developed with parallel rig gardens running at right angles to its main street, and here can be seen the tofts falling down to Tweed Green, the common land between the town and the river. Many High Street buildings have gabled additions extending into their gardens; there is development of separate buildings in some gardens with access from the main street via vennels, and others have new buildings at their ends that can be entered directly from the lane running outside the wall.

The regular line of the foot of the rigs marks the southern line of a wall that once encircled the new town. This was erected shortly after 1568 following a call from the Regent Moray for 'the biggin of ane wall about the burgh to resist the invasioun of thevis'.[3] The earlier 'heid dyke' and town ports gave some protection from English attacks, but, as with other burghs, their principal function was to restrict entry and exit to and from the town in order that customs duties might be controlled. The three ports – located at the east end of the High Street, at its west end above the bridge crossing and to the north – could also be closed in times of plague or attack. The East Port was guarded by a fortified building, the New or East Wark, erected in 1488. This gated structure stretched across the street and artillery was mounted on its upper part. It was demolished in 1656 as an obstruction to traffic, while the West Port was removed in 1758.[4] Regulations were enforced to ensure the repair of the town wall and in 1642 it was strengthened for fear of attack.[5] By the 1720s it had fallen into disrepair, although some fragments have survived on the north side of the town. The bridge over the Tweed dates from the fifteenth century but was extended in 1793 and doubled in width in 1834, just before the date of the painting.[6]

Before the middle of the nineteenth century, Peebles operated principally as a centre for the surrounding agricultural hinterland. The introduction of industry serving more than local needs was slow in comparison to other Borders towns although, in time, textile entrepreneurs from Galashiels and Hawick established works in the town. Improvements

84. Charles A. Blyth, *View of Peebles from Tweed Green*, 1836

to the High Street were undertaken in the 1840s when the surface was lowered by several feet. At the same time, façades were improved through the removal of forestairs and other projections onto the street, new pavements were formed and the last thatched houses were re-roofed in slates from Stobo.[7]

The only large public building is the parish church, constructed in 1784 from dark brown, local whinstone and located close to the elevated site of a long-destroyed royal castle dating from the time of David I. There was always some dissatisfaction with its design and the poor contribution it made to the townscape: 'If a little more architectural taste had been shown, it would have been very ornamental to the High Street' and 'The massive steeple which, by being built inside the church, destroys the uniformity of the gallery, should have been placed outside of the church, and flanked by a few pillars'.[8] A commentator in 1856 wrote of its awkward relationship with the public street and of how 'the fabric generally and the steeple in particular bear the unmistakable marks of the dearth of taste which pervaded during the reign of George III'.[9] The building was eventually replaced in 1885–7 with the crown-spired building known now as the Old Parish Church.

The principal foreground focus of the painting is Tweed Green, which is presented as a community facility upon which a number of public activities are being undertaken. Cattle are grazing, there are poles for drying laundry, and white clothes are lying flat out to bleach in the sun on the green by the millrace, this being the standard method prior to the availability of the patented dry bleaching powder that could be used indoors, developed by Charles Tennant (1768–1838) at his works at Glasgow (see 50). Children also play football on the green, which is not surprising given the location of the two principal schools, the light-coloured English or Burgh School (1766) and the stone-built Latin or Grammar School (1812) on either side of the foot of School Wynd or School Brae. Cabbage Hall, the schoolmaster's house, lies immediately to the right of the wynd. The break in the higher section of wall to the right is marked on early maps as a public privy.[10] The painting shows the family of local mill owner, Walter Thorburn, and is just one of a number of such views in which the artist featured local people to order.[11]

Many other buildings can be identified. On the extreme right can be seen the gable of St Peter's Episcopal Church, a 'broad aisled-less rectangle of 3 bays', c. 1830–3, by William Burn.[12] The large building on the High Street above Cabbage Hall is the Dean's House or Queensberry Lodgings, which was redeveloped as Chambers' Institution from 1857.[13] The Gothic revival Free Church sits on the right side of School Wynd. The Town House of 1752–3 sits across the head of the wynd, a pend beneath providing a link to the High Street. To its left is the mass of the Tontine Inn of 1810, which extends well into its rig with a full-height, bow-ended wing with tall, round-headed windows to light the ballroom, and a pedimented stable onto the green.[14] In the far distance, Neidpath Castle can be seen, and between it and the town are the manse (built in 1770 with a new front added in 1812) on a bank above the Tweed and the elegant Hay Lodge, both houses taking advantage of the riverside setting.

Endnotes

1 According to P. J. M. McEwan, *Dictionary of Scottish Art and Architecture* (Woodbridge, 1994), 80, Blyth exhibited at the Royal Scottish Academy in 1846 and 1849, after which he was resident in Peebles.

2 Pryde, *Burghs*, no. 10.

3 J. W. Buchan and H. Paton, *A History of Peeblesshire*, (Glasgow, 1925–7), ii, 27.

4 *Ibid.*, ii, 51.

5 R. Gourlay and A. Turner Simpson, *Historic Peebles: The Archaeological Implications of Development* (Scottish Burgh Survey, 1977), 5–6.

6 *NSA*, iii, 17.

7 Gourlay and Turner Simpson, *Historic Peebles*, 3; J. L. Brown and I. C. Lawson, *History of Peebles 1850–1990* (Edinburgh, 1990), 43.

8 *NSA*, iii, 17.

9 R. Chambers, *Peebles and its Neighbourhood with a Run on the Peebles Railway* (Edinburgh, 1856), 55.

10 Ordnance Survey, *Peebles* (1856), Sheet 6.

11 I. O'Riordan and D. Patterson (eds), *Scotland's Art* (Edinburgh, 1999), 48.

12 K. Cruft, J. Dunbar and R. Fawcett, *The Buildings of Scotland. Borders* (New Haven and London, 2006), 618.

13 *Handbook to the Chambers Institution, Peebles* (Edinburgh, 1859).

14 Cruft *et al.*, *Borders*, 625.

85   Perth, St Bartholomew, 1557

This painting of St Bartholomew, patron saint of the glovers of Perth, represents one of the few surviving artefacts of pre-Reformation Scotland. The date 1557, crudely inserted in large numerals at the foot of the picture, is a key clue to its provenance.[1] The first craft in Scotland to be awarded incorporated status was the guild of skinners in Edinburgh, given a foundation charter in 1474. The following six decades saw the incorporation of a host of crafts in Scotland's major burghs, including nine in Perth. There, the two 'sciences' of glovers and skinners were amalgamated in a charter of 1534. With incorporation came greater powers for the masters in the craft, including a disciplinary tribunal with an ethos which was a forerunner of post–1560 kirk session discipline. It also resulted in a craft chaplain, missal, vestments and a dedicated altar in the parish church of St John.

The pattern in Scotland that towns almost invariably had only one parish church resulted in very large buildings, which typically housed a large number of images of occupational, biblical and intercessory saints: Aberdeen's St Nicholas had more than forty side altars and St Giles' in Edinburgh had forty-five, each claiming a specific saint or cult. In Perth each of the burgh's nine crafts guilds had a separate altar. The extent of the glovers' altar may be deduced from the size of the painting, which measures some 56½ inches in height by 43½ inches (143.5 × 110.5 cm) in width. The adoption of St Bartholomew as patron saint of the glovers and skinners, which was common throughout much of western Europe, probably owed its origin to one popular tradition which maintained that his martyrdom came about by being flayed alive: hence his depiction in the crimson red of a martyr. Other occupational saints, such as St Eloi, patron saint of goldsmiths and metalworkers, had a more obvious and less gruesome provenance. Although the images of such saints were commonplace in Europe, this picture was probably the work of a local artist.

It is an irony of history that the sole surviving pre-Reformation painting of a saint should have escaped what was the first and the most devastating bout of iconoclasm in the history of Scotland's Reformation – the 'cleansing' of St John's Kirk triggered by an inflammatory sermon by John Knox in May 1559. In the space of three days, the parish church was stripped of its Catholic ornaments and artefacts, and the burgh's three friaries and the large Carthusian

85. St Bartholomew, Glovers Incorporation, Perth, 1557

monastery were sacked. The picture of St Bartholomew survived, probably because it was not in St John's at the time.

The iconoclasts were, it is likely, fewer in number than those whose first instinct was to protect expensive and recent investments in 'altar grayth'. In Edinburgh the burgh council took all of the town's religious ornaments and relics into protective custody at the first rumour of the approach of the Protestant 'Lords of the Congregation'. To ensure a longer-term survival of a religious artefact, some creative thinking was necessary. St Bartholomew, one of the twelve apostles, had the advantage of being a biblical saint, so was less inherently objectionable to the reformers. But changes were made to the painting after 1559. Prayers for the dead, which recalled the doctrine of purgatory, were frowned upon, so the inscription at the foot of the painting must have been obliterated. It is likely that the odd intrusion of gloves beside the canopy above the saint's head was made at this point and it is possible that the tools of the glover craft – the flaying knife and shears at the foot of the painting – were also added at this time. In place of the inscription imploring prayers for the dead is a slab of green paint and the date of 1557 daubed on top of it. This self-inflicted act of selective iconoclasm might be compared with a later, more elaborate example: the pre-emptive desecration in 1640 of the part of the medieval pulpit in St Machar's, Old Aberdeen, displaying Christ's wounds and Passion, to avoid its wholesale destruction when the radical Covenanters reached the burgh.[2] Yet it also suggests a desire to record the past, however unpalatable parts of it might be to some contemporaries.

Green paint was one of the key instruments of the 'cleansing' of Scotland's churches. In St Giles', Edinburgh, twenty-five pillars were painted over with this colour in the summer of 1560. The same happened in St Nicholas, Aberdeen, and in the church of Foulis Easter, near Dundee, though not there until 1612.[3] Why green? The answer, which may seem strange to twenty-first century Scots minds, is that it was a colour which – unlike red, yellow, blue and, of course, purple (the colour of divinity) – did not have associations with either religious 'idolatry' or secular majesty. The Perth glovers' painting represents a rare survival and a cautionary tale that, for many in and after 1560, the preservation of part of the past was at least as important as embracing new beliefs.

A second 'restoration' took place, probably in 1787, when the glovers moved premises. A picture of the old Glover Hall, in Curfew Row, was added to the picture, in its bottom right-hand corner. The notion of the preservation of historic artefacts as seen is a relatively modern instinct. This was rather viewed as a commissioned work, which was intended as an ongoing record. Whether a family portrait or a picture of a craft's symbolic mentor, such work could and was often altered by whim, to keep it up to date.

Endnotes

1 *See* D. McRoberts, 'A sixteenth-century picture of Saint Bartholomew from Perth', *Innes Review*, 10 (1959), 281–6. The picture itself is depicted, in black and white, opposite p. 275.

2 D. Stevenson, *St Machar's Cathedral and the Reformation, 1560–1690* (Friends of St Machar's Cathedral Occasional Papers, no. 7, 1981), 10–11.

3 R. Adam (ed.), *Edinburgh Records: The Burgh Accounts ii, Dean of Guild Accounts, 1552–1567* (Edinburgh, 1899), 94; A. B. Dalgetty, *History of the Church of Foulis Easter* (1933), 69. *See also* D. McRoberts, 'Material destruction caused by the Scottish Reformation', in D. McRoberts (ed.), *Essays on the Scottish Reformation* (Glasgow, 1962), 415–62.

86   Perth, 1783

Both this view and plan of Perth were insets in the four-section map of the counties of Perth and Clackmannan complied by James Stobie (fl. 1775–1804) in 1783.[1] The map was a virtual art gallery, containing a number of specially commissioned engravings of country seats of local aristocracy, including the Duke of Atholl for whom Stobie acted as a factor, as well as a view of Dunkeld (*see* 26). Most of the views, including that of Perth, had the distinctive claim 'J. Stobie delin[t]' and 'Mazell sculp[t]'. Peter Mazell was a London-based engraver (*see* Introduction, 22). The map sold for an ambitious £2 sterling (the equivalent of at least £200 in present-day values) or two guineas if the parish boundaries were coloured in.

Neither of Stobie's productions of 1783 could claim to be the first surviving view or plan of Perth. The military surveyor John Slezer (*c.* 1650–1717) had been commissioned by Perth's town council to draw *The Prospect of the Town of Perth* (1693). It was demonstrably a more carefully composed work than Stobie's. And the Hanoverian government, in the wake of the major Jacobite rising of 1715, had a number of military surveys of the town made.[2] Stobie's plan, however, was much more detailed in depicting buildings and plots, and was the first to show the extent of settlement within the town, in which the population had grown significantly in the previous half century.

The centrepiece of Stobie's view is the new bridge, built by John Smeaton (1724–1792) in 1766–72. It was a replacement for an older bridge of 1617, which had been swept away by floods in 1621, as Stobie's plan duly noted. But there is some carelessness evident in his depiction of the new bridge, in both the view and the plan. The view shows only five of the nine spans, although part of it may be hidden by trees on the east bank, and the plan just seven. Stobie's image of St John's, still in 1783 the parish church of the burgh, is less careful than Slezer's in its depiction of the fifteenth-century octagonal spire and the 150 feet (46 metres) high steeple. There was no other spire to the south (left) of St John's according to the *Statistical Account* of the 1790s.[3] More culpably still, Stobie entitles his view *Perth from the North-west*. The view of the bridge and the area around St John's is, in fact, from the north-east, drawn from north of the village of Bridgend on the east bank of the river.

Like Slezer, Stobie shows the gardens of prestigious houses extending down to the west bank of the Tay. On the east bank he depicts, as the *Statistical Account* confirmed, large

86. James Stobie, *Perth from the North West*, 1783

villas with extensive gardens or 'pleasure grounds' in Kinnoull. On the North Inch, across the river, he draws 'military men' performing their 'exercise'.[4] Beyond these details, Stobie's view is more difficult to interpret than that of Slezer, whose sightlines, more directly from the east, allow a more readily understandable panorama, taking in the extensive policies of the Earl of Gowrie's House to the south (left) of St John's and the quay beyond.

If the angle of the bridge is followed in Stobie's image, it leads into the area of the old Castle Gavel Port or, in modern terms, Charlotte Street, which had still to be laid out in 1783. The Balhousie Mill Lade and the King's Lade, which merged at the waterfront, are shown flowing into the river just to the north (right) of the end of the bridge. Beyond

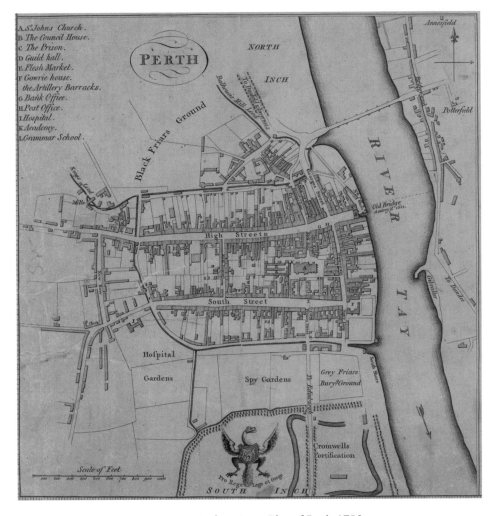

86a. James Stobie, *Street Plan of Perth*, 1783

404

the lade, artistic licence has been employed, or sheer distortion. Stobie's problem – like that to a lesser extent with Slezer – was that the basic shape of the burgh, since the castle on the North Inch had been swept away in the thirteenth century, had turned on its axis to face east–west rather than framing a natural panorama parallel to the north–south flow of the river.[5]

The area to the north of the bridge would have new streets laid out in the 1790s and after. They included the impressive mansions on Athole Place, Athole Crescent and Rose Terrace, shown in John Wood's map of 1823 as standing in splendid isolation with a clear view over the new race course, which first opened in 1791.[6] In the 1780s, however, this area was still open ground and notoriously prey to flooding. So, Stobie's depiction of buildings to the right of the bridge portrays the north and north-western edge of settlement as running virtually parallel to the river. In other words, this part of his view *was* from the north-west. This was the only way he could capture a significant proportion of the burgh's townscape. The large, four-storey building at the extreme right of his picture presumably represents the H-shaped four storeys of the King James VI Hospital as rebuilt in 1749–50, close to the original site of the Carthusian monastery razed to the ground in 1559.

So flawed was Stobie's double-hinged image of Perth, one suspects that this was the reason why it was not reproduced in the later edition of his map of Perthshire, published in 1805.[7] By then, new settlement at the north end of the burgh would have fatally compromised his earlier rearrangements of reality. Ironically, his 1783 plan would be reproduced, with impunity and only minor changes, as an inset in John Thomson's map, *Perthshire with Clackmannan*, in 1827.[8]

Endnotes

1 *See* NLS website, Counties of Scotland, 1580–1961, Perthshire (1783).

2 *See* NLS website, Military Maps of Scotland (18th Century), 1715–16, 1724–45. *See also* C. Fleet, M. Wilkes and C. W. J. Withers, *Scotland: Mapping the Nation* (Edinburgh, 2011), 77–8.

3 *OSA*, xviii, 532.

4 *OSA*, xviii, 297–8.

5 R. M. Spearman, 'The medieval townscape of Perth', in M. Lynch, R. M. Spearman and G. Stell (eds), *The Scottish Medieval Town* (Edinburgh, 1988), 42–59, esp. 49–50.

6 *See* NLS website, Town Plans/Views, 1580–1919: Perth (1823).

7 *See* NLS website, Counties of Scotland, 1580–1961, Perthshire (1805).

8 *See* inset in NLS website, Counties of Scotland, 1580–1961, Perthshire (1827).

87   Perth from Barnhill, 1833

The view of Perth from Barnhill, on the upper slopes of the eastern bank of the Tay, was one of the favourite vantage points for artists. It had been used by David Octavius Hill some ten years before in his *Sketches of Scenery in Perthshire* (1821) to celebrate the new focal point on the waterfront of the recently completed County Buildings and this would become *the* iconic view of the 'fair city'. This oil painting, *Perth from Barnhill*, by the local artist William Brown (1798–1874) was one of two views of Perth which he painted from the same location with an intervening gap of some twenty-seven years. Brown taught drawing and painting at Perth Academy.[1] The painting can be dated with some precision as it was also published in 1833, with the inscription 'To the Citizens of Perth this View of their Fair City is respectfully Inscribed, by their much obliged Serv't, Wm. Brown'. The engraver was also a local man, William Forrest (1805–1889), who was involved in publishing other work by Brown of scenes in Perthshire.

This print has been hailed as a fine example of the art of engraving – good enough for it to be republished by the highly reputable Edinburgh firm of Bartholomew's as late as 1919.[2] Even so, the print could hardly do justice to the detail of the original, which was four times its size, measuring 50 × 72 inches (127 × 182 cm), or have its dramatic impact on the viewer. Unusually, however, the engraver used a copperplate, so the print run cannot have been extensive. For his later production of Brown's artwork, published in *Scotland Illustrated* (1845), Forrest used steel plates, allowing a greater print run.

The painting is a celebration of a burgh which was rapidly increasing in size and in process of physical transformation. It is revealing that another of Brown's better known paintings was devoted to *Queen Victoria's Entry to Perth, 1842*; it was another work driven by local patriotism. In 1755 the population of the town had been 9,019; in 1831 it stood at 20,016.[3] Population increase, however, tells very little of the story of Perth in the half century since our last glimpse of it, in James Stobie's picture of the town in 1783 (86). In the interim, large parts of the old town had been demolished. The Spey Tower on the South Inch and Gowrie House – two of the most iconic buildings in Slezer's view of the town in 1693 – were 'ruthlessly razed'[4] to the ground between 1801 and 1805 to make way for a series of new streets being laid out, including Marshall Place, which effectively removed part of the gardens on the South Inch. The so-called 'Parliament House', where some of James I's parliaments were reputed to have met between 1424 and 1437, was

87. William Brown, *Perth from Barnhill*, *c.* 1833

demolished in 1818. Here was a historic burgh, which claimed pride of place in a nation's history, but, save for its original parish church and some isolated vernacular building, had almost no built heritage of consequence. The old single parish was broken up into four separate congregations in 1807, and by 1835 two more would be added. By 1820 Perth was, in effect, a new town, with a markedly different street plan.

Waterworks

Brown's view is one of a town dominated by its new buildings, both public and private. The distinctive dome of the Waterworks (1830) and the unmistakable shape of the neo-classical County Buildings (1819) on the waterfront, with the sizeable structure of the County Prison visible behind it (1812) are conspicuous. They vie for attention with the church spires of the old parish church of St John's, some 150 feet (46 metres) high, and the new St Paul's (1807), in a straight line behind it at the west end of the High Street. The south end of the town is now sharply defined by the mansions of the new streets, King's Place and Marischal Place (1801).[5] The river provides a contrast between the sail boats and fishing smacks moored in the basin of shallow water beside the old harbour at the end of Canal Street and the primitive paddle-driven steamships – probably including one of the two steamships which plied between Perth and Dundee on a daily basis –

County Buildings

berthed downstream. They lie at the wharves recently built in the marginally deeper water beyond the old Greyfriars burial ground farther along the South Inch. Significantly a map of 1832 referred to this stretch of landing as 'Coal Shore'.

Oddly, in his later painting of 1860, Brown recaptures virtually the same scene, in the same perspective, despite significant changes which had taken place in the intervening years. He made two concessions to change. In his foreground he added a quaint country cottage beside the cows. And in

Steamships

1860, as he depicted it, the steamships have gone, replaced by a variety of sail boats and smacks. By then, most larger shipping had been forced, because of the relentless process of silting up of the river, almost a mile downstream to a new harbour at Friarton.

Endnotes

1 Pigot & Co.'s *National Commercial Directory for the whole of Scotland ...* (1837), 680.
2 http://blogs.nls.uk/bartholomew/?p=5, 'A fine engraving'.
3 *NSA*, x, 86.
4 *NSA*, x, 70.
5 *NSA*, x, 85–6.

88   Peterhead, 1824 and 1790s

Peterhead was created a burgh of barony in 1587 for George Keith, 4th Earl Marischal (*c.* 1549–1623), who also founded Marischal College, Aberdeen.[1] Peterhead stands on the tip of the most easterly peninsula of Scotland jutting out into the North Sea. It was known as the German Ocean when this charming watercolour was painted by the talented but elusive I. (or John) Clark (fl. 1824–8), painter of many Scottish townscapes in the early 1820s (*see also* 18, 38, 82, 100).

Dominating the foreground is the Invernettie Brick and Tile Works. Started by William Forbes in the early nineteenth century, it produced about 250,000 bricks and pantiles a year.[2] This picture illustrates the various processes, including the table where a moulder filled the dampened moulds with clay, trimming off any excess with a piece of wood. The bricks were then dried in sheds for twenty-four hours until at least a quarter of the water content had evaporated. The smoking chimneys show where the bricks were baked in kilns for six days. The process, though labour intensive, did not require many skilled workers.

Tiles were made in much the same way, and Clark includes two men laying tiles out on the ground after firing. These locally produced pantiles were said to be 'equal, if not superior, to those of the Dutch'.[3] They can be seen on the roof of the works and also the house where the Forbes family lived, almost hidden by the smoke from the kilns.[4] Several buildings in the town behind have pantiled roofs. By the end of the century, these would largely be replaced by slates. James Forbes (1797–1881), who took over from his father, was also a talented local painter who exhibited in several major galleries. He sold the Invernettie works in 1857 before emigrating to America.[5]

The townscape behind is so beautifully executed that many individual buildings are clearly defined. The large building with a tall chimney on the far left is Kirkburn Mill. Built in 1812, this originally housed Arbuthnot, Scott & Company, producers of woollen cloth, which used steam power for all but the weaving stage of the process.[6] It is interesting to note the various uses for which this building was adapted. About the time this picture was painted, it became a distillery, run by Alexander Murray, a prominent local businessman. When this venture failed, the building housed Dr Pirie's Meal Mill. Murray took over again in the mid-nineteenth century. Needing stone to carry out building work,

88. John Clark, *The Town of Peterhead*, 1824

he decided to blow up the windmill he had been trying to sell on Keith Inch, a tiny island by the harbour that had been absorbed into the town. Nobody was hurt because everyone had been warned but several local buildings were badly damaged. In 1854 Kirkburn Mill was sold and became a woollen mill once more.[7]

The first spire to the right of Kirkburn Mill is that of the parish church. When it was built in 1803, it was the subject of such bitter legal wrangling that the case went to the House of Lords. The heritors, no longer the Keiths whose estates had been forfeited after the 1715 rebellion, and now led by the Governors of the Merchant Maiden Hospital of Edinburgh, decided to build a larger church and pass the greatest share of the cost on to the town's feuars. This was so unusual that the feuars went to court, many particularly aggrieved because they worshipped in other churches. They lost their case and had to pay but took their revenge by fighting every refinement that might have made the parish church in Peterhead more pleasing to the eye.[8] The church became known as the 'muckle kirk', which may have indicated its greatly increased capacity or perhaps its very solid form.

The spire in the centre is that of the more elegant townhouse on Broad Street, built in 1788. Measuring 125 feet (38 metres), it topped that of the parish church by seven feet. Again, it was the community of feuars who bore the cost of construction.[9] This building housed the parish school where one master taught navigation for those destined to go to sea.[10]

The ships in Peterhead Bay and the masts in the harbours beyond indicate that the port of Peterhead was 'one of the most valuable on the east coast of Scotland'.[11] As a natural

88a. Montague Beattie, *The Harbour at Peterhead*, 1790s

412

anchorage and haven on an otherwise inhospitable coast, it was second to none. While towns like Fraserburgh and Greenock struggled to raise money to update their harbour facilities, many of Peterhead's harbour improvements were funded by government, and three of the country's top engineers, John Smeaton (1724–1792),[12] John Rennie (1761–1821) and Thomas Telford (1757–1834), were employed to work on them. One great advantage was a plentiful supply of local granite, strong enough to withstand the worst storms of the North Sea.

Another advantage enjoyed by Peterhead was its famed, iron-rich, medicinal spring. In a book on the watering and sea-bathing places in Scotland, Peterhead is dubbed the 'Scarborough of the north', with special mention made of the brilliance of its granite buildings twinkling in the sunshine.[13] The town attracted many summer visitors wishing to improve their health like James Beattie (1735–1803), poet, musician, philosopher and professor at Marischal College.[14] Beattie's younger son, Montague (1778–1796), painted the accompanying vignette of the south harbour from Keith Inch with the newly completed townhouse spire in the centre. Although a member of the Church of Scotland, James Beattie, like many in Peterhead, attended St Peter's Episcopal Chapel, tucked behind the tallest of the houses on the foreshore.[15]

Endnotes

1 Pryde, *Burghs*, no. 240.

2 J. Arbuthnot, *An Historical Account of Peterhead, from the Earliest Period to the Present Time* (Aberdeen, 1815), 47.

3 *Ibid.*, 47.

4 D. M. Bertie, *Master and Pupil, An Exhibition on James Forbes (1797–1881) and John Phillip (1817–1867)* (Aberdeen, 1997), 5.

5 *Ibid.*, 1–2.

6 J. T. Findlay, *A History of Peterhead from Prehistoric Times to AD 1896* (rev. edn, Peterhead, 1933), 301–2.

7 *Ibid.*, 301–2.

8 *Ibid.*, 141–2.

9 *Tolbooths and Town-houses*, 167.

10 Arbuthnot, *Peterhead*, 60.

11 Groome, *Gazetteer*, v, 202.

12 Smeaton's plan of 1775 showing his proposed works on the 'town and harbour of Peterhead', is printed in R. Gibson, *The Scottish Countryside: Its Changing Face, 1700–2000* (Edinburgh, 2007), 131–2.

13 W. M. Wade, *Delineations, Historical, Topographical, and Descriptive, of the Watering and Sea-bathing Places of Scotland* (Paisley, 1822), 305.

14 *DNB, James Beattie*.

15 We are indebted to Dr David Bertie, Curatorial Officer, Documentation and Conservation, (Aberdeenshire) for his advice.

89   Pitlessie, 1804

Pitlessie, made a burgh of barony in 1541, is in the parish of Cults in Fife.[1] In 1791 the parish had a population of 534. By 1838 this had risen to 914, but only 516 lived in the village itself. The same period saw agricultural improvement, the establishment of spinning, saw and yarn mills, lime working, malting and an associated rise in average wages.[2] In the eighteenth century there were two annual fairs in Pitlessie for the sale of livestock, principally cattle. By the 1830s there was only one, which was held on the second Tuesday of May. This was a highly popular event and one of the best-attended fairs in the county of Fife.

Recognised as a seminal work in the area of genre painting, this youthful masterpiece, *Pitlessie Fair* by David Wilkie (1785–1841), is also of interest for its townscape content. It is a portrait of the place where the artist was born and brought up, as a son of the manse. The painting's stage-set contains several architectural elements, which, with a high degree of accuracy, illustrate aspects of the local vernacular tradition.

The centrepiece is a cottage roofed in pantiles. The artistic device of a judiciously placed orange-tiled roof, which has precedents in Dutch and other landscape paintings with which Wilkie may have been familiar,[3] draws the eye into the composition in conjunction with the red uniforms of the centrally placed militia and the similarly coloured garments of flanking characters. Of Low Countries origin, and manufactured in Fife from 1714,[4] it may have been well into the nineteenth century before the roofing material was commonly found on modest, rural domestic dwellings such as shown,[5] especially in the part of Fife where the local tradition of thatch had a very late survival. Wilkie, therefore, may have been deliberately recording a village in a state of 'improvement' and modernisation. Unusually, the cottage has a ridge of turf rather than the normally expected half-round tile, and perhaps only one face has been renewed. Alternatively, this might indicate the use of emerging building technique not yet fully absorbed into local practice. Wilkie's characteristic attention to detail is shown in the light lines of lime mortar applied between the tiles, a detail also seen in earlier Dutch painting.

Behind the modernised cottage, rows of older, thatched dwellings, their roofs in differing states of upkeep, are built on the slope in the old Scottish manner, with rooflines parallel with the falling ground. In the distance is a building with a timber gable. On the right, an abandoned cottage, now in use as a byre, has the remains of a 'hingin lum' made

89. David Wilkie, *Pitlessie Fair*, 1804

from timber and thatch, the loss of roof covering exposing rough rafters and purlins of unworked branches. All other habitable properties have stone or brick chimneys. There are also grander two-storey houses in stone and with elegant sash and case windows, but even these are thatched. The two-storey house to the left has crow-stepped gables, another feature common in buildings in the county. The central house with figures at its gable window still exists and local tradition says that it was an inn around the time of the painting. Its garden wall contains traces of infilled windows and a door which may be a remnant of one of the row of cottages in the painting.[6]

89a. David Wilkie, *Background for the Painting for Pitlessie Fair*

In a preliminary sketch, Wilkie captured the juxtaposition of buildings just as painted and, helpfully, noted their construction materials.[7] The masonry of the tiled house and the two-storey building to the left are 'harld' (harled) while the facing two-storey gable and distant cottages are of 'whin stone', igneous rock which would have been quarried locally.

Wilkie's painting demonstrates an understanding of folk traditions and Scottish literature such as Robert Fergusson's (1750–1774) *Hallow Fair* (1772), while owing much to the *kermesse* paintings of the Dutch School in its depiction of fairs. The influence of Alexander Carse's (1770–1843) *Oldhamstocks Fair* (81), where characters are similarly grouped, can also be detected.[8] Here, however, the characters are given a more sympathetic reality and unsentimental identity, with the actors spread across the canvas without any single action taking prominence.[9] The painting contains a wealth of ethnographic detail in the many figures that make up the scene, such as the fiddler and ballad singer or the children playing games. The significance of the blue flag on the house to the left is intriguing but may only exist for artistic effect. The artist introduced into this work a large number of relatives, neighbours and friends of whom he had formerly made thumbnail sketches. When finished, the picture caused quite a sensation with people flocking to Cults to see the work.

Endnotes

1 Pryde, *Burghs*, no. 217.

2 *OSA*, ii, 409; *NSA*, ix, 568.

3 L. Errington, 'Gold and silver in shadow. The Dutch influence on nineteenth-century Scottish painting', in J. Lloyd Williams, *Dutch Art and Scotland: A Reflection of Taste* (Edinburgh, 1992), 49–59.

4 S. Eydmann, 'Pantiles', in M. Jenkins (ed.), *Building Scotland. Celebrating Scotland's Traditional Building Materials* (Edinburgh, 2010), 143–55.

5 On the subject of single-storey cottages in rural east central Scotland, A. Fenton and B. Walker, *The Rural Architecture of Scotland* (Edinburgh, 1981), 65, noted: 'houses with pantiled roofs were very rare prior to the 1850s unless as an inexpensive substitute for thatch. The use of pantiles for houses is a late nineteenth-century feature and their introduction to this class of building caused considerable controversy'. For a photograph of a comparable row of thatched cottages in central Fife, *see ibid.*, 58, fig. 49.

6 We are grateful for valuable local information provided by Charlie and Maggie Lawrie, Pitlessie.

7 NGS, accession no. D 4893.

8 A. G. Williams and A. Brown, *The Bigger Picture. A History of Scottish Art* (London, 1993), 88.

9 N. Tromans, *David Wilkie: Painter of Everyday Life* (London, 2002), 50.

90 Port Glasgow from the South-East, 1768

This print of the tobacco fleet at Port Glasgow was drawn by Robert Paul (1739–1770).[1] Paul had studied at the Foulis Academy in Glasgow, a school of art and design founded by the celebrated printer Robert Foulis (1707–1776). Later Paul specialised in topographical works of Glasgow and the lower Clyde, producing some of the earliest known views of the area by a locally trained artist.[2] He is probably the figure sketching under a tree, on the left, while another man appears to be pointing out places of interest. This picture celebrates the centenary of the foundation of Port Glasgow and the golden age of the tobacco trade.

In the mid-seventeenth century, when new markets were emerging across the Atlantic, it was impossible for all but the smallest vessels to reach the growing mercantile city of Glasgow because the upper reaches of the Clyde were very shallow with many shoals and sandbanks. Ocean-going vessels could reach Greenock, an advantage which that town was quick to seize. To develop new markets on the other side of the Atlantic, Glasgow's merchants needed to find their own deep-water port.

Attempts to buy land at Dumbarton and Greenock were thwarted by the fierce rivalry that already existed among the ports on the lower Clyde. A meeting in the evening of 3 January 1668, between Glasgow's town council and the Laird of Newark and his son, was more successful. Contracts were signed for thirteen acres of land at Newark 'for loading and livering of their ships there, anchoring and building ane harbour there'.[3] New 'port-Glasgow' was erected a free port with harbour and tolbooth less than three weeks later.[4] It lay just above Greenock and opposite Dumbarton, an important step in a growing trade war.

Paul's picture illustrates just how much the town had grown in the intervening century. It had already engulfed the original village of Newark and had also been appointed the principal customs house port on the Clyde. The success of its overseas trade is indicated by the number of large ocean-going ships in the harbour. The main foreign imports were sugar, rum, cotton, mahogany, logwood and staves but by far the most important was tobacco.[5] It was the Union of 1707 that gave the green light to what had been a small-scale, illicit Scottish trade in tobacco. By the time this picture was painted, Glasgow's 'tobacco lords' had acquired the lion's share of the British tobacco market and the bulk of that valuable commodity passed through Port Glasgow.

90. Robert Paul, *A View of Port Glasgow from the South-East*, 1768

Scotland had imported an average of one and a half million pounds (in weight) of tobacco annually when the Union was signed. By the 1740s this had grown to an annual average of nearly ten million pounds by Glasgow alone, a figure that had reached an astonishing thirty-three million pounds by the time this picture was painted.[6] As America's colonists were legally bound to export all their tobacco to Britain, Port Glasgow also enjoyed a lucrative re-export trade to France, Holland, Germany and Ireland. The majority of ships belonging to Port Glasgow, like those anchored in the harbour in this picture, were not owned by local merchants but by business houses in Glasgow.[7]

90a. Dry Dock

In the centre of the picture is Scotland's first dry or graving dock.[8] Up until this time, ships had to be pulled clear of the water for their hulls to be cleaned or careened, a process often carried out on a local beach. A major problem for the tobacco fleet was the teredo worm, a marine creature that bored into submerged wood causing severe damage. In 1758, to speed up the careening process, Port Glasgow decided to build a dry dock and to send a ship's carpenter, John Webb, to study those in Liverpool. This resulting dock did not drain properly, so, in 1767, the famous engineer, John Smeaton (1724–1792) was asked to design a new pump.[9]

Smeaton's pump was driven by the big wheel on the quayside near the centre of this picture. It could empty the dock in four hours if the machinery was operated by six 'good *English* labourers' or in three hours twenty minutes by two ordinary horses.[10] By 1771 Smeaton's more famous colleague James Watt (1736–1819) was proposing further improvements to the dock, including suggestions for clearing the harbour which was constantly silting up.[11] The problem for the merchants of Glasgow was that, at the same time as maintaining the harbour facilities at Port Glasgow, they were also financing the construction of a navigable channel up to Glasgow.

90b. Port Glasgow Rope and Duck Company

The long ropewalk and attached mill in the foreground housed the prosperous Port Glasgow Rope and Duck Company, set up in 1736 by a group of Glasgow merchants to produce rope and sailcloth (duck). The men walking backwards out of the shed are twisting yarn by hand. An explanation of the process is given in a history of this famous company:

> Each man is shown as having a hank or "head" of this hackled yarn round his waist, and once some fibres of this had been attached to a hook on a spinning wheel, he spun his yarn to the specification required. Slung to his belt was a pannikin of whale oil, with which he at once lubricated his hands and the fibre under his fingers.[12]

The company name was changed when it was bought out by the Gourock Ropework Company in 1797 but the operational centre of this highly successful company remained in Port Glasgow.

Endnotes

1 We are indebted to George Woods, Assistant Curator, McLean Museum and Art Gallery, Inverclyde Council, for his advice.

2 G. Fairfull-Smith, *The Foulis Press and the Foulis Academy* (Glasgow, 2001), 68.

3 Groome, *Gazetteer*, vi, 216.

4 Pryde, *Burghs*, no. 381.

5 *OSA*, v, 554.

6 B. Crispin, 'Clyde shipping and the American war', *SHR*, 41 (1962), 124–5.

7 *OSA*, v, 554.

8 *NSA*, vii, 69.

9 R. L. Hills, *James Watt, Volume 1: His Time in Scotland, 1736–1774* (Ashbourne, 2002), 279.

10 NLS, J. Smeaton, *Description of a Pump for the Dock at Port Glasgow*, Austhorpe, 4 September 1767.

11 Hills, *James Watt*, i, 279.

12 G. Blake, *The Gourock: The Gourock Ropework Co. Ltd, Port Glasgow, Established 1736* (Glasgow, 1963), 116.

91   Portobello, *c.* 1850

Portobello has been known for the last 200 years as a favourite seaside resort. Before that, it was an obscure part of the parish of Duddingston, with a few scattered homes of quarriers and miners in the small villages of Figgate and Joppa. Its name changed *c.* 1740, when a veteran of the naval victory over the Spanish at Puerto Bello in Panama in 1739 called his home after the battle.[1] Geography possibly did not work in its favour, the beach facing northwards and at times subject to high winds and stormy seas encroaching on the shore, but this did not deter the people of Edinburgh and later, with better transport, many from farther afield.

This wash drawing by an unknown artist is a delicate description of a leisurely life at Portobello. People are lounging in a relaxed fashion; some, a little more active, have been collecting mussels. The long stretch of sands was a magnet, initially for the well-to-do of Edinburgh, who were gradually abandoning the attractions of Leith (*see* 68). Decorum was at this time of prime importance. Undressing on a public beach would have been unthinkable. And so, bathing machines were introduced. They arrived in Portobello in 1795. As may be seen in this illustration, they were four-wheeled contraptions, hauled by a horse into the water. There were six or so steps to exit, and the horse drew the machine into a depth of about four steps, leaving the occupant with minimal problems to descend to bathe. The horse may be seen tramping back from the water to pull yet another machine into the Forth. Morality was paramount, and machines for males had to be sited at least sixty yards from those occupied by females.[2] Failure to observe this code of conduct would merit a fine in the Burgh Court. Once adequately refreshed, the occupant of the machine would indicate by waving a towel out of a rear porthole that a horse was needed to return to pull the machine back to the sand. This was a luxury pastime in the mid-nineteenth century. To hire a bathing machine cost one shilling per hour, and the newly established stagecoach, the *Edinburgh Courant*, cost 10d each way from Edinburgh to Portobello in 1806. By comparison, housepainters at Messrs Bonnar, George Street, Edinburgh, were at that time paid 3d per hour, so this was decidedly a pastime for the genteel.

The attractions of this length of sand are further highlighted by the building to the right rear of this view. Built in 1785 in stone and Portobello brick as a summer house, bathing hut or folly for a Mr Cunningham, an Edinburgh advocate, it later fell into

91. Anon., *Portobello Beach, c.* 1850

disrepair, but was restored in 1864 by Mr Hugh Paton, the publisher of *Kay's Edinburgh Portraits*. Of eccentric design, it is said to contain carved stone that came from the old market cross of Edinburgh and the old college of Edinburgh University.[3] It is perhaps significant that when Mr Cunningham met financial difficulties in 1806 he advertised the sale of the property as follows:

> The Tower … commands one of the finest views in the kingdom, and the sea beach is well known to be the finest in Scotland for cold bathing. About 100 feet or more of ground on the west can be taken in from the sand at very small expense, which would be exactly on a line with the other grounds lately taken from the sea.[4]

Other householders also sought to capitalise on their position, by walling off sections of the beach, thus making them private. Such efforts were discouraged, and the walkway from Leith to Musselburgh, where the promenade now stands, remained open to all. The attractions of Figgate were supplemented by two natural springs, reputed to have restorative properties, one at the west end of the village, the other at Joppa. This growing popularity meant that the emerging town was graced with elegant villas. Indeed, the author of the *New Statistical Account of Scotland*, written in 1843, maintained that 'in a short time Portobello will be one of the handsomest towns of its size in Britain'.[5]

By 1806 the growing town also boasted hot and cold public baths, with a 'public room … provided with magazines and pamphlets to amuse while waiting'. Invalids might also be transported to the baths in sedan chairs and for those who rode to the baths there was a 'stable for bathers horses'.[6] The facilities would be extended over the next hundred years, with a 'Fun City', a 1,250 feet (381 metres) long pier, opened in 1871 and designed by Thomas Bouch of Tay Bridge 'fame', donkey rides, bandstand, a paddling pool at Joppa and various seaside entertainments.[7]

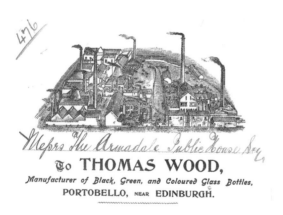

91a. Portobello Glassworks invoice

Portobello beach served another function. The sands proved an excellent drilling parade for the men and horses of the 17th Lancers. For many years cavalrymen would clatter down from Piershill Barracks in the early hours of the morning to drill and exercise their steeds. Portobello would also play an important role in the defence of the country in the twentieth century. The wave-making machine in the open-air public baths was used as a secret practice area for soldiers preparing for the D-Day landings.

Clearly, Portobello was first and foremost a holiday resort. But industry played a vital role in the life of the town. At the west end of the town, close to the old harbour, were the potteries; a flax mill opened in Tobago Street and nearby stood a soap works. These mills were fed by a lade from the Figgate Burn. Glass bottle manufacture began in Portobello in 1848 (*see* 91a). There was also quarrying for clay for brickmaking, a paper mill, manufactories of bricks and tiles and a chemical works. At the far end of the town, near the rocks of Joppa, just faintly visible at the far left, salt panning was a major industry, with at one time about forty carriers, all women, employed retailing salt from the coast to Edinburgh and its environs. Portobello was an eccentric mix of expensive, stone-built villas, seaside entertainments and heavy industry, which somehow co-existed alongside each other.[8]

Endnotes

1 A. J. Youngson, *The Companion Guide to Edinburgh and the Border Country* (London, 1993), 278.

2 M. Munro and A. Foley, *Portobello and Duddingston* (Stroud, 2005), 12.

3 W. Baird, *Annals of Duddingston and Portobello* (Edinburgh, 1898), 299–300.

4 *Ibid.*, 300.

5 *NSA*, i, 392 (Duddingston).

6 Baird, *Annals*, 318.

7 Munro and Foley, *Portobello*, 22.

8 We much appreciate the helpful comments and loan of images from Dr Margaret Munro and Mr Archie Foley.

92   St Andrews, *c.* 1580

This panoramic view of St Andrews, entitled *S. Andre sive Andreapolis: Scotiae Universitas Metropolitana*, was inscribed by John Geddy, or Geddes, probably around 1580. This dating resulted from researches by R. N. Smart, who studied the palaeography of the italic script and the fine French paper on which the view was drawn.[1] Doubts have been expressed, however, as some of the features suggest a pre-Reformation dating. Geddy was probably born in St Andrews to one of the local Geddes families, and was a student at St Leonard's College from 1571 to 1574. He worked as copying secretary to George Buchanan (1506–82), the Scottish historian and poet. Twice in receipt of a royal pension from James VI (1567–1625), in 1577 and 1588, he was secretary to a commission sent to Germany in 1590, and may have served on earlier diplomatic missions. He may also have been secretary to Queen Anne in 1591. In late 1593 or early 1594 he possibly died in a shipwreck on the way to the Low Countries.

Geddy's calligraphic skills were much in demand. This view may have been intended for inclusion in one of the six volumes of G. Braun's and F. Hogenberg's impressive atlas, *Civitatis Orbis Terrarum* (1572–1618), but as this was only a very able sketch plan rather than a surveyed depiction, there are obvious errors, although some detailing is highly accurate and skilled.[2]

The most outstanding feature on the view is the dominance of the cathedral complex, with St Rule's tower clearly shown, if in an exaggerated manner, to the east. The cathedral has lost its roof, the triforium arches being portrayed, so definitely dating the view to the period after the Reformation of 1560. Geddy, however, draws only five of the twelve cathedral nave bays. Adding to the ecclesiastical atmosphere are the religious houses of the Blackfriars and Greyfriars. St Salvator's College tower is seen standing prominently on North Street, thus reinforcing the two intertwined cultural influences in St Andrews – the ecclesiastical and the university. The tower is interesting. Its height is also exaggerated, but, once the depiction of it is magnified, it can be seen that Geddy drew this at 4.50 in the afternoon. Stressing the importance of the university is the further insertion of views of the colleges of both St Leonard's and St Mary's.

Prominent on the edge of the townscape is the Bishop's Castle but, significantly, it stands on an undeveloped street, now called The Scores.[3] The alignment of the streets and positioning of the town gates, or ports, are highly revealing. Geddy draws four parallel

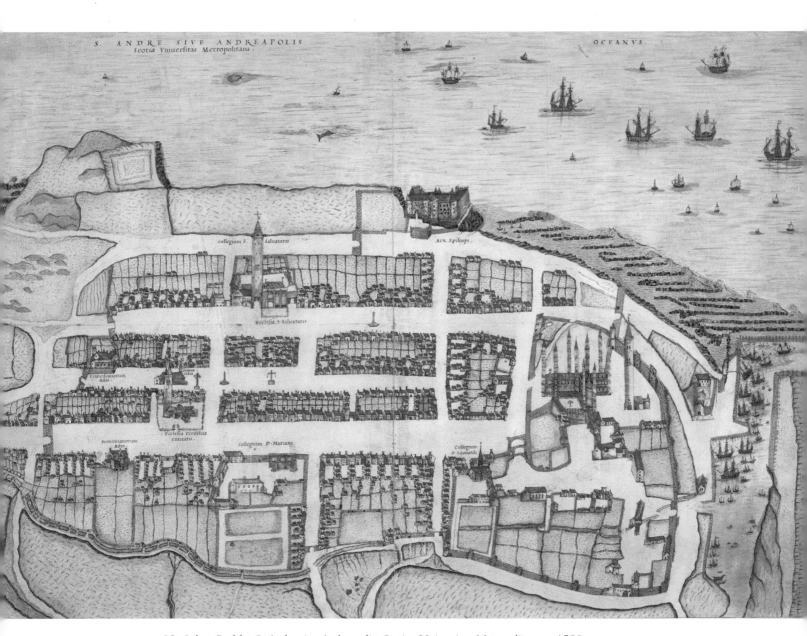

S. ANDRE. SIVE ANDREAPOLIS
Scotiæ Vniuersitas Metropolitana.

OCEANVS.

collegium S. Saluatoris

Arx. Episcopi.

Ecclesia S. Saluatoris

Franciscanorum ædes.

domus vrbis

Dominicanorum ædes.

Ecclesia Perochiæ ciuitatis.

collegium D. Mariani

Collegium D. Leonardi

92. John Geddy, *S. Andre sive Andreapolis: Scotiae Universitas Metropolitana, c.* 1580

streets, all exaggeratedly wide. In fact, North Street and South Street both taper in towards the cathedral complex, with Market Street between them, probably as a later intrusion. This tapering towards the focal point of the cathedral was the work of the master town-planner, Mainard the Fleming, who had previously laid out Berwick.[4] Ports at the end of the four streets indicate much about the development of the town. It is noteworthy that both the Greyfriars and Blackfriars complexes are within the town ports. This is probably an indication that the town had expanded westwards, gradually assimilating the two religious houses within settlement for friaries were normally sited outside a town. Interestingly the siting of the port on the Scores is much farther east, an indication that settlement here was less popular, although archaeological research has shown that there was some occupation here, as well as a tannery.[5] Neither is shown in Geddy's view.

Burgage plots are depicted, not always correctly. He portrays six burgage plots between Blackfriars and West Port, whereas there were, in fact, thirteen. However, a vacant plot seven tofts to the east of St Salvator's chapel has been excavated and shown to have been undeveloped until the nineteenth century.[6] Work probably began on the view at the east end, the more prestigious part of the town where plots and buildings are depicted clearly, whereas in the west plots are foreshortened. The map also gives a clue to the fact that South Street was considered the most desirable area to live: there are more three-storey houses here than elsewhere.

Impressive, too, is the crowded harbour, with ships depicted also out at sea, indicating that, as with all burghs, commerce was the lifeblood of town life. If magnified, it may be seen that Geddy even drew the occupants of boats. Market Street, as the name implies, was the commercial centre of the town. In fact, the market area was much more of an open lozenge shape than is shown. The tolbooth, market cross and tron are shown, the tron in particular being of interest, being one of the few depictions of a medieval weighing machine. Nearby stands the pillory. The fish market cross, however, is to be seen in North Street. Here there may be the remnants of clues to the origins of St Andrews.

92a. Tron

It is known that an earlier Pictish settlement, Kilrimund ('head of the king's ridge'), stood at the east end of the site of St Andrews from at least the mid-eighth century. This was the chief Pictish monastery and, from early in the tenth century, it was the seat of the principal bishopric of Scotland. This monastic site predates the founding of the burgh of St Andrews by Bishop Robert sometime between 1144 and 1153.[7] But what is important is that the monastic site could not have survived without an associated lay settlement for supplies of food and labour. References to the moving of the market cross, from a pre-existing site to that in Market Street, also mention an early 'clachan' or village.[8] It has been thought, although not definitively proven, that this earlier market stood at the east end of North Street, where the roadway opens out into a triangular shape. It is also known from excavation that a boat-shaped structure underlay the plot lay-outs masterminded by Mainard the Fleming.[9] This, allied with ninth- to twelfth-century pottery found in Market Street, is evidence of pre-existing settlement, with an associated market, before the founding of the burgh.[10]

Endnotes

1 R. N. Smart, 'The sixteenth-century bird's eye view plan of St Andrews', *Annual Report. St Andrews Preservation Trust for 1975*, 8–12.

2 N. P. Brooks and G. Whittington, 'Planning and growth in the medieval burgh: the example of St Andrews', *Transactions of the Institute of British Geographers*, new series, 2 (1977), 278–95.

3 For a discussion of occupation to the west of the castle, *see* J. H. Lewis, 'Excavations at St Andrews, Castlecliffe, 1988–90', *PSAS*, 126 (1996), 605–88.

4 A. C. Lawrie (ed.), *Early Scottish Charters* (Glasgow, 1905), no. clxix.

5 Lewis, 'Excavations', *passim*.

6 Personal comment, N. Bogden.

7 Lawrie (ed.), *Charters*, no. clxix.

8 'Black Book', B65/1/1, Sixteenth-century cartulary in the keeping of St Andrews University. B65/23/2 (Burgh Record Series, St Andrews, University of St Andrews and NRS) does not seem to have survived in the original. We are indebted to Dr Norman Reid, Head of Special Collections and Assistant Director of Library Services, Department of Special Collections, University of St Andrews, for his views.

9 Personal comment, N. Bogden.

10 Personal comment, Derek Hall.

93   South Queensferry, *c.* 1860 and *c.* 1887

These two views of South Queensferry, one looking westwards by an unknown artist, the other a watercolour by Charles Bryden (fl. 1880–1901) showing the head of the harbour *c.* 1887, tell us much about this small town. Bryden, or Brydon, was an Edinburgh-based artist and is best remembered for his depictions of coastal scenes.

On the first view may be seen the main road hugging the shoreline, leading to the harbour on the right and the tolbooth on the left. This illustration has been dated to *c.* 1860[1] but is possibly of earlier provenance, given that all the shipping to be seen is sail. By the 1860s the Forth benefited from several steam-powered vessels. The Queensferry Passage had a steam ferry, the *Queen Margaret*, from 1821.[2] On the far right is the Beamer Rock lighthouse, guiding shipping to the inner reaches of the Forth. It has now been removed and is to be relocated at North Queensferry, as the rock itself will form one of the foundations for the new Forth Replacement Crossing.

The tolbooth spire is prominent, with its clockface set high above the town's roofs, most of which appear to be pantiled. The tolbooth was probably built in the seventeenth century, there being a tolbooth in existence by 1635, but was remodelled and the five-storey tower added around 1720. Its original function, as the name implies, was as a collection point for tolls or dues to attend the burgh market, and the beam and weights for the market were housed here. The rest of the building probably functioned as a prison. In due course the tolbooth also became the court-house for the burgh council.[3] The town had received the right to a market when it became a burgh, the first mention being as one of the four burghs dependent on the abbey of Dunfermline in a charter of Robert I (1306–29) dated 1315 x 1328.[4] The other three were Dunfermline, Kirkcaldy and Musselburgh. The right to have a market was an important burghal privilege – it was the only official place for trading for those living in the hinterland of the burgh, and all people from the surrounding countryside would flock to the market cross, which stood in front of the tolbooth, to buy and sell their wares. South Queensferry became a royal burgh in 1636.[5]

Also prominent on the skyline, at the head of the harbour, is the tall chimney of the Glenforth Distillery Company. The second view, by Charles Bryden, shows the malt house of the distillery, to the left of Gote Lane. This building had originally been the

93. Anon., *South Queensferry High Street and Tolbooth, c.* 1860

93a. Charles Bryden, *View of the Harbour Head, c.* 1887

distillery, but by 1854, when the Ordnance Survey map was completed,[6] a new, much bigger distillery had been built on the same side of the lane, nearer the High Street and opposite the tolbooth. The distillery gave employment to some locals, welcome after the decline of the soap-making industry and the herring fishery. The seventeenth-century house opposite the malt house was probably known as Hill's Land.

The harbour is seen as well maintained. When the town became a royal burgh it was described as having a 'haevine and herberie'. By 1693 this seems to have taken the form of a pair of piers which were soon ruinous. In 1710 there was a pier for 'barks and boats' and another at Newhalls (Hawes Inn Pier) for the Queensferry Passage ferry boats. Various works were effected on the harbour during the century, on a number of occasions being ruined by storms. By 1817, on the advice of an engineer named Hugh Baird, the west pier was extended at right angles to run eastwards and a new entrance was made in the north-east corner after the end of the east pier was rebuilt. It is this format that is seen in the first view. The head of the harbour is shown clearly in Bryden's watercolour, displaying little activity where once this would have been the bustling scene for fish-gutting.

The 1832 *Great Reform Act Plans and Reports* indicates that at this time settlement was largely confined to the area around the harbour, there being virtually no houses between the town itself and Newhalls Pier. The first view shows this clearly. Building was largely confined to the level area close to the sea, below the rising ground, which was in the main still agricultural. Rather than build too far up the slope, the High Street became an attractive double-tiered development. The smallness of the town was reinforced in the 1831 census: there were only 684 people in the burgh and the parish, and they lived in a mere seventy-three homes, which suggests a high level of occupancy.

But it is as the southern landing point of the Queensferry Passage that the town is best known. It was from the time of Queen Margaret, wife of King Malcolm Canmore (1058–93) that the ferry crossing gained prominence. John of Fordun, a chronicler writing in the fourteenth century, relates in his *Chronica Gentis Scotorum* that the Pictish king Hungus, after defeating the Northumbrian king Athelstane, displayed the king's severed head on a pike on an island in the middle of the 'Scottish Sea'.[7] Tradition has it that the island was Inchgarvie. If correct, this suggests that this landmark was well known in the busy sea lane. That there were old names for the strait –'Casschilis' or 'Cilis Cassie', meaning 'narrow firth' – further supports the view that this was already a well-established crossing point.

It is recorded that Queen Margaret provided ships for the crossing and endowed hostels on both sides of the ferry.[8] Local tradition has it that The Binks, to the west of the harbour, was the favoured landing place. The nearby Carmelite Priory, not shown on either of these two views, most certainly could have provided suitable accommodation in its guesthouse for travellers. The role of this small burgh became that of the southern crossing point of an ancient routeway – South Queensferry.

Endnotes

1 *Tolbooths and Town-houses*, 185.

2 E. P. Dennison and R. Coleman, *Historic North Queensferry and Peninsula: The Archaeological Implications of Development* (Scottish Burgh Survey, 2000), 30; NRS NRA(S) 0175, Report on Queensferry Passage, 5 April 1828, 13.

3 *Tolbooths and Town-houses*, 184–5.

4 *Registrum de Dunfermelyn* (Bannatyne Club, 1842), no. 346.

5 Pryde, *Burghs*, no. 76.

6 The OS map was published in 1856 as Linlithgow sheet 11.16, with inset 11.12 – Dalmeny, Cramond and Queensferry.

7 *John of Fordun's Chronicle of the Scottish Nation*, translated from the Latin by W. F. Skene, *The Historians of Scotland* (Edinburgh, 1872), iv, 146–7.

8 Turgot, Bishop of St Andrews, *Life of St Margaret, Queen of Scotland*, trans. by W. Forbes-Leith (Edinburgh, 1884), 59–60; Dennison and Coleman, *Historic North Queensferry*, 14–17. See also A. A. M. Duncan, *Scotland: The Making of the Kingdom* (Edinburgh, 1975), 123; P. Yeoman, *Pilgrimage in Medieval Scotland* (London, 1999), 58.

94   Stirling in the Reign of Charles II, *c.* 1679

This is the oldest known full-scale picture of the burgh of Stirling. It was probably painted in the late 1670s or early 1680s, although other dates, such as *c.* 1670 and *c.* 1673–4, have been attributed to it. It is the work of two artists, both Dutch painters closely associated with the court of Charles II (1651–85). One was Johannes Vosterman or Vorstermans (1643–1699), who specialised in landscapes; the other was Jan van Wyck or Wijck (*c.* 1645–1700), who, outwith his own work on hunting and battle scenes, was employed by others to depict figures in their work. His particular speciality lay in depicting horses and domestic pets, buildings and people; in John Slezer's *Theatrum Scotiae* (1693) Wyck was paid ten shillings a time for 'touching and filling up ... 57 draughts with little figures'.[1] In this painting van Wyck included the principal artist, sitting in the left foreground. The other bewigged figure standing nearby may be van Wyck himself (*see* 94b).[2]

Both artists had impressive Scottish connections. Vosterman had been commissioned to paint a view of Greenwich by Anne, Duchess of Hamilton (1632–1716). Van Wyck enjoyed the patronage of the royal favourite, James Scott, Duke of Monmouth and Buccleuch (1649–1685), and painted *The Battle of Bothwell Brig* (1679) to celebrate Monmouth's crushing defeat of the Covenanting rebels. This is why it seems plausible that the painting dates to the period after Bothwell Brig. It is likely that the two travelled to Scotland together to work on it.[3]

Vosterman's landscapes had two particular features: he was fond of painting iconic buildings, such as the royal castles at Windsor and Stirling, and he placed towns within a broader landscape, as with his views of Gloucester and Stirling. There may have been a particular motive for his choice of Stirling Castle as his subject. He had recently completed a large overmantel painting for Whitehall Palace but had not been paid for it. What better iconic symbol of the Stuart monarchy might there be to open the king's purse than the royal castle and palace where Charles II's father had been born? In the picture, the King's Knot, an ornamental garden commissioned *c.* 1630 in the reign of Charles I (1625–49) is prominently depicted, as is the royal deer park. A further reason may have been that Vosterman realised the great weight that the king placed on his ancestry and symbols of it because of the large sums which had been invested in the repair of the castle in the 1670s; £30,000 had been devoted to building work at Holyroodhouse and the castle

94. Johannes Vosterman and Jan van Wyck, *Stirling in the Time of the Stuarts, c.* 1679

in 1670. Unfortunately the repairs were not enough; James, Duke of York, appointed commissioner to Scotland in 1680, recommended further work, especially on the roof of the palace, in 1681.[4]

The picture shows the outstanding defensive position Stirling occupied. Even so, both artists gave free rein to imagination and artifice. Castle and burgh are set high on a volcanic rock with commanding views over the marshy flatlands below and the River Forth, artfully re-routed to the south to give added point. Here is an early version of what commentators on later periods have called the Scottish historical landscape: the boggy carse lands around Stirling are tamed and placed within a scene of settled order; the castle itself is highlighted and placed farther apart from the burgh than in reality. The tower of the parish Church of the Holy Rude and the spire of the tolbooth are, for effect, set further apart from each other than in reality. The burgh is given a more crowded and ordered profile of buildings than it actually had; a military map of 1725 shows gardens and orchards behind the line of 'Back Row' (now Spittal Street) on the western side of the burgh.[5] Van Wyck added a riot of staffage. Deer abound, sail boats adorn the river, and the travellers and laden pack ponies emphasise Stirling's position at a crossroads in the very heart of the kingdom and a natural gateway to the Highlands. Some of the figures are wearing the tartan plaid of the Highlander.

94a. The King's Knot, *c.* 1679

Stirling's strategic importance made it a natural target for invading armies. The impressive walls Vosterman shows surrounding the burgh had been strengthened in the 1540s during the war with England later dubbed the 'Rough Wooing'. Yet the artist probably again exaggerated: one of Slezer's three views of Stirling, drawn barely two decades later,[6]

94b. The two artists

has walling which is less impressive and less geometric. Vosterman's picture shows a town of some distinction with stone buildings, mostly of two storeys, and tiled or pantiled roofs. Another of Slezer's views, by contrast, depicts a mixture of roofing including many thatched houses, with more one-storey dwellings than not.[7]

Three copies of the picture are known to exist. One hangs in the art gallery in Stirling, having been owned by a local laird.[8] Another belongs to the Hamilton family, who served the Stuart dynasty for generations and had for a time been next in line of succession to the Scottish throne. The other belongs to the Portland family. Hans Willem Bentinck, 1st Duke of Portland and Dutch favourite of William III, effectively ruled Scotland from 1689 to 1699. Like his royal master, he never visited Scotland, but much of what he needed to know about Stirling's strategic importance is in this painting.

Endnotes

1 Cavers, Slezer, 9.

2 There are three likenesses of the artist; *see DNB*, van Wyck.

3 *Oxford Art Online*, Johannes Vosterman; *Oxford Art Online*, Jan Wyck; *DNB*, Jan Wyck.

4 *Stirling Castle Palace: Archaeological and Historical Research 2004 to 2008* (Historic Scotland, Level IV Publications).

5 NLS, *John Laye, A Plan of the Town and Castle of Sterling*, 1725.

6 John Slezer, *The Prospect of their Ma'ties Castle of Sterling, Theatrum Scotiae* (1729 edn).

7 *Ibid. The Prospect of the Town of Sterling from the East.*

8 The online catalogue of the Smith Art Gallery and Museum attributes the painting to Vosterman and Thomas van Wyck (1616–1677), father of Jan. Almost certainly the second artist was Jan rather than the father, who probably returned about 1669 to Haarlem, his home city, where he died in 1677.

95   Stirling Bridge, *c.* 1703–7

This illustration is the oldest known surviving view of the stone bridge built in the fifteenth century across the Forth, north of Stirling.[1] It replaced a twelfth-century wooden structure, which was the site of the Battle of Stirling Bridge, where William Wallace defeated the English army in September 1297.

Probably painted between 1703 and 1707, in oil on wood, it was depicted to adorn a room in the townhouse or tolbooth of Stirling, which was rebuilt during these years, to a design of Sir William Bruce. The townhouse stands on the south-west side of Broad Street, at its junction with Jail Wynd, this latter lane taking its name from the fact that the tolbooth was traditionally the town jail. The site had been acquired in 1473 for the construction of a tolbooth.[2] The embellishment of this painting for the new townhouse was designed to assert the town's importance. As such, it can be compared with the flattering painting of Aberdeen from across its estuary commissioned by the town council in 1756 to hang in its townhouse and completed by William Mosman (*see* 2). The painter was probably John Berrihill of Alloa, who had been admitted as a burgess of Stirling *gratis* in 1700, and the purpose of the painting was to display the natural prosperity and resources of the town. The style and types of clothing illustrated are certainly consistent with this dating.

Bridges were important features on the landscape, functioning as key crossing-points on routeways throughout Scotland.[3] At each end of the bridges settlements grew up to service travellers. Unless the traveller traversed the Forth by the Queensferry Passage, this bridge was the main crossing-point north to south over the Forth, which was still tidal here. Although in the countryside, half a mile from the core of the burgh, the bridge had a strategic role to play as an outpost defence as well as an access point. The sentry posts on it attest to this. The bridge itself is guarded by two gateways or ports. The family of Bailie Lapslie, who died around 1684, had been key keepers, and a close guard would have been kept on this strategically important river crossing.

Beyond the bridge, on the north bank, the burgh's parish to landward extended in the form of a narrow strip of land as far as Cambuskenneth Abbey, so the buildings on both banks lay within Stirling's jurisdiction.[4] To judge from a military map of 1725 (95a), there were probably only about six to eight households at Bridgend, and their occupations were probably associated with the nearby mill and the collection of customs from those crossing the bridge to enter the town's precincts.[5] Some of the buildings clustered near

95. John Berrihill of Alloa, *Stirling Bridge, c.* 1703-7

the bridge, at Bridgehaugh on the north bank and at Bridge Mill on the south, may have been inns, where travellers could rest. One of the inns at Bridgend was owned by Janet Bachop, widow of Bailie Lapslie. Some of the other dwellings housed mill workers. They are well built, whether of single or two storeys, and the roofs are slated or tiled, a large improvement on thatch which was always at greater risk of fire. At a time when transport was, at best, on horseback or, for a few, by horse-drawn carriage, a change of horses after a gruelling journey was essential. The horse paddocked close by the bridge may have been a replacement for a weary animal. The map of 1725 seems to show two paddocks on the north side but no buildings. The rural setting is highlighted by the haystack on the north bank and threshers and scarecrows on the south bank. The dog running in the field

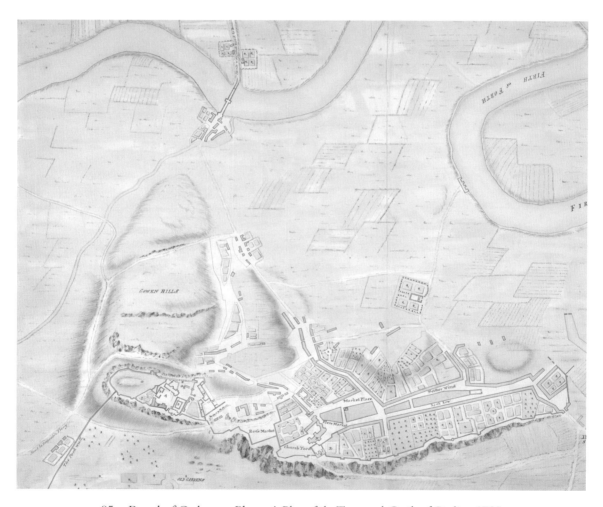

95a. Board of Ordnance Plans, *A Plan of the Town and Castle of Sterling*, 1725

and the dovecot on the north bank were commonplace, both outside and within towns, where animals were free to roam and dovecots provided food for the wealthier members of society.[6]

Fish and shellfish were an important part of the Scots diet, supplementing the simple traditional fare of meat, vegetables, cereal and dairy products. Fishing was also a means of providing food for a family at no cost. The gentleman in this view has just caught a fish. A single-storey building at Bridgend has an unusual, large chimney, reminiscent of a brewery, but it may in fact have been a distillery, malt barn or fish smokery, although the most usual method of preserving fish at this time was by salting.[7]

Water was an important source of power. A mill-race was constructed to increase the flow of water to run the mill wheel, clearly seen here serving the wheel before disgorging itself in to the Forth. Mills were used to grind grain, and the structure just in front of the wheel may have been a storage shed. Fulling mills or waulk mills were also found in rural settings. This painting is in effect a 'publicity' view, extolling the natural resources of an important Scottish town and stressing the vital links between town and countryside at this time.

Endnotes

1 We would like to acknowledge the helpful advice given to us by Elspeth King and John Harrison.

2 *Tolbooths and Town-houses*, 186–8.

3 For a short discussion of the historical importance of bridges, *see* E. P. Dennison, 'Pont's portrayal of towns', in I. C. Cunningham (ed.), *The Nation Survey'd* (East Linton, 2001), 133–4.

4 *OSA*, viii, 272–3.

5 J. G. Harrison, 'The hearth tax and the population of Stirling in 1691', *Forth Naturalist and Historian*, 10 (1985–6), 104–5.

6 A few early dovecots survive in Scotland, as at the south of Linlithgow, which may date to the sixteenth century.

7 For further details on diet, *see* A. J. S. Gibson and T. C. Smout, 'Scottish food and Scottish history, 1500–1800', in R. A. Houston and I. Whyte (eds), *Scottish Society, 1500–1800* (Cambridge, 1989), 59–84.

96   Stonehaven, 1830s and 1805

This bird's-eye view of Stonehaven and its harbour was captured by William Henry Bartlett (1809–1854), a London-born topographical artist and one of the most prolific and widely travelled of the period. It was included in *Scotland Illustrated*, written by Dr William Beattie (1793–1875) and published in 1838.[1]

The view is from Downie Point, a craggy headland towering above the town from the south.[2] The harbour and surrounding buildings look strikingly similar from the same vantage point today. Stonehaven is a natural harbour as its name suggests, the bay sheltered by an arm of land to the north and another, behind the artist, to the south. The original harbour consisted only of the far pier and a great mass of sandstone rock, called *Craig-ma-cair*, roughly where the end of the south pier is in this picture. Both are visible in the accompanying vignette, drawn by a Mr Reid in 1805, which shows why the harbour was a good enough anchorage in summer but too exposed in winter.[3]

The creation of the harbour in this picture began when a new south pier was built in 1826 by John Gibb, an architect and builder from Aberdeen, who also excavated and completely removed *Craig-ma-cair*. Gibb was working on plans prepared by the famous civil engineer Robert Stevenson (1772–1850).[4] His plan included a protective breakwater, but lack of funds prevented its construction, leaving the harbour still exposed to easterly gales. A secure harbour was achieved only when a mid-pier was built, a 'recent' addition in 1842.[4]

The building furthest out on the north quay is the old tolbooth. Most Scottish seaports built their tolbooths away from the harbour, but this large building already existed in 1600, when Stonehaven found itself in need of a tolbooth. Until then the county town was Kincardine, a place which failed to thrive and has since disappeared. When it was decided that Stonehaven would make a better county town, this storehouse belonging to the Keiths, Earls Marischal, the burgh superiors, was converted into a tolbooth providing necessary county court and prison accommodation. It remained the town's tolbooth until 1767. Famously, three Episcopal clergy, imprisoned there in 1748–9, held services and even christenings through the window of their cell.[6]

Another conspicuous piece of civic architecture is the four-storey town steeple rising above the High Street behind the harbour. Built in 1790 at the request of the feuars, it housed the town's bell and clock. Obviously the feuars did not consider that

96. William Henry Bartlett, *View of Stonehaven*, 1830s

the bell added quite enough distinction to their town because they purchased a bigger, better replacement just two years later.[7] Appropriately for a fishing community, a public barometer was added in 1852.

Stonehaven was erected a burgh of barony in 1587 for George Keith (1550–1623), 4th Earl Marischal.[8] Sitting on the northern edge of the parish of Dunnottar, the fortunes of the town were inextricably linked to the famous Keith stronghold of Dunnottar, which lay two miles to the south. The town paid a heavy price for that connection, being an easier target than the castle. Stonehaven was sacked several times by armies opposed to the powerful Keiths. Despite these early disasters, the picture shows a flourishing, mid-nineteenth century town that has long outgrown its humble beginnings around this picturesque harbour.

The man behind this growth was a local landowner, Robert Barclay of Urie (1731–1797), a Quaker and passionate agriculturist whose lineage, though less distinguished, rivalled in length that of the Keiths.[9] Much has been written about Barclay the agricultural improver, but less about his achievements as a property developer and town planner. A man of 'no common powers',[10] Barclay bought a neighbouring estate on which to lay out a fine new town of Stonehaven, its wide streets designed on a grid plan. In 1781 he built a three-arched stone bridge across the Carron Water, clearly visible in the centre of the

96a. Mr Reid, *View of Stonehaven from the South East*, 1805

444

vignette, to join the old town in the parish of Dunnottar to his new one in the parish of Fetteresso.

A description of the new town written about the time this picture was sketched sings the praises of Barclay's town in language that might almost have come from an estate agent's brochure. Its 'many excellent houses to which walled gardens are attached' can be seen over the curve of the hill but houses of 'an inferior description, suited to various classes in society' were also included along with shops 'where goods of every description are always to be obtained'.[11] In the middle was a fine new market square, the elegant market building put up in 1828 by Captain Robert Barclay Allardice (1779–1854), son of the founder.

The smoking chimney stacks are evidence of the town's economic success. A measure of its growth came when it crossed the Cowie Water to embrace the old fisher town of Cowie to the north. Cowie was a burgh of barony in its own right, erected for the Keiths in 1541, nearly fifty years before the town that would one day engulf it.[12]

Above the town stands the parish church of Fetteresso. Out of scale but otherwise accurate, this church was built in 1712 in the same style as the nearby Keith castle of Fetteresso, out of sight on the left of the picture but just visible in the vignette. Fetteresso was the castle where the pretender, James VIII (1688–1766), was proclaimed king in the Jacobite rebellion of 1715. The Keith participation resulted in the forfeiture of their vast estates but it was not the last of this illustrious family. The vignette is dedicated to a famous descendant, George Keith Elphinstone, Viscount Keith (1746–1823). When it was painted, he was Commander-in-Chief of the North Sea, just one appointment in a long and distinguished career that did not end until 1815 when he arranged Napoleon's exile to St Helena.[13]

Endnotes

1 *DNB*, William Henry Bartlett.
2 We are indebted to Gordon Ritchie for his advice.
3 *NSA*, xi, 227.
4 NLS, *Survey of the Harbour of Stonehaven with plans and sections shewing the proposed improvements referred to in a report by Robert Stevenson, Civil Engineer, 1824.*
5 *NSA*, xi, 228.
6 *Tolbooths and Town-houses*, 11.
7 *Ibid.*, 190.
8 Pryde, *Burghs*, no. 241.
9 *DNB*, Robert Barclay Allardice.
10 G. Robertson, *A General View of the Agriculture of Kincardine-shire or, The Mearns, Drawn up under the Direction of the Board of Agriculture* (London, 1813), 323.
11 *NSA*, xi, 244.
12 Pryde, *Burghs*, no. 220.
13 *DNB*, George Keith Elphinstone.

97 Stornoway, 1798 and 1821

This illustration of Stornoway from the south is one of the earliest known representations of the landscape of the Western Isles. Painted by James Barret (fl. 1785–1819), it is a fine portrayal of the town, which was already becoming an important port in Scotland's north-west, with its sheltered inner harbour. Barret inherited the post of Master Painter at Chelsea Hospital, London, from his father George Barret (*c.* 1732–1784), a landscape painter. His two brothers and sister were also artists. James, with his brother George (1767–1842), specialised in watercolour, although James exhibited many oils at the Royal Academy, London. This view was soon to be followed by others with an interest in the area. Notably, William Daniell (1769–1837), also a landscape painter, produced a similar panorama of Stornoway in 1819 and published an eight-volume *A Voyage round Great Britain* (1814–25) in 1825, the result of six separate expeditions between 1813 and 1823.

There is evidence of Viking/Norse settlement on the island (ninety-nine out of 126 village names are of Scandinavian origin, and a further nine contain Norse elements).[1] Perhaps the most famous discovery is the twelfth-century Lewis Chessmen. But the find of a Viking Age silver hoard of the first half of the twelfth century, in the grounds of Lews Castle, suggests that Viking settlement at this protected harbour was more than likely.[2] Barret's view is important for a number of reasons. Firstly, it shows vividly the reason why Stornoway was an important, safe haven from early times. Outlying crops of rocks and a sand bar, not seen on Barret's illustration, offered an element of protection and the jutting piece of land depicted with housing on it, later called the 'Point', gave a further, more secluded, harbouring place. Indeed, with fresh water from the Bayhead River, this was an ideal spot not only for a trading post but also the safest place for an anchorage on the island of Lewis. John Wood's plan of 1821 illustrates this graphically.

A further reason why this illustration is of interest is that it shows the town of Stornoway before major changes took place. The concentration of housing on the Point indicates that this was the core of settlement, now well re-established after the Cromwellian occupation (*see* 7 and Introduction, fig. 11). But housing also stretched along the shoreline by this time. The homes varied in structure and comfort, although most of those depicted would suggest adequately substantial buildings. 'Building works on old castle of Stornoway' might suggest restoration work, but was more probably robbing of stone, which was doubtless

97. James Barret, *The Village of Stornaway with a Shooting Lodge, on the Isle of Lewes*, 1798

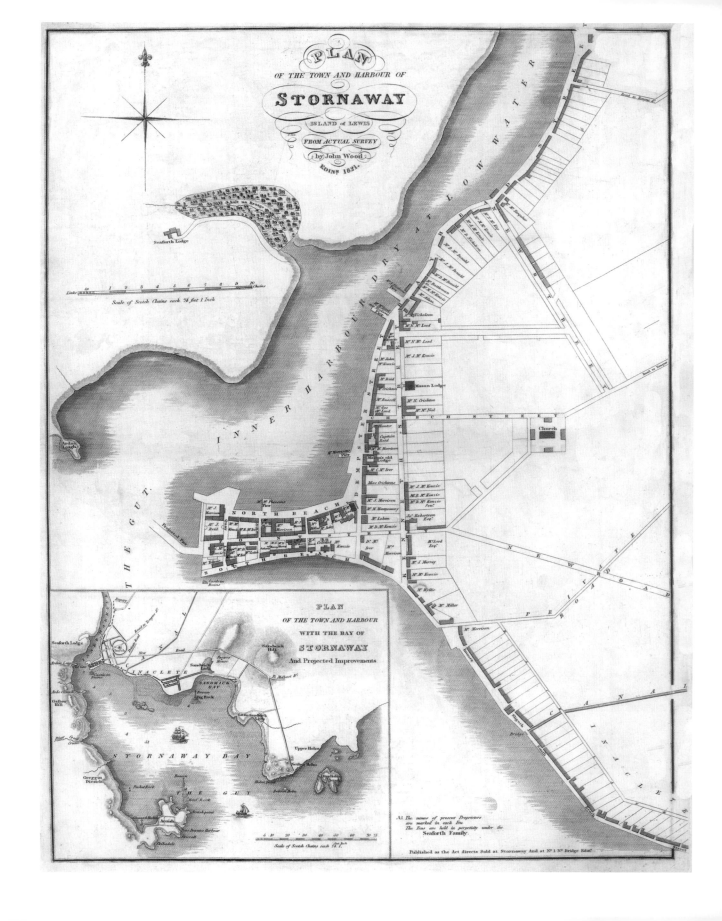

PLAN
OF THE TOWN AND HARBOUR OF
STORNAWAY
ISLAND of LEWIS
FROM ACTUAL SURVEY
by John Wood
Edin. 1821.

Scale of Scotch Chains each 74 feet 1 Inch

PLAN
OF THE TOWN AND HARBOUR
WITH THE BAY OF
STORNAWAY
And Projected Improvements

Scale of Scotch Chains each

N.B. The names of present Proprietors are marked in each Feu. The Feus are held in perpetuity under the Seaforth Family.

Published as the Act directs Sold at Stornaway And at No. 1 No. Bridge Edin.

used in the new houses. It was said that 'the houses [were] built at a considerable cost, because all the materials [were] imported, the stones not excepted'. In consequence, rents were higher than in most other places in the Western Isles, being between £15 and £25 per annum. By 1796 there were sixty-seven slated houses, twenty-six of which had been built in the previous twelve years. Twenty or more houses with thatched roofs, but substantially built, flanked the bay where it narrowed in the north-west of the town, and in the north there were still, in spite of improvements, a great number of 'miserable thatched huts, occupied by sailors, fishers and other people with their families'.[3] It is interesting that Barret does not show these poorer dwellings, so to some extent this is an idealised view.

Ships and boats are seen both in the inner harbour and to the south of the Point. John Knox of the British Fisheries Society visited Lewis in 1786. He noted that the 'noble port [was] without a key, and it appeared still more strange, when [he] was informed that £12–£15,000 had been granted several years [previously], by the trustees at Edinburgh for building a sufficient key'. This would suggest that the pier under construction in the previous decade had not been completed. The lack of an adequate quay was such that vessels loaded and unloaded on the beach or in the bay by means of small boats. In spite of this, Stornaway at this time was one of the largest fish-exporting ports on the western seaboard, sending some 23,000 barrels of herring south each year.[4] To the left, Seaforth Lodge, built in the late seventeenth century as the family home of the Mackenzies, earls of Seaforth, who controlled Lewis, stands prominently. Slightly to the rear of the lodge may be seen a dovecot and nearer the coastline a water tower, described by Daniell as 'erected over a freshwater spring, chiefly for the supply of shipping'.[5] The sandy foreshore shows how a small boat could readily be beached to collect water.

It is noticeable that the Mackenzies set their lodgings apart and secluded from the town, possibly even removing a settlement at Ranal to secure their privacy.[6] This 'apartness' was a policy very much followed by the successors of the Mackenzies – the Mathesons – who bought the island of Lewis in 1844 for £190,000.

Endnotes

1 A full discussion of the place-name evidence is contained in W. F. H. Nicolaisen, 'Scandinavian names' in *Scottish Place-Names: Their Study and Significance* (London, 1976).

2 E. P. Dennison and R. Coleman, *Historic Stornoway: The Archaeological Implications of Development* (Scottish Burgh Survey, 1997), 51–2.

3 *OSA*, xx, 19–20, 22, 35.

4 J. Knox, *A Tour through the Highlands of Scotland and the Hebride Islands, A Report to the British Society for Extending the Fisheries* (London, 1786; reprinted Edinburgh, 1970). Quoted in E. Bray, *The Discovery of the Hebrides* (London, 1986), 140–1; F. Thompson, *In Hebridean Seas* (Leicester, 1994), 37.

5 We are indebted to Ms I. MacLachlan of *Comhairle nan Eilean Siar* (*Museum nan Eilean*) for her advice; and also to Ms M. Davenhill of Leabharlainn nan Eilean Siar.

6 Dennison and Coleman, *Historic Stornoway*, 33.

98   Stranraer, 1880s, 1842 and *c.* 1810

This engaging view of what we now know as Stranraer shows, almost graphically, two separate settlements. Drawn, probably in the 1880s, by a resident, a Mr Baird of Belfast,[1] it displays clearly how the burgh to the east of the burn running through Stranraer to Loch Ryan – once called 'Chapel' or 'the clachan of St John' had more prestigious houses – well built and some relatively substantial. The buildings to the left – in Stranraer itself – appear more modest. The two vignettes give a little more information.

The vignette lithograph portrays the town in 1842 as a relatively wealthy, relaxed place to live, where one could enjoy a certain level of prosperity, besport oneself in fine clothing and be on view on the shore. The Loch Ryan regatta was typical of many seaside towns in Scotland; sailing clubs and rowing clubs, with fiercely fought competitions between neighbouring settlements, were the norm and occasions for fun and jollity.

The lithograph was produced by the Glasgow engravers Maclure and Macdonald after a work by Robert George Kelly (1822–1910). Kelly was a landscape painter, born in Dublin, who was living in George Street, Stranraer, in 1852. He painted a number of Galloway views in the 1850s and 1860s. The *Loch Ryan Regatta* was distributed through *The Galloway Register* and the caption below the image reads 'Printed exclusively for and presented to readers of the *Galloway Advertiser*'. Clearly, for some in Stranraer, life was relatively comfortable.[2]

There were many buildings of substance in Stranraer that would support this claim to modest prosperity. Still standing in George Street is the 1776 townhouse, simple but elegant, in spite of a claim by a visitor in 1877 that it was a 'very plain edifice' and 'like some ladies very much indebted to paint for its good looks'![3] Nearby, on the corner of George Street and Church Street, stood the George Hotel (rebuilt in 1867). This fine coaching inn was a mark of Stranraer's role as a staging post for the short crossing from Scotland to Ireland. An elegant building, offering accommodation for wealthy travellers, with stabling facilities to the rear, a nineteenth-century visitor deemed it as 'capital accommodation for both man and beast'.[4]

A number of imposing private houses indicate the town's growing prosperity in the late eighteenth and nineteenth century. Park House, a three-storey, symmetrical building, stands to the south of Leswalt High Road. Its stables and gateposts reflect its status as a

er and Lochryan from Gallowhill

98. Mr Baird, *Stranraer*, 1880s

98a. Robert George Kelly, *The Loch Ryan Regatta*, 1842

country residence of distinction. Ivy House on London Road, nearby Bellevilla House and Ann House are all testament to the quality of housing appearing on the townscape. Built around 1820 was North West Castle, so called after its owner Sir John Ross, who searched for the North-West Passage. It was also sometimes called 'Observatory House', perhaps after the camera obscura that Ross had built on one of the towers and the lower windows on the north, with their small openings for the insertion of a telescope. The boat-house door lintel, still visible, is a reminder of the proximity of the sea before infilling in the nineteenth and twentieth centuries transformed this area.

Of far greater antiquity, the most prominent building in the town is the Castle of St John. Built around 1520 as an L-shaped tower house, it probably functioned as a family home and an administrative centre for the estates of the Adair family of Kinhilt, who were of Irish origin, arriving in Scotland in the thirteenth century. They were a well-to-do family, unlike many of their countrymen who were immigrants in the nineteenth century.[5] The original entrance was to the north and gave access to two vaulted chambers. An entresol is entered from the wheel-stair and, above this, on the first floor, one large vaulted apartment has two chambers in the thickness of the west wall. Alterations have been made over the centuries, commencing in the seventeenth century when the building was heightened. Its function varied from family home to billet for Graham of Claverhouse's troops in his offensive against Galloway Covenanters in 1679 to a gaol in the nineteenth century, with an exercise area on the open parapeted roof.[6]

What is significant about this anonymous drawing of *c.* 1810 is not merely the excellent portrayal of the castle, but the squalor and poverty of the houses surrounding it – a sharp contrast to the genteel living portrayed at Loch Ryan regatta and the elegant houses being erected nearby. And this was not the poorest area. Stranraer had its slums. The areas of greatest poverty were Little Dublin Street (present Millhill Street), Little Ireland and Mill Street (now Hanover Square). Some moved to Sloss's Close and Pretty Mill Close (later called Rankin's Close). As some of the names suggest, these streets were largely populated by Irish immigrants. These areas soon also became slums, with sub-standard housing that was not demolished until the 1930s.[7]

There are elements of mystery about this illustration; the location of the original is unknown. It appears to be an etching and there might be a faint date of 1811 in the cross-hatching at the bottom right. The view must be pre-1820 as that is when the building became the town prison and the

98b. Anon., *Stranraer Castle, c.* 1810

gabled roof – shown in the picture – was demolished. The juxtaposition of these two vignettes illustrates two facets of nineteenth-century Stranraer. Both are honest, but each tells only a partial story.

Endnotes

1 Baird is not listed in W. G. Strickland, *Dictionary of Irish Artists,* 2 vols (Dublin and London, 1913).

2 We are indebted to John Pickin, Principal Officer, Leisure and Sport, Arts and Museums (Wigtownshire), now retired, for his advice; to Graham Roberts, Dumfries and Galloway archivist; and to Donnie Nelson, Stranraer.

3 E. P. Dennison Torrie and R. Coleman, *Historic Stranraer: The Archaeological Implications of Development* (Scottish Burgh Survey, 1995), 53; *Tolbooths and Town-houses,* 191–2.

4 *Ibid.,* 54.

5 *ER,* xiv, Appendix, *Libri Responsionum,* 537; Anon., *The Castle of St John* (Wigtown District Museum Service, n.d.), 2, 4; *RMS,* iii, nos 325, 869; NLS, Adv MS M.6.15, no. 14.

6 Dennison Torrie and Coleman, *Historic Stranraer,* 53.

7 Personal comment, Mr Donnie Nelson; J. E. Handley, *The Irish in Modern Scotland* (Cork, 1947), 124.

99   Wick, 1875 and 1872

This remarkably detailed view, entitled *Wick's Harbour during the Herring Fishing*, appeared in a supplement to the *Illustrated London News* on 28 August 1875. It was the work of an English watercolour painter Samuel Read (1815–1883), who had regularly published pictures in the *News* since 1844 and had been appointed its first special artist in the eastern Mediterranean in 1853, immediately prior to the outbreak of the Crimean War. Since then he had travelled extensively throughout Europe as well as England, specialising in the depiction of church interiors and urban scenes, which may help explain the attention to detail in this work.[1]

In the 1870s Read turned to landscapes, especially of scenes in Ireland and Scotland, though these were less acclaimed than his other, more specialist architectural work. The particular reason for his interest in Scotland may in part be explained by his relatively late marriage, in 1860, to the daughter of Robert Carruthers (1799–1878), proprietor and editor of the *Inverness Courier*. Carruthers had turned the *Courier* into the most popular newspaper in the north of Scotland; he encouraged local writers to address the condition and changes in the Highlands. Among these was the celebrated geologist, Hugh Miller (1802–1856), who had long had an interest in promoting the herring industry in the Moray Firth. Carruthers published a series of his articles in the *Courier* in the 1820s, which he subsequently republished as *Letters on the Herring Fishery* (1839).[2]

The scene depicted by Read is not of Wick, a royal burgh founded in 1589,[3] but of its upstart rival: the new town and harbour of Pulteneytown, across the river from the royal burgh. Pulteneytown was a creation of the British Fisheries Society, triggered by a report and plan for a new town made by Thomas Telford (1757–1834) in 1807.[4] Pulteneytown was named after its patron, the Governor of the Society and local MP, William Johnstone (1729–1805). His planned new town was as much a grab for status as was his change of name to Pulteney after marrying the cousin of William Pulteney, 1st Earl of Bath. It was an attempt to create a new working-class settlement, recruiting from far and wide across the north and north-east: its men would provide boat builders, repairers, coopers and masons and its women would gut and process the fish in newly built curing houses. The population of Pulteneytown, a one-industry town – which was unusual in itself in Scotland – grew swiftly and by the 1870s was more than three times that of Wick. The *First Ordnance Survey* map of 1872 shows the new town as very different

99. Samuel Read, *Wick's Harbour during the Herring Fishing*, 1875

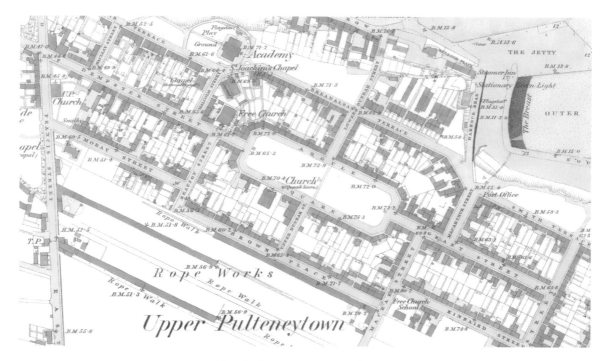

99a. Ordnance Survey, *Wick*, 1872

from the close-knit clustering of streets and wynds in the old royal burgh. Pulteneytown, the last architectural venture of the British Fisheries Society, had two faces: its residential zone was an elegant mixture of fashionable crescents and squares, with Argyle Square and its church as its focal point, in imitation of Bath; its industrial zone was severely practical, constructed in a uniform grid of nineteen plots organised in four rectangular blocks, with names such as Herring Row and Salt Row.[5]

The herring fishery off the coast of the Moray Firth had a long history. Until the second half of the eighteenth century, it was largely dominated by Dutch shipping and industry. The years after the end of the Napoleonic war in 1815 saw a rapid expansion of ports along the Moray Firth as well as Caithness. Although Wick began to lose its near-monopoly hold over the Scottish herring fleet in these years, its production rose rapidly and its pre-eminence became more marked. By 1811 Telford's new harbour had become hopelessly over-crowded. By the 1820s the summer fishings saw more than 600 boats docking at Wick and an annual influx of over 4,000 immigrants. A new harbour extension was completed by 1830 but it, too, quickly became overwhelmed. By 1840 some 765 boats docked at Wick and by 1860 the figure was over 1,100.

These boats were very different from the earlier Dutch 'busses', which typically were of 60 to 100 tons and had a crew of fifteen. The vessels depicted by Samuel Read were small open boats – 'scaffies' – with a keel of only 20–22 feet (6.1–6.7 metres), a skipper owner and a crew of no more than four. Nonetheless, this fleet was the basis for a dedicated industry which smoked, cured and pickled herring for export markets in northern Europe. By 1850 fast schooners also docked at Wick and Fraserburgh, the two main supply centres, bound for Hamburg and Danzig in two or three days. This was an international trade, and Wick was one of the few towns in Scotland which was little altered by the arrival of the railway, which came in 1874. By then, the industry was in decline and, unlike other towns and industries, the railway did not offer alternative markets.[6]

Read's graphic panorama has his characteristic attention to detail:[7] almost without exception, the boats are four-oared scaffies; the harbour, strewn with piles of barrels, is a hive of industry showing fishermen, women gutting the herring in large water butts, and better dressed agents and businessmen negotiating sales and prices. In the background, two sea-going schooners – of two and three masts – are moored at the quay, waiting to transport the cured herring across the North Sea. The date of publication was also relevant: the last week of August typically marked the peak of the season. Yet there are also puzzling features in Read's images. By the 1870s boats were becoming larger with a wider range, with 40-foot keels common. There is no trace of them in Read's picture. The curing houses of Pulteneytown are absent, leaving an impression of primitivism which belies what is otherwise known of a highly organised factory-style operation. The height of the cliffs on the far side of the bay is hugely exaggerated. And the very title is misleading; this is not the harbour of Wick, an ancient burgh in genteel decline, but that of Pulteneytown, for a time one of the most remarkable, unusual and little-known success stories in Scottish urban history.

Endnotes

1 *DNB*, Samuel Read.

2 *DNB*, Robert Carruthers.

3 Pryde, *Burghs of Scotland*, no. 63.

4 D. Maudlin, 'Robert Mylne, Thomas Telford and the architecture of improvement: the planned villages of the British Fisheries Society, 1786–1817', *Urban History* 34, no. 3 (2007), 453–80.

5 *Ibid.*, 473–7. Telford's plan of 1807, showing the layout of the residential and industrial zones of Pulteneytown, is also printed and discussed in R. Gibson, *The Scottish Countryside: Its Changing Face, 1700–2000* (Edinburgh, 2007), 132–3.

6 F. Foden, *Wick of the North* (Inverness, 1996), 270–4, 284, 324, 446–50, 494–5, 499–500, 562. This book has the painting as its cover.

7 The accuracy of Read's detail is confirmed by early photographs of the herring fleet in the harbour, held in the online Johnson Collection, Wick Heritage Museum; *see* for example 'The Schooner *Elba* ready for loading'.

100   Wigtown, 1827 and 1850s

T hese two views of Wigtown, although only two decades apart, suggest a town in a state of transformation.[1] The earlier is a watercolour, *Wigtown from Windy Hill*, on the western edge of the town, where a monument to the Covenanters would be erected in 1855. It looks east, across Wigtown Bay. The main visual feature is the tower and steeple of the Town Hall, built in 1749 and rebuilt with a tall spire added in 1776. The second view is of the High Street, sometime in the 1850s, after it had been widened and paved but before a new Gothic style townhouse was built in 1862. It also shows the tip of the spire of the old Town Hall.[2]

The view of 1827 seems to show a town where there are still a large number of single-storey cottage-style dwellings, some thatched. Although its population had more than doubled, from 1,032 in 1755 to 2,337 in 1831, Wigtown was otherwise still very much as it had been in the eighteenth century, when Samuel Robinson claimed that the 'greatest number of houses were of a homely character, thatched and one storey high'.[3] In 1839 the local minister claimed that the burgh had undergone 'great improvements' in the previous twenty years, with many new houses built. He drew particular attention to the unusual width of the High Street and the 'plantation' of shrubs and trees, bounded by a metal rail, with walks and a bowling green within it.[4]

By the 1850s, certainly, the High Street portrayed in the painting, looking eastwards from the old West Port, has a mixture of architectural styles, including one- and two-storey buildings, at least one with old-style crow-stepped gables, but many seem very new, with fashionable architectural features such as neo-classical door pillars. There is variety, too, in the stone used, with some, more prestigious buildings being built of red sandstone. The large three-storey building opposite the market cross is probably the general post office or the Queen's Arms Hotel which stood next to it.[5] The centrepiece of this elegant new square is the new burgh cross, built in 1816 to commemorate the Battle of Waterloo. It stands some twenty feet high, twice as high as the original market cross, and surrounded by a railing.[6]

The two paintings differ in their approach to townscape. The 1827 view was by John Clark (fl. 1824–8), an artist and engraver, who published widely but about whom remarkably little is known in personal terms. This was one of a series of townscapes which

100. John Clark, *Wigtown from Windy Hill*, 1827

100a. Andrew Farlow, *Wigtown High Street*, 1850s

he drew in the 1820s, including Banff, Edinburgh, Gretna, Hamilton, Inverness, Paisley, New Lanark and Tain (*see* 18, 38, 82, 88). Most appeared in an illustrated volume, *Views in Scotland*, first published in London in 1824 which went through various reprints. Each watercolour, it was claimed, was 'sketched and painted on the spot' and was subjected to the scrutiny of 'Gentlemen of taste, resident on the spot'. Wigtown was not one of the first batch of thirty-five engravings which were completed by February 1826, although it was on an original list of seventy-two views which the publishers announced would be published at regular intervals in batches of two. In one sense, the panorama of Wigtown is typical of Clark's known townscape work, in which he used to highlight one prominent civic building or church. In another sense, it is untypical of him, in that his painting of Wigtown is more in close-up than any of his other known work, with the possible exception of his view of New Lanark. The difficulty for him with Wigtown may have been in finding a vantage point from which he could paint to his regular formula of a linear townscape.

For Clark, the town was the townscape. For others, the town was about life within it. This was the case with the other artist, Andrew Farlow (b. 1839?), almost certainly a local and otherwise unknown. The surname, while unusual in Scotland, was relatively common in nineteenth-century Wigtown.[7] His painting was published in lithograph form by Bruce Kelly, who worked as a bookseller and bookbinder in Newton Stewart between 1837 and 1852, which helps to date the work more precisely.[8] The High Street scene portrayed by Farlow seems a highly didactic attempt to depict 'improvement' in an age of self-conscious elegance, displayed in the picture by an unlikely profusion of fashionable top hats and smartly dressed children. This is not the town almost over-run by Irish labourers and vagrants which the local minister complained about in 1839. As well as the stagecoach – two or three a day operated on the main route from Dumfries to Stranraer until the railway eventually reached Wigtown in 1872 – a well-to-do couple has their own horse and trap. The width of the street, forty-four feet (13.4 metres) in reality, is greatly exaggerated. Street lighting is prominently displayed. What looks like a police constable is casually chatting to another local. There is an irony here. Wigtown in reality did not adopt any of the mid-nineteenth-century acts regularly used by other burghs to initiate improvements in lighting, cleansing and general policing.[9] Yet the unmistakable scene painted here is of a well-regulated, model police burgh. However exaggerated Farlow's picture was, there could hardly be a greater contrast with the town of three quarters of a century before, described by Samuel Robinson as 'humble, unpretentious and untidy'.[10]

Endnotes

1 We are indebted to John Pickin, Principal Officer, Leisure and Sport, Arts and Museums (Wigtownshire), now retired, for his help and advice.

2 *Tolbooths and Town-Houses*, 207.

3 S. Robinson, *Reminiscences of Wigtownshire about the Close of the Last Century* (1872), 20–2.

4 *NSA*, iv, 1–8 (1839).

5 *See* the 1848 large-scale OS map of Wigtown: NLS website, OS, *Wigtown* (1848).

6 Groome, *Gazetteer*, ii, 492–4.

7 *See* International Genealogical Index (British Isles) for the surname Farlow in Wigtown; variants included Furlough (and Andrew F. was born 23 December 1839), Furlaw and Furlow.

8 NLS, Scottish Book Trade Index (online).

9 J. F. McCaffrey, *Scotland in the Nineteenth Century* (London, 1998), 36, 62–3.

10 Robinson, *Reminiscences*, 20.

Index of artists, cartographers and engravers

The entries marked in *italics* indicate an illustration or map.

Index

The entries marked in *italics* indicate an illustration or map.